A Liberal Descent

A
Liberal Descent

*Victorian historians and
the English past*

J. W. BURROW
*Reader in Intellectual History
University of Sussex*

CAMBRIDGE UNIVERSITY PRESS

Cambridge
London   New York   New Rochelle
Melbourne   Sydney

Published by the Press Syndicate of the University of Cambridge
The Pitt Building, Trumpington Street, Cambridge CB2 1RP
32 East 57th Street, New York, NY 10022, USA
296 Beaconsfield Parade, Middle Park, Melbourne 3206, Australia

First published 1981

Printed in Great Britain at The Pitman Press, Bath

British Library Cataloguing in Publication Data
Burrow, J. W.
A liberal descent.
1. Historiography – History and criticism
19th century
I. Title
907.2   D13   81–3912
ISBN 0 521 24079 4

FOR MY FRIENDS, WHO ARE RESPONSIBLE

Always acting as if in the presence of canonized forefathers, the spirit of freedom, leading in itself to misrule and excess, is tempered with an awful gravity. This idea of a liberal descent inspires us with a sense of habitual native dignity, which prevents that upstart insolence almost inevitably adhering to and disgracing those who are the first acquirers of any distinction.

Edmund Burke

Great abilities (said he) are not requisite for an Historian; for in historical composition, all the greatest powers of the human mind are quiescent.

James Boswell, The Life of Samuel Johnson

Contents

Abbreviations

The following abbreviations have been used in the notes:

Stubbs	*Constitutional History of England*	CH
	Seventeen Lectures on Medieval and Modern History	SL
	Lectures on Early English History	EEH
Freeman	*History of the Norman Conquest*	NC
	The Reign of William Rufus	WR
Froude	*History of England*	HE
	Short Studies on Great Subjects	SS
	Waldo Hilary Dunn, *James Anthony Froude. A Biography,*	
	vol. i, *1818–1856*; vol. ii, *1857–1894*	Dunn

The place of publication of all works cited is London unless stated otherwise. The customary abbreviations O.U.P. and C.U.P. have been used for the Oxford and Cambridge University Presses, respectively.

Preface and acknowledgements

The motives of an academic writing a book are naturally mostly unavowable: ambition, vanity, frustration, even possibly an unrealistic avarice. Among the approved if sometimes implausible references to the needs of the subject or the stimulus derived from teaching, however, it is surprising that one quite respectable impulse is seldom if ever mentioned: embarrassment at the well-meant if tactless enquiries of friends wishing to know what one is 'doing', with the implication that only a certain kind of answer will be acceptable. In my own case I know that the importunities and encouragement of friends have been a major, and at times the only, sustaining impulse. In naming them I fasten responsibility: Stefan Collini, Ruth Morse, Larry Siedentop, Quentin Skinner, John Thompson, Patricia Williams, Donald Winch. The book was written in the first instance for them, in the hope that they might enjoy it, and it is to them that it is dedicated, as an inadequate acknowledgement of innumerable kindnesses, both intellectual and practical. They have given me, variously, the services and sustenance of college, foundation grant, audience, critic, editor, literary agent, cakes and ale. I have stood in salutary awe of their fastidiousness and benefited much from their criticisms. For the book's errors of taste and judgement my own obstinacy is solely to blame.

Other scholarly debts call for fuller acknowledgements than those in the footnotes. J. H. Plumb has added to my many debts to him by the stimulus I have received from his *The Death of the Past*. I am also particularly indebted to the work of Duncan Forbes and J. G. A. Pocock. I have learnt much from it; without it the book would have been significantly different and considerably the poorer. I have also learnt much from Sheldon Rothblatt's sensitive studies of English cultural history, and have greatly valued the encouragement and suggestions by which he has added to my debt. I am particularly grateful to Norman Vance for reading and commenting on the section on Froude.

In preparing the manuscript for the press I have been helped by the unfailing kindness of Sheila Brain. My gratitude to Kay Smith, who typed the manuscript beautifully, is heightened by her possession of a rare and, to me, invaluable accomplishment in the ability to read my writing. I am also grateful for a grant to cover the typing costs from the University of Sussex.

To offer one's work as a product of a particular academic environment is risky and presumptuous; one may discredit what one had hoped to adorn. But I can safely admit that the necessarily eclectic work involved in preparing a book of this kind has been made easier by the official recognition – still rare – of Intellectual History at the University of Sussex, and by the absence of disciplinary tribalism, and the close and easy intellectual relations between colleagues in different disciplines, fostered by its academic system since its foundation. For that, and to all the colleagues from whom I have learnt by teaching with them and talking to them, I am grateful.

J. W. BURROW

January 1981

CHAPTER I

Introduction

The thirty years between 1848 and 1878 saw a remarkable flowering of English narrative history and a new intensity and elaboration in the interpretation of what arguably had been the three great crises in the history of the English as a nation: the Norman Conquest, the Reformation and the Revolution of 1688. They were treated, respectively, in three massive historical works: Macaulay's *History of England from the Accession of James the Second* (1848–55), Froude's *History of England from the Fall of Wolsey to the Defeat of the Spanish Armada* (1856–70) and Freeman's *History of the Norman Conquest* (1867–79). These were in one sense traditional works, narrative histories, immense in the old, leisurely fashion of historiography. But though variously successful they each had a density of narrative texture, an imaginative range and a power of rhetorical enforcement and suggestion scarcely approached or attempted before; among histories of England, only Hume's, now a century old, challenged comparison.

To say that these works – together with Stubbs' *Constitutional History of England* (1873–8), which provided the latter part of the nineteenth century with its definitive statement of English constitutional development, as Hallam had provided it for the earlier – form the main subject of this book, though true, says little and may even be misleading. For its subject is neither narrative, nor rhetoric nor scholarship as such. Moreover, though its immediate subject is historians and their works, it is only imperfectly described as an essay in the history of historiography. It is not concerned with the development of historical scholarship, but with historiography in the sense defined by Burckhardt, as a record of what one age finds of interest in another. It is intended as a study in Victorian culture and intellectual history based on the premiss that one of the ways in which a society reveals itself, and

I

its assumptions and beliefs about its own character and destiny, is by its attitudes to and uses of its past. The discussion of each historian specifically considered here has as its central theme the presence of some particular sense of the national past as instructive or inspiring: an idea, in fact, of England and the English, and of the relevance to them of some particular portion of their past. But this in turn implies a concern on their part with the question of the continuity of that past, and it is this which links the various chapters as their common theme.

The concern with continuity relates the book to familiar and larger themes in English intellectual history, in particular to an aspect of nineteenth-century English political thought, approached, as in this case is appropriate, through the study of historiography. From Burke onwards, a self-conscious and influential school of English political thinking has held that political wisdom, and the identity of a society, and hence in some measure the appropriate conduct of its affairs, are found essentially in its history. It would only be consistent with this view to find the subsequent elaborations of it conducted not in treatises of political theory – the normal quarry of the historian of political thought – but in historiography. Burke himself has of course been extensively studied, but the existence of a 'Burkean tradition' is more often referred to than examined. The method adopted here is not the only way of identifying such a tradition – in a comprehensive treatment there would be other works to consider – but it is one way, and an indispensable one.

But though I hope the book may throw light on the notion of a nineteenth-century Burkean tradition, the latter does not provide its central theme. It is subsumed under what is, for our present purposes, a wider concept: the familiar idea of a 'Whig interpretation' of English history. The historians chiefly considered here can all, with one exception to be considered in a moment, be thought of as Whig historians in the sense licensed for us by Sir Herbert Butterfield;[1] a sense, we may observe, which carries no necessary implication that the historian so designated need be a Whig when doing anything else, such as, for example, voting. The idea of a Whig interpretation of English history is simple in outline, complex in detail. Butterfield at one point distinguished as its main original components the concept of an ancient, free Teutonic

---

[1] Herbert Butterfield, *The Whig Interpretation of History* (1st edn. 1931; 1936).

constitution; Magna Carta; the antiquity of the House of Commons; and an idealisation of the 'constitutional experiments' of the fourteenth and fifteenth centuries.[2] But, of the first three, enthusiasm for Teutonic or Saxon freedom was intermittent; it meant little, for example, to such unequivocally Whig historians as Hallam or Macaulay. Magna Carta, as Ann Pallister has shown,[3] waned in significance in the nineteenth century. Again, Macaulay makes little of it. And after the crushing work of Robert Brady in the late seventeenth century,[4] belief in the high antiquity of the House of Commons could not be sustained indefinitely. There was some ebb and flow of confidence and literalness in the Whigs' appropriation of the nation's past, and in the long run a kind of decline, a muting of sturdy claims to know what the constitution definitely was, and to know that it was what Whigs had always known it was, into a more esoteric capacity to detect in English history the continuous presence, sometimes manifest, sometimes rather distressingly occult, of an abiding spirit of liberty.

Despite this, however, one thing that is definitive in the sense of a Whig interpretation that we have all learnt from Butterfield is confidence: confidence in the possession of the past ('Our ancient history', Freeman said, 'is the possession of the liberal');[5] even more confidence, perhaps, in understanding the present. The past may be revered; it is not regretted, for there is nothing to regret. Whig history that earns the name is, by definition, a success story: the story of the triumph of constitutional liberty and representative institutions. But if it is celebration it is not brash or heedless; it is, rather, an invitation to national jubilation at which the shades of venerated ancestors are honoured guests, or, as Burke put it, 'canonized forefathers'.

In the mid-nineteenth century, though the Whig constitutionalist claims may have been subject to some retrenchment, this characteristic jubilation took on a new complexity and richness of presentation. It is this which has determined not only the choice of the subject of this book, but also its treatment, about which something must now be said.

Historiography, above all the narrative historiography consi-

---

[2] Herbert Butterfield, *The Englishman and His History* (C.U.P. 1944), p. 69.
[3] Ann Pallister, *Magna Carta. The Heritage of Liberty* (O.U.P. 1971).
[4] J.G.A. Pocock, *The Ancient Constitution and the Feudal Law* (C.U.P. 1957), p. 197.
[5] E.A. Freeman, *The Growth of the English Constitution from the Earliest Times* (3rd edn. 1870), p. x.

dered here, is a mixed mode. It accommodates, that is, not just occasionally but intrinsically, writing of various kinds: the discursive presentation of constitutional, political and religious doctrines, both those the author writes about and those he professes; psychological portraiture; visual description; the dramatic rendering of a sequence of actions and events. It touches on one side the abstractions of constitutional law and political theory, on the other the full-bodied representations of the novel. It demands correspondingly eclectic treatment.

Any rich and original work of historiography, moreover, is a point of intersection: the simultaneous meeting place of the historian's unique personality, shaped by an intellectual and social milieu, with historiographical and literary models and conventions, with traditional and contemporary views of past events, and with a body of primary sources, some already established as important, others discovered or selected by the historian himself. The historian of historiography ignores any of this at his peril; he will, for example, make a fool of himself if he treats as idiosyncratic what was in fact an historiographical commonplace.

It is these considerations which have determined the arrangement of the chapters of this book, which falls into two distinct types. Each part except the third begins with an introductory or contextual chapter discussing earlier views of the period of English history under consideration and attempting to distinguish the available – and sometimes, of course, coercive – historiographical traditions. (Part III is covered in this way by chapter 5 in Part II.) These are then followed by chapters on individual historians. This arrangement is admittedly a compromise, and runs the usual risk of displeasing all parties. Readers whose interest is in the historians and their works may wish to dispense with some of the more detailed discussion of the varieties of Whig constitutionalism offered in the next chapter, and in that case I would encourage them to begin with chapter 3. On the other hand, academic readers whose interest is chiefly in the history of social and political thought may find the chapters on individual historians clogged with discussion of their personal traits and with biographical detail, and wish for a sparer treatment of the mutations of Whig constitutionalism and conceptions of historical change.

They would, I think, have missed the point, and the point is not marginal to intellectual history but central to it. Obviously there is a price for the arrangement adopted here, but I have thought it worth paying. That understanding a past author or work presupposes attention to his intellectual context is now an orthodoxy of intellectual history and needs no labouring.[6] But contexts also need detailed examination of texts and authors for their fuller illumination. What the essentially classificatory activity of distinguishing forms of discourse or available theoretical languages[7] ideally needs as its complement is a sense of the complex ways in which individuals respond to, assimilate and reshape the materials of their intellectual milieux.

This is particularly necessary in the present case, where we see an older, peremptory and legalistic constitutionalism changing into a subtler political persuasiveness, expressed as much through tone and the presentation of historical characters (see especially chs. 2–4) as through overt injunction. In such persuasive uses of the past, intended as educative rather than directly prescriptive, it is largely through the intensity of a personal vision, through the intersection of personal and public mythologies, that images of, and attitudes to, the past are essentially conveyed, even though we may be able only to guess at the extent of their influence.

The last point is a necessary reservation, because there are dangers more serious than the possible irritation of the purist in the concentration on individuals, even accompanied by an attempt to place them in their intellectual contexts. They may, by their isolation for attention, seem tacitly endowed with a representative status. But the study of an individual author shows us how a particular mind at a particular time *could* respond to and reconstruct its intellectual world; it tells us, in itself, nothing about how others did. Again, the authors considered here, given the decision to concentrate on the three periods in question, are the obvious ones. But they were not unchallenged. Macaulay's account of the seventeenth century had a formidable rival in the work of Samuel Gardiner. Froude's *History* was bitterly attacked, notably by Freeman. Macaulay's *History* was immensely popular, Freeman's not so. Froude's sold well, but seems to have made less impression on more popular versions of the sixteenth century than one might

---

[6] See particularly the deservedly influential article by Quentin Skinner, 'Meaning and understanding in the history of ideas', *History and Theory*, 8 (1969).

[7] J.G.A. Pocock, 'Languages and their implications: the transformation of the study of political thought, in Pocock, *Politics, Language and Time. Essays on Political Thought and History* (1972).

expect.[8] No attempt has been made in this book to measure the possible influence of the interpretations discussed; that would need a work of quite a different kind.

Even in a book such as this, a different choice of historians for attention – Gardiner, Lecky, Seeley, for example – would have given a different and perhaps soberer impression of Victorian historiography. But this book offers a section, not a survey, and it is about some of the more notable Victorian uses of the past, not, except perhaps incidentally, about contributions to the study of it. The least relevant judgement on the historians considered here, in the present context, is how far their methods or results may be vindicated by modern scholarship. There is just one qualification. Ideally the historian of historiography should know the sources available to the authors he studies as well as they did themselves; only in this way can he judge how far the past historian was led – or misled – by them, how far he imposed himself, even to perversity, upon them. Modern historians may occasionally be in this fortunate position for periods they have themselves studied, but as a general recommendation for the study of historiography it is clearly a counsel of unrealistic perfection, and no attempt has been made to follow it here, except occasionally by way of illustration.

As a general consideration, too, however, if a false impression is not to be created, the obvious must be borne in mind: that however clearly we may sometimes see the influence of current enthusiasms and preoccupations in historical writing, the historian does not work autonomously, but in collaboration with his material. It was the state of the evidence that compelled a reappraisal and compromise in Whig history in the late eighteenth and early nineteenth centuries (ch. 2); it was partly at least for the same reason that in the late nineteenth and early twentieth centuries the extension of Whig notions of continuity back again into the early medieval period (chs. 5–8) came to seem extravagant and insupportable. Though this book uses historical writing as a source for intellectual history, and is not concerned with the history of scholarship as such, it is no part of its purpose to endorse an extreme version of historical relativism.

I have said that the authors chiefly considered here are the obvious ones, given the book's intentions. Two, however, may be

---

[8] See Valerie E. Chancellor, *History for their Masters. Opinion in the English History Textbook, 1800–1914* (1970), pp. 51, 76–7, 83–4, 104–5.

debatable. The choice of Froude is questionable because only in the most extended sense can he be described as anything of a Whig historian. The reasons for choosing him will be made clearer in chapter 10, but essentially they are two: first, that no other history of the sixteenth century, in this period, exists really to challenge his; secondly, that he offers the opportunity for some extended consideration of the chief rival to Whig versions of English history, a potent one in the nineteenth century: disaffected, Radical or Tory Radical, and nostalgic. Froude occupies an ambiguous position in relation to both views, and helps us to trace their boundaries and interplay.

In Freeman's case, the obvious rival is John Richard Green. But though Green's was certainly the finer and less eccentric mind, his *oeuvre* is smaller; he died too young. He and Freeman had so much in common that a separate chapter on him would have involved an unacceptable amount of repetition. I have therefore adopted the not altogether satisfactory solution of incorporating some discussion of his work into the section on Freeman.

The book's chronological limits, though obviously there are frequent references backwards, are set roughly between the Reform Act of 1832, clearly crucial to any subsequent interpretation of an evolving constitution, and the emergence of history as a major university subject and a profession towards the end of the nineteenth century. Froude and Freeman became professors, but only late in life; essentially they were private scholars, like Hallam and Macaulay. The book's conclusion in the later nineteenth century is marked by the rise of a new kind of political and constitutional history which, if it was not devoid of social and political implication, was cooler, more self-consciously professional and 'scientific', often preferring an argumentative form of exposition to narrative. But the change itself is not my direct concern. The subject of this book is not the rise of a new outlook but the elaboration, modification and enjoyment of an old one.

I
THE WHIG

Macaulay and the Whig tradition

CHAPTER 2

A heritage and its history

Veneration, allegiance and the construction of a tradition

In his essay on Hallam's *History of England* in the *Edinburgh Review*, Macaulay remarks, not disapprovingly, on Hallam's lack of piety: 'He is less of a worshipper than any historian whom we can call to mind.'[1] The modern reader of Hallam's history is likely to feel that a criterion of piety which denies it to him must be a stringent one. There is an almost liturgical solemnity about his periodic acts of thanksgiving for English history.[2] In fact what Macaulay clearly has in mind is not so much lack of piety as such but Hallam's habitual tone of judicial equability, and the absence of the grosser forms of political partisanship traditionally express-ed in the exaltation of its historic symbols. Assuming that Macaulay's judgement was, in the sense of his time, correct,[3] he was right also to find it noteworthy.

Veneration is, of course, the required emotional register of any conscious attachment to a tradition or the manufacture of one, and nowhere more remarkably than in that tradition of pious and embattled Whig historiography of which Hallam and Macaulay himself were late and in their respective ways relatively cautious adherents. Some aspects of political piety or assertiveness the

---

[1] 'Hallam's Constitutional History' (1828) in Lady Trevelyan (ed.), *The Works of Lord Macaulay*, (1897), 8 vols, v. 164.
[2] More marked, admittedly, in his treatment of medieval history than the later period. See, e.g., Henry Hallam, *View of the State of Europe during the Middle Ages* (1818), 10th edn, 3 vols, (1853), ii, 266, 344.
[3] E.g. William Smyth, *Lectures on Modern History* (Cambridge 1840), p. 166. The chief ground of offence seems to have been Hallam's treatment of Algernon Sydney. See below, p. 13. Cf. Brougham on Hallam, quoted in John Clive, *Thomas Babington Macaulay. The Shaping of the Historian* (1975), p. 88.

English were, it is true, spared by the incomplete or ambiguous nature of the English Revolution of the seventeenth century and the relatively late arrival of the utopian convention of commemorative renaming, except of inns. Covent Garden never became Hampden Square; Whitehall was not even temporarily the Avenue of the Grand Remonstrance or Street of the 30th January. Russell Square commemorates property, not martyrdom. But historical veneration ran strongly enough in English party allegiances and the historiography they helped to form, and they attached themselves particularly to the seventeenth century. Tory fervours on behalf of the royal martyr, in the dedication of churches, or fasting on the anniversary of the king's execution, expiating the nation's guilt, as Macaulay mockingly said, with salt fish and egg sauce,[4] were matched on the other side by an exuberant reverence for the leaders of the Long Parliament. Radical parliamentary reformers could find, in 1815, no better name than the Hampden Club to express their corporate aims and sense of identity. In competitive martyrology, Charles' last parting from his young children was countered by Lord William Russell's pathetic farewell to his wife;[5] the king's speech from the scaffold by Algernon Sydney's dying affirmation of allegiance to the Good Old Cause. In the early nineteenth century such pieties mattered; were, in a sense, definitive.

To an age anxious not to disjoin political principle from moral character, personal reputation mattered too. Charles I was often only reluctantly conceded, if at all, his reputation as a good man though a bad king.[6] The eighteenth century Whig historian Mrs Catherine Macaulay had spoken of the leaders of the Long Parliament as 'the greatest men England ever produced' and asserted that 'in the annals of recorded time never had Fortune reared so tall a monument of human virtue'. She was extreme in her political views – Hallam said she 'had nothing of compromise or conciliation in her temper, and breathed the entire spirit of

---

[4] *Works*, v. 210.
[5] For a list of nineteenth century paintings of this most popular of Whig martyrdoms, see Roy Strong, *And When Did You Last See Your Father? The Victorian Painter and British History* (1978), p. 167.
[6] E.g. George Brodie, *A Constitutional History of the British Empire from the Accession of Charles I to the Restoration* (1823), new edn, 3 vols, (1866), iii, 344. Macaulay, *Works*, v. 207, 209.

Vane and Ludlow'[7] – but scarcely in veneration. The Scottish 'scientific Whig' John Millar wrote that

In the history of the world we shall perhaps discover few instances of pure and genuine patriotism equal to that which, during the reign of James, and during the first fifteen years of the reign of Charles, were displayed by those leading members of parliament, who persevered, with no less temper than steadiness, in opposing the violent means of the court.[8]

Macaulay said of Hampden that 'Almost every part of this virtuous and blameless life which is not hidden from us in modest privacy is a precious and splendid portion of our national history.'[9] Historical characters provided political landmarks and tests of allegiance. Hallam said that 'it may be reckoned as a sufficient ground for distrusting anyone's attachment to the English constitution that he reveres the name of the Earl of Strafford',[10] and Fox made the same point in the opposite sense, about veneration for the memory of Russell and Sydney, the leading martyrs of the Whig canon.[11]

The last was a sensitive point. The revelation by Sir John Dalrymple in the eighteenth century of Sydney's acceptance of bribes from the court of France was still a felt grievance. Millar, for example, while asserting that such questions of personal reputation were politically irrelevant, clearly felt uneasily that they were not, and tried hard to find an explanation consistent with high principle.[12] This chiaroscuro of 'stainless lives' balanced by monsters of cruelty and perfidy, with Strafford and Jeffries as the Lucifer and Moloch of Whig demonology,[13] was of course characteristic of an historiographic idiom in which, even apart from political partisanship, the blackening and vindication of

---

[7] Henry Hallam, *Constitutional History of England from the Accession of Henry VII to the Death of George II* (1827), Everyman's Library edn, 3 vols, ii. 243n. Cf. Macaulay, *op. cit.*, p. 23. For Catherine Macaulay, see T.P. Peardon, *The Transition in English Historical Writing, 1760–1830* (New York 1933), p. 80.

[8] John Millar, *An Historical View of the English Government from the Settlement of the Saxons in Britain to the Revolution of 1688* (1812 edn), 4 vols, iii. 225. For the term 'scientific Whiggism' see Duncan Forbes 'Scientific Whiggism: Adam Smith and John Millar', *Cambridge Journal*, vii (1954).

[9] *Works*, v. 54. Cf. Carlyle, 'best-beatified man we have', *Past and Present* (1843), (Everyman edn), 115.

[10] *Const. Hist.*, ii. 49.

[11] Charles James Fox, *A History of the Early Part of the Reign of James the Second* (1808), p. 50.

[12] Millar, iii. 407, 410.

[13] Macaulay referred to Charles II and James II as Belial and Moloch. 'Milton' (1825), *Works*, v. 36. See also his portrayal of Strafford as something like a fallen angel in the essay on Hampden, *ibid.*, 557.

characters were seen, long before Lord Acton, as a primary task and privilege.

But for seventeenth-century history, in particular, as we have seen, more was involved than historiographic convention. As Hallam said, it was 'the period from which the factions of modern times trace their divergence; which, after the lapse of almost two centuries, still calls forth the warm emotions of party-spirit, and affords a test of political principles'.[14] As late as the 1870s Stubbs thought that the period should not be taught to undergraduates; it was too close to contemporary politics.[15] The seventeenth century, and particularly the Civil War period, held the imaginations of nineteenth-century English people to a degree only second to the Middle Ages. It bequeathed, for example, an iconography which nineteenth-century painters liked to reiterate and amplify: Charles I before his judges in Westminster Hall was joined, willy-nilly, by Yeames' dapper infant in 'And When Did You Last See Your Father?' The latter was a slanted example; Whigs would doubtless have preferred something like 'Alice Lisle before Judge Jeffries'.

According to Lecky, 'We are Cavaliers or Roundheads before we are Conservatives or Liberals.'[16] If so, it was a significant choice, at least earlier in the century, for if one knew a Victorian's view of Charles I or Hampden one could have a strong inkling whether he voted Whig or Tory. When Hallam said that in weighing the merits of the two sides in the Civil War we should be 'judging whether a thoroughly upright and enlightened man would rather have listed under the royal or parliamentary standard',[17] he was not so much introducing a quaintly anachronistic partisanship as speaking of a choice many of his contemporaries seem to have made in any case, no doubt less scrupulously. In the minds of these retrospective recruits to the levies of Essex, Rupert and Cromwell, we may suppose a number of influences at work: social position, snobbery, family tradition – much the same, in fact, as those which direct contemporary political choices, lacking only the cruder forms of self-interest. Many, no doubt, of those who took the cavalier side did so for the reason frankly avowed by Sir Walter Scott: that he considered it the more

[14] Const. Hist., ii. 85.
[15] William Stubbs, Seventeen Lectures on the Study of Medieval and Modern History (O.U.P. 1887), p. 54.
[16] W.E.H. Lecky, The Political Value of History (1892), p. 19.
[17] Const. Hist., ii. 126.

gentlemanlike of the two.[18] But among the agencies overtly making for choice, the most important was the long identification of the Stuart cause with the Established Church and of the opposition with Puritan Dissent. So long as Church and Dissent were categories profoundly struck into the institutional, social and intellectual fabric, memories of the seventeenth century would resonate. Both sides could look to it for records of martyrdoms and persecutions: clergy deprived, churches desecrated, dissenting congregations harried, ministers fined, imprisoned, mutilated. These partisan memories made highly coloured correlatives for modern Anglican anxieties and the continuing grievances of Dissenters. In Scotland and Ireland, of course, the memories were more ferocious still.

The allegiances such historic recollections fostered were clearer cut and more relevant to the nineteenth century than any historical continuity – a continuity, as Hallam admitted, much blurred and confused, and at least partly imaginary – of Whig and Tory parties with their seventeenth-century precursors. And in the first half of the nineteenth century the cry of 'the Church in danger' rang with more plausibility than at any time since the seventeenth century.

There were other correspondences too, historical parallels which acquired a sharper sense of relevance from the intensified political fears and hostilities of the period between the French Revolution and the Reform Act of 1832. The habit of drawing such parallels was formed early, in some contexts even from necessity. Conditions in England in the early years of the century, though repressive, were not, like those in France after the Restoration,[19] such as to make it prudent to refer to current political issues under a veil of historical allusion. Young men still under educational discipline, however, were subject to sterner constraints. The Cambridge Union, in Macaulay's time, was allowed to debate only the public questions of previous centuries. Naturally, historical parallels were eagerly sought. It requires little imagination to conceive the excitement with which, in the same period, in the mid-1820s just prior to Catholic Emancipation, the Eton Society of Gladstone's day must have debated whether the conduct of England to Ireland from the Revolution 1688 to 1776 was justifiable, or 'Was Queen Elizabeth justified in her persecu-

[18] J.G. Lockhart, *The Life of Sir Walter Scott* (abridged edn 1898), p. 28.
[19] Stanley Mellon, *The Political Uses of History. A Study of Historians in the French Restoration* (Stanford, Calif. 1958).

tion of the Roman Catholics?'[20] England's troubled relations with Ireland continued to give an edge to the events of the seventeenth century. When Macaulay said that to write of Ireland was to tread on a volcano on which the lava was still glowing, he no doubt expressed merely the perennial feelings of an Englishman about to write on Irish history,[21] but the issue of Catholic Emancipation gave them in some respects an additional sensitivity in the first third of the century. As Macaulay was to point out in his *History*, the coronation oath for the sake of which George III baulked Pitt's project of reconciliation was the one drafted for William and Mary.[22] The precedents of the seventeenth century were for Whigs, moreover, for once uncomfortably ambiguous. English Whigs were for Emancipation, but in Ireland the hero of the Protestant ascendancy was also the Whig hero of the Glorious Revolution, William III. Tories wished to stand by the Anglican establishment, so that, as Macaulay said in his essay on Milton (1825), 'The very same persons who, in this country never omit an opportunity of reviving every wretched Jacobite slander respecting the Whigs, have no sooner crossed St George's Channel, than they begin to fill their bumpers to the glorious and immortal memory.'[23]

The other central issue of the period, parliamentary reform, was equally confusing. The constitution on which the Tories wished to stand pat was, after all, largely the creation of the Revolution of 1688. They could praise the Revolution as conclusive, while Whigs committed to reform could only consider it as an instance of a necessary constitutional adjustment made just in time. It was necessary for the latter to argue, as Macaulay did in the Reform Bill debates,[24] that the Whigs of 1688 had legislated for their own times and the present generation should do the same; it was necessary, in other words, for Whigs to detach their notion of the spirit of the Glorious Revolution from the letter. John Clive has shown admirably how, in the essay on Milton and in his 'Dialogue between Cowley and Milton' Macaulay attempted to deprive the Tories of their new-found enthusiasm for the Revolution by asserting its essential continuity, which no Tory would be disposed

---

[20] Sir George Otto Trevelyan, *The Life and Letters of Lord Macaulay* (Popular edn 1899), p. 58; M.D.R. Foot (ed.), *The Gladstone Diaries* (O.U.P. 1968), i. 45, 96.
[21] Macaulay, *History of England*, *Works*, i. 619.
[22] *Works*, ii. 489.
[23] That is, of William. *ibid.*, v. 35.
[24] 'Speeches', *ibid.*, viii, e.g. p. 16; Cf. 'Sir James Mackintosh' (1835), *ibid.*, vi. 93.

to allow, with the Parliamentarians in the Civil War and even the regicides.[25]

Of course, in dwelling in this way on the relevance to contemporary politics of these allusions to the conflicts of the seventeenth century we are running some risk of misunderstanding. The mode of political discourse in the early nineteenth century was still strongly marked by historical allusion and by the sense of historic party identities. Sydney Smith was driven to protest in the *Edinburgh Review* against the habit of arguing 'a Gulielmo', that is by treating every issue in terms of the hypothetical question what would the men of 1688 have done.[26] But appeals to precedent were in no way overriding as they had been in the seventeenth century itself. In the historical memories of English people of the constitutional conflicts of the seventeenth century, and their long, slow slackening from the unappeasable resentments of Jacobites, Non-Jurors and Old Commonwealthmen, to the cheerful scufflings of the Sealed Knot Society in our own time, the first half of the nineteenth century is a kind of middle point: the memories and sense of identity were certainly not all-absorbing or even dominant, but they were not yet trivial or irrelevant. They still provided symbols of political identification; indeed, Clive has suggested that in a period of confused political allegiances and policies they offered an important means of political self-definition, 'supplying touchstones and confrontations lacking in the contemporary situation'.[27]

It was no doubt a help that an allegiance largely defined by an historic symbolism by no means necessarily implied any particular knowledge or detailed interpretation of English seventeenth-century history. As Macaulay admitted, 'the cause for which Hampden bled on the field and Sydney on the scaffold is enthusiastically toasted by many an honest radical who would be puzzled to explain the difference between Ship money and the Habeas Corpus Act'.[28] Within wide limits, the more imprecise a political myth the better it can perform its functions. But for the more reflective what was desired and often assumed was not merely sacred events and revered heroes and martyrs but a whole tradition, of which the faithful of the present day were the only

---

25 John Clive, *Macaulay*, pp. 91–2. I am much indebted to this work, above all for its illuminating analyses of Macaulay's early writings in relation to contemporary politics.
26 *Edinburgh Review*, xli (1813), quoted in John Clive, *Scotch Reviewers. The Edinburgh Review*, 1802–1815 (1957), pp. 99–100.
27 Clive, *Macaulay*, p. 95.   28 *Works*, v. 165.

true heirs and preservers. Macaulay's famous Edinburgh election speech, with its Miltonic vision of a great Whig party stretching its mighty length back through English history, from the Reform Act to the Elizabethan parliamentary opposition to monopolies, is his version of such a tradition,[29] which, in the essay on Mackintosh he had extended back in the name of 'progress' to Magna Carta;[30] even Macaulay, though he involved Peter Wentworth and Algernon Sydney in the general election of 1839 – an election the Whigs fought with the fervent support of their sovereign – baulked at flatly calling the Magna Carta barons Whigs.

It is striking that four leading Whig politicians in the first half of the nineteenth century wrote histories of England devoted to, and largely concerned with, the later seventeenth century,[31] while Disraeli's attempt to restate a philosophical and historical basis for Toryism included a rehabilitation of the policies of Charles I, of whose reign his father had written a sympathetic history.[32] An intellectual Whiggism – and Disraeli felt the same about Toryism – was necessarily pressed to provide an interpretation of English history both before and since the revolution of the seventeenth century.

Before, because the political claims of the seventeenth century had themselves been framed so notably in terms of versions of the national past, in which the Norman Conquest, Magna Carta and the antiquity of Parliament were points of the highest sensitivity.[33] If the Parliamentarian version had been wholly mistaken – and it had become clear that in some respects at least it could not be historically sustained – there would be an uncomfortable sense in which, on the Parliamentarian's chosen ground, the Stuarts were entirely vindicated. The case was not, in fact, so dire, but it remained a matter of continuing importance to nineteenth-century Whigs to justify, in part at least, the constitutional claims as well as the achievements of the seventeenth-century Parliamentary leaders whose political heirs they claimed to be. Macaulay noted the consequences for historical writing of the vital role played in English political controversy by constitutional precedent and

[29] 'Speech to the Electors of Edinburgh', *Works*, viii. 158.   [30] *Works*, vi. 96.

[31] Charles James Fox, Lord John Russell, Sir James Mackintosh and Macaulay himself.

[32] Disraeli, *Sybil*, bk iv, ch 1. Isaac Disraeli, *Commentaries on the Life and Reign of Charles the First* (1828), 5 vols.

[33] See particularly J.G.A. Pocock, *The Ancient Constitution and the Feudal Law* (C.U.P. 1957), and Quentin Skinner, 'History and ideology in the English Revolution', *Historical Journal*, 8 (1965).

hence by the political annexation of the past: 'in our country the dearest interests of parties have frequently been staked on the results of the researches of antiquaries. The inevitable consequence was that our antiquaries conducted their researches in the spirit of partisans.[34] The implication of the tense was not entirely justified in the first half of the nineteenth century. Maitland, commenting on this remark of Macaulay's half a century later, observed cheerfully: 'Well, that reproach has passed away.'[35] Even then his confidence was a trifle excessive;[36] at the time of Macaulay's initial remark it would have been decidedly so.

But the Whig was driven forward, as well as backward, from the seventeenth century, by the need to establish, as all claimants to the possession of a tradition must do, the authentic, unimpeachable line of descent. We can see this claim embodied, in this case resentfully, in the early eighteenth century use of the term 'True Whig' for the radical, republican Commonwealthmen.[37] We see it, from the opposite camp, in Burke's distinction between 'old' and 'new' Whigs, in his attempt to discredit the latter.[38] Every tradition acquires its polemical commentary, each side claiming sole legitimate descent. But the connection between commentary and tradition is a peculiarly intimate one: commentary which becomes canonical becomes part of the tradition it qualifies and explicates. The nineteenth-century Whig historian, in choosing his English history, had also to choose his historiographical tradition, the version of historical Whiggism to which his allegiance was given. It is to his available choices that we shall shortly have to turn. First, however, it is necessary briefly to restate what we may, with an inevitable oversimplification, think of as the 'classic' seventeenth-century Parliamentarians' and common lawyers' version of the national past. Some distinguished scholarship has been devoted to reconstructing this in recent years[39] so we can be brief.

With minds bent to a tense grasp of rights, the Parliamentary leaders and common lawyers of the early seventeenth century had

---

34 Macaulay, *History, Works*, i. 21.
35 F.W. Maitland, 'Why the history of English law is not written', *Collected Papers of F.W. Maitland*, ed. H.A.L. Fisher (C.U.P. 1911), 3 vols, i. 492.
36 See my discussion of this, in '"The village community" and the uses of history in late nineteenth century England' in N. McKendrick (ed.), *Historical Perspectives. Studies in English Thought and Society in Honour of J.H. Plumb* (1974).
37 For this see Caroline Robbins, *The Eighteenth Century Commonwealthman* (Cambridge, Mass. 1957).
38 Edmund Burke, 'An appeal from the New to the Old Whigs'.
39 See particularly Pocock, *Ancient Constitution*; Skinner, 'History and ideology'.

approached the problems of constitutional rectitude in a manner
that was legalistic rather than pragmatic. However anxious they
may have been to settle their differences with the crown, their
theoretical idiom dictated that the questions at issue should be
seen not as adjustments of powers but as questions of historic
right. Paradoxically, it was their very belief that a legal solution, in
which the prerogatives of the crown and the rights of the subject
were harmonised, must already, in a sense, exist, as well as their
subscription, in some cases, to the extremer tenets of Protestant
theology, which led them to see the conflicts of their time in
somewhat Manichaean terms. If the solution did not answer, it
must be because someone was wilfully rejecting it, just as the
kindred belief that the Bible, read with a pure heart and mind, was
of unequivocal import, tended to deny to theological opponents
any claim to good intentions. It was a habit of mind which the
later historians who adopted their cause inherited, with less
justification; in the young Macaulay's case the Manichaeanism
could be almost literal: in the essay on Milton he spoke of the
seventeenth century as 'the very crisis of the great conflict between
Oromasdes and Arimanes'.[40] It was an historiographical tradition
not rich in a sense of history's tragic ironies.

But despite this continuing intransigence it was found in the
long run impossible to argue that the view held of English
constitutional history by the seventeenth-century Parliamentarians
and common lawyers was literally correct. It was not true that an
ancient immemorial constitution had descended, essentially un-
changed, to the early seventeenth century, to be plotted against
and subverted by the early Stuart kings. In particular, the demonstration by the royalist Robert Brady that the writs of summons to
the House of Commons could not be traced back beyond the
thirteenth century, though at first bitterly contested, eventually
won general acceptance. Some, it is true, continued to believe, like
the seventeenth century Levellers, in an ideal ancient constitution
forfeited much earlier in English history, destroyed by the conquering Normans or overlaid by feudalism.[41] Such a belief,
locating a lost constitution in a twilight past, provided it remained
unperturbed by the mere lack of evidence, was more or less
invulnerable to historical criticism, as the Whig idea of continuity

[40] 'Milton', Works, v. 23. In his Reform Bill speech six years later, however, he recognised
Charles I's predicament, Works, viii. 74.
[41] See Christopher Hill, 'The Norman yoke' in Puritanism and Revolution (1958).

was not. The Harringtonian 'True Whigs', and the Country Party Tories of the Walpole period, under the guidance of Bolingbroke, located their ideally balanced 'Gothic' constitution in a more recent past, in the later middle ages or even in the reign of Elizabeth.[42] But though such beliefs retained their polemical usefulness, they became in the long run increasingly difficult to sustain historically.

The variety of Whiggisms and the Humean challenge

The appeal to an ancient constitution came to be significantly supplemented and even in some cases supplanted among Whigs and their historical apologists, by other lines of argument. There was, first, the assertion of the ahistorical philosophical doctrine of original natural rights of man, which could be allowed either to support or replace the analogous 'historical' claim to ancient constitutional rights. Secondly, sometimes in association, some-times in rivalry with the philosophical claim, there was the eighteenth-century idea of the progress of society, which signifi-cantly inverted the prestige hitherto attached to antiquity and innovation. It was an idea which seems to have been first used in political polemics by the ministerialist writers employed in defend-ing the government of Walpole. Leaving to the intransigent 'True Whigs' and to Bolingbroke and the Tories any enthusiasm for the 'ancient constitution' supposedly finally corrupted by Walpole, they flatly asserted the value and justification of modernity and constitutional innovation. Liberty was modern, not ancient; the admired 'Gothic' constitution was a feudal anarchy in which no ordinary citizen's rights were secure.[43] The Glorious Revolution had not restored or confirmed the free English constitution but brought it about. Divested of its obvious crudities, this use of the concept of the progress of society is the key to the interpretation of constitutional history provided by the eighteenth-century Scottish school of 'sociological' or 'philosophical' historians, most notably

[42] Issac Kramnick, *Bolingbroke and His Circle. The Politics of Nostalgia in the Age of Walpole* (Cambridge, Mass. 1968). Also J.G.A. Pocock, *The Machiavellian Moment. Florentine Political Though and the Atlantic Republican Tradition* (Princeton 1975); Duncan Forbes, *Hume's Philosophical Politics* (C.U.P. 1975), ch. 8; for Harrington, see Pocock (ed.) *The Political Works of James Harrington* (C.U.P. 1977).

[43] Kramnick, pp. 127ff. See also Quentin Skinner, 'The principles and practice of opposition; the case of Bolingbroke versus Walpole' in McKendrick, *op. cit.*

David Hume, Adam Smith and John Millar, though it did not preclude in their writings elements of ambiguous feeling, and misgivings about the political consequences of 'the progress of opulence' analogous to the condemnation of them in the Harringtonian radical Whig tradition.[44]

Finally, the English common law tradition itself developed – most strikingly in the hands of Burke – a subtlety in its interpretation of the ancient constitution which, though it remained as distinct as ever from theories of divine right or royal absolutism, allowed it to treat in a more flexible spirit the notion of constitutional change. It might, therefore, be no longer necessary to deny that the constitutional developments of the seventeenth century were at least in some modified sense innovative. The notion of continuity, always a necessary feature of the Parliamentarian's – though not of the disgruntled 'disinherited' radical's – conception of the ancient constitution, proved susceptible of a creative elaboration: an accommodation to the idea of change. This is of course the Burkean[45] notion of change-in-continuity, of the sequence of precedents seen as itself a flexible, creative and enriching process.

With the first of these additional possible Whiggisms mentioned above – the ahistorical conception of natural rights, usually spoken of in this context as Lockean – we are not directly concerned, though it was formally accepted, often alongside the newer ahistorical ideas of utility, as an ultimate political justification by the late eighteenth- and early nineteenth-century Whig historians we shall have to consider; the availability of Lockean and utilitarian arguments as an ultimate justification helped, one might say, to take some of the pressure off the still eagerly desired demonstration that the English Revolution of the seventeenth century had preserved an essential constitutional continuity.

Ideas of progress and the Burkean conception of tradition, however, are the warp and woof of all those nineteenth-century interpretations of English history which, in contrast to the lamentations, whether Tory Radical or simply radical, for a forfeited or corrupted social and constitutional idyll located somewhere in the Saxon or medieval past, may safely if loosely be described as Whig interpretations. The innovation that is most

---

[44] See Donald Winch, *Adam Smith's Politics. An Essay in Historiographic Revision* (C.U.P. 1978), esp. chs 3 and 4.
[45] Pocock, 'Burke and the Ancient Constitution', *Politics, Language and Time* (1971).

immediately striking in both the Scottish conception of progress and the Burkean notion of a political tradition creating itself through time is the repudiation of antiquarianism as the approved mode of political argument, though this implication is muted and sometimes obscured in the more Burkean lines of argument by the continuing respect for precedent. The characteristically Scottish conception of stages of the history of civil society, on the other hand, though it fostered classification and comparison, and even, as for example in the work of Adam Ferguson,[46] provided the basis for a critique of modern commercial society, allowed, obviously, for no appeal to earlier 'stages' to determine questions of right. When respect was paid to the past it was done in the eighteenth-century manner, as a kind of profit and loss balance sheet applied to the development of civilisation, not as an appeal to the past as authority. As Millar said, the criterion which had supplanted the authorisation of the past was utility: 'The blind respect and reverence paid to ancient institutions has given place to a desire of examining their uses . . .. The fashion of scrutinizing public measures according to their utility has now become very universal.'[47]

But the English Whig too, though sometimes less obviously, had distanced himself from the older constitutional antiquarianism. Political tradition was a living thing, prompted and nourished by its past moments but not circumscribed by them. Burke himself had contrasted the search for the constitution 'in rotten parchments under dripping and perishing walls' with the constitution made active in the traditions of the great political families, 'in full vigour and acting with vital energy and power in the characters of the leading men and natural interests of the country'.[48]

The historians learnt the lesson; indeed, in some cases were eager to learn it. Whig supporters of parliamentary reform, for example, were necessarily committed to a flexible view of constitutionality. A sovereign people represented by a sovereign parliament might wisely choose to respect the past but could not be confined by it. As Macaulay put it in the Reform Bill debates: 'Sir, we are legislators not antiquaries.'[49] Hallam declared that the

---

[46] Adam Ferguson, *A History of Civil Society* (1767).
[47] Millar, *Historical View*, iv. 305.
[48] Edmund Burke, 'Letter to the Duke of Richmond, in Lucy Sutherland (ed.), *The Correspondence of Edmund Burke* (C.U.P. 1960), ii. 377.
[49] Quoted Clive, *Macaulay*, p. 181.

right to a free government could not be tried by a jury of antiquaries.[50] Hallam's own enthusiasm for the English love of precedent was tempered by a sense that it had made English law as a whole unmanageably complex and unsystematic: 'England must find her Tribonian.'[51]

Indeed, the Whigs in this period paradoxically, while continuing to insist, as we shall see, that the ancient constitution was essentially one of liberty, accuse Tories of an excessive attachment to constitutionality – a development understandable in the years leading up to the Reform Act. The Scottish Whig historian George Brodie, for example, speaks of 'Writers' – he probably, though absurdly, means Hume (he *usually* means Hume) – 'who have espoused the cause of prerogative – as if they deemed it a sufficient reason for consigning the people to slavery, that they can plead the precedents of former times.'[52] Hallam identified as the perennial characteristic of the Tory that for him 'the constitution was an ultimate point . . . from which he thought it altogether impossible to swerve' while the Whig 'deemed all forms of government subordinate to the public good, and therefore liable to change when they should cease to promote that',[53] while Fox based his characterisation of the parties on a similar antithesis, between 'the natural rights of man on the one hand, and the authority of artificial institution on the other'.[54]

In fact, as this last remark reminds us, for all the English and Scottish Whig historians considered so far, the ultimate appeal in political questions was to Lockean or utilitarian first principles; often, as with Millar, a loose combination of the two, though in his case utilitarianism seems predominant; adherence to natural rights *and* utility is for him the defining Whig characteristic.[55] All in fact, were, in terms of Burke's distinction, New Whigs . Yet they also show every inclination to wish to be Old Whigs as well, at least in the flexible sense which Burke himself had done so much to define. In innovating one *was* acting in the spirit of one's constitutional ancestors: as Russell put it, giving a fair imitation of Burke: 'It was part of the practical wisdom of our ancestors, to alter and vary the form of our institutions as time went on; to suit them to the circumstances of the time and reform them according

[50] Hallam, *View*, iii. 158.
[51] *ibid.*, ii. 339.
[52] Brodie, i. 4.
[53] Hallam, *Const. Hist.*, p. 176.
[54] Fox, *James the Second*, p. 60.
[55] Millar, iv. 294, 298.

to the dictates of experience'[56] – and he goes on to draw the contemporary moral. Yet it was not enough that the Whig's ancestors had innovated; they must also have been respectful of constitutional precedent and form, to license and enjoin a similar respect in their descendants. As Russell also put it, 'the abuses of our constitution are capable of amendments strictly conformable to its spirit'.[57] The Whig *via media*, with its belief in the value of continuity and the associated virtue of piety, placed heavy demands on those it chose to claim as ancestors: they must have been unafraid of necessary innovation, yet also deeply versed in, and observant of, constitutional precedent.

For of course the Whig was conscious not only of the obstinacy of the Tory attachment to the existing constitution but of the vehemence of the radicals' repudiation of it. At a time when the language of radicalism incorporated both the abstract, historical rights of man and the nostalgia of renewed appeals to the democratic rights supposedly enjoyed under the ancient constitution, it made equal sense for the Whig to distance himself from constitutional antiquarianism and to qualify his Lockean or utilitarian arguments of last resort by a continuing appropriation of the historic past. The Whig, in rejecting a mere constitutional antiquarianism, had not, characteristically, renounced his possession of English history as a heritage, but merely claimed to hold it on easier terms. Hallam's declaration of independence, referred to earlier, was significantly and typically followed by a reservation in favour of piety: 'it is a generous pride that entwines the consciousness of hereditary freedom with the memory of our ancestors'.[58] But for the ancestors to be proper objects of piety they should ideally themselves be Whigs, venerating as well as venerable. Their own attachment to the ways of constitutionalism must have been profound, and their view of what the historic constitution they venerated actually was must have been fundamentally correct. The Whig could not comfortably lay claim to the possession of English history as a heritage if his alleged political ancestors had not done so also, and this they could not have done if their own view of English history was a mistaken one. The trouble was that, as we have seen, in a number of ways it did appear mistaken. A rescue operation was clearly necessary.

The chief obstacle to the Whig's pious appropriation of the

[56] Russell, p. 18.   [57] *ibid.*, pp. xv–xvi.   [58] *View*, iii. 158.

national past, the obstinate litigant who blocked the undisputed enjoyment of his inheritance, was above all, and for nearly a century, Hume. Hume affected the Whig historians of the early nineteenth century, to reapply a simile of Macaulay's, like a hair in the mouth: inescapable and intolerable. His offences were manifold and rank.[59] He had claimed, notoriously, that under the Tudors the English had as little public liberty as the subjects of the Grand Turk. There was no established free constitution for the Stuarts to transgress or attempt to overthrow.[60] The actions of the Long Parliament were clearly innovative and in many respects unreasonable. Hume had presented a sympathetic account of Charles I's predicament, and condemned Strafford's attainder. And, as might be expected of a well-known atheist, he had lacked piety, finding the leaders of the Long Parliament uncouth and fanatical.[61]

The dominance of Hume's history for over half a century at least, in defiance of almost every Whig prepossession, was remarkable. Each of the historians mentioned here announced at some point his intention of refuting the distortions of Hume; indeed, for most of them it figured as the central object of their work. Hallam, in pursuit of the Whig middle way, proclaimed his intention of steering between the errors of the radical libertarian ancient constitutionalists on the one hand, and Hume's indulgence to the royal prerogative on the other.[62] George Brodie published in 1822 a three-volume history which is a protracted, point-by-point refutation of Hume. Charles James Fox, according to Lord Holland, was largely inspired to write his own history in order to correct the errors of Hume.[63] Macaulay was obviously flattered as well as amused when, after the publication of his *History*, he saw in a bookseller's window an edition of Hume advertised as 'valuable as an introduction to Macaulay';[64] it was almost a century since Hume's first volumes had been published. Hume was a felt presence for every subsequent historian of England, and of seventeenth-century England in particular, up to and including Macaulay: he was important both in what they absorbed and what they consciously and strenuously rejected.

[59] The account of Hume here is heavily dependent on Duncan Forbes, *Hume's Philosophical Politics*.
[60] David Hume, *The History of Great Britain. The Reigns of James I and Charles I*, ed. Duncan Forbes (Penguin edn 1970), p. 134.
[61] *ibid.*, p. 418.   [62] Hallam, *View*, iii. 155–8.   [63] Fox, *op. cit.*, pp. ix–x.
[64] Trevelyan, *Life*, p. 522

Hume's position is initially similar to that of the early eighteenth-century Whig apologists for Walpole, in that it incorporates a conception of progress and holds liberty to be on the whole modern rather than ancient. Of course Hume's version was far subtler, having nothing of that stark political Manichaeanism which Walpole's pamphleteers had perforce taken over from Bolingbroke and the Country Party polemics when standing their arguments on their head. For Hume, as Forbes puts it, there was not one ancient constitution, but several and ample precedents could be quoted on both sides,[65] though the period immediately preceding the conflicts of the seventeenth century had been one in which the royal prerogative was supreme. He drew the obvious inference – and it was this, as Forbes points out, which was largely responsible for his 'Tory' reputation – from the Walpolean apologists' view that liberty is essentially modern, though it was not one which Whigs generally cared to see proclaimed: namely that if liberty is modern the Stuarts could hardly be blamed for not conceding it. This is presumably what he meant by saying his history was Whig as to measures but Tory as to men. The general Whig outcry against this shows, as Forbes again points out, how far Whigs generally were from having abandoned the 'ancient constitution'.

Another ground of offence was the cool, Scottish cosmopolitanism, inimical to the pious enthusiasms of the 'vulgar' Whig tradition, with its fervours about the Good Old Cause and the 'matchless constitution', which characterised Hume's notion of the progress of civil society.[66] The latter was for Hume a general European phenomenon, of which English constitutional liberties were only a local, welcome, though eccentric manifestation. He did not, like so many English Whigs in the eighteenth and early nineteenth centuries, condescend to the French because French civilisation was flawed by a despotic form of government. There could be a distinction between political and personal liberty: the latter was a function of civilisation; the former might also be, under favourable conditions, but its relation to civilisation is ambiguous, and England's development of parliamentary supremacy in the late seventeenth century made her an anomaly in the European comity of nations.[67] This development owed more, it seemed, to circumstance and geography, and to the religious

---

[65] Forbes, *Hume's Philosophical Politics*, p. 267.   [66] *ibid.*, p. 298.
[67] Hume, *History*, Forbes' introduction, p. 23.

fanaticism of the Parliamentary opposition than to any abiding 'spirit of liberty' in the constitution.

Progress and the constitution: the Whig compromise

In the Whig historians of the late eighteenth and early nineteenth centuries, Millar and Brodie, and the English, Fox, Hallam and Russell, it is tempting to see these emphases continued; Scottish cosmopolitanism set against English nationalism, the Scottish conception of the growth of liberty as part of the history of civilisation against an English Burkean conception of the English people weaving the fabric of a free constitution, spider-like, out of its own entrails. Up to a point these correlations hold, but only with qualifications. Millar is certainly even more overtly cosmopolitan than Hume; comparison is a constant preoccupation with him in his history, as one might expect from the author of the 'sociological' *Origin of the Distinction of Ranks*. Millar was the heir of that whole characteristic and impressive late eighteenth-century Scottish enterprise, the reconstruction and explanation of the History of Civil Society through a typology of 'stages'. He is clearly heavily indebted not only to Hume but to Adam Smith. In his history he boldly distinguishes, in the Scottish manner, three steps in the development of English society: pastoral, at the time of the Saxon settlement, feudal and commercial; the advent of the latter is placed in the reign of James I, with the union of the crowns of England and Scotland – for once a slightly unjustified Caledonianism, perhaps.[68] The English Revolution of the seventeenth century is firmly related to social, economic and geographical conditions: the new spirit associated with commercial society kindles the love of liberty; England's insular position and absence of a standing army make the crown vulnerable, at a time when elsewhere in Europe professional armies are tilting the balance in favour of absolutism.[69]

Similarly, if one turns to Brodie, it is not hard to relate his intentions, at least, to the Scottish tradition; he has a conception of social and economic history rare at the time in England, and clearly derivative from an eighteenth-century conception of 'civil society'. Yet though Millar and Brodie are recognisably Scottish historians, and though Millar's history, at least, clearly owes much

[68] Millar, iii. 1.   [69] *ibid.*, iii. 120–2.

to Hume as well as to Smith, they are not Humeans but Whigs; Millar dedicated his *History* to Fox. Both are in fact critics of Hume; Brodie, indeed, his severest critic. To both of them, it is unmistakably important – to Brodie it is vital – that Hume *must* be wrong in his views on the state of the constitution in the Tudor and Stuart period. It cannot be allowed to be the case that the constitutional precedents were contradictory, or even on balance favourable to the prerogative. There must be a line of essential constitutional practice and theory, intermittently interrupted though it may have been; and that line must exhibit constitutional liberty and representative government.

When we turn to the English historians, we again find, not surprisingly no doubt, that just as the sociological bent of the Scots did not relieve them from the standard partialities of the Whig view, the English historians, or some of them, have learnt from Hume a certain guardedness, albeit unwillingly. Whether they have imbibed very much of the Scottish bent towards comparison and typology is more questionable. Russell boldly announces at the beginning of his *History* that there are four stages in the history of 'society',[70] but these categories prove to be more narrowly political than this might lead one to expect. Russell's 'sociology' in fact derives much more from the older Machiavellian[71] theories of the civic humanist tradition than from the distinctively Scottish notion of social and economic stages, though this is a line of thought also perceptible in Millar. For both Millar and Russell the initial problem is the difference between ancient and modern liberty. The former belonged essentially to the city state, and was lost when conquests brought an extended dominion and eroded military vigour and public spirit. As Russell succinctly put it, 'the very force and strength which their form of government produced tended, by increasing the commonwealth, to destroy the laws and manners which gave them birth'.[72] How has it come about that England has escaped this fate, reconciling liberty with opulence and power?

This older, Machiavellian and Harringtonian political sociology was cyclical and pessimistic; it was obviously the fruit of long meditation on the fate of Rome, history's greatest cautionary lesson, and the extension of a diagnosis into a law of the decay of

[70] Russell, p. vii.
[71] He prefixes a maxim from *The Prince* to his chapter on the Revolution. *ibid.*, ch. x.
[72] *ibid.*, Preface. Millar, i. 6–8.

states and the loss of liberty, as a result of the corruption of public virtue by opulence and luxury; Montesquieu and Gibbon both make extensive use of it. By contrast, the Scottish account of the development of society through distinct social and economic stages was equally obviously hinged on the emergence in Europe during the last three centuries of a new social type, the commercial stage of society. It was, by comparison and despite reservations, optimistic. But the older account was still challenging enough for Millar and after him Russell to use in formulating the case of England as a problem, though neither shows any of the character-istic civic humanist enthusiasm for ancient republican patriotism which had normally accompanied it. For Millar, Roman patriot-ism 'was far from being directed by a liberal spirit'.[73] His work makes in fact a sustained attempt to solve the problem posed by England, in terms set not by the older Machiavellian ideas but by the new Scottish explanatory context provided by the history of civil society.

Russell, though he poses the problem, makes no serious attempt to solve it. Explanation soon gives way to incantation in the vulgar Whig manner: 'At whatever time it originated, the early preva-lence of freedom is nobly characteristic of the English nation' – and he goes on to speak of its capacity for resisting 'degrading institutions and customs imported from other countries'.[74] Rus-sell's work is, as he in places admits, heavily dependent on Hallam. It is not easy to extract any general explanations from Hallam. He mentions, for example, the growth in wealth in the sixteenth and seventeenth centuries as part of the background to the Civil War,[75] but essentially his *History* is pitched in another key; legalistic, constitutionalist and insular. English liberty is indigenous: 'the character of the bravest and most virtuous among nations has not depended on the accidents of race or climate, but has been gradually wrought by the plastic influence of civil rights, transmit-ted as a prescriptive inheritance through a long course of generations'.[76] This is, of course, the authentic voice of insular English Whiggism.

If Hallam has a general explanation it is in terms of the early establishment of civic equality. The nobility never enjoyed the immunities it possessed elsewhere, while the gentry enjoyed no special privileges. 'There is no part of our law so admirable as this

---

[73] Millar, i. 10. Cf. Russell, Preface.   [74] Russell, p. 8.
[75] Hallam, *Const. Hist.*, ii. 73–4.   [76] *View*, iii. 158.

equality of civil rights'[77] – there is an echo, here, perhaps, of the old Harringtonian theme of the independent freeholder as the indispensable basis of freedom. Hallam presents this at least in part as a paradoxical benefit of the Norman Conquest. The feudal barons, held more strictly in check by a strong monarchy, were driven, as at the time of Magna Carta, to make common cause with their inferiors. But often Hallam is content to leave causality to a higher power; as when reflecting on England's preservation from violent revolution by her early conquest of constitutional liberty and civil rights:

It is, I am firmly persuaded, to this peculiarly democratical character of the English monarchy, that we are indebted for its long permanence, its regular improvement, and its present vigour. It is a singular, a providential circumstance, that, in an age when the gradual march of civilisation and commerce was so little foreseen, our ancestors, deviating from the usages of neighbouring countries, should, as if deliberately, have guarded against that expansive force, which, in bursting through obstacles improvidently opposed, has scattered havoc over Europe.[78]

Of course, a period of continental revolution and a generation of European warfare was an unlikely time for the elaboration of a sceptical, 'philosophical' cosmopolitanism of the mid-eighteenth-century Humean kind. It is understandable that there should have been comfort in an older kind of insular self-congratulation. The passage from Hallam above contains much, old and new: the notion of commerce as an ' expansive force' with consequences for the political and social order; the belief in an ancient liberty, seen here as the equality of civil rights, and not, of course, in the radical manner, as Saxon democracy; and the insistence on the unique, indigenous character of that liberty, in association with a notion of special divine protection. The reference to the latter was no mere isolated flourish. Elsewhere Hallam speaks of 'destined means' and of 'the chain of causes through which a gracious providence has favoured the consolidation of our liberties and welfare'.[79] The groundswell of Hallam's *History* is gratitude for English history and a rather nervous insistence on national unity, on the absence of fundamental barriers or clashes of interest between ranks. Those historians (like Millar) who took a cool view of Magna Carta as an essentially feudal document are accused of being 'ungrateful'.[80] Participation in the fellowship of the constitution becomes almost sacramental: 'We do not argue from the creed of

[77] *ibid.*, ii. 344.　[78] *ibid.*　[79] *Const. Hist.*, iii. 83, 46.　[80] *View*, ii. 323.

the English constitution to those who have abandoned its communion.'[81] To emphasise both the inclusiveness and the providential uniqueness of that communion was the central impetus of Hallam's *History*. It is for that reason that Magna Carta is so important to him; it is the first 'national' event; it is for the same reason that he dwells proudly on the absence of legal distinction between gentry and freemen. It was a contention which, in the agitation for extensions of the franchise – to which Hallam refers in the conclusion to his *History* – could have a useful duality, enjoining mutual trust on both haves and have-nots. English liberty was unique but also capacious; the message of Hallam's *History* is a justified sense of shared privilege.

To English Whigs, characteristically, England is related to the fate of Europe not, as in Hume and Millar, as the sharer of a common advancing civilisation, which in England, because of peculiar circumstances, has developed distinctive political features, but, if at all, as the bearer of a political mission. It was not a new idea, but the times gave it an additional urgency; it was a national response to the vigorous ecumenism of the French Revolution. The belief that, as the young Macaulay put it, in the seventeenth century 'the destinies of the human race were staked on the same cast with the freedom of the English people',[82] did nothing to moderate the stridency with which that period was usually discussed. It is a pleasing irony that such proclamations of an ecumenical national mission, though here predicated on the uniqueness of English history, are one of the things which, rather unexpectedly, stamp English Whigs as participants in the European political culture of their time; in the years after the Congress of Vienna there seems to have been virtually no country or ethnic group so obscure that it failed to find publicists ready to claim for it the role of the messiah of the nations.[83]

In England, even those who looked more sympathetically on the political turmoil of the continent than Hallam were concerned to emphasise the indigenous character of English libertarian thought and traditions; it was, no doubt, the most prudent as well as perhaps the most congenial way of recommending the cause of liberty in the revolutionary years. We have seen what Russell thought of importations. The language of natural rights, indeed, assimilated to the English heritage by its Lockean and Whiggish

---

[81] *Const. Hist.*, ii. 126.   [82] Macaulay, *Works*, v. 23.
[83] See, e.g. J.H. Talmon, *Political Messianism* (1960), pp. 242ff.

associations, was not discredited by its conceptual association with the revolutionary rights of man; all the Whig historians continued to employ it freely, and none more explicitly than Hallam. What was not accepted, as we have seen in Millar and Russell, was the neo-classical rhetoric of republican patriotism made fashionable by the French Revolution. Fox, perhaps the most overtly libertarian of these writers, was at pains to stress that the seventeenth-century Parliamentarians 'never conceived the wild project of assimilating the government of England to that of Athens, of Sparta, or of Rome'.[84] Phrygian caps and classical pseudonyms were not wanted at Westminster; the habit of clothing the statues of deceased statesmen – including Fox himself – in togas descended from more urbanely Augustan notions of civic dignity and virtue. It was reassuring to return to the pieties of the Whig tradition, to Hampden, the Petition of Right and the Convention Parliament.

But Hume had to be answered. In the attempts to frame an answer it is possible to see the emergence and formation of an historiographical consensus; what we may call the Whig compromise. There are differences of emphasis on various events and institutions, but in essence it is the same in Millar, in Brodie, in Hallam, and in Russell – who takes most of his version from Hallam – and in Macaulay, who, in the first chapter of his *History*, clearly also owes a heavy debt to Hallam. The constitution was not ancient, in the sense of Saxon, but it was certainly not merely modern. It took its rise in the twelfth and thirteenth centuries, with Magna Carta and the summoning of the burgesses and knights of the shire to Parliament. It was initially imperfect, with the incoherence and imprecision characteristic of a barbarous age. But its essential character was clear: monarchy was limited, the sovereign was below the law; kings could not tax, or legislate without Parliament. The Lancastrian constitution of the later Middle Ages was not merely an episode but normative for the future. There were contrary precedents, but they never became accepted or established, and constitutional progress was essentially a matter of giving greater security and definition to what already existed. The despotic innovations of the Tudors – Henry VIII's Statute of Proclamations, for example – were not merely innovations but usurpations, aberrations which never became a settled, accepted part of the constitution. Thus, in a sense, ancient

[84] Fox, *James the Second*, p. 9.

constitutionalism was valid in the seventeenth century; there was a free constitution for Parliament to defend, and in defending to add to and improve, though it was only the parent of the constitution enjoyed today.

Hence the seventeenth-century Parliamentarians were allowed, and even, by the exacting Whig requirements, obliged, to have, as it were, both the past and the future in their bones; to be better constitutional lawyers and historians than the royalists, and also to sense, without full comprehension, the current of progress, the great surge of England's destiny and perhaps the world's. It was essentially the requirement of the Burkean political style, tutored in precedent, sensitive to needs; and the seventeenth century, in this case, and particularly the Revolution of 1688, was the historical proving ground of that style. Hallam even half-faced the anachronism implicit in the Whig interpretation of history:

A time, perhaps, was even then foreseen, in the visions of generous hope, by the brave knights of parliament, and by the sober sages of justice, when the proudest ministers of the crown should recoil from those barriers, which were then daily pushed aside with impunity.[85]

The attraction of this restatement, in its modified form, of the doctrine of ancient liberty is, in the context of its time, easily understandable. Though its ancient constitutionalism is not literal and static in the characteristic seventeenth-century fashion, but developing, it does in a high degree, compared with Hume or with Walpole's pamphleteers, represent the re-establishment of a connection with older ways of thinking. In one sense the most theoretically radical, though also arguably among the most complacent, of the Whig interpretations of history we have considered, was that of the apologists for Walpole. Theoretically radical because they grounded their case on a universal philosophical principle – natural rights – and on a successful revolution: that of 1688. And despite the obvious crudity of their view of England as sunk in anarchy, despotism and servility in all ages prior to the seventeenth century, it did allow them a bold consistency which more pious Whiggisms found harder to achieve. But of course it was one thing in the 1730s to ground one's case exclusively on a successful revolution; it would have been quite another to do so after 1789.

In the later period some compromise was imperative. The

[85] *View*, iii. 146.

Revolution of 1688 was, it was admitted, innovative as well as conservative; its justifying principles were thought to have been general and philosophic as well as legalistic. But the English liberties it affirmed and secured, it also in a sense confirmed; their prior existence, wilted at times but still vital, constituted the essential thrust and meaning of English history and was a precondition of the Revolution's lasting success: of the stable, ordered liberty it had so effectively promoted. The history of England was that of a deeply, almost, it seemed, providentially favoured country; favoured by circumstance, by the spirit of its people and institutions from an early date, and by its history. In constitutional essentials England was qualified to be the tutor, not the pupil, of a more distracted world. This, in outline and in much of its detail, was the version of English history inherited by Macaulay, and displayed by him with all the imaginative energy of a copious, unperplexed mind.

CHAPTER 3

Macaulay: progress and piety

The sociology of liberty

Macaulay's conception of the historian's opportunities was, as is well known, a deliberately extended one. Though he admired Tacitus and almost idolised Thucydides, it was to the narrative and descriptive precedents of the novel, and particularly the work of Scott,[1] that he most turned for examples of what a modern historian might accomplish. If he did not altogether succeed in fulfilling the programme he sketched for the ideal historian to follow,[2] the attempt, as made, was not simply a matter of applying surface colour. Macaulay's place in any notional tradition of Whig historiography has to be assessed in the broad and challenging terms he himself announced; to do otherwise would be to leave out most of Macaulay. It is true that his own essays in recreating the social past continued to be restricted by an overriding concern with public affairs. But in recommending, in his essay on History, a new kind of historiography, Macaulay was speaking of things which are separable though intelligibly related: of a justification for 'social history' and of the availability to the historian of the novelist's discoveries in rendering reality. It is the latter which is relevant here, for it is obvious that the insinuation of a particular view of the nation's past and its politics becomes more potent, not less, when that past is dramatically re-enacted and rich with evocative circumstance and possibilities of empathy.

Yet argument could not be abandoned either. Macaulay, aspiring to evoke emotions and images of the past outside the range of the rational assent and concurrence of feeling sought by Hallam's constitutional homilies, could hardly avoid finding the latter arid. But Macaulay's innovatory achievement was also a vehicle for

[1] E.g. 'History', *Works* v. 157–9; 'Hallam', *ibid.*, pp. 162–3.
[2] *ibid.*, pp. 157–9.

profound and abiding convictions. Theoretically attached to the
role of showman of later seventeenth-century English society,
Macaulay remained, inescapably, the impresario of the Whig
version of the constitution. It would be simply mistaken to
represent him as sacrificing any coherent conception of the
development of the English constitution to the exigencies of
picturesque narration. There is such a conception, though it is not
a particularly original one, and, apart from the first chapter of the
History, it has to be looked for mainly in his essays. The review
articles, known now as Macaulay's essays, on Burleigh, Bacon,
Hallam, Hampden and Temple, constitute a kind of history of
England from the reign of Mary to the end of the seventeenth
century; those on Mahan, Horace Walpole, Chatham, Pitt, and
the two great Indian essays on Clive and Warren Hastings give us
essentially all that we can know, apart from Macaulay's own
statements of his project, of the unwritten section of the *History*,
which he intended to run from the reign of Anne to the death of
George IV.[3]

Of course, there are dangers in making the essays stand for the
unwritten history. Writing for the *Edinburgh Review* allowed,
even exacted, a more dashing, polemical tone than Macaulay
thought proper to use in the *History*. There are dangers too in
quoting promiscuously, as will be done here, from works written
at different periods in an author's life. Though some critics, from
Bagehot onwards, have thought otherwise,[4] Macaulay did change,
in his tone and sympathies, if not in fundamental views. The early
essays are highly polemical and, as John Clive has shown,[5] closely
related to the contemporary political situation even when dealing
with the events of the seventeenth century. India, the shocks of
1848, and the patriotic fervours of the Crimean War did not leave
the tone of Macaulay's mind unaltered. The mellowing of age,
coinciding, in his case, with the more equable pulse of public
life – as he himself noted[6] – of the middle years of the century,
mitigated the vivid delight in partisanship and polemic. Occasionally, comparisons of the earlier and later Macaulay will be
relevant here, but for the most part these changes need no more
than a *caveat*; we are concerned here with the range within which

---

[3] Trevelyan, *Life*, pp. 344; Cf. *History*, *Works*, i. 1.
[4] Norman St John Stevas (ed.), *Collected Works of Walter Bagehot*, 8 vols, i (1965), 400;
Cf. Sir Charles Firth, *A Commentary on Macaulay's History of England* (1964), p. 275.
[5] Clive, *Macaulay*.   [6] Preface to 'Speeches' (1853), *Works*, viii. 5.

his historical opinions and sympathies flowed, with the quality of their appeal for him, and hence perhaps, when exhibited for them in a rhetoric at once coercive and seductive, for his readers; according to Acton, Macaulay's essays were 'a key to half the prejudices of our age'.[7]

Least of all do we need the *caveat* in discussing Macaulay's conception of English constitutional history, for there are here no signs of any fundamental change; only of changes, at the most, of emphasis, and a voice modulating from strident to sonorous. Essentially, Macaulay's view of English history was a version of the Whig compromise considered in the last chapter. There was no stress on the constitution as ancient, that is, Saxon. On the contrary, its history is one of almost continuous improvement. It was in the thirteenth century that England became a nation, and from there that English history and with it English liberties take their origin. It was one of the class of medieval European constitutional monarchies, though it was the best.[8] But though not abrogated by a Tudor absolutism, the constitution was rude and ill-defined, imperfect and insecure. In the seventeenth century it needed both confirmation and preservative innovation; without the latter it would have perished.[9] But the triumph of Parliament in the late seventeenth century brought a new danger: the possibility of a parliamentary executive tyranny, secured by a corrupt House of Commons and an alliance between crown and Parliament against the nation at large.[10] Corruption could for a while do what the prerogative had failed to do. Until other forms of control, by party discipline and an enlightened electorate, had developed, Macaulay was prepared to concede the necessity of corruption as the only possible form of executive control over Parliament. He was for Walpole against Walpole's opponents.[11] The emergence of party loyalty, the publicity given to Parliamentary affairs, and the enlargement of the franchise in 1832 had, however, finally removed the deplorable necessity, and ended the conflict between Parliament and the nation, as 1688 had ended that between the crown and Parliament.[12]

---

[7] Quoted Firth, *Commentary*, p. 3.
[8] *History, Works* i. 22. Cf. 'Hallam', *Works*, v. 148.   [9] *History, Works*, i. 34.
[10] *ibid.* p. 39. This was a constant theme; cf. the essay on Hallam, and the 'Speeches on the Reform Bill', *Works*, v. viii.
[11] E.g. 'Horace Walpole' (1833), *Works*, vi, esp. pp. 19–28.
[12] Again a favourite theme. E.g. Trevelyan, *Life*, p. 344.

The similarities, indeed the debts – particularly in the first chapter of Macaulay's *History* – to Hallam, are obvious enough. The indigenous character of English liberty, which Hallam had emphasised, was loudly proclaimed by Macaulay.[13] Hallam's reverent gratitude for a heritage of constitutional freedom, reconciling liberty with order, was something Macaulay enthusiastically shared; Hallam would find no difficulty in admitting him to the communion rail. For both, to be English was to belong to a people privileged in its history and worthy of its privilege. The chief point on which Macaulay takes issue with Hallam in his review of the latter's *History* is his unsympathetic treatment of the more radical and undeniably innovative measures of the Long Parliament in 1642, in particular the proposal to assume control of the militia, and the Nineteen Propositions. Hallam's sympathies were with Clarendon and the Parliamentarians who changed sides at that point; Macaulay's were resolutely with the Parliamentary leaders. Hallam saw, as Hume had done, that once the ground of strict constitutionality was given up, and measures admittedly unprecedented taken under plea of necessity then that plea was as much available to Charles I as to his opponents.[14]

It is easy to see this difference of view as a reflection of the younger man's radicalism compared with Hallam's caution. In 1825, when Macaulay wrote his essay on Milton, or in 1828, when he wrote his review of Hallam, this may indeed be correct, though it will hardly, as we shall see later, account for the differences in the treatment – Macaulay's, of course, written much later – of 1688 in their respective histories. There is, however, a small but significant dispute which places Macaulay's objections in a larger intellectual context. It is a point on which Macaulay's defence of the Long Parliament becomes strikingly Whiggish in the full, Butterfieldian sense, while Hallam, at this point, may be thought to keep better faith with his historian's conscience. Wishing to insist that necessity knows no law, Macaulay is led, that is, to make the test of legitimacy not constitutional propriety as the mid-seventeenth century would have understood it, but the as yet undiscerned course of future constitutional development. Hallam had written that deprivation of the royal right of veto 'was in this country as repugnant to the whole history of our laws, as it was incompatible with the subsistence of the monarchy as any

---

13 'History', *Works*, v. 137–8.   14 Hallam, *Const. Hist.*, ii. 124.

thing more than a nominal pre-eminence'. Macaulay's rejoinder
was:

> We are surprised, we confess, that Mr Hallam should attach so much importance
> to a prerogative which has not been exercised for a hundred and thirty years,
> which probably will never be exercised again, and which can scarcely, in any
> conceivable case, be exercised for a salutary purpose.[15]

Charitably, we could assume that Macaulay intended here
merely to deny that the deprivation of veto was so damaging to the
monarchy as Hallam had asserted, though it is hard to understand
his grounds. But in context the effect is of Macaulay judging the
constitutionality of acts done or contemplated in the seventeenth
century by subsequent constitutional practice. Macaulay is led to
this anachronism by what seems in other respects a merit in his
view of the seventeenth-century crisis: he places it, more emphatically than Hallam, in the general context of transformations in
society. That it should lead him, at this point, to see less merit than
Hallam in the royalist case is paradoxical, because the enlargement of his view of the seventeenth-century crisis brings his
account, in many respects, much closer to that of Hume, and it is
indeed very probably owed to him. It betrays him here, however,
into an inconsistency of which the anachronism is the symptom.
Macaulay, in fact, wishes to have it both ways. Hallam had
admitted that the free constitution needed strengthening as well as
merely defending in the seventeenth century, but, confining himself largely to strictly constitutional history, he was under less
temptation to judge the case for Charles anachronistically. Hume,
on the other hand, believing both that there were profound social
reasons for the crisis and that the constitutional precedents were
heterogeneous, was able to do full justice to the Stuarts' dilemma.
Macaulay is caught between the two. He is sufficient of a Humean
to see that the social and economic changes of the period would be
reflected in profound constitutional changes; on the other hand he
remains sufficient of an English Whig constitutionalist to want to
continue to get the better of the strictly constitutional argument
and to retain his reasons for hating Charles I. The remark on the
veto, insignificant though it may seem, shows him awkwardly
trying to combine, in a particularly unpromising instance, the two
strands of the nineteenth-century Whig case: conflating an argument about what was progressive with an argument about what

---

[15] Macaulay, *Works*, v. 200. Of course Macaulay may have had in mind, in insisting on its
obsolescence, that the royal veto could again become a constitutional issue.

was constitutional by invoking the criterion of what future
constitutional practice was to be.

But the claim that Macaulay was strongly influenced by the idea
of the history of civil society, though not a new one, needs some
elaboration, as does the further claim that it makes his account of
seventeenth-century history, in some respects, more distinctively
Humean than Hallam's. In fact, where Macaulay's account of
English history, though briefer and more fragmentary than Hallam's, has sharper outlines and a greater explanatory urgency, it
achieves this because he, much more emphatically than Hallam,
has embraced the Scottish conception of the progress of society
through distinct stages.

John Clive has shown how much Macaulay's early essays,
particularly those on Milton and Machiavelli, are imbued with the
idea of stages of society.[16] The leading assumption of what Dugald
Stewart called 'conjectural history' and which in the nineteenth
century came to be called 'the Comparative Method'[17] is that
different societies at different times may be at essentially the same
stage of social development, while societies co-existing in time
may represent 'earlier' or 'later' stages respectively. In Macaulay's
History it is a standard point of reference, a conceptual pigeon-
hole almost as much frequented by him as historical reminiscence,
Baconian induction, or assertion of the unique intellectual, social
and economic progress of Europe since the sixteenth century. It
provides, of course, his chief resort in explaining to his readers the
alien complexities of Irish and Scottish seventeenth-century politics and social antagonisms. The English and the Irish were 'in
widely different stages of civilisation',[18] the native Irish 'almost as
rude as the savages of Labrador'. Elsewhere there are comparisons
with Red Indians and Hottentots,[19] while the feelings of the
French troops in Ireland send Macaulay back to the gazetteer: for
them it was like banishment to 'Dahomey or Spitzbergen'.[20] The
Scottish Highlands (one of the sources of the eighteenth-century
Scottish interest in the conception of 'stages of society' in the first
place) were in 'a state scarcely less savage than that of New

16 Clive, *Macaulay*, pp. 105–7.
17 See J. W. Burrow, *Evolution and Society* (C.U.P. 1966), ch. 1. The main channel of
transmission for the Scottish conception of stages of society to Macaulay seems likely to
be the early numbers of the *Edinburgh Review*, with whose outlook he came to have so
much in common. He was said to have known Jeffrey's articles by heart. Clive, *Scotch
Reviewers*, pp. 45–6.
18 *History*, *Works*, i. 620.   19 *ibid*., ii. 505, 521.   20 *ibid*., iii. 319.

Guinea'.[21] More significantly, a half-civilised Scottish noble like
the Earl of Breadalbane

united two different sets of vices, the growth of two different regions and of two
different stages in the progress of society. In his castle among the hills he had
learned the barbarian pride and ferocity of a Highland chief. In the Council
Chamber at Edinburgh he had contracted the deep taint of treachery and
corruption.[22]

Generally, however, the Highlanders were treated more generously than the Irish, being allowed more honourably Homeric
parallels.[23] Lochiel was 'the Ulysses of the Highlands' and the
contentions of the chiefs in the campaign of 1689 would have
afforded to a Highland bard 'subjects very similar to those with
which the war of Troy furnished the great poets of Antiquity'.[24]
There is even an odd circumspection, an uncharacteristic refusal of
the opportunity for judgement, in Macaulay's summing up of the
clan way of life:

The time when a perfectly fair picture could have been painted has now passed
away. The original has long disappeared: no authentic effigy exists: and all that is
possible is to produce an imperfect likeness by the help of two portraits, one of
which is a coarse caricature and the other a masterpiece of flattery.[25]

This is so untypical that it cries out for explanation. It is perhaps
significant that Scott is not mentioned at any point in this section
of the *History*, though he seems omnipresent. Donald Bean Lean,
Evan Dhu and Vich Ian Vohr stalk even in the modern reader's
mind through the descriptions of Highland manners, and
Macaulay and his Victorian audience were more profoundly
saturated in Scott than almost any modern reader is likely to be.[26]
The character of Breadalbane drawn by Macaulay, quoted above,
echoes the divided nature of Scott's Fergus Mac-Ivor, just as, in
another section of the *History*, the account of the Covenanters is
haunted by Scott's Balfour and Mucklewrath.[27] In his ultimate
and uncharacteristic equivocation, quoted above, about the clan
way of life, it is tempting to see a kind of deference to a more
intimate knowledge, a subtler balance of sympathy and judgement, already well known to his readers in the pages of Scott, by
which he may have sensed without acknowledging it, that his own
brisker certainties would stand rebuked.

In considering Macaulay's notion of the history of society, it is

[21] *ibid.*, p. 520.   [22] *ibid.*, p. 511.   [23] *ibid.*, p. 348.
[24] *ibid.*, p. 71.   [25] *ibid.*, pp. 51–2.   [26] E.g., Trevelyan, *Life*, pp. 22–3, 71, 343.
[27] Scott, *Waverley*; *Old Mortality*. For Macaulay on the latter, see *Works*, v. 158.

needless to illustrate in detail his more general, more celebrated and celebratory remarks on progress. It is amusing, though, to find him even invoking his favourite concept to deal with a kink in the Whig genealogy. The disturbance caused to the Whig canon by the revelation of Algernon Sydney's dealings with France has already been mentioned. Some, like Millar and Fox, resolved to brazen it out. Hallam, consoled no doubt by Sydney's republicanism, decided to face it like a man.[28] Only Macaulay used the occasion to draw a characteristic moral:

> Yet it is some consolation to reflect that in our time, a public man would be lost to all sense of duty and of shame, who should not spurn from him a temptation which conquered the virtue and the pride of Algernon Sydney.[29]

More seriously, of course, it was the conception of the progress of society which formed the ground of Macaulay's pleas to the House of Commons in the debates on the Reform Bill: the progress of society had outgrown the constitution; the constitution was therefore again in danger, and must be amended to be brought again into harmony with the condition of civil society.[30] It was his resort too when explaining the 'imperfections', potentially embarrassing to Whigs, of the constitution in early times; Macaulay sets these in context by contrasting the precision of constitutional ideas 'in a refined and speculative age' with their inevitable vagueness and relative crudity 'in rude societies'.[31] To admit these imperfections and speak of the constitution in its full bloom as necessarily the work of time had become a standard feature of Whig historiography, but Macaulay is unusual in the emphasis and directness with which he amplifies this explanation with the concepts and diction of eighteenth-century 'sociological' history.

Most significant of all is his use of concepts drawn from this tradition in his various defences of the innovations of the Long Parliament and in his general characterisation of the crisis of the seventeenth century. The resemblances to Hume, in particular, are far more striking than in any of the English Whig historians discussed in the last chapter. Macaulay sees the Stuarts' predicament in essentially Humean terms, though he does not draw the same charitable conclusions. Both see the seventeenth century as a transition, between a governing authority founded on large executive discretion and its later, eighteenth-century form, based on the

---

28 Hallam, *Const. Hist.*, ii. 371, 418.   29 *History, Works*, i. 180.
30 'Speeches', *Works*, vii.   31 *History, Works*, i. 23.

control of the members of Parliament though various forms of 'interest'. As Hume had written, 'It was the fate of the house of Stuart to govern England at a period when the former source of authority was already much diminished, and before the latter began to flow in any tolerable abundance.'[32] For Hume the seventeenth century offered the opportunity 'of a more regular plan of liberty'.[33] Hume had stressed, and Macaulay agreed,

> that it was not sufficient for liberty to remain on the defensive, or endeavour to secure the little ground which was left her. It was become requisite to carry on an offensive war, and to circumscribe within narrower as well as more exact banks, the authority of the sovereign.[34]

Essentially, behind both Hume's and Macaulay's accounts lies the older, neo-Harringtonian idea of a medieval 'balance' – Hume uses the word – in which the power of the crown was checked by the military force of his vassals, a balance which was disturbed by the decline of the peerage, destroying the harmonious working of the 'old' constitution. Neither Hume nor Macaulay subscribed to the myth of the ancient, ideal constitution which the older view embodied, but common to both was the notion that old checks had been removed with the decline of feudal military power,[35] and that new ones would therefore have to be provided if England was not to follow in the wake of the continental powers towards a despotic version of what Hume called 'some new form of government, more uniform and consistent'.[36] As Macaulay succinctly put it:

> The history of England during the seventeenth century, is the history of the transformation of a limited monarchy, constituted after the fashion of the Middle Ages, into a limited monarchy suited to that more advanced state of society in which the public charges can no longer be borne by the estates of the crown, and in which the public defence can no longer be entrusted to the militia.[37]

To both, the crucial issue was the military one. Both, that is, stressed in the old Harringtonian fashion the way in which the threat of armed insurrection acted as a check on the central power, though Hume spoke more unflatteringly of the resultant 'balance', as an alternation of authority and anarchy, than Macaulay's Whig commitments allowed him to speak of the ancient constitution.[38] Both saw the professionalisation of the art of war as the crux.

---

[32] Hume, *History of England* (Penguin edn), p. 390.   [33] *ibid.*, p. 108.
[34] *ibid.*, pp. 185, 260.   [35] *ibid.*, p. 108. Cf. Macaulay, *History, Works*, i. 29–33.
[36] Hume, p. 134.   [37] Macaulay, *History, Works*, i. 119.
[38] Hume, p. 169. Macaulay, i. 27.

Because of it, as Macaulay put it, 'the old constitution could not be preserved unaltered . . . the introduction of a new and mighty force had disturbed the old equilibrium, and had turned one limited monarchy after another into an absolute monarchy'.[39]

If there is a difference in emphasis in the ways Hume and Macaulay handle this theme it is one which links Macaulay to the fuller elaborations, in the hands particularly of Adam Smith and Millar later in the eighteenth century, of the general Scottish conception of the history of civil society. Hume places his references to the decline of the military check provided by the armed vassal in the context of a notion of the decline of feudalism which, while it looks forward to Smith and the concept of commercial society, also looks back to Harrington and the idea of balance: 'After that both the statute of alienations, and the increase of commerce had thrown the balance of property into the hands of the commons.'[40] The latter was a tradition of which Hallam too was a beneficiary,[41] while Millar eulogised Harrington's *Oceana* by name.[42] In Macaulay, however, the rise of professional armies is singled out and more heavily stressed, partly, perhaps, because the chief seventeenth-century Parliamentary innovation he had to defend was the attempt to seize control of the militia. Yet it became something of an obsession with him; any reference to professional armies, or the militia, or even military operations generally, tended to evoke a disquisition on the subject; they are scattered throughout his writings.[43]

This is not to say, of course, that his treatment of it is original; on the contrary, it seems strikingly dependent on Smith and, possibly more directly, on Millar, who had made the rise of professional armies a major theme in his own *Historical View*.[44] It was, to both Millar and Macaulay, an aspect of the growth of commercial society, with the division of labour and specialisation as the latter's natural consequence; in commercial society war becomes a trade like any other. As we have already seen, as a polemical, political argument this was an idea with a long history, standing at the centre of the neo-Harringtonian civic humanism of the early eighteenth century. As polemic, Macaulay had no use for it; he had no sympathy with the arguments for the militia, and his

---

[39] Macaulay, i. 35. Hume, p. 171.   [40] Hume, p. 108.
[42] Millar, *Historical View*, iii. 286.   [41] Hallam, *Const. Hist.*, i. 56–7.
[43] Macaulay, *Works*, i. 449, 477; ii. 432; iv. 24, 63, 331-2, 336–8, 340, 347ff.; v. 55ff.; vii. 76.
[44] Millar, iii. 112–24.

references to Harrington and his political disciples were invariably hostile.[45] His own source, clearly, was the more relativist Scottish, Smithian idea of commercial society as a stage in the history of civilisation. Even his diction proclaims it: any discussion – and he gives many – of standing armies, citizen militias, the professional-isation of warfare, speckles his prose with Scottish eighteenth-century hallmarks: 'stages of society', 'rude ages' and so on.[46]

We have seen, in the last chapter, how the application of these Scottish conceptions to English history, to what might be called 'the sociological history of English liberty', could produce a new, more explanatorily satisfactory version of the uniqueness of England's constitutional development. The Harringtonian warn-ing was real. England was threatened in the sixteenth and seven-teenth centuries by the same fate as that experienced by the other European mixed constitutions: the loss of liberty as a result of the loss of the balance formerly provided by the military power of the feudal nobility. The Scottish version of the political consequences of opulence, however, was subtler and more equivocal; it could promote either liberty or despotism, depending on circum-stances.[47] In England the circumstances had favoured a libertarian solution; the levelling effects of the Conquest, the nature of English law and the strength of libertarian constitutional prece-dents, and England's insular position, which deprived the crown of a standing army, were variously weighted in different histo-rians' accounts of England's good fortune. Macaulay, more expli-citly and eagerly than any English Whig historian hitherto, adopted the sociological context provided by the Scots for his account of the uniqueness of English constitutional liberty; he was able to do so the more readily after the 1832 Reform Act, by which the problem posed by civilisation to historic liberty seemed to have been solved. Older qualms about corruption seemed no longer relevant; earlier they had still been lively enough to trouble Millar deeply, and to find a place in Macaulay's own view prior to the Reform Act.[48]

What makes Macaulay's position slightly unusual, and creates stress in his assimilation of the Scottish notions into his version of English history, is the strength of his determination to retain the Whig pieties and animosities which really belonged to a more

[45] See below, pp. 57–8. [46] See above, p. 45 and n.43.
[47] Winch, *Adam Smith's Politics*, esp. ch. 4.
[48] Millar, iv. 78, 84, 95. Macaulay, 'Hallam', *Works*, v.

insular, legalistic and moralising tradition. We have seen a combination of this kind in Millar. It is at least as evident in Macaulay. In one respect, of course, the Scottish contribution could even heighten Whig pride and thankfulness, by sharpening the sense of England's uniqueness – even if considerably dependent on good fortune – and enlarging an understanding of the dangers faced by English Parliamentarians in the seventeenth century. But there were tensions, and they show in Macaulay's writings: between a general historical explanation of the seventeenth-century crisis and a traditional Whig hatred of Charles I;[49] between a strong assertion of the need for constitutional innovation in the seventeenth century in order to accommodate or even, in a sense, to counteract, the general course of social change; and a persisting Whig desire to have the better of the constitutional argument even in strictly constitutional terms. Some charges could, of course, be made out against the Stuarts without difficulty; for example, that of resisting 'necessary' change, in other words not being Whigs. At other times Macaulay was driven to the more local expedient of blaming Charles I's 'duplicity' in reviving practices he had foresworn in assenting to the Petition of Right.[50] But the interest of the tension between what Forbes would call 'scientific' and 'vulgar' Whiggism in Macaulay, between a conception of the progress of civilisation and its consequences, and even a modified ancient constitutionalism, extends beyond these rather trivial judgements.

Some elements of this tension were, as we saw in the previous chapter, felt and in a fashion reconciled in what it there seemed appropriate to call the early nineteenth-century Whig compromise, to which Macaulay was certainly a subscriber. The strains are more obvious in Macaulay, however, because he experienced the pull of both traditions so strongly and expressed them in a rhetoric of such pride and circumstance. Without either, the *History* might in places have a greater consistency of tone, but it would almost certainly have had a narrower appeal. No one could celebrate progress as Macaulay could, but then, few could celebrate the Good Old Cause as he could either. His belief in progress created some difficulties for traditional Whiggism of which he was to some extent aware; he was self-consciously a modern Whig, not an ancient constitutionalist. But his adeptness at comparison, his

---

[49] E.g. 'Speech on Second Reading of the Reform Bill', *Works*, viii. 74–5. Contrast this with the essays on Milton and on Hallam, *Works*, v.
[50] 'Milton', *Works*, v. 29.

interest in historical explanation of a general, sociological kind, in no way seriously qualified the essential simplicity of his faith in progress or moderated his pride in his country and his party, or the mode of historic piety in which they claimed his allegiance. If all his life Bacon and Adam Smith stood at one elbow, Somers and Burke stood no less squarely at the other. If the result was sometimes less than entirely consistent, for his readers the confusion was surely a rich one in which they were willing accomplices.

A demonstration, such as the one given here, that Macaulay was a believer in progress as well as a Whig is unlikely, perhaps, to count as a vital despatch from the frontiers of knowledge; still, ordnance surveys are sometimes useful even in the home counties, and for the sake of completeness it may, before venturing something possibly more contentious, be worth similarly confirming the existence of those elements of Whig pride and Whig caution which shared the furnishing of Macaulay's mind with contrasts of rude and opulent societies, with modern schoolgirls better informed than Renaissance scholars, and with seaside boarding-houses and rumbling factories embellishing landscapes once squalid with timber and thatch.

Civil prudence and civic virtue

It would be churlish to grudge an extended quotation, familiar though it may be, to one of the high moments of Macaulay's *History*:

As our Revolution was a vindication of ancient rights, so it was conducted with strict attention to ancient formalities. In almost every word and act may be discerned a profound reverence for the past. The Estates of the Realm deliberated in the old halls and according to the old rules. Powle was conducted to his chair between his mover and his seconder with the accustomed forms. The Sergeant with his mace brought up the messengers of the Lords to the table of the Commons; and the three obeisances were duly made. The conference was held with all the antique ceremonial. One one side of the table, in the Painted Chamber, the managers for the Lords sat covered and robed in ermine and gold. The managers for the Commons stood bareheaded on the other side. The speeches present an almost ludicrous contrast to the revolutionary oratory of every other country. Both the English parties agreed in treating with solemn respect the ancient constitutional traditions of the state. The only question was, in what sense those traditions were to be understood. The assertors of liberty said not a word about the natural equality of men and the inalienable sovereignty of the people, about Harmodius or Timoleon, Brutus the elder or Brutus the younger. When they were told that, by the English law, the crown, at the moment of a demise, must descend to the next heir, they answered that, by the English law, a living man could have no heir. When they were told that there was no precedent for declaring the throne vacant, they produced, from among the records in the Tower, a roll of parchment, near three hundred years old, on which, in quaint characters and barbarous Latin, it was recorded that the Estates of the Realm had declared vacant the throne of a perfidious and tyrannical Plantaganet. When at length the dispute had been accommodated, the new sovereigns were proclaimed with the old pageantry.[51]

This eulogy – why are we so sure it is a eulogy? – of the 1688 Revolution may well seem to be an epitome of the favourite clichés of the Whig tradition, and so in a sense it is. But the Whig tradition could accommodate perceptible nuances, and Macaulay's treatment of the Revolution differed markedly from Hallam's, for example, and perhaps even more markedly from his own earlier references to it in his review of Hallam's work. Hallam had been at pains to stress the unprecedented character of the Revolution, even at the cost, at times, of making it sound doctrinaire. While admitting that the 'liberal tenets' of the Revolution were maintained 'rather, perhaps on authority of not very good precedents in our history than of sound general reasoning',[52] Hallam's treatment of the Revolution in general is not merely strikingly 'new Whig' in the sense of Burke's distinction, in his insistence on abstract principle,[53] but also somewhat sectarian.[54] Rejoicing, predictably, that in the Revolution 'Nothing was done by the multitude' he also rejoices, more surprisingly, that James' return after his first flight, by making the fact of his deposition manifest, split the nation and strengthened the Jacobite faction. Hence,

while the position of the new government was thus rendered less secure, by narrowing the basis of public opinion whereon it stood, the liberal principles of policy which the Whigs had espoused became incomparably more powerful, and were necessarily invoked in the continuance of the revolution settlement. The ministers of William III and of the house of Brunswick had no choice but to respect and countenance the doctrines of Locke, Hoadley, and Molesworth.[55]

Macaulay's emphasis, by contrast, is not merely traditionalist but also markedly ecumenical. It had not always been so, however.

---

[51] *Works*, ii. 395–6.   [52] Hallam, *Const. Hist.*, iii. 83.
[53] The Convention 'proceeded not by the stated rules of the English government, but by the general rights of mankind. They looked not so much to Magna Carta as to the original compact of society, and rejected Coke and Hale for Hooker and Harrington.' *ibid.*, p. 87.
[54] *ibid.*, 79.   [55] *ibid.*, p. 81.

In his review of Hallam twenty years earlier he had spoken disparagingly of the Revolution, of its lack of boldness and principle. The Revolution was useful but inglorious; only William gained glory from it. 'The transaction was, in almost every part, discreditable to England.' He is contemptuous of the precedent-hunting of the Parliamentary leaders: 'In all the proceedings of the Convention; in the conference particularly, we see that littleness of mind which is the chief characteristic of the times.'[56] The differences are not, in fact, difficult to account for. Macaulay himself provides a large part of the explanation when he concludes the passage on the observance of tradition quoted above by remarking that

To us, who have lived in the year 1848, it may seem almost an abuse of terms to call a proceeding, conducted with so much deliberation, with so much sobriety, and with such minute attention to prescriptive etiquette, by the terrible name of Revolution.[57]

The chapter on the Revolution concludes with Macaulay at his most vehement, comparing the English Revolution with the recent insurrections in Europe, in which 'The proudest capitals of Western Europe have streamed with civil blood.'[58] In 1828 his denigration of the Revolution had presumably been an aspect of his attempt, as John Clive describes it,[59] to counter the Tory endeavour to treat it as definitive for all time. Too severe an attachment to precedent was incompatible with the principles of Parliamentary reform to which he was committed.

Hallam's motives may have been rather different: his history was a war on two fronts. The radicals must be confounded, but Whig principles must also be unmistakably asserted against any surviving supporters of the prerogative. Whig suspicions of the crown had not yet become a retrospective indulgence, and there is an admonitory note in Hallam's declarations, made perhaps a little too emphatically for complete conviction, that the house of Brunswick is bound by the origin of its tenure of the throne to respect the principles of the Revolution.[60] But of course there is no fundamental cleavage, at the theoretical level, between Macaulay and Hallam or Macaulay and his earlier self. Hallam mentions also the continuities respected by the Revolution; Macaulay declares in the *History* that 'The Whig theory of government is . . .

[56] Lord John Russell, *A History of English Government* (1823), p. 227.
[57] *History, Works*, ii. 396.
[58] *ibid*., p. 397.   [59] Clive, *Macaulay*, p. 92.   [60] Hallam, *Const. Hist*., iii. 80–1, 161.

a Lockean contractarianism,[61] and though he was undoubtedly badly shocked by 1848, he had taken much the same line in the *History* as in the undergraduate prize essay on William III he wrote in his youth, where it was stressed that William had

imparted to innovation the dignity and stability of antiquity. He transferred to a happier order of things the associations which had attached the people to their former government. As the Roman warrior, before he assaulted Veii, invoked his guardian gods to leave its walls, and to accept the worship and patronise the cause of the beseigers, this great prince, in attacking a system of oppression, summoned to his aid the venerable principles and deeply seated feelings to which that system was indebted for protection.[62]

Protection, one is inclined to ask, from whom? But that passage, apart from the self-conscious classical allusion, could have been written by Macaulay at any age.

Moreover – since we are trying to see at precisely what point the balance was struck – the chapter on the Revolution settlement in the *History* is not so uniformly eulogistic as its peroration quoted above. Macaulay had not unlearned the knowledge that members of Parliament were legislators not antiquaries, and though the attachment of the Revolution to tradition is unmistakably applauded, there is enough ironic distance in Macaulay's account, as well as in occasional explicit statements, to save it from endorsing archaism. Consider the passage on the debate between the Lords and Commons, the proceedings he had castigated twenty years earlier for their 'littleness of mind':

A full report of the speeches of both sides has come down to us. There are few students of history who have not taken up that report with eager curiosity and laid it down with disappointment. The question between the Houses was argued on both sides as a question of law. The objections which the Lords made to the resolution of the Commons were verbal and technical, and were met by verbal and technical answers. Somers vindicated the use of the word abdication by quotations from Grotius and Brissonius, Spigelius and Bartolus. When he was challenged to show any authority for the proposition that England could be without a sovereign, he produced the Parliament roll of the year 1399, in which it was expressly set forth that the kingly office was vacant during the interval between the resignation of Richard the Second and the enthroning of Henry the Fourth. The Lords replied by producing the Parliament roll of the first year of Edward the Fourth, from which it appeared that the record of 1399 had been solemnly annulled. They therefore maintained that the precedent on which Somers relied was no longer valid. Treby then came to Somers' assistance, and laid on the table the Parliament roll of the first year of Henry the Seventh, which repealed the Act of Edward the Fourth, and consequently restored validity of the record of 1399. After a colloquy of several hours the disputants separated.[63]

[61] *Works*, ii. 407.   [62] Trevelyan, *Life*, p. 63.   [63] *Works*, ii. 384.

The substance is almost the same as that of the quotation, from the same chapter, with which this section opened; the difference in tone between the two is therefore the more striking. Where the repetitiveness of the former passage conveys solemnity and reassurance, here the pattern of assertion and counter-assertion insinuates pedantry. Where the alienness of Harmodius and Timoleon implied a threat, the barbaric names of Somers' jurists have a touch of Swiftian mock-heroic which sets the tone of the whole passage, reflecting their quaintness on to the remote Plantaganet kings, giving a hint of crabbed obsessiveness to the Lords' response in kind, and of Homeric burlesque to Treby's charge to the rescue, and reducing the final solemn colloquy of several hours to absurdity. It is not so much disapproving as condescending, the indulgence of the Burkean Whig who knows what value to attach to old rotten parchments but also knows how to value the valuing of them. In disparaging ancient constitutional-ism as political doctrine while applauding its influence on political practice, Macaulay exhibits a kind of sophistication not uncommon in the riper years of the Whig tradition; Sir Herbert Butterfield condemning Whig history in *The Whig Interpretation* and celebrating its political consequences in *The Englishman and His History* offers a parallel example. One is reminded of Bagehot applauding only half ironically the stupidity of the English as the foundation of their liberties.

For of course the Burkean, modern Whig has a sophisticated, second-order defence of the veneration for precedents – usually accompanied by a reservation about the inconvenience of a slavish devotion to them. As Macaulay for once rather drily put it:

that profound reverence for law and prescription which has long been character-istic of Englishmen, and which, though it runs sometimes into pedantry and sometimes into superstition, is not without its advantages.[64]

History, in other words, provides an empirical demonstration of the political value of a respect for precedent not carried to excess. Considered as an induction this claim easily becomes circular: the empirical proof that the observance of continuity is more politi-cally successful than radical revolution is less than impressive if continuity is taken as the measure of success. Still, the difficulty can no doubt be surmounted by redefining success in terms of goods observedly or at any rate plausibly attached to continuity

---

[64] *ibid.*, p. 421.

rather than revolution. Respect for precedent thereupon becomes one of the 'maxims of civil wisdom' the quest for which Macaulay had contrasted with the political antiquarian's search for rights as one of the two main motives for the study of history.[65]

The contrast becomes blurred, though not effaced, however, when respect for ancient right itself figures as an established maxim of civil wisdom: we then have a modified ancient constitutionalism recommended in the rival language of historical induction. The habit of conducting political argument by claims to indefeasible historic rights modulates into the respectful and pragmatic political style enjoined by a civil prudence learnt from history. But if the justification is inductive, the mode of feeling and historic allusion by which this necessary modulation is accomplished, and an uncompromising legalism transformed into a sceptical, flexible, essentially cautious temper of mind and habitual political practice, is, above all, piety.

It clearly cost Macaulay nothing to make the pragmatic case for piety; in his endorsements of it there is much genuine complicity and only, as we have seen, a touch of ironic distance, of the condescension that comes from approving self-consciously of what others do unself-consciously. Even while establishing the distance, he admits, with considerable self-knowledge, the all but inescapable complicity. In the passage quoted above at the beginning of chapter 2, in which he professes his astonishment at Hallam's exemption from the influence of vulgar political piety, he acknowledges its power, though holding it at arm's length with an ironic religious analogy and a slightly juvenile parade of learning in association psychology:

Every political sect has its esoteric and its exoteric school, its abstract doctrines for the initiated, its visible symbols, its imposing forms, its mythological fables for the vulgar. It assists the devotion of those who are unable to raise themselves to the contemplation of pure truth by all the devices of Pagan or Papal superstition. It has its altars and its deified heroes, its relics and pilgrimages, its canonized martyrs and confessors, its festivals and its legendary miracles.[66]

Again one is reminded of Bagehot, of the 'efficient' and 'dignified' parts of the constitution.[67]

It is a large part of Macaulay's strength as a proponent of the Whig interpretation of English history that he himself belonged to both schools, the esoteric and the exoteric. He may have held

[65] *ibid.*, i. 20.   [66] 'Hallam', *Works*, v. 164–5.
[67] Walter Bagehot, *The English Constitution* (1867).

himself aloof in the *History* from the cruder forms of partisanship
in the interests of a more eirenic political mythology, but he was
not the man, like Gibbon's Roman aristocrats, simply to view
'with a smile of pity and indulgence the various errors of the
vulgar', and to conceal 'the sentiments of an Atheist under the
sacerdotal robes'.[68] As he went on to admit,

> as in religion, so in politics, few even of those who are enlightened enough to
> comprehend the meaning latent under the emblems of their faith can resist the
> contagion of the popular superstition. Often, when they flatter themselves that
> they are merely feigning a compliance with the prejudices of the vulgar, they are
> themselves under the influence of those very prejudices.[69]

Here, indeed, Macaulay for once seems more sophisticated than
Bagehot, who, in *The English Constitution*, tends to make the
distinction between the enlightened and the vulgar an absolute
one.

But Macaulay was much more naturally a worshipper, to use his
own word, than Bagehot. Though he might sneer at Horace
Walpole's antiquarian connoisseurship, his searches for Queen
Mary's comb and Wolsey's red hat,[70] his own was, even by the
standards of his time, a sensibility eminently pious and associative.
He speaks in the essay on Milton of personal attachment to
childhood objects;[71] in that on 'Madame D'Arblay' he obviously
feels for her the veneration due to a relic. Trevelyan says that in
later years 'he positively lived on the associations of his own
past'.[72] His sister Hannah said that on his travels he responded
rather to the associations of a landscape than to the landscape
itself.[73] Much given to brooding on the illustrious dead, he was
predictably moved, in Florence, by the tombs in Santa Croce.[74]
The antiquity of the Catholic Church drew from him a reverence
he expressed in his essay on Ranke's *History of the Popes*.
Devoted to Trinity College, he would memorise the names of past
senior wranglers, and held in grateful recollection the names of
some fellows of the college several generations back who had been
responsible for a minor reform from which he had benefited[75] – a
degree of piety almost awesome to contemplate.

Even the passion for ranking and comparison – 'the greatest
man since Milton'[76] – which can seem coldly arrogant and in-

---

[68] Edward Gibbon, *The Decline and Fall of the Roman Empire* (ed. W. Smith 1854),
8 vols, i. 168.   [69] Macaulay, *Works*, v. 165.   [70] 'Horace Walpole', *Works*, vi. 2.
[71] *Works*, v. 10.   [72] Trevelyan, p. 569.   [73] *ibid.*, p. 349.
[74] *ibid.*, p. 353.   [75] *ibid.*, p. 60.   [76] Burke, in fact. *ibid.*, 613.

appropriately mechanical, as though recording the batting averages of the master spirits of the ages, actually lent itself to the purposes of veneration, establishing a canonised hierarchy of the elect. Touched by Macaulay's wand, the Rockingham Whigs became, slightly implausibly, 'men worthy to have charged by the side of Hampden at Chalgrove, or to have exchanged the last embrace with Russell in Lincoln's Inn Fields'.[77] No writer was more keenly alive than he to the political value of such associations; indeed, judging others by his own memory and feelings, he may even have exaggerated it. They formed, for example, along with other such desiderata as property, social order and civilisation, part of the vital interests he appealed to the House of Commons to save by passing the Reform Act: 'reform now, while old feelings and old associations retain a power and a charm which may soon pass away'.[78] Political myths and the emotions they stirred might, of course, divide as well as unify. The Tory myths, indeed, he seems to have regarded as simply ridiculous; veneration of the royal martyr merely aroused his derision. Some, however, like those of the Protestant ascendancy in Ireland, were too heroically imposing for disdain, too fierce for comfort:

It is impossible not to respect the sentiment which indicates itself by these tokens. It is a sentiment which belongs to the higher and purer part of human nature, and which adds not a little to the strength of states. A people which takes no pride in the noble achievements of remote ancestors will never achieve anything worthy to be remembered with pride by remote descendants. Yet it is impossible for the moralist or the statesman to look with unmixed complacency on the solemnities with which Londonderry celebrates her deliverance, and on the honours which she pays to those who saved her.[79]

But there was one class of political myths which aroused his unvarying, frequently expressed and unmitigated distaste: the myths of classical, republican liberty, patriotism and stoic civic virtue. Outcrops of denunciation of this political mythology, and its modern adherents, chiefly, of course, the neo-Harringtonian True Whigs and Bolingbrokian 'patriots' of the eighteenth century, and after them the French revolutionaries, litter Macaulay's writings: in the denunciation of 'Plutarch and his school' in the essay on History, in his essays on Machiavelli and Mirabeau, in his youthful review of Mitford's *History of Greece* for *Knight's*

[77] 'Chatham', *Works*, vii. 253.   [78] *Works*, viii. 24.   [79] *History, Works*, ii. 585.

Magazine, and at various points in the *History*. It was a distaste
which encompassed True Whigs of the late seventeenth and early
eighteenth century, like Sir Patrick Hume and Fletcher of Saltoun,
and modern revolutionary 'patriots' in the manner of Saint Just.
The ground of Macaulay's objection was that theirs was the
mythology of the politically inexperienced and disinherited: an
ancient political creed and its symbols were detached from the
social and political context which had given them meaning, the
small city state, and naively applied to the very different conditions of modern Europe. Plutarch and his imitators were cosmopolitan subjects of a despotic empire who looked back to and
idealised the patriotism of the small city state. 'These writers, men
who knew not what it was to have a country, men who had never
enjoyed political rights, brought into fashion an offensive cant
about patriotism and zeal for freedom.'[80] In that patriotism there
was in fact much that was narrow and repressive; the Spartans, so
admired in the republican tradition, enjoyed little or no personal
liberty.

   'In almost all the little commonwealths of antiquity, liberty was
used as a pretext for measures directed against everything that
makes liberty valuable.'[81] We seem to hear a distinct echo here of
the Humean distinction between political and civil liberty.[82]
Continental political thinkers in modern times, deprived, like
Plutarch and his school, of contact with a vital political tradition,
developed similar enthusiasms. The writings of the Plutarchian
school 'were read by men placed in circumstances closely resemb-
ling their own, unacquainted with the real nature of liberty, but
inclined to believe everything good which could be told respecting
it'.[83]

   The self-conscious literary 'patriotism' of the Plutarchians,
ancient and modern, was in fact the antithesis of the Whig's
enjoyment of his political heritage:

We have classical associations and great names of our own which we can
confidently oppose to the most splendid of ancient times. Senate has not to our
ears a sound so venerable as Parliament. We respect the Great Charter more than
the laws of Solon. The Capitol and the Forum impress us with less awe than our
own Westminster Hall and Westminster Abbey, the place where the great men of
twenty generations have contended, the place where they sleep together.[84]

[80] *Works*, v. 137.   [81] *ibid.*, p. 136.   [82] See above, p. 27.
[83] *ibid.*, p. 139. For analogies with the French Revolution, *ibid.*, 40, 139, 619, 635.
[84] *ibid.*, pp. 137–8.

The desire, even the need, to have accessible a modern and native Pantheon to match or surpass that of the ancients is a distinct theme in the Whig celebration of the past; we find it, in a slightly different form, in Freeman as well as Macaulay.[85] Macaulay's conclusion here is clearly admonitory as well as complacent:

Our liberty is neither Greek nor Roman; but essentially English. It has a character of its own – a character which has taken a tinge from the sentiments of the chivalrous ages, and which accords with the peculiarities of our manners and of our insular situation. It has a language, too, of its own, and a language singularly idiosyncratic, full of meaning to ourselves, scarcely intelligible to strangers.[86]

The Plutarchian school and its modern imitators, instead of providing emotional access to a tradition of political experience, exalted an antique form of polity which was culturally remote and socially irrelevant. To the progressive Whig, the modern classically inspired 'patriots' exhibited the double offence of being both archaic and revolutionary; like the English radicals who continued to appeal to an idealised ancient constitution, they praised the past at the expense of the present, saw as corruption what should be regarded as progress, or at least as its concomitant, and cherished utopian notions of revolutionary political transformation. Macaulay's attacks, in particular, on their exaltation of the citizen-in-arms as against the professional soldier, in the neo-Harringtonian and Country Party polemics in favour of the militia, are among his most sustained and successful pieces of political and sociological argument. In the early essay on Machiavelli he had shown how the civic patriotism of the city state was related to a specific social setting and specific conditions of warfare: not only to the absence of the professionalisation which comes with commercial society, but to a fragility of small states and a ruthlessness in the treatment of a vanquished people which stakes the lives and freedom of the whole community on the outcome of a decisive battle.[87]

Macaulay's distaste for the Harringtonians and for all theoretical, neo-classical republicanism is a minor but recurrent theme in the *History*.[88] Together with his dislike of the more extreme forms of Protestant enthusiasm, his disapproval of the republican cult of liberty significantly shapes his accounts of the Monmouth and

[85] See below, p. 198.   [86] *ibid.*, p. 138.

[87] 'Machiavelli', *Works*, v. 78–9. Cf. 'History', *ibid.*, p. 136 and Clive, *Macaulay*.

[88] *History*, *Works*, i. 421; ii. 353; iii. 455; iv. 334–5, 352. Cf. 'Essays', *Works*, v. 160; vi. 27.

Argyll rebellions, particularly the latter; his account of the dissensions of the leaders, though it seems to owe something to Scott's picture of the Covenanters in *Old Mortality*, also stresses the impractical and stubborn ungovernability of a classical republican like Sir Patrick Hume.[89] Explicit in Macaulay's account of both rebellions is the contrast between disciplined professional armies – which the royal troops, as he points out, were only imperfectly – against amateurs and fanatics. The Western Rebellion fails, essentially, because feudalism is over. It is the militia debate over again, with a practical demonstration.[90] Elsewhere in the *History*, in his invariably unsympathetic references to the ideals of classically inspired neo-Harringtonian or True Whig idealists like Fletcher of Saltoun or Molyneux, Macaulay stresses their stiff aristocratic arrogance,[91] while the 'patriotic' neo-classical allusions in which the opposition in Parliament conducted the militia controversy are mocked for their puerility.[92]

Puerility, personal and political inexperience combined, is such a constant theme in Macaulay's references to the cult of patriotism, liberty and virtue expressed through classical allusion that one can hardly avoid suspecting that the exorcism of some juvenile guilt of his own may have shared, with a mature distaste for political utopianism, the responsibility for his consistent hostility. In his review of Mitford's *History of Greece* for *Knights' Magazine* (1824) we find the recently graduated Macaulay recommending Mitford's book as a corrective 'For the young gentleman who talks much about his country, tyrannicide, and Epaminondas.'[93] It was a topical and striking coolness, six months after Byron's death at Missolonghi. In any case, it is not implausible – to speak mildly – that school and undergraduate debating societies should provide eventide homes for a decaying political rhetoric; and Macaulay knew his debating societies. There is even some slight evidence that he may not always have been hostile to the civic humanist cult of the citizen-in-arms. In his essay on Dante, earlier in the same year, he had written, uncharacteristically, that 'there is no sword like that which is beaten out of a ploughshare', and that 'It was something that the citizen of Milan of Florence fought, not merely in the vague and rhetorical sense in which the words are

---

[89] *Works*, i. 422, 436.   [90] *ibid.*, pp. 424, 477.
[91] *ibid.*, i. 421; iv. 370ff.   [92] *ibid.*, iv. 331ff.
[93] 'Mitford's Greece' (1824), *Works*, vii. 687. For the philhellene political enthusiasm and rhetoric provoked by the Greek War of Independence, see W. L. St Clair, *That Greece Might Still be Free* (O.U.P. 1972).

often used, but in sober truth, for his parents, his children, his lands, his house, his altars.'[94] Of course, this involved no retraction of the key notion of successive stages of society in which past arrangements and even virtues became irrelevant or possibly pernicious. But emotionally it was a significant concession:

> And how can man die better
> Than facing fearful odds,
> For the ashes of his fathers,
> And the temples of his Gods . . .[95]

The Lays of Ancient Rome could not have been written but by a man whose mind, or at least the more childlike side of it, had been warmed by the legends of ancient civic patriotism. Of course it made some difference that the *Lays* were inspired by Livy, and Macaulay exempted Livy from his charges against Plutarch: Livy was a Whig. 'He contemplated the past with interest and delight, not because it furnished a contrast to the present, but because it had led to the present.' While sharing something of the Plutarchian's cant, he was blessedly chauvinistic: 'He does not seem to think any country but Rome deserving of love: nor is it for liberty as liberty, but for liberty as a part of the Roman institutions, that he is zealous.'[96]

In any case, of course, the *Lays* were a *jeu d'esprit* which could be disavowed without embarrassment. Yet it would not be surprising, despite Macaulay's hostility to the rhetoric of republican patriotism and liberty, if there were aspects of the rich and various tradition of what, following Hans Baron and J. G. A. Pocock, we may abbreviate as 'civic humanism', which were by no means alien to Macaulay. His was a youth, as Trevelyan says, passed in an atmosphere of great public causes, though the idiom of discussion was evangelical. Trevelyan connected this, and the disinterestedness of the Clapham saints, with Macaulay's mature judgements of the actions of statesmen, framed in terms 'of ardent public spirit and lofty public virtue'.[97] But, more relevant here than the early excitements of the anti-slavery campaign, is the whole weight – not Evangelical – of Macaulay's culture and sympathies. He was, after all, the most Augustan of the great Victorians. It is one of the things which most distinguishes him from the historians who came to maturity in the mid-century,

---

[94] *Works*, vii. 607.   [95] Macaulay, 'Horatius', xxvii, *Lays of Ancient Rome*.
[96] 'History', v. 141.   [97] Trevelyan, *Life*, p. 52.

Freeman and Froude, whose minds were formed in the shadow of the great early Victorian sages whose thought and sensibility were suffused with the influences of the Romantic movement, Thomas Arnold, Newman and Carlyle. Yet it can be argued that the appeal of Macaulay's *History* to his contemporaries was actually enhanced by the Augustan quality of a mind soaked in the classics, above all perhaps in Cicero,[98] and in the English literature of the eighteenth century, and by a diluted civic humanism, found there not as part of an explicit political creed but as a sense of values and of the significance of certain kinds of achievement. It gave the *History* a dimension which we shall now have to consider; without it, the *History* could not have fulfilled the unique role it occupied in the transmission of aspects of the Whig tradition to a wider Victorian public.

[98] *The Marginal Notes of Lord Macaulay*, selected by Sir G. O. Trevelyan (1907), pp. 37–54. Cf. Trevelyan, *Life*, pp. 60, 620.

CHAPTER 4

Macaulay's res publica

'The height of human glory'

One point of access to Macaulay's sense of what value the public realm might hold is his admiration for a certain kind of man of action: energetic, vast-conceiving, above all stoical. Of course, in itself such admiration proves nothing; thousands, millions, of his countrymen felt the same; the stiff upper lip is so assimilated a Victorianism that to speak of neo-classical origins seems pedantic. Macaulay was hardly unusual, in the mid-century, in finding the glory of the nation's greatest living hero enhanced by a characteristic trick of laconic speech.[1] And such examples of taciturnity in men of action lend themselves, of course, as readily to the Carlylean apocalyptic mode as to older, neo-classical and stoic concepts of civic virtue. Macaulay sympathised with neither, or rather, he had for the latter, as we have seen, an aversion which did not altogether exclude possibilities of collusion. He certainly disliked what he felt to be an affectation of stoic philosophy: it grated, clearly, on his natural exuberance, his confidence in progress, even his utilitarianism. He spoke of Romilly, for example, as 'a fine fellow; but too stoical for my taste. I love a little of the Epicurean element in virtue.'[2]

Yet he warmed, in fact, to what he felt to be genuine stoic imperturbability, when combined with grand designs and great achievements with which to feed his imagination. Macaulay's monument to William III is constructed of a subtle combination of Romantic and stoic materials: the indifference to danger, and even to life; the physical frailty and the iron will; the inner torment masked by impassive self-control; the dry, laconic utterance which Macaulay himself compared to the Iron Duke's.[3] Washington was

[1] Trevelyan, *Life*, p. 539.   [2] *ibid.*, p. 535.
[3] *ibid.*, p. 539. Cf. eg. *History, Works*, iv. 260.

another of the type, whom Macaulay also admired.[4] But most striking, because half-unwilling, and because it resulted in a literary monument scarcely less impressive than the one to William himself, is his admiration for Warren Hastings. In the famous essay Macaulay gives him a tragic grandeur, not only because of the Roman scale of his achievements, and the splendour of the talents arrayed against him at his trial, but because his stoicism in adversity makes him a worthy antagonist and victim. Parliamentarian and Whig though he was, there was a side of Macaulay that liked to see matters carried with a high hand; we have already noted, for example, his Miltonic portrait of Strafford as fallen angel.[5] Privately he described Hastings as 'in the highest degree striking and majestic ... one of the greatest men England ever produced', significantly praising his 'heroic equanimity in the midst of adversity and danger. He was a man for whom nature had done much of what the stoic philosophy pretended, and only pretended, to do for its disciples.'[6]

India, in fact, and Indian themes, always, quite naturally, called up Roman connotations for Macaulay. In India, middle-class Englishmen like himself had made conquests rivalling those of the Caesars – he compares them with those of Trajan.[7] Once in India, his imagination was kindled by the grandeur of the proconsular role.[8] Again, these are, or became, stock Victorian responses, though no doubt it was in part Macaulay who had helped to make them so. But in his references to Indian society before the Company's conquests, and his depiction of the Bengali character, there is a more distinctive, indeed, a more old-fashioned note, a flavour of diction and literary trope which identifies the eighteenth-century sources of his categories and imaginative response: notions of luxury and corruption, and oriental despotism, which were central to the neo-classical, Machiavellian, civic humanist complex of ideas, and which enjoyed a wider currency and vitality than the political prescriptions most closely associated with them, which, as we have seen, Macaulay repudiated. They strongly inform, for example, Montesquieu's and Gibbon's explanations of the rise and fall of empires, with their cycle of liberty – civic

[4] He compared Hampden to him, and also Cromwell, of whom, too, he always spoke highly. *Works*, v. 34, 586.   [5] See above, p. 13 and n. 13.

[6] Quoted, Trevelyan, *Life*, p. 398.   [7] 'Clive', *Works*, vi. 453.

[8] 'If he put up at a collector's bungalow, he liked to think that his host ruled more absolutely and over a larger population than "a Duke of Saxe-Weimar or a Duke of Lucca".' Trevelyan, *Life*, p. 265.

virtue – conquest – luxury – corruption – loss of liberty. It is striking how uncharacteristically Gibbonian – Macaulay disliked Gibbon's style[9] – Macaulay's language and periods become when he writes of Moghul India; it is as though there were only one way to write of oriental luxury: 'A succession of nominal sovereigns, sunk in indolence and debauchery, sauntered away life in secluded palaces, chewing bang, fondling concubines and listening to buffoons.[10] The Gibbonian parallels here were no doubt conscious, though not the style: Macaulay compares the successors of Aurungzebe to those of Theodosius and Charlemagne.[11] But any notion of a parasitic, luxurious, courtly indolence, it seems, woke, inadvertently, the Gibbonian chimes: 'the crowd of beautiful faces and light characters which adorned and disgraced Whitehall during the wild carnival of the Restoration'. Charles II's favourite concubines were 'three women, whose charms were the boast, and whose vices were the disgrace of three nations'.[12]

In the *Decline and Fall*, the civic humanist cycle of corruption, so often repeated in Gibbon's history, was balanced by another and newer theme, the Enlightenment's conception of the development of civilisation, which surrounds the work with an optimism which the story it tells, by itself, could hardly warrant.[13] The notion of the gradual progress of the useful arts, through human industry, is one aspect of that optimism: Gibbon owes a debt, reflected in his footnotes, to Smith's *Wealth of Nations*. It is true that this version of progress is not heavily stressed; in the *Decline and Fall*, the most obvious antithesis is still the old one of republican patriotism and barbarian hardihood set against the 'indolence', 'luxury' and 'effeminacy' of supine Asiatics and of once energetic former barbarian conquerors enervated by their own success. Yet there is clearly another possible antithesis to indolence and luxury: industry and a permissible (if still dangerous) civilised opulence.[14]

This latter development is only hinted at in the *Decline and Fall*. In Macaulay, of course, it is in full, assertive bloom. The opulence and comfort of civilised peoples compared with the squalor of savagery and the discomforts and ignorance of barbarism is

---

[9] *ibid.*, p. 324.   [10] 'Clive', *Works*, vi. 389.   [11] *ibid.*

[12] *History, Works*, ii. 75. *ibid.*, i. 335. Cf. e.g. 'the palace, nay the bedchamber of the pope was adorned, or polluted, by the visits of his female favourites'. Gibbon, *Decline*, viii. 80.

[13] *Decline*, iv. ch. xxxviii, 'General observations'.

[14] See Donald Winch, *Adam Smith's Politics*.

notoriously one of his favourite topics, a subject for celebration, not apprehension. Looked at in one way, Clive and Hastings in India are like Gibbon's hardy barbarian conquerors, masters of servile and 'effeminate' Asiatics by right of superior energy and valour, though subject to the solicitations of corruption as the price of success. But there is an obvious difference; 'the bold and energetic children of Europe'[15] are the representatives not of barbarism but of civilisation.

For the energy and stoic qualities of middle-class conquerors like Clive and Hastings, Macaulay has only admiration. With 'industry' however we move into an area of some ambiguity. For the civic humanist idea of public life as the highest of man's pursuits implied a traditional condescension towards the useful arts. Industry stood under the classical stigma of servile activity, narrowing the faculties of man while participation in the public life of the *polis* fulfilled them.

It may at first sight seem unacceptable to suggest that Macaulay inherited this distaste, or, at best, ambivalence; is he not notorious for his enthusiasm for industrial prosperity, and his explicit opposition, as, for example, in his review of Southey's *Colloquies*, to the notion that it might be humanly impoverishing? Yet it would, of course, have been astonishing had there been no condescension. He himself had yearned for a public career; public life shared with literature and his family virtually all his allegiances. He approved of industrious artisans; we hardly suspect him of wishing to be one. Only when communities of traders and artisans became, as sometimes in seventeenth-century Ireland[16] or eighteenth-century India, an embattled polity under threat of extinction, and hence entered, perforce, the realm of public life and history, was his interest really aroused. This ambivalence may help to explain what has usually and surely correctly been seen as one of the rhetorical failures – perhaps the only serious one – of the *History*: the interruption of the narrative at dramatic moments – William's landing at Torbay being only the most famous[17] – for extensive comparison of the scene as contemporaries saw it with the prosperity and industry which greeted the Victorian observer on the same spot a century and a half later.

---

[15] 'Clive', *Works*, v. 405. Also 'Warren Hastings', *ibid.*, p. 555.
[16] E.g. Londonderry. See also the story of the English settlement at Kenmare in the *History*, ch. XII.
[17] *History*, *Works*, ii. 253–4; cf. *ibid.*, iii. 10, 65, 282, 287, 322.

Macaulay no doubt thought of this as a legitimate and traditional epic device; Johnson had proclaimed it the duty of the writer of epic to 'diversify by retrospection and anticipation'.[18] Yet few, surely, of Macaulay's readers can have found the amount of the customs dues of modern Greenock,[19] though doubtless impressive in their way, anything but an embarrassing lurch into bathos in the presentation of the savage tragedy of the Argyll rebellion. Macaulay was, of course, pointing a moral by contrast, fulfilling the pledge at the opening of the *History* to refute those who sighed for a past superior to the present; conversely, in joining the prosperity of Torquay to the landing of William, he was achieving another of the objects of the *History* announced in his exordium, to extend the Whig glorification of the growth of English liberty to include the consequent and no less glorious growth of British prosperity.[20] Future factories and hotels followed William's banner as trade followed the flag, and Macaulay, invoking their attendance, was calling on the arts and sciences, as though in some baroque apotheosis, to hover joyfully around the spirit of rational liberty enthroned.

Through these deliberate anachronisms, as well as in the contrasts in the third chapter of the *History*, Macaulay made a bid to incorporate the industrial revolution into the Whig interpretation of English history. It was a significant attempt, because, increasingly, the evils of industrialisation and the heartlessness of industrial and commercial society were taking over from the Norman Conquest or political corruption as the central grievance of nostalgic radicals for whom, as against Whig notions of continuity, the pattern of English history was a fall and a future redemption, paradise lost and one day regained. We cannot, of course, know for what proportion of his early readers Macaulay's attempt succeeded; certainly it did not do so universally; Kingsley, for example, wrote a cutting semi-parody of it in *Westward Ho!*[21] To the extent that it failed, the failure was a pregnant one, not merely a lapse of taste; it is not fanciful to see it as an early defeat for industry and the idea of progress in their long failure to establish a rapport with what we shall have to call here, for brevity's sake, the English literary mind.

18 Samuel Johnson, 'Milton', *Lives of the English Poets* (ed. John Wain, Everyman's Library edn), p. 92.
19 *History, Works*, i. 431.   20 *ibid.*, pp. 1–2.
21 Charles Kingsley, *Westward Ho!*, ch. xxx.

Macaulay was attempting to find a rhetoric in which to celebrate industry and the legitimate opulence it created, as an established rhetoric of Whig piety celebrated England's political glories. Yet it is surely not only our own reservations, if we have them, about the industrial revolution – or about coastal housing developments for that matter – which make the attempt seem a failure. The comparison with Carlyle is instructive, because Carlyle, in a highly individual way and with far more reservations than Macaulay, did, in *Past and Present*, achieve something of the kind. For all the talk of Arkwright and the captains of industry, his imagination was able to respond appropriately to two features of industrial production, its Titanic energy and its essential anonymity. Despite Macaulay's love of energy and bustle, his eager response to the multifarious glitter of the Great Exhibition (which Carlyle, of course, despised), or – a harder test for a Victorian – to the grubby southern vitality of the Naples streets,[22] his mind and imagination and the language he commanded easily were essentially tuned to a society of public men who knew each other by name, whether in the high literary and political world of Holland House and the House of Commons, or the humbler one of great philanthropic causes in the Clapham of his boyhood, as well as to that wider and yet more distinguished society of dead statesmen and men of letters among whom he moved, as Trevelyan said, as if he knew them personally.[23]

In his essay on History, and in the *History* itself, he protested against older, essentially classical and Augustan notions of the 'dignity of history', which excluded the common life of men; he was for the mixed mode of the novel, and demanded that the historian should go into the Exchange and the coffee house as well as the senate.[24] He recognised, too – it was part of the notion of the unplanned, unlegislated changes in the history of civil society – that great transformations like the extinction of personal slavery in the early medieval period were essentially imperceptible, and that men could be happy in bad reigns and miserable amidst national glory.[25] Yet the *History*, of course, despite the famous third chapter on the state of England at the accession of James II, remains obstinately political. Among the losses, there is one kind of deepening and intensification of the sense of the past which

[22] Trevelyan, *Life*, pp. 550–1, 368–9.   [23] *ibid.*, pp. 645, 677.
[24] 'History', *Works*, v. 157; cf. 'Temple', *Works*, vi. 258–9.
[25] *History*, *Works*, iv. 189.

characterises the nineteenth century but in which Macaulay's *History* scarcely shares, though it would have been crucial in the famous passages on 'then and now'; it is its absence which determines their failure. It is the romantic intensification of antiquarianism into a kind of imaginative archaeology, a sense of man's shaping and penetration of the landscape through many generations. Carlyle possessed it in a high degree; Hardy and Kipling, at the end of the century, made it the imaginative possession of every English reader who cared to acquire it. Macaulay, for all his love of past associations, did not. We have already noted his response to the associations in landscape rather than landscape itself; we can be sure that they were associations with names or events, in a word, with identities. Macaulay's sensibility was, in any case, essentially urban – unkindly, one might say, suburban – but his feeling for the past in cities was essentially of the same kind.

There is a note by Carlyle on his travels in Belgium which points the contrast:

Sand downs and stagnating marshes, producing nothing but heath, but sedges, docks, marsh-mallows, and miasmata – so it lay by nature; but the industry of man, the assiduous unwearied motion of how many spades, pickaxes, hammers, wheel-barrows, mason's trowels, and the thousandfold industrial tools have made it – this! A thing that will grow grass, potherbs, warehouses, Reubens' pictures, churches and cathedrals. Long before Caesar's time of swords the era of spades had ushered itself in and was busy. Tools and the Man! 'Arms and the Man' is but a small saying in comparison. Honour to you, ye long forgotten generations, from whom at this moment we have our bread and clothing![26]

The industry and prosperity of the Low Countries, the gardened quality of its landscape, was a favourite theme of Macaulay's too, but such imaginative archaeology escapes his insistent didacticism and even his love of associations. The anonymous lay, for the most part, outside his range. Because of this, and perhaps too because he does not know quite in what terms he wants to make the triumphs of industry and commerce imaginatively acceptable, when he approaches the problem of celebrating the transformation of a landscape, his only resort is a mechanical inversion of a familiar eighteenth-century *topos*.

Images of decayed grandeur amid present desolation were

---

[26] J. A. Froude, *Thomas Carlyle. A History of His Life in London 1834–1881*, 2 vols (1902), i. 280. It was, of course, a recurrent theme in Carlyle's writings, especially in *Past and Present*. See below, p. 251.

imprinted on eighteenth-century imaginations above all by the topographical etchings of contemporary Rome: an infinitely suggestive iconography of broken and scattered columns and architraves; triumphal arches half buried in the dusty roads; artisans' sheds leant against vast crumbling walls tufted and draped with spurts and fronds of vegetation; peasants goading oxen past ancient greatness; beggars with arms theatrically outstretched. And swarming, of course, over the ruins, tricornehatted, pensive or exclamatory, were what Gibbon called 'a new race of pilgrims from the remote and once savage countries of the North'.[27] Gibbon himself made unforgettable use of this image in presenting and dignifying the conception of his *Decline and Fall*.[28] It may have provided the genesis, as it certainly provided the imagery, of Macaulay's famous New Zealander in the essay on Ranke, sketching the ruins of St Paul's from a broken arch of London Bridge.[29] Two years earlier, in Rome in 1838, he spoke of 'a reflection into which I often fall here, [that] the day may come when London, then dwindled to the dimensions of the parish of St Martin's, and supported in its decay by the expenditure of wealthy Patagonians and New Zealanders . . .'[30] But it was an image always congenial to him. Years before, in his review of Mitford, reflecting on the fate of Athens, he had envisaged 'savage hymns chaunted to some misshapen idol' amid the ruins of St Paul's.[31] In the same vein is his anticipatory threnody for Holland House, swallowed up by the growth of London and peopled only by distinguished ghosts.[32] He was not, of course, the first to put such images to melancholy – or minatory – prophetic use. Gray, for example, had done so in a passage Macaulay cites.[33] The nineteenth century added new motifs to an essentially classical and Gothic repertoire; some were provided by Egyptian and near-Eastern archaeology, as in Shelley's 'Ozymandias'; in 'The Burden of Niniveh' Rossetti envisaged a Londoner borne, as an Egyptian mummy now is into the British Museum, by 'Some tribe of the Australian plow'. Clearly some Victorians found a pleasureable

---

[27] Gibbon, *Decline*, viii. 288.
[28] Gibbon, *Memoirs of My Life and Writings*, in *Decline*, i. 85–6.
[29] Macaulay, 'Ranke', *Works*, vi. 455; cf. Gibbon: 'New Zealand may produce in some future age the Hume of the Southern Hemisphere.' *Decline*, iii. 270.
[30] Trevelyan, *Life*, p. 359.   [31] *Works*, vii. 703.
[32] 'Lord Holland', *Works*, vi. 541–2.
[33] *ibid*., 537. Geoffrey Carnall, *Robert Southey and His Age* (O.U.P. 1960), pp. 112–13, gives several interesting parallel examples for the early nineteenth century, and mentions Volney's *Les Ruines* as a source.

excitement in the prospect of being one with Niniveh and Tyre. And in Ruskin's hands history's most powerful cautionary tale became for Victorian England neither Rome nor Egypt but Venice. Macaulay, in the moments of topographically inspired jubilation in the *History*, employs the convention and simply stands it on its head. The aesthetics of the Picturesque delighted in the accretions of time; so, in his fashion, did he: tall-chimneyed factories, 'crowded marts and luxurious pavilions'[34] where once stood the hovels of cottagers and fishermen; industrious populations gloried and drank deep – especially the latter – on the sites of a vanished desolation. It is not so much the celebration itself that jars, though the irrelevance does, as the languid perfunctoriness of an almost rococo diction ('luxurious pavilions'), grating against a nineteenth-century reality for which no adequate rhetoric had been found.

If this view is correct, then at the level of imaginative sympathy Macaulay's fusion of Whig political history and material progress was less than complete. The relative failure to incorporate the latter is made the more striking by the vivid realisation of the former. Macaulay was undeniably excited by the vigour and the novelties of his century; he was enthusiastic, not without reason, about the improvements in comfort and health they brought or promised, but he saw them, as he saw India – the India of the Indians, that is – essentially externally, as an exhilarating spectacle which he saw and described through categories and a language that was stale and inapposite. To the face-to-face world of public life and the drama of parliamentary occasions, the stage for the display of civic virtue, he brought the full resources of his historical imagination and a mind easily and confidently possessed of every relevant descriptive and argumentative convention, founded on the ancient orators and historians and continued in England through centuries of public debate, vigorous pamphlet hostilities, and much political satire and posthumous eulogy. Adapting these and investing them with a Romantic sense of detail, circumstance and pathos, much of it learnt from the novel, he was able to offer a recreation of periods in the history of English public life that was both recognisably, traditionally, humanist and Whig and intensely individual.

But the precondition of that achievement was an unquestioning confidence in the value of public life, the dignity of public men,

[34] *History, Works*, ii. 254. Cf. iii. 282, 287.

and the validity of the fame that was their ultimate reward. Macaulay was sometimes ironical about politicians, never about politics. He could never have thought of Parliament, in Carlyle's or Dickens' terms, as a talking shop. Personally, it is true, his feelings about his own political career were complex, and in the long run not strong enough to hold him at the centre of the stage which for much of his life he loved. The young man who had haunted the gallery of the House of Commons when he should have been learning the law in his chambers,[35] and who, as a member of Parliament in 1832, had felt with such exultation at the Reform Bill vote that he was witnessing history ('like seeing Caesar stabbed or Cromwell taking the mace from the table')[36] was already, by 1835, writing from India to his friend Ellis contrasting the peaceful search for truth and the pleasures of friendship and conversation with the slavery of politics:

In England I might probably be of a very different opinion. But, in the quiet of my own little grass-plot, when the moon, at its rising, finds me with the Philoctetes or the De Finibus in my hand – I often wonder what strange infatuation leads men who can do something better to squander their intellect, their health, their energy, on such subjects as those which most statesmen are engaged in pursuing.[37]

The image is almost too consciously, elegantly classical, and both he and Ellis would have known it: the scholar in his quiet garden communing with the ancients and viewing from afar the futile bustle of the capital. The pursuit of literature and philosophy was, of course, covered by as much classical authority as that of public life, and Macaulay, with his strong feeling of participation in the great republic of letters – a state like St Augustine's City of God, linking the living and the dead[38] – responded fully to a sense of its combination of ease and dignity; one is reminded of Machiavelli putting on his courtly clothes to read the classics.

Various causes probably co-operated in Macaulay's growing distaste, if not for the idea, at least for the inevitable limitations and discomforts of politics: late nights, dull speeches, 'pestiferous rooms'.[39] There was a waning of youthful zest and awe, blunting political ambition and the excitement of privileged access to historic scenes; the more mundane character of political life in the

---

[35] Trevelyan, *Life*, p. 80.
[36] Thomas Pinney, (ed.), *The Letters of Thomas Babington Macaulay*, ii (C.U.P. 1974), 9; cf. Trevelyan, p. 146.
[37] Pinney, *op. cit.*, iii (C.U.P. 1976), 158.
[38] E.g. 'Milton', *Works*, v. 45; 'Bacon', *ibid.*, v. 137.
[39] Trevelyan, p. 320.

1840s and 1850s after the almost unbearable tensions of the Reform Bill battles – he can hardly have hoped – or wished – to see Caesar stabbed a second time; the death of his sister Margaret and the break-up of the family audience that meant so much to him.[40] India was inevitably distancing in a more than literal way, ensuring future affluence and leisure. If Macaulay was not quite like the later Anglo-Indians who have been described as deriving from their Indian official experience an authoritarian impatience running counter to their English liberalism,[41] he could hardly fail to contrast the facility of public life in India with the noisy contentiousness, discomfort and tiresome Scottish constituents which had to be endured after his return to the House of Commons.[42]

Given his growing distaste for active politics, in fact, it is remarkable that he could never, until forced by illness, bring himself entirely to let go; even after his life was dedicated to the *History*, he remained, obviously rather to Trevelyan's regret, a member of Parliament and even a minister. But though, in transferring his real allegiance to writing, he became the celebrant of the sacrifices he was no longer fully willing to make in person, the faith and the dogmas remained essentially unaltered. Public life remained close to his sense of essential human dignity; it seems, for example, to be the key to the difference in the treatment the *History* accords to the Highlanders and the native Irish. The former had a barbaric form of public life in which civic virtues were displayed; a man like Lochiel possessed, and was able to display, senatorial quality.[43] The Irish Chief he portrays as merely sunk in ignoble rusticity and sensuality, with no autonomous polity worthy of the name; cut off by the English penal laws from the possibility of improvement, his existence is merely animal: 'shooting, fishing, carousing, and making love among his vassals'.[44]

Public life offered not merely human dignity but, at its highest, possibilities of sublimity. In the letter to Ellis quoted above, Macaulay deplored, in line with his argument with himself, that Burke, in wasting his energies in party politics, had forfeited the

---

[40] See Clive, *Macaulay*.
[41] J. P. C. Roach, 'Liberalism and the Victorian intelligentsia', *Cambridge Historical Journal*, xiii (1957), 64.
[42] See e.g. Trevelyan, pp. 404, 469–70.   [43] *History, Works*, iii. 47–8, 72–4, 87.
[44] *ibid.*, ii. 558. Macaulay's own notorious incompetence in field sports may have coloured his view of gentlemanly rusticity, whether of the Irish or English Tory varieties.

chance of writing 'some great and durable work'.[45] Yet there is a glow, a complicity touched with envy even, in the view he imputed to Burke himself, in the essay on Southey: 'To plead under the ancient arches of Westminster Hall, in the name of the English people, at the bar of the English nobles, for great nations and kings separated from him by half the world, seemed to him the height of human glory.'[46] To those indifferent to such sublimity or even to public dignity Macaulay was habitually severe. In the essay on Sir William Temple, though, rationally, the charge against Temple's indolence rests on his alleged special responsibilities and opportunities, the tenor of the letter to Ellis is effectively reversed. The scholar in his garden becomes an epicurean dilettante, tepidly self-indulgent and selfish.[47] Only literary achievement of the highest kind could match the responsibilities of office. To him someone like the (third) Earl of Shaftesbury had unmistakably chosen the lesser path in giving to philosophy what was meant for the House of Lords: 'He soon left politics to men whose bodies and minds were of coarser texture than his own, gave himself up to mere intellectual luxury, lost himself in the mazes of the old Academic philosophy, and aspired to the glory of reviving the old Academic eloquence.'[48] His comment on the Earl of Dorset is in the same vein.[49] These judgements are reminiscent of Gibbon on the contrary instance of Boethius: 'From these abstruse speculations Boethius stooped – or, to speak more truly, he rose – to the social duties of public and private life.'[50] Macaulay was gratuitously harsh to the private diversions even of energetic men of affairs; Montague's poetasting, Schomberg's china, Frederick the Great's flute clearly seemed to him derogatory to the dignity which should hedge a statesman.[51]

A firm notion of the behaviour proper to public men is of course one of the beacon lights by which Macaulay sets the course of his *History*. But even the examples given so far are not trivial, and their possible interest goes beyond a perhaps pedantic insistence on the continuing presence of a strain of civic humanist sentiment. They lead us to the existence, in the *History*, of a set of polarities

---

[45] Pinney, *Letters*, iii. 159.   [46] *Works*, v. 331.

[47] *Works*, vi. e.g. p. 314. Macaulay himself spoke of his 'cross between Stoicism and Epicureanism'. Trevelyan, p. 226. For the Epicurean image of the scholar in his garden, and attitudes to it, see Sheldon Rothblatt, *Tradition and Change in English Education* (1976), pp. 69–71. I am much indebted to this stimulating and subtle book.

[48] *History, Works*, iv. 204.   [49] *ibid.*, ii. 129.   [50] *Decline*, v. 29.

[51] E.g. *History, Works*, ii. 422; iv. 57. 'Frederick the Great', *Works*, vi.

which are vital to the sense it conveys of the governing arrangements proper to a free but sober people, and of the value of that
open, energetic yet ordered and responsible public life which for
him lies at the centre of the Whig tradition, though individual
Whigs may often have betrayed it. His feeling for its value, by
contrast with the irresponsible frivolities and extravagances of
other political manners, both courtly and demagogic, expressed
itself at many levels and often in contexts apparently remote from
his central public concerns; in his judgements of style and character, and in the resonances of such words as 'manly' and 'social':
there is, for example, a whole complex of values implied in the
Augustan adjective when he speaks of the Covenanters' 'unsocial'
superstition, and in the kindred terms he applies to the Puritans;
the judgement is essentially that of Gibbon on the Jews and the
early Christian fanatics, and the vocabulary is the same.[52]

To Macaulay, in fact, both royal absolutism and political and
religious radicalism have their associated styles of character and
expression: artificial, frivolous, dissimulating; coarse, uncontrol-
led, licentious, canting and fanatical. Between them, along the line
of the Whig middle way, lies ordered parliamentary government
and the rational control of honest feeling: openness and accountability stabilised by senatorial gravity and a high sense of public
honour, by a style of public character and utterance suited to an
ideal constitutionalism. As a standard, of course, it has some
affinities with the austere, over-strained, neo-classical notions of
stoic republican virtue and Spartan simplicity which Macaulay
consciously repudiated, but it is balanced and up to a point
humanised by an Augustan feeling for a decorous, polite and
tolerant sociability, as well as by more typically Victorian ideas of
sexual and financial propriety: in short, a Victorian Whig compromise still able to draw nourishment from older, eighteenth-
century and even classical sources.

We have already seen how images of courtly luxury, indolence
and corruption call up unconscious Gibbonian echoes, rare
enough to be significant, in Macaulay's prose, and how they
emphasise by contrast, in the Indian essays, the virtues of the
energetic middle-class Europeans. In the *History*, though the class
dimension is absent, the trivial absurdities of precedence and

---

[52] *History, Works*, iii. 352. Cf. Gibbon, 'that unsocial people' (the Jews), *Decline*, ii. 155.
On sociability as a value in the eighteenth century, see Rothblatt, *Liberal Education*,
ch. 7.

protocol at the peace conference at Ryswick offer a similar contrast to the grand designs and stoic indifference of William and Bentinck's common sense.[53] So far the contrasts are of an almost Carlylean kind, between insubstantial tinsel and the dictatorial energy of stern men of action. But the farcical treatment of the European conference, the meeting-place of petulant petty sovereigns and the corrupt representatives of arbitrary governments, also throws into relief the description immediately preceding it of the bitter, factious, but unquestionably real debates of the English Parliament. The difference is ontological; discreditable though the proceedings of Parliament had been, they had substance.

It is a characteristically Victorian antithesis, not least in the way Anglo-Dutch solidity is pitted against Latin frivolity – though at Ryswick the Germans and Austrians share much of the obloquy. It is a contrast reinforced by deep-running religious and class sympathies and antipathies; Protestantism is obviously one feature of it. It enters into a characteristic preference for Dutch realism to baroque allegory or rococo elegance,[54] the latter having strong connotations of artificiality and even corruption; a baroque ceiling formed a fitting setting for Dickens' feline lawyer, Mr Tulkinghorne.[55] Thackeray, to whose view of history dualities of surface and moral substance were, as one would expect, fundamental, concluded *The Four Georges* with the thoroughly Macaulayan contrast of the ball at Carlton House to celebrate the Prince of Wales' (George IV) coming of age with the resignation of Washington.[56] In Macaulay's *History* the military exploits of Louis XIV, arriving with his full retinue to receive the keys of fortresses about to fall,[57] have only a little less unreality than the baroque diplomatic ballet at Ryswick, with its mimic battles over precedence. In the essay on Madame D'Arblay we are given a variation, which sometimes appears in the *History* in the characterisations of James and Louis: the subordination, at court, of public questions to private passion, contrasted with Pitt's responsible, essentially public view of the Regency crisis.[58] We are invited to see this as characteristic, though Macaulay's own

[53] *History*, ch. xxii.   [54] E.g. George Eliot, *Adam Bede*, ch. xvii.
[55] *Bleak House*, ch. x.
[56] Thackeray, 'George the Fourth', *The Four Georges* (1861).
[57] Macaulay, *History*, chs xix, xx.
[58] 'Mme D'Arblay', *Works*, vii. 31–2.

experience of cabinet government, as one might expect, furnished examples of similar pettiness.[59]

Courtly triviality was compounded, for him, when it was associated with Catholicism; the converse was also true. Macaulay was not, judged by contemporary standards, particularly anti-Catholic. There was a side of him that found the institution venerable from its longevity and enjoyed the colourfulness of its ritual.[60] It was a sympathy not in any way dependent on the medievalism which appealed to so many of his contemporaries. Though his judgements of seventeenth-century taste in the arts are often disparaging, a man of his dramatic and expansive temperament could hardly escape a sneaking sympathy with Mannerism and the Baroque. Castle Howard he called 'the best specimen of a vicious style',[61] but St Peter's seems to have provided the central aesthetic experience of his life, in marked contrast to his feelings about Chartres.[62] His culture, his literary tastes, in so far as they were not English, were, after all, essentially classical and southern rather than Gothic; Dante and Milton were his poets, French, Spanish and Italian his modern languages; he learnt German later, and, it seems, in a mood not wholly serious.[63]

But despite these avenues of sympathy, the combination of court and Catholicism was more than Whig flesh could endure; it brought to the surface in him all the Protestant folklore about wily Jesuit intriguers, just as the use of Latin as a living language always evoked the scornful condescension of the Fellow of Trinity. English seventeenth-century prose was bad enough, before men like Sprat and Addison began to set it to rights,[64] but seventeenth-century Popish Latin was intolerable. Macaulay's account of the Castelmaine mission to Rome, with its accompanying festivities and compliments, reads like the marginal notes of an irascible schoolmaster:[65] florid declamation, 'insipid and hyperbolical adulation', 'turgid and impure Latinity', 'detestable hexameters' – these, the reader is made to feel, are the inevitable and dreadful consequences of the unblessed union of courtly and clerical insincerity, and of a public life essentially ornamental and performative, unchastened by the habits acquired in the public

[59] Trevelyan, p. 460.   [60] 'Ranke', *Works*, vi; Trevelyan, pp. 354–67.
[61] *History*, *Works*, iv. 178.
[62] Trevelyan, pp. 358–442. He also loved the churches of Genoa. *ibid.*, p. 352.
[63] *ibid.*, p. 333.
[64] *History*, *Works*, i. 596; iii. 171. Also 'Dryden' and 'Bacon', *Works*, v, vi.
[65] *History*, ii. 84–5.

transaction of business. Read against such a contrast, Macaulay's reference elsewhere to 'that keen, weighty, manly logic, which is suited to the discussion of political questions'[66] becomes itself triple-weighted. The public face of courtliness and papistry is florid eloquence, its private one is the hypocritical dissimulation which reaches its acme in the politician made out of an impious priest. Macaulay's gives his readers his portrait in the *History* in the character of the Spanish minister Portocanero,[67] just as in the essay on Barère he painted that of the archetypal demagogue. The priest's profession emancipates him at once from family affection, religious awe and the gentlemanly code of honour; dealing in daily hypocrisy, coldly studying in the confessional the secret hearts of men and women, he is a figure of terror from the Romantic imagination. For all the vulgarity of its elements, or perhaps because of them, the portrait has a certain mythical power; it is Balzac's Vautrin in one of his incarnations, or what Julien Sorel would have wished to be able to become; it is also tempting to think that Macaulay may have drawn for it on Talleyrand, whose company he enjoyed.[68]

A whole essay could be written on Macaulay's attitude to duplicity. It is, of course, for him a distinguishing characteristic of the Stuarts: Charles I's false dealings with Parliament; the Treaty of Dover and Charles II's covert Catholicism; James II's breaches of his pledged word. Sunderland and Marlborough are made monsters by it, as though by a disease or obsession. It relates to many things, besides the folklore of Jesuit casuistry and traditional Whig accusations against the Stuarts. It was an understandable preoccupation in a man who had thought much about Oates and the Popish Plot and still more about the Indian law of evidence. It touched one of Macaulay's own most sensitive points: his almost finicking touchiness about his political independence and integrity.[69] It provides, in the Indian essays, a distinction as vital as the antithesis of energy and indolence: it is, in fact, one of the chief criteria by which the scale of civilisation is established; fair dealing, trustworthiness, is the distinctive virtue of modern commercial society, as loyalty and honour are those of chivalry.[70] That

---

[66] Applied by Macaulay to the elder Fox. 'Chatham' (first essay), *Works*, vi. 57.
[67] *History*, *Works*, iv. 470–1.   [68] Trevelyan, pp. 167–8.
[69] *ibid.*, pp. 206, 249, 364.
[70] The contrast is not made directly, but compare, e.g. the remarks on the National Debt below with the portrait of 'the honest old Cavalier' in the essay on Milton. *Works*, v. 40–1.

is why Macaulay seems much more disturbed by Clive's stooping to duplicity to save lives and accomplish desirable objects than by Hastings' alleged cruelties and extortions. Clive had let England and civilisation down by not playing the game:

English valour and English intelligence have done less to extend and to preserve our Oriental empire than English veracity. All that we could have gained by imitating the doublings, the evasions, the fictions, the perjuries which have been employed against us, is as nothing when compared with what we have gained by being the one power in India on whose word reliance can be placed.[71]

Public honesty, governments and merchants standing by their bond, was, as Macaulay understood it, the foundation of that combination of commercial prosperity and honourable public life which he saw as essentially fused in the Whig creed. Through it he managed to give the idea of the growth of civilisation a value more than simply material. The National Debt, that Whig creation which had so often seemed to eighteenth-century critics and moralists to epitomise the insubstantial values of commercial, as distinct from landed, wealth, as well as an intolerable burden on the latter, was to Macaulay the exact reverse: the epitome at once of honourable conduct and of the invisible but profound moral consensus upon which civilisation itself rested, and a source of power which no despot could match:

The inclination of a society to pay debts is proportioned to the degree in which that society respects the obligations of plighted faith. Of the strength which consists in extent of territory and in number of fighting men, a rude despot who knows no law but his own childish fancies and headstrong passions, or a convention of socialists which proclaims all property to be robbery, may have more than falls to the lot of the best and wisest government. But the strength which is derived from the confidence of capitalists such a despot, such a convention, never can possess. That strength . . . flies, by the law of its nature, from barbarism and fraud, from tyranny and anarchy, to follow civilisation and virtue, liberty and order.[72]

If the mark of civilisation is trust, the mark of a free government is accountability. It is this which gives such force to the famous description of the trial of Warren Hastings, for Hastings, in Macaulay's account, was a man out of whom a Carlylean hero might easily be made: a strong man doing what had to be done, halting a Gadarene rush and dispelling with brusque authority the unhealthy vapours of two societies, one decadent and the other

---

[71] 'Clive', *Works*, vi. 419.
[72] *History*, *Works*, iii. 621; cf. iv. 456. Also 'Southey', *Works*, v. 345, 368.

corrupt. Macaulay in fact disapproved of attainder as a judicial procedure;[73] he admitted, too, that after a while Hastings' trial became a bore.[74] But in the great set-piece description of Hastings' arraignment the surge of the rhetoric sweeps away, for a while, all qualifications.[75] Given Macaulay's sympathies it is a moment full of symbolic suggestion: the stoic man of action, accustomed to executive command and unused to debate, called to account by the masters of language, themselves the heroic guardians of the traditions of government by discussion. There is no doubt that Macaulay regards this, whatever the merits of the case, as one of the great moments of a free constitution: the display of all its talents and its historic associations, and the central meaning of it, the idea of accountability.

It is also one of the high moments of mid-nineteenth-century prose rhetoric, and what is most striking about it – and may seem to give Macaulay's achievement an old-fashioned air, though it is hard to think of anticipations of it – is that the other examples which spring most readily to mind present mostly images of confusion and disaster, even delirium: dreams, nightmares, riots, saturnalia; Carlyle's descriptions of the march to Versailles and the September massacres; Hugo's grotesque parliament of beggars in *Nôtre Dame de Paris*; the Gordon riots in *Barnaby Rudge*, and the sub-Carlylean crowd scenes in *A Tale of Two Cities*; even, in its subtler way, the opening of *Bleak House*; Balzac's description of the Palais Royal in *Les Illusions Perdues*, and the terrible banquet in *Le Peau de Chagrin*. Even in Scott, the Porteous riots in *Heart of Midlothian* leave perhaps a more lasting impression than hierarchical images of order, like the muster of Mac-Ivor's clan in *Waverley*. Nor do trial scenes redress the balance; the most deservedly famous are burlesque (Bardell *versus* Pickwick) or surreal: the trial of the Knave of Hearts in *Alice in Wonderland*. Only Macaulay attempts a rhetorical *tour de force* that is intended as the celebration of a rational freedom, founded on accountability and made almost hieratic by historic precedent and association. It is the literary and parliamentary equivalent of a great allegorical Renaissance state pageant; in the nineteenth century itself the only fair comparisons are pictorial or, still more, operatic.

Macaulay begins with an implied sidelong sneer at more purely ceremonial and courtly occasions; probably he had in mind the lavish banquet in Westminster Hall at the coronation of George

---

[73] *History, Works*, iv. 362; also vi. 634.   [74] *Works*, vi. 633–4.   [75] *ibid*., pp. 628–31.

IV, which had caused so much ill-feeling. He assembles his extras: the guards, the judges, the peers in gold and ermine; the audience in the galleries: beautiful women, royalty, foreign ambassadors, celebrities: Mrs Siddons, Gibbon, Reynolds, the Duchess of Devonshire. Then the principals, a Homeric roll-call: Fox and Sheridan, 'the English Demosthenes and the English Hyperides', Burke and Windham and the unconsciously prophetic figure of the young Charles Grey, Grey of the Reform Act. But the central figure is really the Hall itself, the very symbol of accountability:

the great hall of William Rufus, the hall which had resounded with acclamations at the inauguration of thirty kings, the hall which had witnessed the just sentence of Bacon and the just absolution of Somers, the hall where the eloquence of Strafford had for a moment awed and melted a victorious party inflamed with just resentment, the hall where Charles had confronted the High Court of Justice with the placid courage which has half redeemed his fame.[76]

There is here, expressed not philosophically but rhetorically, a high idea of the state and the law as the enduring public thing in the lives of men, and of the dignity, at its highest even the glory, of the men who minister in its rituals and shape and transmit its precedents. Government by discussion, under the law, takes on the form of epic. And if this seems obvious enough, it is not, after all, one of the ideas one tends most readily to see as dominant in mid-Victorian England. For Macaulay, public men unworthy to participate in such rites disqualify themselves, and in a healthy state of the polity are seen to do so, by conduct, even by style, as well as by political opinion or public crime. Of course, on the right side and in evil times even rogues like Tom Wharton had their uses.[77] But the concomitant of despotism is the systematic unfitness of public men; the low standard of public morality both before and immediately after the Revolution is explained by the lack of an orderly continuity in the recent past, the sudden transformations and the nefarious habits acquired in surviving arbitrary reigns and government by cabal.[78]

The *History*, as we have it, chronicles only the beginning of better things. The original plan, to take it up to the eve of the Reform Act, was more ambitious and optimistic. Yet there is a sense in which the Reform Act would not have been the end, because the consummation of Macaulay's *History*, like that of Hegel's philosophy of history and of *A la Récherche du Temps*

[76] *ibid.*, p. 629.   [77] *History, Works*, iv. 59–63.
[78] 'Temple', *Works*, vi. 252–3. Cf. 'Hallam'.

Perdu, is its own conception: the final act of the projected *History* is the *History* itself. Of course, this was not a literal intention of Macaulay's in the sense in which it can be attributed to Hegel or to Proust. Yet the connection between a political tradition and the commentary on it is intimate enough to save the suggestion from absurdity; what grounds there might be for making it we shall have to consider in the final section of this chapter.

Reconciling Parliament and the nation

In the volumes of the *History* which deal with the reign of William III a picture gradually begins to establish itself which is, quite naturally, the reverse of the one presented in the account of the events leading to the Revolution. What begins to emerge with the constitutional settlement of 1688, despite the frequently deplored conduct of Parliament and of politicians, is a respectable idea of public life, capable of uniting all men of goodwill. There is again, to use the old metaphor, a ship of state; battered, ill-officered, its crew undisciplined, but still identifiable, in whose perils from external hazard and simmering mutiny the reader can take a sympathetic interest. There are even moments, when the colours are broken out, for a gulp of pride. The debate on the restoration of the currency, for example:

one of the proudest days in the history of the English parliament. In 1796, Burke held up the proceedings of that day as an example to the statesmen whose hearts had failed them in the conflict with the gigantic power of the French republic. In 1822, Huskisson held up the proceedings of that day as an example to a legislature which, under the pressure of severe distress, was tempted to alter the standard of value and to break faith with the public creditor.[79]

The tradition is again in working order, capable of bequeathing precedents that are valid rather than merely cautionary, and the subject, significantly, is that of government standing by its bond.

In the latter part of James' reign it had been very different: the growing consensus of the men of goodwill inclining to desperation and ultimately resistance: 'Actuated by these sentiments our ancestors arrayed themselves against the government in one huge compact mass.'[80] The great moments are extra-parliamentary: the Magdalen election, the trial of the Bishops, the refusal of the clergy to read the Declaration of Indulgence. The story is one of a nation

[79] *History, Works*, iv. 266.   [80] *ibid.*, ii. 183.

all but hopelessly corrupted and prostrate, purged and united by suffering, and recovering its soul by a stubborn adherence to its law and its religion. It is only the extent of the resistance to James which prevents Macaulay's account of William's invasion from taking on the character of a classic Machiavellian *renovatio* of a corrupted nation by a strong prince; in the essay on Hallam, a quarter of a century earlier, in fact, that is precisely the account Macaulay offers, though not in those words.[81] In the *History*, by contrast, the nation's resistance takes on an epic grandeur: the lords lieutenant of the counties who defy James and are dismissed are introduced one by one in full panoply of title, lineage and attainment, as though by a Shakespearian monarch marshalling his support.[82] When Macaulay exultantly tells us that in the hundred or so London churches only four clergymen obeyed the Council's order to read the Declaration, it is rather a relief to be spared a Homeric recital of the names and parishes of the disobedient, as in some protracted game of oranges and lemons.

But the rottenness, of course, is at the centre; it is, as Macaulay's significant phrase 'the carnival of the Restoration' implies, a world turned upside down: saturnalia. The characterisations of James' favourites reinforce the lesson to weariness: the incessantly swearing, frenziedly bragging, Tyrconnel; the lying Jermyn, the snivelling turncoat, and pandar Rochester;[83] the frantically ranting, scurrilous, debauched Jeffries. And so it goes on, down to the Popish interloper at Magdalen College, the drunkard and pimp Anthony Farmer. The more disreputable and extreme of the Whigs are merely the other side of the same coin; the Catholic courtiers are in their way as fanatical and revolutionary as the radical Whigs and covenanters: they were 'fanatics, who were ready to break through all rules of morality and to throw the world into confusion for the sake of propagating their religion'.[84] On the other side are the heirs of Shaftesbury, who himself had lived to see, as Macaulay wrote in his denunciation of him in the essay on Temple, 'a mighty ruin wrought by his own ungovernable passions'.[85] There was his creature Oates, a fit witness for such a Chief Justice as Jeffries; the half-demented demagogue Ferguson,

---

[81] *Works*, v. 227. Speaking of Cromwell, and comparing him with Caesar and Napoleon, Macaulay wrote: 'No men occupy so splendid a place in history as those who have founded monarchies on the ruins of republican institutions.' *ibid.*, p. 211.

[82] *History, Works*, ii. 126–31.   [83] *ibid.*, i. 573, 578–9.   [84] *ibid.*, ii. 136.

[85] *Works*, vi. 305.

turning the tragedy of the Western rebellion to farce[86] as Jeffries
turned the majesty of the bench to buffoonery. 'In every age the
vilest specimens of human nature are to be found among
demagogues.'[87]

The gallery of characters in Macaulay's *History* is various
enough to constitute a *comédie humaine*. Macaulay's own
apprehension of human character, however, is limited in a way
that was actually of value to the overall design. His response to
saturnalia is, of course, essentially civic and disapproving: shocked, as Bernard Shaw wrote of some excessively Victorian stage
extras witnessing a Shakespearian duel scene, 'to see gentlemen of
position so grossly forgetting themselves'.[88] Macaulay's response
to the merely human ran typically, as in his notorious essay on
Johnson, to caricature as the alternative, and sometimes the
complement, to disdain; his ways of putting things were pitched,
like those of Henry James' fake medium, 'altogether in the key of
public life'.[89] The latter was a category which, in his meditations
on public execution and on the contrast between burial in the
Tower and in Westminster Abbey subsumed even death.[90] But the
relative crudity of Macaulay's grasp of human character outside
the realm of public honour and repute was nothing but advan-
tageous to the artistic completeness of the dualistic, almost
Manichaean, vision on which, despite all prosaic qualification, the
imaginative economy of the *History* is based.

Ferguson points the moral. Attempting to join the invading
army of William, he is repulsed. Ferguson 'had been a great man in
the knot of ignorant and hotheaded outlaws who had urged the
feeble Monmouth to destruction: but there was no place for a
lowminded agitator, half-maniac and half knave, among the grave
statesmen and generals who partook the cares of the resolute and
sagacious William.'[91] Ferguson's rejection by William is also
Macaulay's rejection of the populist traditions of English Whiggism. The crushing of the Western rebellion had been the bloody
purge of the fanatical, Shaftesburian element in Whiggism. After
the Revolution the world is again the right way up, though
precariously. It is convenient for Macaulay's vision, or part of its
justification, that the extremes he rejects so readily meet. Ferguson, unable to leave his métier, turns to plotting as a Jacobite,[92]

[86] E.g. *History, Works*, i. 415, 480.   [87] *ibid.*, p. 460.
[88] *Plays and Players* (O.U.P. 1952), p. 46.   [89] *The Bostonians*, ch. 10.
[90] *History, Works*, i. 488–9.   [91] *ibid.*, ii. 235.   [92] *ibid.*, iii. 236.

just as Shaftesbury had been both courtier and demagogue: 'the Shaftesbury who, in office was the chief author of the Declaration of Indulgence, was the same Shaftesbury who, out of office, excited and kept up the savage hatred of the rabble of London against the very class to whom that Declaration of Indulgence was intended to give illegal relief.'[93]

Under James 'the worst members of the Whig party ... men who were plotters and libellers by profession' lay hidden 'in cocklofts and cellars';[94] the suggestion of rats is irresistible. In the new reign the Jacobite plotters, mostly men identical in type and sometimes even in person, gnaw at the foundations of re-established public order. Their occasional discovery lifts, each time, a corner of the subterranean, twilit world of the dangerous classes; it provides, in fact, much of what 'social history' the latter part of Macaulay's work contains: Hunt, the smuggler of Romney Marsh; the renegade Fellow of Magdalen; the highwayman; and Goodman, actor, gigolo, poisoner and forger.[95] Of the same world are the false-witnesses, 'that vile tribe of which Oates was the patriarch', like Robert Young, the scandalous priest, bigamist, forger, gaolbird.[96] Oates' instruction of his apprentice Fuller in the arts of false witness[97] is like a scene from a Restoration comedy: Brazen and Swearwell whispering together in a garret. The failure of the various sub-plots enhances the sense both of danger and achievement in the main one, the overt, parliamentary conduct of public business.

Mundanely, there were qualifications enough to keep Macaulay's work within the bounds of a realistic, enthusiastic prose, and the judiciousness of responsible history: the factiousness of the Whigs in Parliament, the corruption, self-seeking and treachery of the great Whig nobles, the tensions between the nation and its deliverer. But in the dimmer shapes suggested to the imagination there are greater and more dramatic simplicities. The historian might have unlearnt some of the more naively partisan assertions of the young reviewer and Whig polemicist, and no longer talk, as in the essay on Milton, of the conflicts of the seventeenth century in terms of Oromasdes and Arimanes,[98] but their presences still hovered over the *History*, no longer identified with the overt protagonists of party conflict – even Tories had

[93] *ibid.*, vi. 302.　　[94] *ibid.*, i. 409.　　[95] *ibid.*, iv. 146–7, 208.
[96] *ibid.*, iii. 354–5.　　[97] *ibid.*, iii. 498ff.　　[98] *Works*, v. 23.

their uses[99] – but with more plausibly perennial interests: the reassurances provided by civilisation, property, public trust, liberty under the law, the outward sign of which was a decent gravity of public demeanour; and below, the turmoil of lawless ambition, fanatical delusions akin to delirium, the negligence or hatred of all boundaries to will, passion and appetite.

At the Revolution, civil society itself was menaced by a return to a state of nature:

Never, within the memory of man, had there been so near an approach to entire concord among all intelligent Englishmen as at this conjuncture; and never had concord been more needed. All those evil passions which it is the office of government to restrain, and which the best governments restrain but imperfectly, were on a sudden emancipated from control; avarice, licentiousness, revenge, the hatred of sect to sect, the hatred of nation to nation. On such occasions it will ever be found that the human vermin which, neglected by ministers of religion, barbarous in the midst of civilisation, heathen in the midst of Christianity, burrows among all physical and all moral pollution, in the cellars and garrets of great cities, will at once rise into a terrible importance.[100]

Historically speaking, the most interesting feature of this passage is the substitution of the word 'intelligent' for the word 'propertied' which had normally formed the basis of a stake in civil society; it is the criterion of a society disposed to rate education as highly as property in qualification for the franchise. It is, in Macaulay, untypical in the explicitness of its fears, but it sets the tone for the whole: the Revolution is respectability clamped down on universal riot and licence, a return of chaos and old night.

It is an antithesis generally expressed in a spatial metaphor, which locates at the emotional centre of Macaulay's *History*, though it never insistently or aggressively dominates it, a characteristic nineteenth-century drama, both psychological and social. It is a drama of nightmare and reassurance in which blind instincts and dangerous classes meet in a frightening subterranean moral equation whose outward symptoms and symbols are the slums of great cities: Macaulay's Whitefriars,[101] Carlyle's Faubourg Saint Antoine, and the murky, teeming landscape of Dickensian courts and alleys. Fears for one's own rational identity and apprehensions of social revolution seem often bound together by the same moral and imaginative geography, and it was one which made the prospect of a world turned upside down, even in retrospect, difficult to contemplate calmly. No one would claim

---

[99] *History, Works*, i. 79.   [100] *ibid.*, ii. 311–12.   [101] *ibid.*, iv. 301–3.

that this fearful landscape was Macaulay's habitat: it is apparent mostly in its absence; he could never be counted as one of its explorers, like Dickens or Eugène Sue, yet he must, in his incessant ramblings through London, have seen many sights which, if recorded, would have been jarringly intrusive included in Trevelyan's *Life*. But equally, his not infrequently expressed anxieties about revolution indicate that he knew its terrors; they give force and gravity to his presentation of public life on its proper course, and they help to dramatise or overdramatise his vision of the consequences of Restoration licence and of James' wilful, arbitrary rule. It was the crime of the Stuarts, in wantonness and the exercise of a perverse will, to have allowed the creatures of the deep, epitomised in men like Tyrconnel and Jeffries, to bore through the surface and all but overspread it.

Historical myths are never, we may take it, more potent than when subliminally linked to some archetypal pattern, of which the most obvious is death and renewal; since, in history, things are usually getting either worse or better, it is a pattern almost perennially available. And a new version of the myth is, of course, made more potent still when it is implicitly related to some of the older myths and symbols in which the pattern has been embodied. Macaulay used the symbols of the Whig tradition, but significantly enlarged their range of suggestion, adapting the apocalyptic political myths of seventeenth-century Puritans to the cause of an Augustan sense of order and profound nineteenth-century feelings about respectability. There were other available archetypes. But to see one historical character as a type of another, as precursor or reincarnation, as medieval historians saw Adam, Noah or Moses as anticipatory types of Christ, and as, in the courtly festivals of the Renaissance, similar flattering identifications were instituted for contemporary princes and emperors,[102] was not in Macaulay's idiom, any more than was the *renovatio* wrought by a Machiavellian prince. The nineteenth-century empiricist and believer in progress was always uppermost.

But no history which has at its centre, and takes seriously, the idea of a Great Deliverer, can altogether escape Messianic echoes, and in the ways he draws his central antitheses Macaulay's *History* inevitably takes on something of the shape, if not the idiom, of apocalypse. The Old Commonwealthman, as John Clive remarks in another context, was not extinct in Macaulay.[103]

[102] See Frances Yates, *Astrea* (1975).   [103] Clive, *Macaulay*, p. 94.

England had been given over for a space to Belial and Moloch,[104] and deliverance was at hand. Beneath the Augustan–Victorian surface of Macaulay's *History*, it seems not extravagant to suggest, an early education in Biblical fundamentalism, in the knowledge of the courts of Babylon and Zion, continued to provide shapes and outlines for the drama of the imagination, though its expressive language was the reasoned appraisal of the performances of public men.

Public life in the last part of the *History* is of course still venal and factious, but there is at least an institutional framework, preserved intact, for the consensus of the respectable part of the nation, and occasionally the consensus manifests itself. Stated at its barest, the shape of the *History* as we have it is the agony of the constitution followed by deliverance and partial renewal. But there is also a repeated pattern within this: moments of reconciliation, enforced by a common danger – the Restoration, the trial of the Bishops, the Revolution – followed by a return to factiousness when the danger is past. Macaulay gave it the status of a law: coil and recoil.[105] It is these moments, above all, that the *History* celebrates, while recognising the inevitability of the recoil. But there were also longer-term reconciliations. In Macaulay's conception of the historian's task the traditional forensic associations were strongly present: he was prosecutor, defendant and judge. But these roles were qualified, in two ways, by the fact that in history the only ultimate victor is time: the historian in the grand manner is both a frequent obituarist and, if he is also a Whig, a celebrant of outcomes. Macaulay welcomed both roles. There is a passage in 'Warren Hastings' which is the balancing pendant to the great trial, where Westminster Hall is set in opposition to Westminster Abbey: the contests of the living and the quiet, involuntary ecumenism of the dead.

In that temple of silence and reconciliation where the enmities of twenty centuries lie buried, in the Great Abbey which has during many ages afforded a quiet resting place to those whose minds and bodies have been shattered by the contentions of the Great Hall, the dust of the illustrious accused should have mingled with the dust of the illustrious accusers.[106]

But the mood of eirenic melancholy is more prominently matched by that of eirenic optimism. The growth of nationhood is also the triumph of enduring reconciliation. Ireland, of course,

---

[104] *Works*, v. 36.   [105] *ibid.*, vi. 97, 151; vii. 290.   [106] *ibid.*, vi. 643.

remained intractable, even to an enlarged, conciliatory Whiggism, with Catholic emancipation on its banner;[107] the history of Scotland by contrast, was an object lesson in the burying of old hatreds between Celt and Saxon. Typically, Macaulay sees the distinction in terms of rival or blended historic pieties, one fostering continued hostility, the other the symptom and cement of an achieved unity. 'In Scotland all the great actions of both races are thrown into a common stock, and are considered as making up the glory which belongs to the whole country.'[108] It is a pity that Macaulay was unfortunate with his example. According to him, Scott's enthusiasm at the victory of the Highlanders at Killie-crankie over Lowlanders of Scott's own blood and lineage was a triumph of national over merely clannish feeling. In fact, as Lockhart makes clear, Scott's enthusiasm was actually based on clannish feeling; 'my ancestor was a Killiecrankie man'.[109]

In England, the theme of reconciliation was to have been more evident in the *History* as it was originally planned, taking in the Hanoverian period, than it is in its actual, truncated form. Macaulay intended, of course, that it should cover the whole period from 1688 to the eve of the Reform Act, 'between the Revolution which brought the crown into harmony with the Parliament, and the Revolution which brought the Parliament into harmony with the nation'.[110] In the exordium of the *History* he speaks of 'a new class of abuses from which absolute monarchies are exempt'.[111] meaning, of course, the control of the Commons by the executive through corruption. A constant and understandable theme of disquiet throughout the eighteenth century, and still of deep concern to a Whig historian like Millar, it had also been treated by Macaulay himself, writing before the Reform Act, with a strong sense of urgency.[112] These fears were, for Macaulay, stilled for ever by the extension of the franchise, by the publicity of parliamentary proceedings, and by the growth of an informed public opinion.

But there was a sense in which the reconciliation of Parliament and the nation depended not only on the accountability of Parliament to the electorate, but also on the character of that electorate itself, on its willingness to accept the necessary restraints of self-government. In the cultivation of that restraint nothing was, as we have seen, more important to Macaulay than the

---

[107] *History, Works*, iii. 458.   [108] *ibid.*, p. 93.   [109] Lockhart, *Life of Scott*, p. 202.
[110] Trevelyan, *Life*, p. 347.   [111] *Works*, i. 2.   [112] See above p. 46 and n. 48.

preservation of continuity, the continuing veneration for the political experience of the nation embodied in its history and institutions. It is, of course, the standard Burkean position. But the older political traditions of the country were in some measure arcane; the House of Commons had only recently allowed the publication of debates; the new electorate might be fully informed of the state of contemporary politics while the past which gave it form and stability remained barely known and alien. It is in this sense that the conclusion of Macaulay's *History* would have been only overtly the Reform Act; that in a profounder sense the conclusion was the *History* itself. Through it, the electorate and Parliament, by sharing a common political memory, could be united in a common political culture.

The appropriateness of this view of Macaulay's *History* is, unfortunately, most apparent in its 'unwritten' part, in the essays on eighteenth-century English politics. It is easy to forget that these should have been merely adumbrations of the second part of the *History*; Macaulay himself came to regret, for example, using the great scene of Hastings' attainder in the essay; he wished he had saved it for the *History*.[113] But the role imputed to the latter is most visible in these essays because the period they cover is the one in which memory merges into history, and what is required, essentially, is to put history at the service of tradition by making it the guardian of political memory.

The society to which Macaulay obtained entrance through Holland House and the House of Commons, that exclusive, tightly knit circle of which Parliament was the hub, was one in which political oratory, for example, was still one of the appropriate objects of connoisseurship; a notable orator 'up' and going well was like a *diva* in fine voice. It was a competitive, appraising, ranking society, imbued with a classical feeling for the canonical performances. Past speeches and orators provided the standard against which to measure the aspiring. Macaulay himself received for his maiden speech what seems to have been at the time the standard alpha mark: 'nothing like it since Plunket'.[114] He, with his love of ranking and comparison and his more profound historical knowledge, may even have exaggerated this trait with an outsider's indiscretion; there was surely something ostentatious, even in a recognised critical genre, about a comparison, across

---

[113] Trevelyan, p. 413.   [114] *ibid.*, p. 125.

eighty years, which ranked Lord Holland with Granville as supreme among debaters in the Lords who had never sat in the House of Commons.[115] But clearly connoisseurship, even if not aided by historical comparison, was one of the aspirations of a politically stage-struck young Whig. Earlier in the century we find Francis Horner, parvenu and Edinburgh reviewer like Macaulay himself, comparing, for his father's benefit, the points of Pitt and Fox like a trainer appraising a racehorse. Horner had stamina as well as taste: 'All the world is going to the debate on Monday, which, it is expected, will last two days. There will be great difficulty in obtaining a seat; but I am to make the attempt with two very agreeable companions, Mackintosh and Lord Webb. If we get into the gallery, their conversation will lighten the ennui of waiting seven or eight hours.'[116] Sometimes, for the latecomer, there were only the faint, celestial strains wafting through closed doors: 'You are indebted for this letter to a severe disappointment I met with in not getting into the H. of C. A great display is expected . . . they are now in the very heat and pride of the debate . . .'[117]

But though a charmed world, it was accessible to talent; both Horner and Macaulay, after all, got through the stage door. To a man of Macaulay's capacity for veneration and epic sense of the past, the aristocratic dinner tables and the rooms of the House of Commons of the early 1830s were places of instruction as well as delight. Above all there was Holland House, and Lord Holland himself, carrying with him, through his own experience and links with an earlier generation, the parliamentary memory of half a century. As Macaulay said after his death, 'While he lived, all the great orators and statesmen of the last generation were living too.'[118] From Holland, if his *Memoirs* are any indication, one could hear recollections of Gibbon, Fox, Sheridan; of Pitt's quarrel with Tierney and Canning's with Castlereagh; of hearing from the Lords the shot that killed Prime Minister Perceval and of reading the eighth book of the *Aeneid* to the dying Fox; of the hush when Grattan first rose to address the English House of Commons, and 'the strange and long deep-fetched whisper in which he began'.[119]

[115] 'Lord Holland', *Works*, vi. 539.
[116] *Memoirs of Francis Horner* (Edinburgh 1849), p. 129.
[117] *ibid.*, p. 130. I am most grateful to Donald Winch for drawing my attention to these very apposite quotations. [118] Trevelyan, pp. 394–5.
[119] Henry Richard Lord Holland, *Memoirs of the Whig Party during my time* (1852), 2 vols, i. 199, 264–5. Also *Further Memoirs of the Whig Party, 1807–21* (1905), p. 128.

Macaulay caught the tone of easy, intimate political reminiscence of the society to which his talents as reviewer and speaker had
given him entry, touching it with an epic solemnity perhaps only
possible to a parvenu: 'old men who lived to admire the eloquence
of Pulteney in its meridian, and that of Pitt in its splendid dawn,
still murmured that they had heard nothing like the great speeches
of Lord Halifax on the Exclusion Bill'.[120] In this tone Macaulay
presented parliamentary history as the folklore of the governing
class, and made it accessible. It must have been flattering to
the provincial readers of the Edinburgh Review, this assumed intimacy of shared political memory. They were inducted, as
Macaulay himself had been; reminded – the verb seems appropriate even if untrue – of the aged Chatham and the young Burke
speaking together for the repeal of the Stamp Act: 'a splendid
sunset and a splendid dawn';[121] of the former's voice in his prime,
rising 'like the swell of the organ of a great cathedral';[122] of Burke
moved to tears by the younger Pitt's maiden speech.[123] At times
we seem to be listening to some tribal bard chanting the deeds of
ancient heroes, or Scott's aged minstrel without his wistfulness,
hearing of ' "the great Walpolean battles" ... nights when
Onslow was in the chair seventeen hours without intermission,
when the thick ranks on both sides kept unbroken order till long
after the winter sun had risen up them, when the blind were led
out by the hand into the lobby and the paralytic laid down in their
bed-clothes on the benches.'[124]

> For shivered arms and ensigns
>   Were heaped upon the ground
> And corpses stiff and dying men
>   That writhed and gnawed the ground.[125]

Macaulay, as a boy, had tried to write epic poetry.[126] Here he
found a subject, an idiom, almost a persona even – there is a hint
of inverted commas – suited to his talents and his time: the gouty
veteran parliamentarian's recollections of far-off political battles
and past heroes of debate.

Of course, he knew that the play was in part a comedy: Sheridan
falling back exhausted, handkerchief to his lips, into the arms of

---

120 'Temple', Works, vi. 307.   121 'Chatham' (second essay), Works, vii. 260.
122 'Chatham' (first essay), ibid., vi. 48.   123 'Pitt', ibid., vii. 365.
124 'Lord Holland', ibid., vi. 539.
125 'The Battle of Lake Regillus', xix, Lays of Ancient Rome.
126 Trevelyan, pp. 22–3.

the admiring Burke, after his opening speech against Hastings,[127] is only a half-thought away from the Victorian genre scene of the young lady, smelling bottle to her nose, swooning into the arms of her admirer. Macaulay recognised the contrivance, if not the analogy. Chatham's affectations turn even age, illness and greatness half to burlesque: coming down to the House 'in all the pomp of gout', swathed in flannel, crutch in hand.[128] He was compared to Garrick: Macaulay said he would have been the finest Brutus or Coriolanus ever seen.[129] Government by orators, Macaulay recognised, had its disadvantages (the shades of the laconic men of action look gratified). Chatham was no great strategist; his son a poor war minister. All their genius was given to the House of Commons. Oratory, Macaulay wrote in the essay on Temple

has stood in the place of all other acquirements . . .. This is the talent which has made judges without law, and diplomatists without French, which has sent to the Admiralty men who did not know the stern of a ship from her bowsprit, and to the India Board men who did not know the difference between a rupee and a pagoda.[130]

But these were the defects of a system imperfectly worked out, the product of an all-powerful Parliament divorced from the nation. By the Reform Act the remedy of greater public accountability had been applied, but the wider public had itself to learn the rules of the game. In the *History*, the high parliamentary occasions are given a gravity which enforces the lesson of continuity. Oratory, for the remoter period all but irrecoverable, is not even necessarily involved. It delighted Macaulay, for example, that the thanks of Parliament were conveyed to Schomberg for his military services on the same spot and with the same ritual as was done over a century later to Wellington.[131] We have seen how the currency debate of 1696 derives an added solemnity from its citation as a precedent by Burke in 1796 and Huskisson in 1822. This is epic but it is also gossip, the kind of gossip, founded on shared reminiscence, found in united families and helping to make them so. Macaulay was certainly not unaware of the educative possibilities. The reviews may be *pièces d'occasion* but the *History* is weighty with meditated lessons.

A favourite theme of Macaulay's was the speed of modern communications and its effect on the spread of political information. Words spoken in the House of Commons were read from

[127] 'Hastings', *Works*, vi. 633.   [128] 'Chatham', *ibid.*, p. 69; vii. 277.   [129] *ibid.*, vi. 48.
[130] *ibid.*, p. 295.   [131] *History*, *Works*, ii. 253.

Penzance to Penrith within hours – to render down the sense of a number of possible quotations.[132] The gallery of the House of Commons was now the respectable breakfast tables of the nation; political information ingested as readily as marmalade. But such knowledge was unballasted by political memory, by a vital sense of the past and its inspiring and admonitory precedents. This was the necessary dimension which Macaulay's *History* supplied, and which, if completed, it would have done still more weightily. Of course, it is possible to argue – though at this distance of time only unprofitably – that given the still restricted franchise and the number of English people who were still in more than one sense poor relations, Macaulay's extended political family was a sham; that the *History* is a fake eirenicon, offering only a covert sectarianism masquerading as the fellowship of all men of good-will. Macaulay himself, of course, would not have disputed the facts, only the gloss put on them, and he would certainly have retorted that the wider electorate provided a genuine check on parliamentary misconduct.

One thing at least is clear; the *History* is not simply partisan; a judgement, like that of Firth, that Macaulay was always the Whig politician[133] could hardly be more inapposite. Of course Macaulay thought that the Whigs of the seventeenth century were correct in their fundamental ideas, but the hero of the *History* was William, who, as Macaulay says, was certainly no Whig. Macaulay hated Shaftesbury as much as Laud and liked the Whig Shrewsbury less than the Tory Danby. Some, it is true, Covenanters, Non-Jurors, Jacobites, republicans – 'the bigots who still clung to the doctrines of Filmer . . . the enthusiasts who still dreamed the dreams of Harrington'[134] – were, as Hallam said, outside the communion. If this was Whiggism it was so only, by the mid-nineteenth century, in the most extended and inclusive sense, requiring only an acceptance of parliamentary government and a sense of the gravity of precedent. Butterfield says, rightly, that in the nineteenth century the Whig view of history became the English view.[135] The chief agent of that transformation was surely Macaulay, aided, of course, by the receding relevance of seventeenth-century conflicts to contemporary politics, as the power of

132 *Works*, i. 537; vi. 48; vii. 81.
133 Firth, *A Commentary on Macaulay's History of England*, p. 275.
134 *History*, *Works*, ii. 353.
135 *The Englishman and His History*, p. 2.

the crown waned further, and the civil disabilities of Catholics and Dissenters were removed by legislation. The *History* is much more than the vindication of a party; it is an attempt to insinuate a view of politics, pragmatic, reverent, essentially Burkean, informed by a high, even tumid sense of the worth of public life, yet fully conscious of its interrelations with the wider progress of society; it embodies what Hallam had merely asserted, a sense of the privileged possession by Englishmen of their history, as well as of the epic dignity of government by discussion. If this was sectarian it was hardly, in any useful contemporary sense, polemically Whig; it is more like the sectarianism of English respectability.[136]

---

[136] The view that Macaulay occupied a central, rather than a partisan Whig, position, is not, of course, new. See, e.g., H. A. L. Fisher, *The Whig Historians* (1928), and also the most recent comprehensive study of Macaulay, Joseph Hamburger, *Macaulay and the Whig Tradition* (Chicago 1976).

II
THE TORY
Stubbs and the Ancient Constitution

CHAPTER 5

The German inheritance: a people and its institutions

The modern historian and the ancient constitution

If the study of periods of History is to become part of a school education, I trust that due care will be taken not to dwell unnecessarily on, or to choose for exaggerated illustration, those periods which are connected most closely with the questions and controversies of today. Of all things in the world except a controversial woman, a controversial boy is the most disagreeable.[1]

The speaker is William Stubbs, Regius Professor of Modern History at Oxford in 1876, celebrating a decade of tenure of his chair by a lecture on 'The Present State and Prospects of Historical Study'. The delivery we may think of as firm (the evidence does not quite warrant the obvious adjective 'gruff', which was applied to his friend Edward Freeman),[2] by a Yorkshireman whose modesty had no trace of hesitancy, and whose strong sense of the difficulty of historical judgement was compatible with, perhaps even made possible by, an imposing harmony of character and principle. Stubbs was of a piece; that the historical writing of the Tory High Churchman and future Bishop of Oxford should lie so squarely along the line of the Whig tradition was a sign, not of any waywardness or unresolved tension in him, but of the kind of capaciousness that tradition could now exhibit, while remaining still clearly identifiable and a source of important satisfactions.

Before we consider these, however, and before returning to the specific issue Stubbs raised at the end of his lecture, it is worth attending to the occasion itself. For Stubbs' position as Regius Professor and the review of his subject which he offered in the lecture were symptoms of the ways in which the discipline of

---

[1] W. Stubbs, *Seventeen Lectures on Medieval and Modern History* (O.U.P. 1887) (henceforth cited as *SL*), p. 53.
[2] W. L. Hutton (ed.), *Letters of William Stubbs, Bishop of Oxford, 1825–1901* (1904), p. 67.

history was being transformed. It was not only that with the exception of Thomas Arnold no Regius Professor of History at either university, since the foundation of the chairs by George I, could plausibly be called a great historian. They had not needed to be historians at all. As Stubbs said in his Inaugural lecture of his early predecessors, 'I do not find that they were men to whom the study of History, either English or foreign, is in any way indebted.'[3] Contrasting Stubbs' appointment in 1866 with 'the promotion of a popular novelist [Kingsley] to the historical chair at Cambridge', John Richard Green remarked that 'It is the first merit in the appointment of an historian to the chair of History, in the case of Mr Stubbs, that it is at any rate a confession that such a study as that of history exists.'[4] Stubbs' immediate successors in the chair were to be Freeman and J. A. Froude, though neither lent it quite the same distinction. When Stubbs was appointed he was not the author of a great synthetic, much less narrative, work of history, but he had already won a reputation as an outstanding editor of and commentator on the obscure and difficult documents of the early medieval period.

In this he was a portent, as was the survey, European in scope, which he offered to his Oxford audience in 1876. History was becoming a professional, even a co-operative, discipline, with international networks of information and standards of perform- ance. Another sign of this was the foundation in 1886 of the *English Historical Review*, largely at the instigation of Green. Moreover, Stubbs was not only a scholar and historian; he had to concern himself, as Macaulay or Hallam had not, with historical education. The passage quoted above concerned history in schools, but much of the lecture had dealt with the state of historical teaching in Oxford. For there were now, since the inception of the Oxford History School, initially as part of a joint School of Law and History in 1850,[5] undergraduates to be taught, and, to the regret of professors, since they took no part in the necessary coaching, examined; Stubbs, Freeman, and Seeley in Cambridge, all hated examinations. The constraints of examining, with the necessity it imposed of choosing set periods for examina- tion and hence for study, made the advocacy of one's own 'period' a piece of academic politics. Stubbs' remarks would almost

[3] *SL*, p. 7.
[4] *Saturday Review*, 2 March, 1867. Reprinted in *Stray Studies* (2nd series, 1903), p. 195.
[5] See *SL*, pp. 39–41.

certainly have been taken as such by the more sophisticated members of his audience.

Stubbs went on – it was his peroration – to specify the dangerous periods and prescribe the antidote: 'The judgement must be trained in cooler air and by milder methods than are found in the battle-field of modern politics.' Under 'modern politics' we find

the struggles of puritanism and absolutism, or the deep religious discussions, that for three centuries have separated Christendom into two camps and do so still. Let them learn the history of early England and early France before they are called on to exert their tender judgement on the Great Rebellion or the French Revolution. If the teachers had been so taught the experiment had never been tried.[6]

For an Oxford audience the sting was perhaps in the final sentence. The original proposals for an Oxford History School had provided for 'at least a knowledge of the history of England, or France, or Germany during the sixteenth and seventeenth centuries'.[7]

Stubbs was not alone in thinking the choice undesirable. Freeman also, who, after his resignation of his Trinity Fellowship on his marriage in 1847, retained his connection with Oxford as an examiner, agreed. It was, according to him, the worst choice that could have been made; it was altogether too controversial. The Council of Trent or the Long Parliament aroused partisanship as fierce as that provoked by the Reform Bill or the Corn Laws.[8] Stubbs wrote similarly in his *Constitutional History* of 'the two theories which have been nursed by the prejudices of ten generations'.[9] It is a striking testimony to the persisting intractability, in the third quarter of the nineteenth century, of the Reformation and the history of the seventeenth-century England, and the difficulty of assimilating them to an increasingly reconciliatory and 'national' version of Whig history. Perhaps Macaulay had, in a sense, written in vain. All the large-minded concessions, the recognition of the balancing necessity of Tories and Whigs, the celebrations of the moments of national unity, when the old Abhorrer took the old Exclusionist by the hand and the candles burned in the windows of the City for the acquittal of the

6 *ibid.*, pp. 53–4.
7 W. R. W. Stephens, *The Life and Letters of Edward A. Freeman* (1895), 2 vols, i. 124.
8 *ibid.*, p. 125.
9 Stubbs, *The Constitutional History of England in its Origin and Development* (O.U.P., 2nd edn 1875) (henceforth cited as *CH*), 3 vols, iii. 639.

Bishops,[10] were unavailing; regicide and religion were not yet uncontentious.

Of course, Stubbs and Freeman, as medievalists, had a vested interest. Stubbs, too, in declaring his intention of avoiding political preaching, was paying his tribute to a growing sense of professional responsibility, and proclaiming his dedication, in a manner later to become fashionable and even mandatory, to the cause of pure truth.[11] In fact, Stubbs was in this respect a transitional figure, disclaiming the kind of prophetic office, when he spoke *ex cathedra*,[12] which Arnold had assumed as a matter of course, yet also himself regarding the study of history as 'thoroughly religious'.[13] His advocacy of the Middle Ages was symptomatic of that compromise. The ancient world – 'the dead world of Greece and Rome' – was too remote from modern concerns to be truly instructive,[14] just as the seventeenth century was too close to them. Yet there was more in the aversion to the latter than either professional jealousy or professional inhibition. The terms in which Freeman confessed to his uneasiness with what he called 'the nuisance of the seventeenth century' do not suggest an overriding concern with objectivity: 'One can't go unreservedly with any side as one can with our friends in the thirteenth. My political and my religious sympathies are divided. I go with the Parliament as Parliament; but I can get up no sympathy with the Puritan as Puritan.'[15] Freeman's dilemma, revealed with characteristic naiveté, was particularly acute, but his blend of liberalism and High Church sympathies was less idiosyncratic than it would once have been, and was to become much less so as the century wore on; it was shared, for example, by Green and Gladstone. Since the beginning of the Oxford Movement, the boundaries of High Churchmanship had been extended; it was no longer 'High and Dry' or even necessarily Tory. But in any case, broadly, Freeman was right in the contrast he drew between the thirteenth century and the seventeenth. No defiant supporters of the prerogative toasted the memory of King John or fasted for the misfortunes of Henry III.

It is worth remembering this as we turn to consider the possible significance, in mid-Victorian England, of the period Stubbs and Freeman made their own. It helps to soften a paradox: the revival of what looks like a version of 'ancient constitutionalism'. For the

---

[10] Macaulay, *History*, ii. 182–4.   [11] See Rothblatt, *Liberal Education*, ch. 13.
[12] *SL*, p. 15.   [13] *ibid.*, p. 10.   [14] *ibid.*, pp. 16, 109.   [15] Stephens, *op. cit.*, ii. 266.

mature Whiggism or, as it might now be more accurately called, Parliamentarianism, of Macaulay had, after all, left 'the ancient constitution' far behind. The sacred *corpus* of the seventeenth-century lawyers had been etherealised – it is a familiar process – by critical commentary into, at best, a pervasive spirit; the cult of the constitution, with its heroes and martyrs and its witness to centuries of evolving but reminiscent piety, had, as it were, turned back on itself and become the object of its own veneration, rather as the votive offerings and worn footprints of pilgrims grow in time to be themselves objects of reverent attention. We might, accordingly, expect some of the dogmas of earlier Whiggism simply to slip quietly out of the canon: the freedom born in the German woods, the 'free' Anglo-Saxons, and the anguished denial that the Norman Conquest, by breaching the continuity of English constitutional life, had marked it with an 'indelible stain' of absolutism.[16] In the late eighteenth and early nineteenth centuries, in fact, these tenets had seemed increasingly to be abandoned to intransigent radicals, losing any claim to respectability as sober history. For Hallam and Macaulay Magna Carta was the true beginning of the national history: the constitution derived essentially from the thirteenth century, though Hallam, like Millar and Hume before him, admitted that English law was Saxon in origin. The development of a reverent, minute and enthusiastic study of the early Middle Ages, which is the great mid-Victorian achievement in historiography, would have seemed highly improbable fifty or a hundred years earlier.

Of course, we must not exaggerate the sense in which this revived attention to early institutions can be called 'ancient constitutionalism'. The repudiation of any belief in a strictly normative past by the new generation of historians is as emphatic as Hallam's refusal to allow the right to freedom to be tried by antiquaries.[17] Stubbs said that 'the past has no power, no moral right, to dispose of the present by a deed in mortmain'.[18] Freeman wrote of the significance once attached to the interpretation of the Norman Conquest with at least the ostensible detachment of retrospect: 'Time was when the whole fabric of our liberties was held to depend on the exact nature of the entry made by William

[16] Quentin Skinner, 'History and ideology in the English Revolution', *Historical Journal*, 8, (1965), 168.
[17] See above, p. 24.
[18] *SL*, p. 25.

the Bastard.'[19] In the nineteenth century such considerations had largely lost their relevance. A full-hearted acceptance of parliamentary sovereignty as a doctrine and the practical supremacy of the House of Commons as a political fact makes politically inspired ancient constitutionalism irrelevant and politics a pragmatic activity. Even among radicals, as Christopher Hill showed in his classic essay, the significance of 'the Norman Yoke' waned in the early nineteenth century.[20] Ann Pallister found the same of radical appeals to Magna Carta; the newer political idioms of the rights of man or of utility largely supplanted political claims based on a version of English history.[21] It is true that in the Romantic–medievalist social criticism of the second quarter of the century we find claims still emphatically made to ancient rights – the cottagers' rights of common and the right to poor relief – but these claims were social and economic rather than constitutional; Disraeli's was the most overtly constitutionalist version of such Tory Radicalism.[22]

Of course, to cherish the past while denying it binding force had become, as we have seen earlier, part of the Whig tradition; it is a formula which applies as readily to the mid-Victorians as to their predecessors. Freeman, while asserting the political irrelevance in modern times of the nature of the Norman Conquest, was nevertheless ready with the eager claim that, 'As far at least as our race is concerned, freedom is everywhere older than bondage . . .. Our ancient history is the possession of the liberal,'[23] and he began *The History of the Norman Conquest* with a vehement denial that the Conquest had been an essential breach in the continuity of English history: 'the Norman Conquest was the temporary overthrow of our national being. But it was only a temporary overthrow . . . in a few generations we led captive our conquerors.'[24] The stance, pious but repudiating any binding legalism, is a familiar one. But compared with the earlier historians we considered in previous chapters under the heading of 'The Whig compromise', the mid-Victorians were irridentists, reclaiming the partially abandoned or neglected Saxon heritage for the

[19] Edward A. Freeman, *The History of the Norman Conquest of England* (O.U.P., 3rd edn 1870), 5 vols, i. 71. (Henceforth cited as *NC*.)
[20] Christopher Hill, 'The Norman yoke', *Puritanism and Revolution* (1958), p. 110.
[21] Ann Pallister, *Magna Carta. The Heritage of Liberty* (O.U.P. 1971), pp. 4, 65–6, 76–7, 82–3.   [22] See below, p. 240.
[23] Freeman, *The Growth of the English Constitution from the Earliest Times* (3rd edn 1890), p. x.   [24] *NC*, i. 2.

exercise of Whig piety. Hence – it would be as natural to write 'because' – their piety was differently accented : more consciously national, even racial; more potentially critical and reactionary; more democratic or populist.

To understand the satisfactions of such a Whig historiography it helps to turn again to what might be found uncomfortable, restrictive or insufficient in the version of Whiggism to which Macaulay had given such full and satisfying expression. We have begun by noting that even Macaulay may have failed to process the seventeenth century for almost universal national consumption; Stubbs found him too partisan.[25] But there is also the larger question how much of the nation's past Macaulay had succeeded in rendering in the ways he, almost uniquely, had developed. We can begin by noticing the obvious: that historic Whiggism requires a difficult feat of sustained poise. To maintain complacency in a vale of tears is a more heroic achievement than it is often given credit for. The Whig must be fond of the past, but not too fond; satisfied with the present, but not so satisfied as to preclude trust in the future. More than most men he needs a consistently fair wind, and can survive relatively little disappointment; an embittered Whig historian is a contradiction in terms. Part of the security of the progressive Whig, in Macaulay's sense, lies in the belief that modernity is essentially homogeneous and therefore exacts no agonising choices. This belief, as we have seen, was not universal. The old notion of corruption and its eighteenth-century derivative, the critique of luxury, set up a standing opposition between liberty and progress. We have seen in the first two chapters how that opposition was largely overcome: how, given favourable conditions, liberty and progress could be seen as reconcilable or even complementary. Political disaster, revolution, was the revenge taken by liberty on progress when the accommodation had not been effected soon enough; when, progress having corrupted liberty, the latter took redress in abrupt and doctrinaire forms which threatened the security and prosperity of society.[26] But for the early-nineteenth-century English Whig, the chief, indeed virtually the only, challenge presented by modernity to an inherited liberty was the imbalance of property and education and political representation: the solution was the extension of the franchise. How soon, and

[25] *SL*, p. 124.   [26] E.g. Macaulay, *History*, ii. 392–3, 398.

how much, were debatable but pragmatic questions; they in no way rendered the concept of modernity itself equivocal or pejorative, as 'corruption' and 'luxury' had done. The use of brakes as well as accelerator implies no criticism of the route.

Increasingly, however, in the Whig historians of the mid-Victorian years, we become aware, from time to time, of a sense of strain, of an awareness of modernity as problematic or even in some aspects menacing, not merely in the *outré* form of the revolutionary demagogue, but in the nature and tendency of modern government itself. We come at times close to something by which Macaulay was quite untouched, a critique of bureaucracy, and with it tendencies – it hardly seems to matter whether we call them potentially radical or reactionary – which have more in common with the eighteenth-century Country Party creed, with Harringtonian 'True' Whigs and Georgian radicals, in their suspicious provincialism and distrust of government as such, than with the proudly, even unthinkingly metropolitan Whiggism of Macaulay.

Of course, in using Macaulay himself as a point of reference and departure in this way we are consulting our own convenience; no implication is intended that mid-Victorian historians held him constantly and consciously in mind. But the differences are instructive, and most of all between the man of the centre and the man proudly aware of roots and locality; Macaulay's roots, if anywhere, were in the parliamentary traditions he constructed for himself out of the available materials. In making the Whig tradition personal,[27] dramatic and heroic, he necessarily emphasised the centre: Parliament, Westminster, London. In giving it greater exemplary force and vividness there was a loss of generality. The populace makes, of course, periodic irruptions into the *History*, mostly, naturally, the inhabitants of the capital: turning the camp at Hounslow into a fair; crowding Westminster Hall for the trial of the Bishops and lining the river to see them pass; attending scaffolds; hounding Jeffries; welcoming Charles and William. There are the portraits of the Cavalier and the Roundhead, and the descriptions of the delusions and the fate of the West-Country peasantry ('clowns', Macaulay sometimes calls

[27] Strictly one should say 'more vividly personal', for he was only developing an existing trait, fostered by the Ciceronian element in education. Schoolboy declamation, as we see from Trevelyan, and from Gladstone's diaries, was much concerned with the moral and personal qualities of statesmen. The young Macaulay mentions choosing to do one 'in the character of Lord Coningsby impeaching the Earl of Oxford'. Trevelyan, *Life*, p. 43.

them). In general, however, apart from the third chapter, and the Monmouth rebellion, Scotland and Ireland receive more attention than the English shires, whose members of Parliament, even, are usually mentioned, at the best, with irony; scorn for the county member was one of the ways in which Macaulay revealed his Whiggism in the narrower sense. All the Augustan as well as the rootless suburbanite in him drew him to eighteenth-century notions of 'The Town' as the source and site of all happenings, and to disdain for the provincial as a form of rusticity. We have already attended to the absence in Macaulay, despite his pretensions as a social historian, of any acute sense of the significance of the anonymous.

True, the wider political nation can be thought of as inducted into English history by reading Macaulay's *Essays*. But even the reader's possession of the franchise can hardly disguise the fact that he is essentially a spectator. In fact, of course, he is at a double remove from political action; he is a spectator not a mover of events, and it is only Macaulay's legerdemain which can make him momentarily forget that he is not even that; not a club gossip but his distant auditor. There is, of course, an irony in this; dramatically we may be tempted to call it the central irony of English history, if we take seriously the populist element in the Whig tradition. For the original seventeenth-century common lawyer's and even the Burkean Whig's conception of the constitution is essentially, not indeed democratic, but national. The common law is not a creation of heroic judges or legislators but the slow, anonymous sedimentation of immemorial custom; the constitution is no gift but the continuous self-defining public activity of the nation.[28]

There are, of course, ambiguities. It would be possible to debate endlessly – and no doubt impossible to debate other than endlessly – the respective roles to be assigned to nature and nurture in the traditional process in which a determinate entity both confronts and bends to circumstances and creates itself in its negotiations with them. Burke himself speaks with a deliberate eclecticism of the way a country's constitution 'is made by the peculiar circumstances, occasions, tempers, dispositions, and moral, civil and social habitudes of the people, which disclose

---

[28] See especially Pocock, 'Burke and the Ancient Constitution' in *Politics, Language and Time*, and *The Machiavellian Moment*.

themselves only in a long space of time'.[29] In this formulation
'circumstances' and 'occasions' are balanced by 'tempers' and
'dispositions', which may be thought of as pre-existing, while the
word 'disclose' may or may not hint at a paradigm which often
haunts traditionalist discourse: not open-ended evolution but
embryology: a teleology. It may make a difference whether we
think of the identity concerned as existentially creating itself *in*
traditional activity or as a programme which works itself out or
discloses itself through it. The latter in turn is capable of nuance,
depending on whether we think of it as expansive or refining, as
expanding like a flower or disclosing the statue in the mould.
These ambiguities were not taken up directly, but they will be
worth bearing in mind when we come to consider Stubbs, who
gave the matter some general attention, in more detail.

Ambiguities apart, the idea of a people making its institutions
through the spontaneous creation of custom was a pregnant one.
As the central conception – though compatible with an eloquent
justification for aristocracy – of the Burkean notion of an evolving
constitution, which was to exercise such a profound influence on
the historiography of the nineteenth century, it offered large
opportunities of development in the form of a more inclusive,
national historical myth. It had been part of Macaulay's achievement to make the past, the more recent past at least, intensely
personal, and hence accessible; to read his essays was like making
a tour of the tombs in Westminster Abbey with an incomparable
guide. Yet extending and deepening this possession of the past was
to require a transcendence of the personal, and the disclosure of a
plausible and moving collective subject, the nation. 'Constitutional History', Stubbs wrote in his preface (and here he may indeed
have had Macaulay consciously in mind),

has a point of view, an insight, and a language of its own; it reads the exploits and
characters of men by a different light from that shed by the false glare of arms,
and interprets positions and facts in words that are voiceless to those who have
only listened to the trumpet of fame. The world's heroes are no heroes to it, and it
has an equitable consideration to give to many whom the verdict of ignorant
posterity and the condemning sentence of events have consigned to obscurity or
reproach.

But in compensation for its austerities it 'abounds in examples of
that continuity of life, the realisation of which is necessary to give

---

[29] Undelivered speech on Representation, 1782, quoted Pocock, 'Burke and the Ancient
Constitution', p. 226.

the reader a *personal hold on the past* and a right judgement of the present' (italics mine).[30] It meant, in part, going beyond the more accessible world of the capital to the locality, and back beyond the Homeric parliamentary battles of the more recent past to a point at which the constitution could be thought of as made, as men made the landscape, anonymously, and by uncountable unplanned acts of improvisation and adjustment, unrecorded except in their results. To write such a history called not only for the severest scholarship but for another kind of sensibility, not dramatic but archaeological.

We recognise such a sensibility as one we rightly think of as characteristically mid-Victorian, in its feeling for the obscure and provincial, and its fascination with the structures fabricated, coral-like, by countless almost imperceptible creatures, or, in human terms, in a famous formulation, by 'the number who lived faithfully a hidden life, and rest in unvisited tombs'.[31] We find it in diverse examples: in the complex ecological chains of *The Origin of Species* and the awareness of the teeming, hidden yet consequential life of 'an entangled bank';[32] in the feeling, in *Middlemarch*, for the subtle movement of old provincial society; in Stubbs' typical call for a collection of surviving manorial customs, 'such a codification in fact as is possible, of the ancient unwritten popular law as it is preserved in these most ancient shadows and skeletons of the early life of our fathers'.[33] In historiography, without question, its greatest single monument is Stubbs' *Constitutional History of England*.

This sensibility itself owes much, of course in its origin to a Romantic, Wordsworthian feeling for humble and obscure life; much, too, probably, by the mid-century, to the schooling the age had received in the understanding of economic and industrial processes and the division of labour, and even to economic theories themselves indebted to earlier eighteenth-century ideas: Stubbs' preface is full of 'unintended consequences' and private vices as public benefits.[34] It certainly owes something to physiology and natural history and to the immense imaginative challenge represented by the processes and time-scales of the new Lyellian geology. But it also, of course, as we have already partly seen,

---

30 *CH*, i. p. iii.
31 George Eliot, *Middlemarch*, bk VIII, ch. LXXXV. Cf. *Adam Bede*, ch. XIX.
32 Charles Darwin, *The Origin of Species* (Penguin ed), p. 459.   33 *SL*, p. 73.
34 'The world owes some of its greatest debts to men from whose memory it recoils.' *CH*, i. p. iv.

attaches itself readily to older modes of thought and feeling; above all, to Burkean traditionalism and its attendant aesthetic, the late-eighteenth-century concept of the Picturesque,[35] from which the nineteenth century was to derive its love of encrustation, of the modulations of light and shade on mossy thatch,[36] of crumbling stonework and its natural concomitant, ivy. This love of a patina, a delight in the effects of attrition and accretion, was obviously not without political resonance: the imagination 'doing a little Tory-ism on the sly' – again George Eliot is our aptest witness.[37]

But an inclusive national myth of the kind a reverent anti-quarianism requires needs an identifiable collective protagonist for its historical story. Compared with Macaulay's heroic, epic mode, it exacts a twofold shift of focus, narrowing from Parliament to the minute local details of repeated administrative and customary practice, and widening to grasp the national identity which these both manifest and help to constitute, and of which Parliament is only the highest, conscious expression. The veneration for ancient laws and institutions was intensified, but it was widened by a feeling for other continuities and grounds of identity which had hitherto meant less: continuities of language and race. The tradi-tions of Westminster Hall and St Stephen's Chamber might be esoteric, Macaulay's *Essays* and daily newspapers notwithstand-ing, but anyone who spoke the English tongue and came of stock not palpably immigrant had as good a claim as anyone else to those of the shire-moot and the township, to the English Conquest of England and the freedom brought from the German woods, and to the more stirring events of early English history: 'it is something to know ourselves of the blood and speech of the actors of that day and its morrow'.[38] English historiography became, more urgently than ever before, a search for 'ourselves', for, in the words of Green's title, the history of the English People.[39]

A stout and vigorous nation

The impulse to self-definition had been one of the chief motives in writing English history as far back as the fabrications of Geoffrey

---

[35] Christopher Hussey, *The Picturesque, Studies in a Point of View* (1967).
[36] *Middlemarch*, ch. XII.   [37] George Eliot, 'Amos Barton', *Scenes from Clerical Life*.
[38] Freeman on the day of Godwin's return from exile. NC, ii. 33.
[39] J. R. Green, *A Short History of the English People* (1874).

of Monmouth in the twelfth century. It is an understandable preoccupation in a land so marked by successive invasions and conquests, Celtic, Roman, Teutonic and Norman. Geoffrey's neo-Virgilian legend was an attempt to link Celtic Britain to the classical world.[40] His great kings, Brutus, Belinus, Arthur, are, understandably in a work written in the reign of Henry II, potentates on a European scale, members, even if antagonistically, of the imperial world of Rome. It was the Reformation, the event which most decisively separated England from the political and religious legacy and domination of Rome, which first prompted interest in the invading Saxon barbarians as 'our' forbears.[41] The immediate occasion was theological and polemical: the Anglo-Saxon studies patronised by Elizabeth's Archbishop of Canterbury, Mathew Parker, were, as Maitland put it, to reveal 'the title-deeds of a national church'.[42] The change was more than a matter of religious polemic; it was cultural. England was in a sense withdrawing into a proud, defensive insularity. Coincidentally, the authenticity of Geoffrey's account of the Britons' Trojan origin was under attack by sceptical historians, notably Polydore Vergil.[43] The Classical, Celtic, Chivalric historical mythology of the later Middle Ages, promoted by Geoffrey and centring around the figure of King Arthur, was increasingly supplanted by another, derived not from Virgil but from Tacitus.[44] Its conceptual core was not *imperium* but, for the first time, 'freedom', the native possession which 'this warlike, victorious, stiffe, stout and vigorous nation', as Camden called the Saxons,[45] had brought from Germany. 'The Saxons were to replace the Britons, just as King Alfred replaced King Arthur as a model king.'[46]

The appeal of Tacitus' *Germania* to Englishmen as an account of their ancestors was to be a lasting one; its influence is still obvious in the high-Victorian scholarship of Stubbs, Freeman and Green. Indeed, some aspects of Tacitus' picture of German institutions and manners had to wait for nearly two millennia

---

[40] Geoffrey of Monmouth, *History of the Kings of Britain*.
[41] D. C. Douglas, *English Scholars, 1660–1730* (1951), p. 19.
[42] F. W. Maitland, 'The laws of the Anglo-Saxons', *Collected Papers*, ed. H. A. L. Fisher (C.U.P. 1911), 3 vols, iii. 452. Cf. F. J. Levy, *Tudor Historical Thought* (San Marino, Calif. 1967), p. 117.
[43] See T. D. Kendrick, *British Antiquity* (1950).
[44] See Samuel Kliger, *The Goths in England. A Study in Seventeenth and Eighteenth Century Thought* (Cambridge, Mass. 1952).
[45] Quoted Stuart Piggott, *Ruins in a Landscape. Essays in Antiquarianism* (Edinburgh 1976), p. 40.   [46] Levy, *op. cit.*, p. 122.

for full scholarly exploration and political exploitation, most notably the system of annual land redistribution among the members of what came to be called the *mark*-community (*Markengenossenschaft*).[47] Stubbs, on taking up his Oxford chair in 1866, announced his first lecture course as 'Constitutional History from Tacitus to Henry II', and the second chapter of the *Constitutional History* itself is 'Caesar and Tacitus' (Caesar's Commentaries being, of course, the other major contemporary source for the early Germans). As a piece of ethnography, Tacitus' work has much charm, sowing in the mind images from heroic life: the lightly dressed warriors, bound by a touching loyalty to their chief, urged on in battle by their chaste wives; the assemblies, held in the open at new or full moon, clashing weapons as a sign of assent; the investiture of the young warrior with shield and spear; the villages of scattered houses, each surrounded by a clearing; everywhere the surrounding forest. Tacitean society is not one of absolute equality; there are important hereditary distinctions of rank. But the general impression is one of a hard, in some respects savage, but simple, spacious and independent life, and a society essentially transparent and free, bound together by intelligible, strong, yet largely voluntary loyalties.

It was, of course, particularly important that though some tribes had a form of kingship there was nothing like a system of hereditary monarchy. In the nineteenth century Tacitus' descriptions were to provide a programme of historical research; to earlier generations they offered confirmation that the English constitution was, from the beginning, popular rather than monarchical, 'nor can any nation upon Earth shew so much of the ancient Gothique law as this island hath'[48] – an idea that was to be much canvassed of by English and German scholars in the nineteenth century.[49] It is not surprising that the Dutch scholar Dorislaus was deprived of his Cambridge chair in 1627 for a lecture on Tacitus.[50] That English laws were largely German or 'Gothic' in origin became established doctrine. When Algernon Sydney, towards the end of the seventeenth century, claimed that 'the Saxons, coming into our country, retained to themselves the same rights',[51] he was already speaking within a tradition of

[47] See Burrow 'Village community' in McKendrick (ed.), *Historical Perspectives*.
[48] Nathaniel Bacon, *The Laws and Government of England* (1647), quoted Kliger, *op. cit.*, p. 7.
[49] See Charles E. McClelland, *The German Historians and England* (C.U.P. 1971).
[50] Hill, *Puritanism and Revolution*, p. 64.   [51] Quoted Kliger, p. 190.

'Gothic' constitutionalism, though the old notion of immemorial indigenous custom enforced some respect also for the Britons, an eclecticism which can still be seen flickering in Blackstone a century later.[52] Sydney hedged his bets, noting that Caesar describes the Britons as 'devoted to liberty' and observing that 'whether we deduce our original from them, or the Saxons, or from both, our ancestors were perfectly free'.[53]

The Saxons had played their part in ecclesiastical politics and constitutionalist polemic; in the eighteenth century they became garden ornaments. Saxon motifs were an inelegant variation from a standard repertoire of classical legend and mythology: props for a limping muse. Lord Cobham's gardens at Stowe held a 'Gothic Temple' adorned with Saxon gods, described in verse by Gilbert West, including, for example, 'scepter'd Tiw':

> Ancient Monarch of remotest Fame
> Who led from Babel's Tor's the German Name
> And Warlike Woden, fam'd for Martial Deeds
> From whom Great Brunswick's noble line proceeds.[54]

Used in this way, no doubt, the Saxons, though retaining their association with liberty ('A Nation, valiant, wise and free/Who conquered to establish Liberty!')[55] lose virtually all specific historical provenance – levelled by a self-confident age, along with a miscellany of similar medieval and Celtic bric-a-brac, hermits, bards, Druids, into the bland category of the exotic. Yet such examples, of which Samuel Kliger in his *The Goths in England* provides many, dispose of any notion of a necessary and automatic Augustan contempt for savage ancestors.

It is true, however, that where devotion to the ancient constitution is felt to be largely irrelevant, and is decisively subordinated, as by the Walpolean Whigs and among the Scots, to the idea of progress, the Saxons are left exposed as merely barbarians.[56] With no strong constitutionalist vested interest to protect their reputation, their liberty became turbulence, their simplicity ignorance and indolence, their bravery a savage ferocity: traits common to barbarian peoples of every race and time. The doctrine of legal continuity in its vaguest form, certainly, was not abandoned. Gibbon, in a passage on the Saxon invasions whose weary loftiness, not really characteristic of his treatment of barbarians,

---

[52] Sir William Blackstone, *Commentaries on the Laws of England* (15th edn 1809), 4 vols, i. 64.
[53] Kliger, pp. 191–2. [54] *ibid.* p. 280. [55] *ibid.* [56] See, e.g., Skinner, *op. cit.*, p. 155.

seems deliberately to flaunt an enlightened superiority to patriotic prejudice (and thereby testifies to its existence), acknowledges that the Saxons are, for an Englishman, 'the barbarians from whom he derives his name, his laws, and perhaps his origin';[57] there are similar acknowledgements in Hume and Millar, who otherwise provide some of the severest eighteenth-century treatments of the Saxons.[58]

But unquestionably the notion of the English as a Germanic or Gothic people, preserving or enriching their ancestral freedoms through a continuous tradition of practice, was placed in a new light by the Scottish conception of the History of Civil Society, the idea of a general development of civilisation, seen comparatively and sociologically rather than patriotically and legalistically. We have seen in earlier chapters how the Whig tradition accommodated the idea of progress, but it was able to do so only because Parliament, the protagonist of Whig political history, could be seen from early Stuart times, and with some effort even back to the thirteenth century, as the actor around whose fortunes and deeds the plot of English history revolved. The Saxon Witenagemot, with the greatest goodwill – and it was not lacking – was too vague a body, its connection with the later Parliament too tenuous, to be equal to the role. Instead, the two dominant, paradigmatic historical stories of the eighteenth century, the Augustan civic humanist cycle of corruption, and the Scottish 'scientific Whig' version of social development, dealt not with the nation and its cumulative exploitation of its political heritage, but with something more abstract and general. The former, though its protagonist was a polity, which might in the given instance be the English constitution, was not cumulative but cyclic and pessimistic. In the richest form of the story whose crisis is the fall of Rome, the hardy barbarian has his part in history's greatest and most exemplary drama:

> Hence many a people, fierce with freedom, rushed
> From the rude, iron regions of the North.[59]

Essentially this was a somewhat – though not, as we shall see, invariably – secularised version of the role the Saxon plays in the

[57] Gibbon, *Decline*, iv. 386. Cf. i. 349.
[58] Hume, *History of Great Britain* (ed. Forbes), p. 169. Cf. Hume, *The History of England from the Invasion of Julius Caesar to the Revolution* (repr. of 1786 edn, 1875), 3 vols, i. 110. Millar, *Historical View*, i. 6.
[59] James Thompson, *Liberty* (1735–6), quoted Kliger, p. 33.

first work of British history, Gildas' *De excidio Britanniae*,[60] as the agent of divine vengeance on the corrupted Romans. It does not preclude admiration for the barbarian; in some measure it requires it, but he plays the second lead, not the hero: Bolingbroke to the Roman Richard.

Rome, in earlier versions of the cycle of corruption, Machiavelli's for example, or even Montesquieu's, had been essentially a polity, *Senatus Populusque Romanus*. In Gibbon's larger telling, less austerely republican and vitally informed not only by an acceptance of the value of civic virtue but also by an exalted sense of all that the eighteenth century meant by an enlightened and polished society, we are of course still further away from national Whig history. The protagonist or tragic hero is more than a national polity; it is not even just the Empire, or Rome, *urbs aeterna*, but a concept, civilisation, the precariously held treasury of mankind.

As we have seen, Gibbon's work incorporates both civic humanism and Scottish 'scientific Whiggism'. The civic humanist cycle is evident: Goths and Franks, Vandals and Arabs, Arabs and Turks, successively replay the original roles of corrupted Roman and hardy invading Goth. But beyond that there is civilisation, whose fall and restoration gives *The Decline and Fall* the shape of optimism. In this, of course, it is akin to Scottish scientific Whiggism, in which the concept of civilisation is also central. Unlike the civic humanist's story, the Scientific Whig's is cumulative; it is therefore a variety of Whig history in the broad sense. But its historical protagonist is, even less than in the story of Rome, a nation or concrete body of institutions; it is an abstraction, 'Civil Society' whose 'history' is not strictly a story but a sequence, a way of arranging sequentially a set of social types or stages abstracted from a range of similar societies at various times and places; a sequence whose essential principle of arrangement is a notion of improvement. In the story of the progress of mankind from rudeness to refinement, the barbarian loses his role as antitype, agent of nemesis, and even renovator, which the cycle of corruption could assign him; he becomes merely the exemplar of a stage, pastoral and nomadic, whose destiny is to be surpassed, and whose part in the process of improvement, though in fact he represents an advance on mere hunting-and-gathering savagery, is

---

[60] See Robert W. Hanning, *The Vision of History in Early Britain. From Gildas to Geoffrey of Monmouth* (1966).

usually thought of as negative; he irrupts into general history, rather like a counter-revolution in a Marxist historical scheme, as the temporary recrudescence of an earlier stage. The latter is, so to speak, the scientific Whig's version of the civic humanist's nemesis of corruption.

Of course, we have been speaking typically; individual works and authors are never so pure and schematic, and in practice, in an author like Millar, there is much interweaving of ideas, including the Whig constitutionalist ones. Similarly no anthology of harsh eighteenth-century judgements of England's Saxon invaders can simply stand for eighteenth-century attitudes, though they may be fairly representative of Scottish scientific Whiggism in particular. There was too much that was itself classical and neo-classical in an admiration for hardy, simple and virtuous barbarism for contempt to be the only eighteenth-century response to barbarism. The condemnation of luxury and the idea of the cycle of corruption was itself derived from Polybius and the Latin satirists. There was, however, another source, particularly important in the later eighteenth century, which contained the nucleus of a more positive view of Northern Europe's heroic age: the Homeric epic. Paradoxically, the growing interest in the barbarian mythologies and epic literature of Northern Europe in the later eighteenth century seems to have owed something to the Enlightenment's impulse to categorise and compare, and to the concept that different societies might at different times be in the same social and cultural stage. The Homeric epics could be seen, after the publication of James Macpherson's *Ossian* (originally of course assumed to be a genuine ancient Celtic epic), not as unique except for such obvious imitations as the *Aeneid*, but as the foremost representative of a class. But categorisation took, as we know, second place to a quickened emotional response; *Ossian*, like Percy's *Reliques of Ancient Poetry*, tapped apparently dormant sources of feeling, and among the first beneficiaries of this awakening was the Scandinavian and German literature of the early middle ages. Paul-Henri Mallet's work on ancient Scandinavian literature published in England, in a translation by Bishop Percy as *Northern Antiquities* (1770), was a portent and a major influence.[61]

It was not only the direction of interest which was new. Though Augustan anxieties about luxury and admiration for Sparta and

---

[61] See T. P. Peardon, *The Transition in English Historical Writing* (New York 1966), p. 106.

Livy's Romans[62] have recognisable affinities with the primitivist enthusiasms of the later eighteenth century, there was a perceptible difference in the nature of the fears by which each was in part inspired. Earlier it is corruption and enervation; later it becomes enervation, not only of civic virtue and martial spirit, but of feeling, not merely of social feeling, though that might be included – and earlier social critics had of course feared the erosion of patriotism and social ties in a commercial society – but of strong feeling of any kind, and imaginative resource. To consider what sense of malaise in European culture was expressed here would be outside our scope. What is relevant, however, is the reappraisal of the idea of progress which it prompted. One version, for example, of the story of 'progress', a version which, though not necessarily rejecting the concept, surrounds it with inverted commas, was that of an evolution from a poetic to a prosaic age.[63] In the light of a retrospective patriotism, to draw on the imaginative poetic heritage of one's race could seem appropriately inspiring and therapeutic.[64] It was a new way of relating to the past and claiming one's inheritance; earlier ages, proud of indigenous legal and constitutional traditions, had been largely content to draw on classical or Biblical mythology and legend for the vocabulary of the imagination. Since the newly esteemed poetic heritage derived from times when modern nationalities were still unformed, the conceptions of identity it encouraged were necessarily often, albeit vaguely, racial and linguistic rather than national. The race became the collective poet and storyteller as the nation had been the collective lawgiver.

There was naturally a particular appeal in this for peoples whose national self-fulfilment could be seen as in some way undervalued or aborted, notably, of course, the Scots and the Germans. The Scottish cultural self-assertion which, in *Ossian*, helped to inspire the creation of a supposedly archaic Caledonian epic, in turn promoted an historiography which could well be called Ossianic. Not since Geoffrey of Monmouth had Celtic Britain been so idealised or seen in terms so conditioned by classical epic literature. James Macpherson, *Ossian*'s author, himself wrote an *Introduction to the Ancient History of Great*

---

[62] Caroline Robbins, *The Eighteenth Century Commonwealthman* (Cambridge, Mass. 1957).

[63] Macaulay's 'Milton' (*Works*, v) is a good example of the development of this theme.

[64] See Peardon, *Transition*.

Britain and Ireland (1771) in which the Celts were eulogised.[65]
The predictable rejoinder came in John Pinkerton's *Dissertation on the Origin of the Scythians or Goths* (1787): the Celts were by nature an inferior race; the Goths were noble, wise and virtuous; it was deplorable that 'the name of Goths, the sacred name of our forfathers, is an object of detestation'. But Pinkerton was only drawing to a new pitch of racialist excitement a long tradition of exalting the ancient Germans, which had begun to produce an historiography, though its racial speculations were often confused. Gilbert Stuart, for example, in his *Historical Dissertation concerning the Antiquity of the English Constitution* (1768) stressed the peculiar virtues and liberty of the Germans, and took up the claim that the English constitution was now the best representative of the ancient German polity, but he also seems to have thought that the Germans were of Celtic origin. It was left to Bishop Percy to establish that the Germans were not Celts.

The self-congratulatory racialist historiography of the later eighteenth century was fanciful and ephemeral, but the cult of barbaric ancestors produced more permanent results in a heightened scholarly interest in early Celtic and Teutonic literatures, making available a range of sources previously unknown or little used by historians. Moreover the scholarship originally developed in editing and translating literary works could be turned to the study of early law. England's foremost Anglo-Saxon scholars in the first half of the nineteenth century were, quite naturally, involved in both. Benjamin Thorpe, the pupil of the Danish philologist Rask, and J. M. Kemble, the pupil of Jacob Grimm, both worked on *Beowulf* (first published in 1815) as well as editing documents and chronicles.[66]

Before turning, however, to consider briefly the more energetic exploration of these sources in Germany, there is one English work with an inescapable claim to attention, as the first modern full-length history of Saxon England. Since the early eighteenth century, Saxon scholarship had been neglected. Sharon Turner, the author of *The History of the Anglo-Saxons* (1799–1805), wrote that when his first volume appeared 'the subject of the Anglo-Saxon antiquities had been nearly forgotten by the British public'.[67] Turner's work, as he claimed, was the beginning of the

[65] For the references in this paragraph and the next, see *ibid.*, pp. 112–15, 131–41.
[66] *ibid.*, p. 303.
[67] Sharon Turner, *The History of the Anglo-Saxons, Comprising the History of England from the Earliest Period to the Norman Conquest* (4th edn 1823) 3 vols, i. p. 111.

revival. It is interesting, too, because of the moment it occupies in the development of historiography; on the verge of the new archival scholarship of the nineteenth century but not really part of it. It was a genuinely pioneering work, and was much admired, and not without reason. A summary, which is all that can be offered here, is hard on an historian like Turner, especially an account whose chief interest is in doctrines and opinions rather than in facts and the sources for them. Turner's merits are those of a scholar; the constitutional and political views interpolated into his masses of factual information are essentially unoriginal; they have the interest which, in history, attaches to the commonplace. His career is, however, one example of the connection between the Celtic self-consciousness of *Ossian* and the revived interest in ancient epic literature generally, including that of Scandinavia, and the development of Anglo-Saxon studies. A London attorney, friend of Southey and Isaac D'Israeli, he was led to Scandinavian heroic literature by reading Hugh Blair's *Critical Dissertation on the Poems of Ossian* (1763) and discovered there a neglected source for Anglo-Saxon history.[68] Yet though the direction of his 'patriotic curiosity'[69] to the Anglo-Saxons, and to some extent his exploration of sources, clearly owes something to the racialist interests of the later eighteenth century, what the tone of his history reveals, above all, is how readily such curiosity about primitive origins could be accommodated and rendered innocuous by eighteenth-century ideas of progress.

At the level of simple declaratory statement, Turner's position has a good deal in common with that of his contemporary Sir Walter Scott (who used Turner's work for *Ivanhoe*);[70] without the element of imagination, however, it wholly lacks Scott's suggestive ambiguities of feeling and his Jacobite sense of the poignancy of defeat. Turner, though in contemporary terms no less a Tory, is in historiography a Whig of Whigs; for him the proved capacity of the past to beget the present, often somewhat mysteriously or at least providentially, becomes its sole claim to sentimental regard. His tone, complacent, Whiggishly conservative, anticipates Hallam's, though Turner's vocabulary speaks more loudly of the Enlightenment. He is no racialist: Pinkerton 'disfigured his work by an abuse of the Keltic nations'.[71] The Saxons belong, for him, to the wider category of the barbaric or, as he prefers to call it, the

---

[68] Turner, *Anglo-Saxons*, i. p. iv. [69] Turner, *Anglo-Saxons*, i. p. iv.
[70] Scott, *Ivanhoe*, Dedicatory Epistle. [71] Turner, i. 3.

Nomadic peoples.[72] In so far as the Saxons are distinguished from other barbarians of German stock it is primarily as the instruments of a power also evident in Hallam's work, and, for that matter, in Gildas', Divine Providence:

the Saxons were one of the obscure tribes whom Providence was training up to establish more just governments, more improving institutions, and more virtuous, though fierce, manners in the corrupted and incorrigible population of imperial Rome.[73]

But the Lord giveth and taketh away, and the same Providence in due course favoured the designs of William the Norman. The terms in which Turner refuses to repine for the Conquest suggest that Providence has foreseen and approved the foreign policy of the Younger Pitt:

it was ordained by the supreme director of events, that England should no longer remain insulated from the rest of Europe; but should, for its own benefit and the improvement of mankind, become connected with the affairs of the continent.

To ordain was to execute:

The Anglo-Saxon dynasty was therefore terminated; and a sovereign with great continental possessions was led to the English throne. By the consequences of this revolution, England acquired that interest and established that influence in the transactions and fortunes of its neighbours, which have continued to the present day, with equal advantages to its inhabitants and to Europe.[74]

As well as refusing to regret the Conquest, Turner is as concerned as Hallam to guard against radical, egalitarian interpretations of the ancient constitution; Anglo-Saxon society was hierarchical, and the better for it, for inequality is the cause of progress, thanks to which 'our common farmers now fare better than the thegns and knights of the Anglo-Saxon days'.[75] The connotations of Saxon 'freedom' must not be mistaken. To be free was simply not to be a slave. Again, it is true that 'the popular part of our representation seems to have been immemorial', but 'those classes only who now elect members would then have been allowed to elect them', for modern artisans and labourers would then have been slaves.[76] Not surprisingly a parliament so elected seems to have consisted of cautious constitutional pragmatists: 'not bound in the chains of an obsolete antiquity, but . . . always

---

[72] *ibid.*, i. 9. This is not, as one might expect, a reflection of the Scottish notion of stages of society. For him 'The Nomadic were originally but branches of the civilised' – migratory groups. *ibid.*, p. 19.
[73] *ibid.*, i. 116.   [74] *ibid.*, p. 418.   [75] *ibid.*, iii. 78.   [76] *ibid.*, pp. 181–2.

living, feeling, and acting with the population and circumstances of the day'.[77] And

After many years consideration of the question I am inclined to believe that the Anglo-Saxon Witen-agemot very much resembled our present parliament, in the orders and persons that composed it; and that the members, who attended as representatives, were chosen by classes analogous to those who now possess the elctive franchise.[78]

Radicals idealised the ancient constitution and mourned its loss; Turner warned against such idealisation, asserted the benefits of progress and refused to be bound by the chains of an obsolete antiquity; he also managed to identify an ancient constitution almost indistinguishable from an idealised version of the modern one. He had, we have to conclude, a generous or perhaps attorney-like reluctance to see a good argument wasted.

'Die Germanische Rechtsgeschichte'

The half century in England that followed Turner's work came with a hindsight conditioned by new standards of scholarship and industry to seem largely barren. As Maitland put it: 'Then in the nineteenth century came the critical moment. Would Englishmen see and understand what was happening in Germany? Would they appreciate and emulate the work of Savigny and Grimm? . . . It can hardly be said that they rose to the occasion.'[79] From the 1830s onwards there was some — it came to seem scandalously little — editing and translating of Anglo-Saxon materials, most notably by Thorpe and Kemble. There was the important though scrappy work of the Clerk of the House of Commons, Sir Francis Palgrave. There was even some effort, negligently carried out, towards properly arranging and housing the national archives.[80] It was in the 1830s and 1840s, too, that the influence of Germany first began to be felt by intellectual England: through Coleridge and Carlyle, in Marian Evans' translations of Strauss and Feuerbach, in Hare and Thirlwall's translation of Niebuhr's *History of Rome* and — a lesser contribution — Thorpe's translation in 1845

---

[77] *ibid.*, p. 174. [78] *ibid.*, p. 180. [79] *Collected Papers*, iii. 455.

[80] Peardon, *Transition*. See also the useful historical summary in Paul Vinogradoff, *Villeinage in England* (O.U.P. 1892), Introduction, and J. W. Thompson, *A History of Historical Writing* (New York, 1942), 2 vols, ii. LII. For Palgrave see the full and important discussion in P. B. M. Blaas, *Continuity and Anachronism* (The Hague 1978), ch. II.

of Lappenberg's *History of England under the Anglo-Saxon Kings*. By the mid-century, his immunity to any German influence was one of the things which marked Macaulay as a man of the older generation. But the first English work on early English history to be deeply affected by German scholarship was Kemble's *The Saxons in England* (1849). It was a watershed: for the rest of the century, the work of English students of this period was to be interwoven with the contributions of German historians, including some of the greatest names of nineteenth-century German scholarship: Savigny, Grimm, Konrad and G. L. von Maurer, Waitz, Liebermann, Gneist, Pauli, Gierke. To try to trace their influence at every point on Stubbs, Freeman, Maitland and others, would be an immense and probably unrewarding undertaking, while a further account of the German historians themselves has been made unnecessary here by the recent work by Charles E. McClelland.[81]

But apart from particular German contributions to the study of early English history, there is the more general question of a German intellectual influence imparted to the views and attitudes of English historians as, in professional duty, they absorbed the specific results of German historical scholarship. It is possible to exaggerate. Stubbs and Maitland, in particular, were generous with acknowledgements. Petit-Dutaillis said of Stubbs that 'He had formed himself, in his youth, under the patriotic German scholars who saw in the primitive German institutions the source of all human dignity and of all political independence.'[82] But Freeman tended, perhaps not quite fairly, to play down his debts to German scholars,[83] perhaps mentally excluding what he had learnt from such English interpreters as Kemble and Henry Maine. But German intellectual influences on the mid-Victorians were incalculably diffuse as well as, in some cases – and early English historiography was one of them – specific and powerful. For the fact that the intellectual and historiographical world of Stubbs and Freeman was very different from that of Turner or Millar or Hallam, despite the inevitable persistence of some perennial ideas of English history, the influence of ideas developed if not originated in Germany was unmistakably in part responsible. There

---

[81] McClelland, *The German Historians and England*.
[82] Charles Petit-Dutaillis, *Studies and Notes Supplementary to Stubbs' Constitutional History*, trans. W. E. Rhodes (Manchester 1908), p. xiii.
[83] Stephens, *Life*, ii. 380.

were French influences too: Thierry, Sismondi, Tocqueville, Guizot, and later Fustel de Coulanges, and some of these we shall have to consider briefly later, but except for Thierry the French did not, as the Germans did, concern themselves specifically with early English history. The idiom of English historiography was German, not French accented in the second half of the century, as the study of Anglo-Saxon law came, as Maitland put it, to be seen as 'part of a much larger whole: *Die Germanische Rechtsgeschichte*'.[84] Some understanding of the intellectual foundations of the German historiography of institutions is an indispensable part of the story of the historiography of early England in the later nineteenth century.

It was, of course, in Germany that the idea of primitive and poetic ages as sources of imaginative and emotional renewal was pressed furthest in the late eighteenth and early nineteenth centuries, and with it the notion of the race as the anonymous collective author of its language, culture and law. It offered to Germans an obvious emancipation from the French, neo-classical canons of polish and correctness established in the age of Louis XIV. Escape from the formal and rational was also, for young Germans, a declaration of national cultural independence. Folk poetry and epic provided the new paradigms of creative activity, and their study by German scholars and poets was of fundamental and ramifying importance for the scholarship of the nineteenth century. As F. A. Wolf had dissolved Homer into a collective author, Niebuhr sought to uncover the ancient Roman ballad literature which he thought underlay the legendary stories of Livy, and David Friedrich Strauss later referred the New Testament stories to the collective mythopoeic faculty of the people among whom they arose. But the aspect of this assertion of the collective creativity of the race which is relevant here is its application to the history of law. (The study of folklore and folk-poetry and of ancient law could, of course, be combined, as it was in the case of Jacob Grimm.)

The study of German legal antiquities had begun to be undertaken with some urgency before the French Revolution and under pressures similar to those which had been felt by the English common lawyers of the seventeenth century and the French scholars who had defended the value of customary law against the sharp systematic definitions of revived Roman law in the

---

[84] *Collected Papers*, iii. 457.

sixteenth.[85] Then the defence of customary law had implied the existence of an anonymous collective lawmaking authority, whose habitual practice secreted its shell of custom. But from that point onwards the intellectual character of resistance to the advance of central authority had diverged. In France, in the eighteenth century, it had taken an essentially neo-feudal form, a defence of local independence and constitutionality pivoted on the position of the great nobles;[86] in England, in the Country Party doctrines of the early eighteenth century even an essentially provincial resentment of the capital and of government had still expressed itself in essentially parliamentary terms; in a society of growing commercial prosperity it was a form of resentment which found an apt formula in moralistic, neo-classical, Machiavellian notions of civic virtue and corruption: the power of money disturbed the balance of the constitution, and, by destroying the virtue of the legislators, subverted the representative element.[87]

No such diagnosis, clearly, in terms of the proper functioning of a central, historic, national institution like Parliament was available to the Germans. The classical cycle of corruption and regeneration had nothing to offer them; Germany after the Thirty Years' War was not a prosperous commercial society, and there was no single German institution, no *res publica*, upon which such a diagnosis could fasten. Yet in Germany in the eighteenth century historic local institutions of various kinds possessed a vitality which the old imperial symbols of centrality did not. When the pressures of the newer kinds of centralising tendency were felt in the form of a rationalising bureaucracy and the 'enlightened absolutism' of the rulers, the Germans reproduced and developed the traditionalist defences of customary law, elaborating, in doing so, the notion of anonymous collective creativity which was proving so fruitful in other directions.[88] With the aid of this conception, German scholars developed a new intensity and historical sophistication in the study of their legal antiquities.[89]

---

[85] Pocock, *The Ancient Constitution and the Feudal Law.*

[86] F. L. Ford, *Robe and Sword: The Regrouping of the French Aristocracy* (Cambridge, Mass. 1953).

[87] Kramnick, *Bolingbroke*; Pocock, *Machiavellian Moment.*

[88] See Geraint Parry, 'Enlightened government and its critics in eighteenth century Germany', *Historical Journal*, vi (1963). I have learnt much from this valuable article.

[89] For German historiography in this period, see Herbert Butterfield, *Man on His Past* (C.U.P. 1955); G. P. Gooch, *History and Historians of the Nineteenth Century* (2nd edn 1952); Thompson, *A History of Historical Writing*, ii, chs xxxix, xl; Lord Acton, 'German schools of history', *Historical Essays and Studies* (1907) and in *English Historical Review*, i (1886).

Intellectual resistance to legal rationalisation begun under the Ancien Régime could be deployed against the similarly centralising and despotic policies of the new French Republic, or proposals for a German legal code analogous to the Code Napoleon. Germany, like England to a lesser extent, evolved in reaction to the French Revolution a patriotic mode at once populist and traditionalist, very different from the neo-classical model worn during the revolutionary years in Paris.[90]

Schematically, we can distinguish three closely related strands of argument in this: a defence of local autonomy and initiative – Justus Möser, one of the leading spokesmen of German traditionalism in the later eighteenth century and a pioneer in the history of ancient German legal institutions, employed the expressive term *Lokalvernunft* (local reason as opposed to reason of state);[91] secondly, an assertion of the value of practical reason and experience as against abstract systems;[92] thirdly, which in a sense comprehends the other two, the claim, associated above all with Savigny, that a people's historic legal institutions are, like its language, the expression of its unique identity.[93] The affinities with contemporary English arguments are obvious enough, and made Burke popular in Germany, but again it was important that for the German there was no single focus of veneration such as Parliament provided; his range of reverent historical curiosity had to be wider and to reach further back. The investigation of archaic German law became a patriotic duty, and England, as the country in which Germanic law had evolved free from the influence of Roman imperial ideas and Roman law which had become so powerful in Germany, acquired a peculiar interest.[94] The German scholar sought his national identity in legal origins, in the manifestations of the folk-spirit, rather as devout English naturalists attempted to read the mind of God in the design of nature. The combination of minute descriptive particularity and mystical import is one of the forms taken by Romanticism in its later stages: the work of German historians – Ranke, for example –

---

[90] See J. Droz, *L'Allemagne et la Revolution Francaise* (Paris 1949); G. P. Gooch, *Germany and the French Revolution* (1927); R. Aris, *History of Political Thought in Germany, 1789–1815* (1936); H. S. Reiss (ed.) *Political Thought of the German Romantics* (Oxford 1955). For the history of legal thought see Peter Stein, *Legal Evolution. The Story of an Idea* (C.U.P. 1980), esp ch. 3.

[91] Parry, 'Enlightened government', p. 189.   [92] *ibid*.

[93] Reiss, *German Romantics*, pp. 38–40 and ch. VI; Stein, *Legal Evolution*, ch. 3.

[94] McClelland, *The German Historians*.

provides instances. It is a trait we have learnt to think of as characteristically Victorian, Ruskinian and Pre-Raphaelite; painting, with a scrupulous literalness, the feathers of angelic plumage. The comparison with Stubbs' *Constitutional History of England* is not so strained as it may appear.

It was in the third quarter of the century that English scholarship felt the impact of the German legal historians. Partly it was a matter of encouragement and example; as Stubbs put it, 'the devotion with which, since the days of Grimm, the local and municipal institutions of Germany have been studied sets us a fine example'.[95] Partly it was direct contributions of German scholars to English history.[96] But above all it was the sense of a common enterprise and the belief in a common set of institutions; it was *Die Germanische Rechtsgeschichte*. Following a work like Jacob Grimm's *Deutsche Rechts Altertümer*, it seemed possible to reconstruct what Stubbs called 'the primeval polity of the common fatherland'[97] in some detail, giving historical precision to traditional references to the freedom brought from the German woods and supplying a scholarly gloss to the cryptic descriptions of Tacitus. In particular

the laborious investigations of recent scholars have successfully reconstituted the scheme of land tenure as it existed among the Germanic races, by careful generalisations from charters, records of usages, and the analogies of Scandinavian law and practice, which, at a later date reproduces, with very little that is adventitious, the early conditions of self-organising society.[98]

This was the theory of the *mark*-community as the foundation of all Germanic society, which Kemble learnt from Grimm, and made the Saxons bring with them to England.[99] In its political aspect, as the free village-community, rather than as a system of communal agriculture,[100] Freeman and Green treated it as the basis of the old English polity.

Despite some earlier antiquarian work on Saxon institutions, it was nothing less than the possibility of a new kind of history that

[95] SL, p. 72.   [96] McClelland, *op. cit.*   [97] CH, i. 11.   [98] *ibid.*, i. 48.
[99] John Mitchell Kemble, *The Saxons in England. A History of the English Commonwealth till the Period of the Norman Conquest* (1849), 2 vols, i. ch 11. For Kemble and Grimm, see Raymond A. Wiley (ed.) *John Mitchell Kemble and Jacob Grimm. A Correspondence, 1832–52* (Leiden 1971), esp. p. 225, and Bruce Dickins, 'John Mitchell Kemble and Old English Scholarship', in *Two Kembles, John and Henry* (priv. pub. Cambridge 1974). For the earlier history of the idea of the *mark*-community, see particularly Alfons Dopsch, *The Economic and Social Foundations of European History* (New York 1969), ch. i, and Vinogradoff, *Villeinage in England*, Introduction.
[100] Burrow, 'Village community' in McKendrick, pp. 269–70.

seemed to be revealed. The dubious narrations of the Saxon conquest, derived from the ancient British historians Gildas and Nennius and from Bede,[101] the incomprehensible dynastic and diplomatic affairs of the Heptarchy, the arid recitals of battles which Milton had compared to those of kites and crows, the Saxon annals which Hume had pronounced obscure and tedious[102] and the story of the Saxon conquest which Gibbon had called 'familiar to the most illiterate and obscure to the most learned',[103] were to be replaced by another story, by definition uneventful. The history, or perhaps the embryology, of the constitution was to be the putative story of a continuous process of cellular multiplication, amalgamation and expansion, whose code was contained in its nuclear primal cell, 'the original basis on which all Teutonic society rests',[104] the *mark*-community, *vicus* or self-regulating township. 'It is with a reverence such as is stirred by the sight of the head-waters of some mighty river,' John Richard Green wrote in his *Short History of the English People*,

that one looks back to these tiny moots, where the men of the village met to order the village life and the village industry, as their descendants, the men of a later England, meet in Parliament at Westminster, to frame laws and do justice for the great empire which has sprung from this little body of farmer-commonwealths in Sleswick.[105]

It is a more striking piece of piety than anything in Hallam or Macaulay, this extension of Whig reverence to the primitive social arrangements of North German farmers. The assimilation, here accomplished metaphorically, of this democratic and populist account of constitutional origins to Whiggish notions of continuity was to be the central synthetic task of the new constitutional history.

[101] Hanning, *The Vision of History in Early Britain.*
[102] Hume, *History of England,* i. 1.
[103] Gibbon, *Decline,* iv. 386.
[104] Kemble, *Saxons,* i. 53.
[105] Green, *Short History,* p. 4.

CHAPTER 6

Autonomy and self-realisation: Stubbs' Constitutional History

The new constitutional history was, as we have seen in the previous chapter, at once populist and Whig: populist in the assumed primitive democracy of the folk-moot, Whig and Burkean in its insistence on continuity, on the creation of the constitution without design or even, until later, any formal legislation, by a long, spontaneous, almost imperceptible process of consolidation and registration of custom.

Of course, in one sense there was always an underlying populism in historic Whiggism: the constitution was popular at least in the sense that it did not derive from the royal prerogative. But in the elaborations of the Whig tradition, with their emphasis on Parliament and on the later periods of history, it had become, as we have seen in Macaulay, to some extent heroic, even in a broad sense aristocratic. Even a poetic meditation devoted to the theme of obscurity had to borrow the names and roles of the heroic tradition to dignify and identify its humble subjects, creating village Hampdens and innocently rustic Cromwells. If the first national act was Magna Carta, it was most obviously seen as an act of the feudal tenants-in-chief. The House of Commons was not, unfortunately, immemorial; it owed its origin, if not, except formally speaking, to the crown, then to Earl Simon de Montfort. The gentry in the House of Commons had preserved the constitution by their opposition to Charles I; a handful of Whig peers had saved it again by issuing the invitation to William of Orange. All this might have been done in the name of the nation and with its goodwill and support; it was harder to claim that, except very intermittently, it had been done literally by it.

The problem might seem to be overcome by going back in time; the Saxon conquest and settlement was plausibly a national act. But there was another difficulty. It was not just that there was a perennial problem of continuity created by the Norman Conquest and the tenuousness of any suggested links between the Saxon Witenagemot and the thirteenth-century Parliament. The study of the Saxon records, meagre though it had been, had been enough to show eighteenth-century historians that Saxon society in later centuries had become more aristocratic and, incipiently, feudal even before the Conquest.[1] And subsequently England had surely been a feudal society, differing from others of the type chiefly in the greater power of its kings. To this the Whig Parliamentarians' hopeful reservations, the possible continuity of the Witenagemot with the Norman Great Council, the reaffirmations by the Norman kings of the laws of Edward the Confessor (a point made by Coke in the seventeenth century and reiterated by Blackstone),[2] were little offset. The radical believer in a 'Norman Yoke', however idealised his view of the 'free' Saxon constitution, seemed at least on firmer ground in his belief that the latter had been lost, and needed not preservation but restoration.

The new generation of 'Whig' historians of early England made no attempt to deny the development of Saxon society towards feudalism and a more aristocratic and exclusive polity. Kemble and Green were sufficiently close to being radical ancient constitutionalists in sentiment to regret it. Kemble lamented to his old master Grimm that his own work on English legal antiquities was less attractive than Grimm's on German ones: 'everywhere kingly power in place of free institutions'.[3] A generation later we find Green writing to Freeman of his book *The Conquest of England* (1883):

> The truth is the subject tempts me less and less the more I work at it. The more I study the two centuries before Ecgberht, the more I can see the old free constitution crushed out by the political consolidation, the old Folk-moot dying with the folk themselves into local shire and shire-moot; and by the extinction of the old Ætheling class and the upgrowth of the big kingdoms into a small royal council. After Ecgberht this only grew worse; and closer study of the law and administrative acts convinces me that the conquest was continuous from Hengest to William.[4]

The sense of dismay or urgency prompted by this recognition varied from author to author. Freeman, for example, though one

---

[1] E.g. Hume: 'the Anglo-Saxon government, in the period preceding the Norman Conquest, was become extremely aristocratical', *History of England*, i. 113. Millar, *Historical View*, i. 3, 376; Turner, *Anglo-Saxons*, iii, bk VII, ch. IX.
[2] E.g. Blackstone, *Commentaries*, ii. 52 and bk IV ch. 33.
[3] *John Mitchell Kemble and Jacob Grimm. A Correspondence*, p. 264.
[4] Leslie Stephen (ed.), *Letters of John Richard Green* (1902), p. 481.

of the most vehement proponents of an original Teutonic democracy, relied chiefly for his confidence in 'The Continuity of
English History' (the title of one of his essays) on eloquent
reassertion, drawing, with never exhausted resources of rhetorical
solemnity, on the familiar reservations: the continuity of Witenagemot and Great Council and the Norman reaffirmations of the
laws of King Edward.[5] He happily accepted the recruitment of the
Norman barons to the cause of English liberty – the Normans
were 'a band of worthy proselytes'[6] – and though he made less of
Magna Carta than some Whigs had done, Simon de Montfort was
one of his great heroes.

Freeman was helped too in making the case for continuity by the
fact that for him the most deeply felt oppression was always
national or racial. The Normans, by virtue of their Norse descent,
were Teutons, and within a century of the Conquest had been
assimilated. 'The English', no longer a subject people, had surmounted their greatest crisis.[7] There was, it has to be admitted, a
certain sleight of hand, or at least a complacency of tone not
always warranted by the admitted facts, in Freeman's combined
belief in an abiding spirit of liberty and in an essential continuity.
He took a Burkean pleasure, that is, in pointing out that no design
or specific body of legislation had transformed the English society
of the early settlement into the feudal society of the twelfth
century. The pleasure seemed little mitigated by the direction
taken by the change: 'An assembly in which at first every freeman
had a right to appear has, by force of circumstances, step by step,
without any one moment of sudden change, shrunk up into an
Assembly wholly hereditary and official.'[8] Elsewhere, he faced the
Burkean–libertarian paradox directly, claiming it as a positive
virtue in the despotism of Imperial Rome that it encroached by a
kind of Whiggish stealth. The Augustans' dread, the corruption of
a free government, had few terrors for him compared with
revolution. The Polybian cycle is confronted with an unshaken
Burkean cheerfulness:

as in this way the Roman state changed, as we may roughly say, from monarchy
to aristocracy, from aristocracy to democracy, without any sudden or violent

[5] 'The continuity of English history', *Historical Essays*, 1st series (1871; 5th edn 1896).
   Cf. *The Growth of the English Constitution from the Earliest Times*, ch. II.
[6] *Hist. Ess.*, 1st series, p. 52.
[7] E.g. 'in a few generations we led captive our conquerors; England was England once
   again', etc. *NC*, i. 2. Cf. *Growth of the Constitution*, p. 73.
[8] *Growth of the Constitution*, pp. 64–5.

sweeping away of things old or setting up of things new, so the like happened when the commonwealth changed back again from democracy to monarchy. The Roman empire owed its wonderful permanence to the fact that it was not brought in by a revolution.[9]

Burkeanism becomes, in fact, almost a Machiavellian maxim (the Machiavellianism of *The Prince*, not *The Discourses*) of political science, available to the just and unjust alike:

a republic can supplant a monarchy; a monarchy can supplant a republic; and both can do the work all the more thoroughly and all the more lastingly by keeping as much as possible, by destroying as little as possible, of the institutions which it supplants.[10]

It was a rare lapse from Freeman's usually unremitting political moralism, produced in this case by following the argument, almost certainly inadvertently, whithersoever it led. We cannot pause here to consider in more detail how Freeman rescued his libertarianism from his Burkeanism, in face of the known character of English history from the Heptarchy to Magna Carta: arguably continuous, if one was prepared to explain away its most striking discontinuities, but not even in the most unqualified Whig account a story of the growth of liberty. That must be left to a later chapter; Freeman's account came in any case, to rely on Stubbs,[11] to whom we now have to turn. It is not really fair to compare the two as constitutional historians. Freeman acknowledged Stubbs as his master here, and his own *Growth of the Constitution* is a slight work, written as lectures, and not to be compared with Stubbs' *Constitutional History*, a deeply meditated, immensely detailed and yet in its way epic work of history.

The fact that Stubbs' great work so long dominated its field of learning may in some measure have prevented its being sufficiently appreciated as a book: one of the great books, in fact, of the nineteenth century. The closest parallel, not, of course, in the extent of its influence but in the impression it makes on the reader, is with *The Origin of Species*. Few readers can have begun reading Stubbs' *Constitutional History* as Maitland did, picking it up casually in a club and reading on 'because it was interesting'.[12] Few of its readers, in fact, in the days of its greatest authority – and these must have been the majority of all its readers – can have read it as a book at all, but rather, piecemeal, as a source for a

---

[9] 'The growth of Commonwealths', *Historical Essays*, 4th series (1892), p. 363.
[10] *ibid.*, p. 364.   [11] See below, p. 193.
[12] Maitland, 'Stubbs', *Collected Papers*, iii. 503.

specific assignment, some overdue essay on frankpledge or the Provisions of Oxford, and under duress. It would be quite beside the purpose of the present work to give a list of Stubbs' assertions which have been subsequently rejected or modified by the general consensus of medievalists. But though Stubbs' work is first and last a work of scholarship, it can now be seen independently of its immediate value as an authority. It can still be read as an intellectual experience – and the quality of that experience is an integral part of the story we have to tell, not merely an embellishment of it – because of its combination of weight and judiciousness with a filigree-like intricacy of detail, and because of the exhilarating way in which the whole mass is propelled and given life by a guiding conception, even, as we shall see, a single expanded metaphor. And though it has come to be regarded as a premature and overenthusiastic synthesis,[13] it never strikes the reader as merely the imposition of an opinion.

Moreover Stubbs' book does not, at least in English terms, stand at the end of a tradition of historical writing whose virtues it incorporates; it creates one, virtually single-handed, apart from help from the Germans. English lawyers had written disquisitions on ancient institutions and points of legal history. Palgrave and Kemble ('my pattern scholar' Stubbs called the latter)[14] had written histories of the early constitution which were essentially a succession of loosely connected antiquarian monographs;[15] this is truer of Palgrave than Kemble, but Freeman spoke of the latter, not altogether unjustly, as more an antiquary than an historian.[16] Stubbs' work, while improving, with German help, on their scholarship, giving it scope and subtlety and coherence, was emphatically a book, a work of history in the fullest sense. It

---

[13] In the subsequent development of medieval scholarship a good many of Stubbs' conclusions have naturally been revised or found untenable, especially in the first volume of the *Constitutional History*, on which attention is chiefly concentrated in the present chapter. See Petit-Dutaillis, *Studies*, and for a later and more critical view, Helen Cam, 'Stubbs seventy years after', *Cambridge Historical Journal*, ix, no. 2 (1948). Kemble's theory of the *mark*, which Stubbs took over with reservations and diluted in successive revisions, has been discredited, and Stubbs' own conception of the English people as a political protagonist in the twelfth and thirteenth centuries came to seem a liberal anachronism. But we are concerned here not with the subsequent history of scholarship, but with Stubbs' book as it might have been read by a mid-Victorian – or by Maitland in his club.   [14] *Letters*, p. 76.

[15] Sir Francis Palgrave, *The History of Normandy and England* (1851). Also *The Rise and Progress of the English Commonwealth* (1837). See Freeman's review of the former, *Edinburgh Review*, CCXLVII (1865), attrib. Freeman (*Wellesley Index of Victorian Periodicals* (Toronto 1966), p. 514.   [16] Stephens, *Life*, i. 115.

remains, in fact, the most perfectly achieved expression of a cast of mind which, in an available shorthand, we may call Burkean. Maitland's was a comparable mind, sharper, finer, more theoretical and impressionable,[17] but in Maitland's case, though the *oeuvre* may be as impressive, there is no single work which is so obviously the summation of his talents and learning. Although, as we shall see, its conceptual centre, as well as much detail, seems to owe something to German ideas, Stubbs' history is the most fully realised embodiment of English, Burkean political ideas. There is always an incongruity in expressing these ideas in abstract or declaratory terms; to be true to themselves they need to be exhibited, to use a metaphor of Stubbs', in solution: embodied, and absorbed instance by instance. It is in historiography rather than in theoretical statement that we find the fullest expressions of Burkean political ideas in nineteenth-century England. This creates problems of exposition. As with a great novel, a summary of the plot conveys little of Stubbs' history; it is only in detail that it can be measured or even properly understood, and, unlike a novel, the detail is ineluctably and intractably technical. An attempt to trace the book's contours for others is inevitably both more laborious and more superficial than one would wish; the outlines may be clear but the texture is lost.

Stubbs would not have wished it otherwise. Historians can be divided (among other tempting categorisations) in architectural terms into functionalists and classicists – there is of course a closely related distinction between positivists and humanists: into those who like the girders showing and those who do not; those proud of honest sweat and those who prefer *soigné* results (as usual when presenting antitheses the mean begins to look desirable). Stubbs may be described as a moderate functionalist with a firm sense of classical decencies. What he claimed to want above all from the study of history was not so much conclusions as 'that experience of critical difficulties and moral incompatibilities' which Thomas Arnold had found in it.[18] Horror of the facile ran deep in Stubbs' nature; it was a hard fate that made him so long an instructor of youth. He had, as we saw in the opening words of the previous chapter, something like Matthew Arnold's distaste for that opinionatedness which Tocqueville had marked down, for his own and the ensuing generation, as a characteristic democratic

---

[17] See his comment on Stubbs' relatively poor grasp of abstractions, 'William Stubbs', *Collected Papers*, iii. 509.   [18] *SL*, p. 8.

trait, and one therefore likely to increase.[19] Stubbs was in some
ways a prejudiced man as well as a man of firm faith but he was
not an opinionated man. He drew a sharp line between what he
knew well enough to pronounce on (and his standards were
predictably exacting) and what he did not; it makes his letters
rather uninteresting. It distressed him when others did not observe
the same reticence: when opinions were proffered with a tail-
wagging pride of mere possession.[20]

To him, at the heart of historical study, as its central difficulty
and its essential value as education, was judgement.[21] It was not
quite the historian's judgement in Lord Acton's sense; he has
harsh, Actonian-sounding words about condoning wrong[22] but
the cases which came before Stubbs were civil rather than
criminal; there is no sign that, like Acton or even Macaulay, he
dearly loved a posthumous hanging. Judgement for him meant
judicious appraisal, a fine sense of the complexity of things, and
even a proper respect for the mysteriousness of the workings of the
superintending Divine Providence in which he so firmly believed.[23]
Philosophers of history seemed to him to wish to circumscribe by
supposed laws the historical discretion of the Almighty.[24] Generalisation is an aspect of our imperfection. We cannot study history
without it, but God, being omniscient – it is plainly suggested – is
a nominalist.[25] Belief in divine Providence has not, of course,
traditionally been strongly associated with habits of cautious
historical judgement: Stubbs was perhaps more unusual among his
contemporaries in his practice than in his belief, though Green,
who was present, countered with an almost audible drawing-in of
breath the religious aspiration in the conclusion of Stubbs' Inaugural lecture, with its depiction of world history leading up to God: 'I
remember when this was my clue to history once – I am afraid I
have lost it without gaining another. But conceive the thoughts of
Young Liberalism!'[26]

History, then was the antidote to a newspaper-bred
opinionatedness; Stubbs took a disparaging view of newspapers,[27]

---

19 Alexis de Tocqueville, *Democracy in America* (tr. Bowen, 1892), pt. II, bk I, chs I–III,
    XIII. Cf. Matthew Arnold, e.g. 'The literary influence of academies', *Essays Literary and
    Critical* (Everyman edn), p. 42, and *Culture and Anarchy*, passim.
20 E.g. *SL*, pp. 20, 53, 275.   21 *SL*, pp. 8, 19–21, 83–4, 100, 103, 109, 426.
22 *ibid.*, p. 20.
23 E.g. 'the guidance of a Higher Hand . . .' *CH*, ii. 261.
24 Stubbs, *Lectures on Early English History* (1906) (hereafter cited as *EEH*), pp. 94–5.
25 *ibid.*, 95.   26 Stephen (ed.) *Letters of John Richard Green*, p. 176.
27 *SL*. pp. 26, 103, 121–2, 275, 426.

in marked contrast to Macaulay. Certainly it is hard to imagine anyone waxing opinionated on the basis of Stubbs' *Constitutional History*. Maitland meant high praise when he said that one could read it without being able to guess how its author would vote in an election;[28] still, there are clearly some things he is not; it would be hard to envisage him as some old Benthamite radical. What would exclude this is not only the absence of radicalism but the specific balance of particularity and generalisation. Stubbs shared the interest of his generation in inductive comparison and its possibilities, as the first chapter of the *Constitutional History* testifies, but he maintained, if not exactly a divine nominalism, at least an abhorrence of the oversystematic and the purely theoretical.[29] On philosophers his views were, as he darkly told his Inaugural audience, 'short and concise'; he did not particularise.[30] It was an aspect of his suspicion of ancient history as a study that it was a kind of theoretician's playground.[31] Most of all, however, he suspected lawyers; he and Freeman carried on a protracted campaign against them.[32] Relations between law and history were, of course, at the time peculiarly close, and Bryce commented favourably on Stubbs' own taste for and handling of legal issues;[33] Stubbs recognised the taste himself.[34] It was only after 1871 that Modern History at Oxford had ceased to be a partner in the joint School of Law and History; the repudiation of lawyer-like habits of mind was a kind of declaration of intellectual independence.

Stubbs' and Freeman's disparagement of lawyers had two targets, closely related: their historic role and their allegedly characteristic and, in the study of history, incapacitating inclination to system and definition. As Stubbs put it, 'The essence of the historical study is in the working out the continuity of the subject, while the essence of the legal study is in the reducing of it all to certain theoretic principles.'[35] Theoretic principles, once applied, prove to exhibit, moreover, their usual affinity with despotism. It seems to have been something like a tradition among English lawyers themselves to speak of 'the chicanes and subtleties of Norman jurisprudence' – the phrase is Blackstone's[36] – as the accomplice of tyranny. Lawyers were Freeman's almost invariable

---

[28] *Collected Papers*, iii. 508.   [29] E.g. *SL*, pp. 103, 275, 335.
[30] *ibid.*, p. 15.   [31] *ibid.* pp. 16, 19.
[32] Hutton (ed.), *Letters of Stubbs*, pp. 67, 188, 208–10, 215, 305. Cf. *EEH*, pp. 37–8, 260. For Freeman, see Stephens, *Life*, ii, 262, 270.
[33] Quoted Hutton, *op. cit.*, p. 146.   [34] *SL*, p. 275.
[35] *EEH*, p. 37.   [36] Blackstone, *Commentaries*, ii. 416.

scapegoat whenever English constitutional history particularly conspicuously failed to exhibit the continuity of liberty which for Freeman constituted its essence;[37] it was a habitual device which drew from Dicey the irritated and reasonable protest that if a country's lawyers at a particular time systematically interpreted its constitution in a certain way there are good grounds for holding that that is what the constitution actually was.[38] Freeman's 'England' is undoubtedly at times in danger of becoming a metaphysical entity as divorced from its terrestrial attributes as General de Gaulle's 'France'.

Stubbs' way with the Norman lawyers in particular was more condescending; he seems to have regarded them rather as incompetent colleagues who failed to understand the facts they found in Domesday.[39] But their incomprehension was ominous, though ultimately beneficial to England, as well as a nuisance to the modern historian; they might have sterilised English constitutional development by fixing it as a closed homogeneous system; it was only by inadvertence and ignorance that they failed.[40] Stubbs' view of the Norman feudal lawyers was complemented by his even stronger dislike of more formidable foes, the civilians, who had in a sense succeeded, on the continent,[41] while the former had failed in England and proved no more than a passing nuisance. Dislike of Roman law had a further dimension in Stubbs as an aspect of his detestation of the Roman empire,[42] a feeling Freeman in no way shared. Civil law aroused in him a kind of respectful horror. 'Bryce's Inaugural was beautifully written and clever,' he wrote to Green,

but I, and I suppose you, am not disposed to forget that the Civil Law, with all its exquisite perfection, has been one of the greatest obstacles to national development in Europe, and a most pliant tool of oppression. I suppose that no nation using the Civil Law has ever made its way to freedom; whilst wherever it has been introduced the extinction of popular liberty has followed sooner or later. As an engine of legal Education it has its merits; but I prefer in Historical training something more human and inconsistent.[43]

The hard, sharp categories of Roman law readily become a prescriptive social discipline, confining and sterilising the irregular

---

[37] E.g. Growth of the Constitution, pp. 26–9, 145–7.
[38] A. V. Dicey, Introduction to the Study of the Law of the Constitution (7th edn 1908), ch. 1. Cf. Law and Public Opinion in England during the Nineteenth Century (2nd edn 1914), p. 459 n. 1.
[39] CH, i. 166.   [40] ibid., p. 168.   [41] Hutton, Letters, pp. 67, 208–10, 305.
[42] EEH, p. 334, also p. 237.   [43] Hutton, p. 159.

but vital movements of a society capable of spontaneous development and destroying the flexibility conferred by anomalies. The
chief cautionary example was medieval Germany, where, in the
absence of an effective central legislature, the result was

to leave the law to the mercy of the lawyers . . . .. The lawyers became a privileged
caste, and as the tendency of the lawyers always was to adopt the hard and sharp,
the lucid and definite, principles of the Roman laws, the Roman laws gained a
general, though not universal, acceptance, to the exclusion of the ancient but
varying and obsolete traditions.[44]

History was a discipline in a different sense, a schooling in alert
and respectful attentiveness to the vibrations of social change, felt
in the language of charters, fiscal and court records, original
documents of all kinds. Stubbs was an editor as well as an
historian, and editorial practice can be seen behind the constant
probing and questioning in the *Constitutional History*: what do
the words mean? how would they have been understood? to what
kind of practices do they refer? would they always have borne
such a meaning? A good example of Stubbs' analytic method is the
use he makes of the classic text: Tacitus. The Roman historian
describes not a system but a society in transition: 'Among the first
truths which the historical student, or indeed any scientific
scholar, learns to recognise, this is perhaps the most important,
that no theory or principle works in isolation.'[45] So in the
Germanic society described by Tacitus

We have not the mark system, but we have the principle of common tenure and
cultivation, on which, in India, the native village communities still maintain a
primitive practice much older probably than the Germania, and of which very
distinct vestiges still exist in our own country, in Switzerland and in Germany.
We have not the village system in its integrity, but we have the villages
themselves, their relation to the *pagi*, and through them to the *civitas*, and the fact
that they were centres for the administration of justice. We have not the manor,
but we have the nobleman, we have the warlike magistrate with his attendant
comites, whose services he must find some way of rewarding, and whose energies
he must even in peace find some way of employing.

But though there is no single principle

we have the germs and traces of all. The military *princeps* has but to conquer and
colonise a new territory, and reward his followers on a plan that will keep them
faithful as well as free, and feudalism springs into existence. The members of the
village society have but to commute their fluctuating shares in the annual
redistribution of land for a fixed allotment with definite duties incumbent upon
them as independent owners, and we have the allodial system of village life.[46]

[44] *EEH*, pp. 260, 251.   [45] *CH*, i. 32.   [46] *ibid.*, i. 34–5.

A society at any moment is an unstable compound. The constant presence of anomalies is intellectually chastening for the historian but it is also the mark of life. The technicalities and peculiarities which grow with the increasing complexity of English society and government carry their own lessons. In England

It is far from easy to determine the mutual relations of the courts of the hundred and the shire, and those of manor and honour, or the co-ordinate departments of the bench, the pleas, and the exchequer, or the rival merits of the chancery, the house of lords, and the judicial committee of the privy council. But that very complexity is a sign of growth; simplicity of detail signifies historically the extinction of earlier framework. That which springs up, as our whole system has done, on the principle of adapting present means to present ends, may be complex and inconvenient and empiric, but it is natural, spontaneous, and a crucial test of substantial freedom.[47]

In the gradual development of that complexity the elements of social organisation expand and contract, shift and bend with the pressures they mutually exert. Traces of the past remain as archaic survivals, sometimes, under altered circumstances, pregnant with new life. A society in spontaneous movement – its 'natural' state – ripples with a motion which concepts, including those in use in the society itself, imperfectly grasp, though there can be no doubting the strenuousness of Stubbs' attempts to label and understand. In Anglo-Saxon England

There are no constitutional revolutions, no violent reversals of legislation; custom is far more potent than law, and custom is modified infinitesimally every day. An alteration of law is often the mere registration of a custom, when men have recognized its altered character. The names of offices and assemblies are permanent, while their character has imperceptibly undergone essential change.[48]

In fact there are different names, different legal terminologies for the same things, while things that were once distinct become virtually identical. As the power of the crown grows, a nobility of blood becomes a nobility of service, indistinguishable except by name from the older service nobility of thegns and gesiths; with the growth of hereditary fiefs, the reverse progress is also seen.[49] The older court officials, the chamberlain, constable, steward, pass through several incarnations under the same names: as superior menials – as their names imply, as high officers of state, and eventually as the empty hereditary titles of great feudatories. These are only the most obvious examples. And throughout the society the asymmetries of hereditary status, tenurial rights and

[47] EEH, p. 326.   [48] CH, i. 166.   [49] ibid., i. 166ff.

obligations, and wealth, with numerous barely perceptible and changing gradations in each, draw intersecting and shifting lines of stratification, precluding any simple representation of the social order.[50] And there was individual mobility; early medieval English society was not a system of caste.[51]

No general account or anthology of quotations can at all convey the cautious yet precise richness of Stubbs' analyses or the fine, educated sensitivity to the tremors of social and institutional change, in names and procedural forms, in administrative, fiscal and judicial devices, in franchises, suits, fines, exactions, the growth and waning of privileges, the assumption and desuetude of functions. It is because Stubbs' own poise and control hardly falter, despite revisions;[52] because each detail is illustrative and placed, and the steady authorial voice moves with unforced assurance from confident assertion to admitted conjecture, from bold suggestiveness to tentative generalisation and occasional admissions of defeat, that this mass of discriminated complexity is felt as exhilarating rather than overwhelming.

Stubbs offers his readers not a system or a sequence of them, but a constant process of piecemeal transition. This does not mean, however, that Anglo-Saxon history has not a central story:

> The general tendency of the process may be described as a movement from the personal to the territorial organization; from a state of things in which personal freedom and political right were the leading ideas, to one in which personal freedom and political right had become so much bound up with the relations created by the possession of land, as to be actually subservient to it.

Finally

> the land becomes the sacramental tie of all public relations; the poor man depends on the rich, not as his chosen patron, but as the owner of the land that he cultivates, the lord of the court to which he does suit and service, the leader whom he is bound to follow to the host: the administration of law depends on the peace of the land rather than that of the people; the great landowner has his own peace and administers his own justice.[53]

The mid-nineteenth-century historian, we may say, has his own version of the forfeiture of liberty; whereas the earlier, Georgian, neo-Harringtonian version was much to do with the severance of the tie with the land and the supplanting of the freeholder by the rentier, Stubbs and his contemporaries saw it as being essentially

---

[50] *ibid.*, i. 79–81.   [51] *ibid.*, i. 161–2, 181.

[52] The treatment of the *mark* system was one point, as Maitland noticed, where Stubbs' treatment became more obscure as he tried in successive editions to adapt his account to criticisms of the theory. See *CH*, i. 50–1, 82–3.   [53] *ibid.*, i. 166–7.

involved in the establishment of that tie. Of course, 'corruption' or any such term would be too severe for what they have in mind. 'Progress' and 'freedom' had to be held in a fine balance, within the general Whig category of continuity.

So far, of course, there has been no obvious tension; there has been no difficulty in seeing Stubbs' idea of the growth of institutions as a story of free development; gradual, unplanned, spontaneous institutional growth and transformation is itself a manifestation of free collective activity.[54] This is the classic Burkean and Savignian account of custom solidifying into law.[55] But at this point the paradox we considered earlier becomes embarrassing. For the first six hundred years of the existence of the English as a people, the general thrust of their free institutional creativity seems to have been resolutely away from institutions which it makes sense to call free. The manner of advance may be paradigmatically Burkean, the destination is dependence and serfdom.

No legislation turned the free owner into the feudal tenant: whatever changes in that direction took place were the result of individual acts, or of very gradual changes of custom arising indirectly from the fact that other relations were assuming a territorial character.[56]

No matter that Stubbs regards the process as part of the necessary transformation of nomadic, predatory tribes into a settled, governed and unified agricultural population: this is merely to recreate, in an earlier historical context, the classic dilemma of the Whig historian over the equivocal or antagonistic relations between freedom and civilisation. The decision of Whig historians earlier in the century to begin the story of constitutional continuity and liberty not in the German woods but essentially in the thirteenth century seems fully vindicated.

Yet there was, of course, even among them, a residual tendency to refer vaguely to Saxon origins, to the independent freeholder and the jury system.[57] It was this tendency which Stubbs, following Palgrave[58] and the Germans, decisively amplified. In his account the Norman Conquest was actually of dramatic assist-

---

[54] E.g. *EEH*, pp. 201–3, 332–3, 352. Cf. *CH*, i. 6, 11.
[55] E.g. *CH*, i. 165, 'its simple organization easily adapted itself to the circumstances of the five centuries of its history; it was capable of development and liable to much internal modification according to the variations of the balance of its parts, and the character of its regulative or motive force.'
[56] *CH*. i. 188.   [57] E.g. Hallam, *View*, ii. 274, 277; *Const. Hist.*, i. 5–7.
[58] For Palgrave, see Vinogradoff, *Villeinage*, pp. 12–16.

ance, raising the possibility of a yet deeper serfdom, unfulfilled. In the light of this, the account of English liberties in the Norman and Angevin periods could begin to look like a success story. The *Constitutional History* is in one aspect a post-revolutionary work, a parable of the survival of flexible conservatism through revolutionary times. But since the 'revolution' – the Norman Conquest – was unquestionably a despotic one, and since the older traditions were by contrast 'free', the cause of conservatism was also the cause of freedom. This, of course, was the standard seventeenth-century Whig position – the original Whiggism: the ancient constitution was popular; the kings who threatened it were innovators. But in Stubbs the conservative defence was conducted not by parliamentary heroes but by the combination of inarticulate persistence and malleability in the institutions themselves; it is the conservative – Whig epic not of the defence of the free constitution but of the free constitution itself.

The first volume of Stubbs' *Constitutional History* then, culminating in Magna Carta, is a record not only of growth, the growth of feudalism and territorial monarchy, but of survival. The dormant seeds of future liberties lie embedded in the local institutions bequeathed by the English settlement, in which the representative traditions of the folk are preserved.[59] They are saved by their local and rudimentary character (as the obscure have the best chance of surviving a revolution). Some survive still, as in the supposed survival of the primitive assembly of the township in the vestry meeting of the parish: 'As the national customs which belong to the lowest range of machinery are subject to the fewest organic changes, these courts have continued to exist until the present day.'[60]

For Stubbs – there was some contrast with Freeman here – it was not in the continuity of the Witenagemot (whose official as well as aristocratic character he stressed) with the later Parliament, that the continuity of English history and English liberties rested, but in the vigour of the humbler institutions of local government. English landholding was feudalised, but not English local government; the courts of the shire and the hundred, with their vestiges of the representative principle, continued to lie alongside the franchises of the feudal lords.[61] The feudal pyramid never

[59] Hallam and Palgrave had both stressed this. See Vinogradoff, *ibid.* and Hallam, *View*, ii. 277. Cf. e.g. Stubbs, *CH*, i. 210.
[60] *CH*, i. 91.   [61] *ibid.*, p. 257, cf. *EEH*, p. 265.

became the sole form of relationship; the king remained king of the nation as well as, in Norman times, the feudal overlord of the land.[62] Under the Normans the national life seemed crushed: 'Yet there was life; although it lay deep now, it would be strong enough when it reached the surface; nor had the Conqueror any wish to break the bruised reed.'[63] It was, Stubbs variously implied, the incomprehension of the Norman lawyers of anything not manifestly feudal,[64] and the policy of the Conqueror in retaining a direct link between himself and his subjects,[65] which allowed the lower courts to survive:

In the preservation of the old forms, – the compurgation by the kindred of the accused, the responsibility for the wergild, the representation of the township in the court of the hundred, and that of the hundred in the court of the shire; the choice of witnesses; the delegation to chosen committees of the common judicial rights of the suitors of the folkmoot; the need of witnesses for the transfer of chattels, and the evidence of the hundred and shire as to criminals and the duty of enforcing their production and punishment, and the countless diversity of customs in which the several communities went to work to fulfil the general injunctions of the law, – in these remained the seeds of future liberties; themselves perhaps the mere shakings of the olive tree, the scattered grains that royal and noble gleaners had scorned to gather, but destined for a new life after many days of burial. They were the humble discipline by which a downtrodden people were schooled to act together in small things until the time came when they could act together for great ones.[66]

English society was feudalised, but England never became, like France, a pure case of 'the feudal system'; the saving grace of anomaly was preserved and at work.

Respect for local initiative and community, and hostility to what was seen as the brutal centralisation exemplified, above all, in France, was a recurrent and deeply felt theme among English historians of the middle and later nineteenth century. It is a Burkean and Romantic trait; by the mid-century we should certainly be prepared to recognise it also as a Tocquevillian one. We find it in Stubbs, Freeman, most powerfully in Green, and, with characteristic modifications, in Maitland. The Francophobia of Macaulay and his generation focussed, above all, on the figure of the revolutionary demagogue, and is epitomised in Macaulay's essay on Barère. For the later generation he has been largely replaced, not by the Communard – for whom Green at least felt considerable sympathy as an advocate of local self-government[67] –

---

[62] *CH*, i. 168, 257.   [63] *ibid*., i. 214.   [64] *ibid*., p. 168.   [65] *ibid*., p. 267.
[66] *ibid*., p. 210. Cf. *EEH*, p. 270.
[67] Stephen, *Letters of John Richard Green*, pp. 288, 298.

but by Napoleon III and Baron Haussman and the French provincial bureaucrat and petty official. The increased opportunities for foreign travel brought by peace, affluence and railways may well have had something to do with the change; minor bureaucrats are a more likely hazard for English travellers in France than sans-culottes, even if Walter Bagehot was nearly shot at in 1848.[68] On his frequent French travels, the word 'Préfet' on a poster was enough to throw Freeman into a bad temper.[69] Maitland spoke of France as the country 'where we may see the pulverising, macadamizing tendency in all its glory, working from century to century reducing to impotence and then to nullity, all that interferes between Man and State'.[70]

Stubbs mourned, in his lectures, over the old localities of France:

The old map of France is full of memories – recollections of Gaul and Rome, the empire of the Caesars, Burgundians and Acquitainians, Franks and Armoricans – Clovis, Charles the Great, and St Louis – knights, troubadours, saints and heroes. The history of the land was written on its face. The map of modern France is a catalogue of hills and rivers, a record of centralization, codification, universal suffrage, government by policemen. Probably the work of simplification will never be carried so far in England, but there is a tendency towards it, which is a sign of the decline of independent thought and character.[71]

One of these signs, which touched him closely, he had noted a moment earlier: 'The tendency of the present day is to destroy these historical specialities: the Ecclesiastical Commission has done for our ecclesiastical fabric what phonetic science was to have done for our language and what certain persons want to do for our Prayer Book.'[72] Green too was eloquent in condemnation of the historical insensitivity of the Ecclesiastical Commission.[73] The spirit of system and centralisation was abroad, even in England.

'Independence of character' was a cardinal virtue for Stubbs. It was the self-confidence that comes from rootedness and continuity: a capacity for initiative without direction and a stubbornness in the face of smart modernity, system and rationalisation. But such independence is of course a small-scale and in part negative virtue. Stubbs was too political an animal for it to be all-sufficient; least of all, of course, did he mean by it, in Matthew Arnold's phrase,

[68] Mrs Russell Barrington (ed.), *The Works and Life of Walter Bagehot*, 9 vols (1915), i. 79.   [69] Stephens, *Life of Freeman*, ii. 306.
[70] *Collected Papers*, iii. 311.   [71] *EEH*, p. 2.   [72] *ibid.*
[73] J. R. Green, *Stray Studies from England and Italy* (2nd series) (1903).

'doing as one likes'.[74] It was, it could be said, the characteristic form of Anglo-Saxon freedom, the freedom of the ancient constitution, but it was narrow and sluggish.

The individual Englishman must have been formed under circumstances that called forth much self-reliance and little hearty patriotism. His sympathies must have run into very narrow and provincial channels. His own home and parish were much more to him than the house of Cerdic or the safety of the nation. As a Christian, too, he had more real, more appreciable social duties than as an Englishman. He could accept Sweyn or Canute, if he would be a good lord and not change the laws or customs that regulated his daily life. There was a strong sense of social freedom without much care about political power.[75]

The contrary vice to centralisation was an unthinking, custom-bound independence, a failure, it could be called, to rise to the level of political action and national consciousness. This latter was, for Stubbs, to be the achievement of Englishmen in the century and a half between the Norman Conquest and Magna Carta.

It was not only an achievement, it was a fortunate or providential escape. France and Germany demonstrated the other menacing and opposite possibilities. The conquest of the Gauls by the Franks parallels the Norman Conquest of England (the earlier Saxon invasion was not, for Stubbs, a conquest but an extirpation or eviction of the Britons and a colonisation).[76] Feudalism was the natural adaptation of the original Germanic institutions to the situation of a conquering race.[77] The Franks 'developed the idea of feudal subordination in the organisation of government unmodified by any tendencies towards popular freedom. In France accordingly feudal government runs its logical career'. The only checks on royal power having been the feudal ones, France had only the alternatives of feudal disintegration or despotism. In fact it was the latter, 'and its logical result is the explosion which is called revolution'.[78] The import of Stubbs' French parable is the same as Macaulay's, but Stubbs places the crisis earlier, tracing the French predicament not to the decline of feudalism, the failure of medieval constitutionalism to survive through the ensuing crisis of the sixteenth and seventeenth centuries, but to the manner of feudalism's establishment in the first place, in the character of the Frankish conquest: neither a total expropriation such as the Saxons inflicted on the Britons, nor a relatively superficial and

[74] *Culture and Anarchy*, ch. 2.   [75] *CH*, i. 211.   [76] *ibid.*, i. 61.
[77] *ibid.*, i. 3.   [78] *ibid.*

transitory imposition like the Norman Conquest. German history, of course, exhibits the penalties not of centralisation but of particularism: 'The weakness of the imperial centre, the absence of central legislature and judicature, allows the continued existence of the most primitive forms; the want of cohesion prevents at once their development and their extinction.'[79]

From these fates England was saved by the Norman Conquest. The growth of the great fiefs at the close of the Saxon period threatened England with disintegration and the feudalisation of her polity.[80] It was the Conquest which imposed unity on the nation and, by reaction, made it conscious of that unity.[81] Meanwhile the feudal relation at the lower levels provided, according to Stubbs, the loyalty and discipline[82] by which the nation, united under the Norman barons who were themselves too weak individually to challenge the crown, was able ultimately to assert its freedom of collective action in a more coherent and self-conscious fashion, in the constitutionalist movements of the thirteenth century.[83] Saxon England had left its base of local institutions; the Norman state had provided a powerful administrative machinery. The subsequent history of the constitution consists essentially in their fusion, 'the growing together of the local machinery and the administrative organisation'.[84]

There was nothing particularly original in the notion that the Norman Conquest had been in some measure beneficial to England; Turner, Hallam, Kemble and Palgrave had all held this view in various forms. Stubbs himself was fond of quoting with apparent approval Carlyle's opinion that without the Normans and Plantagenets the English would have remained 'a gluttonous race of Jutes and Angles, capable of no grand combinations; lumbering about in pot-bellied equanimity; not dreaming of heroic toil, and silence, and endurance, such as leads to the high places of this universe'.[85] But this gives no idea of the complexity of Stubbs' own argument. There was discipline of a sort from the beginning, in the obligations, narrow though they were, of the independent freeholder. It was this which distinguished Saxon freedom from a mere raw tribalism, Gibbon's 'wild independence', and provided 'a more likely basis of freedom than the community of land, the close tie of patriarchal or family unity, the enormous and disproportionate estimate of blood nobility and the clannish spirit that

[79] *ibid.*, i. 5.　[80] *ibid.*, i. 202–3.　[81] *ibid.*, i. 216.　[82] *EEH*, pp. 16, 18–19, 262.
[83] *CH*, i. 247–8.　[84] *ibid.*, i. 544; 278.　[85] *ibid.*, i. 216n. Cf. *EEH*, p. 18.

one finds in the Highland Scot and Irishman, or in the Pole and Hungarian'.[86] The Conquest gave this capacity for ordered self-government an effective national organisation, and because English freedom was not won from the central authority as sectional privilege, but achieved by taking over that powerful organisation as its own instrument it was not the possession of a class or classes[87] but the matured, embodied freedom of a constitution which was the political, institutional expression of the nation itself.

Stubbs does not, then, merely describe a strong Conqueror imposing unity and discipline on a turbulent or sluggish people, any more than he offers an organic, simply teleological account of the growth of national self-government; his account is more like a pilgrim's progress, with dangers and vicissitudes on either hand, and a kind of self-transcendence. Stubbs himself freely used the word 'education' in this context,[88] and, of course, if not a simple teleology his history is a Whig history in its allowance of premonition, in the sense it conveys at times, not obtrusively, of ordained preparation and a kind of striving at once unconscious and purposive.[89] He would have admitted as much. History for him was written by the hand of God and it is not forbidden – it could be said to be required – for God to know where he is going. Stubbs' *Constitutional History* is Whig history, but written with a scrupulous respect, in detail, for the integrity of the historian's materials and for the social arrangements of the past: the schematic account given above inevitably travesties the dense subtlety of the text itself.

How far Stubbs' work is from any crude determinism or superimposition of a teleology can best be seen in brief in the highly successful eclecticism of his vocabulary at its most abstract. The creation of such a vocabulary for what was virtually a new

---

[86] *EEH*, p. 204. The contrast was a well-established one, e.g. Gibbon on the 'wild independence' of the Caledonians (*Decline*, i. 141) or Millar's reference to men in the savage state as 'impatient of all restraint' (*Historical View*, i. 61), which is clearly distinct from the public virtue and patriotism associated with civic liberty, based, in the Harringtonian tradition, on the independent freeholder. Froude, also, held up the Irish as the antithesis (see below, p. 262). Cf. Tennyson on

> ... freedom in her regal seat
> Of England; not the schoolboy heat
> The blind hysterics of the Celt. (*In Memoriam*, CIX)

[87] E.g. *EEH*, pp. 36, 352.
[88] *SL*, p. 18. Also, even more significantly perhaps, 'moral training', *CH*, i. 289.
[89] E.g. *CH*, ii. 621; iii. 612.

kind of history ('Constitutional History has a point of view, an insight, and a language of its own')[90] is itself a considerable achievement; the controlled vigour, flexibility and appositeness of its rhetoric is one of the excellences of Stubbs' *History*. It creates a characteristic terminology which reflects as accurately as abstractions can do the complexity of his understanding of institutional change. Organic, mechanical and chemical terms are threaded into a prose both magisterial and supple, whose mixed metaphors have a kind of elegant inevitability. Mechanical metaphors are in fact more common than distinctively organic ones: 'Force', 'weight', 'accretion', 'elasticity', 'balance', 'consolidate', 'counteract'. The old 'mechanical' doctrine of constitutional balance is not dead but transcended. There is no question, of course, of a closed cycle of corruption and restoration; instead, from the self-interested and often countervailing expedients of selfish men[91] 'forms most beautiful and most wonderful have been, and are being, evolved' – the concluding words of *The Origin of Species* rise unbidden, but appositely, when speaking of Stubbs' *History*. To imply influence might be unjustified; the doctrine of unintended consequences was already a platitude, and Stubbs, with Providence as guarantor, had no need of Darwin to underwrite it. All the same, it is not incongruous, nor, clearly, in this minor instance fortuitous, when Stubbs uses the phrase 'natural selection'.[92]

Many passages, obviously, could be chosen to illustrate the distinctive qualities of Stubbs' rhetoric as an historical instrument. Take – more or less at random – the general characterisation of the thirteenth century at the opening of the second volume of the *Constitutional History*. Except in a certain heightening, natural in a preamble, and in its pure generality, it is sufficiently typical:

The prolific luxuriance of the age furnishes in politics, just as in architecture and in science, inventions which the rapidity of its movements and the involution of its many interests will not allow it to test. Hence the political ideas of the time produce on the fabric of society less effect than might reasonably be looked for, and the strong and ancient groundwork on which the edifice has already been begun outlasts the many graceful but temporary superstructures that have been raised upon it ... The life which the heroes of the age breathe into the constitutional body tends to invigorate the whole; their spirit remains whilst their designs perish. Slowly and steadily the old machinery gathers strength and works out its own completeness. It shakes off the premature accretions which would anticipate the forms towards which it is ultimately tending. Hence the political and mechanical sides of the story must be looked at separately; the growth of the

[90] *ibid.*, i. p. iii.   [91] E.g. *ibid.*, p. 446.   [92] *ibid.*, p. 170.

spirit of liberty apart from the expansion of the machinery; for the spirit works in forms which it has soon to discard, the machinery grows in its own proper form in spite of the neglect or contempt of the men by whose force it subsists. Their genius lives, but with a life which runs in other channels than those which it might itself have chosen.[93]

Read in isolation this may perhaps seem vaguely rhetorical; it is not, it is exordium. Each metaphor represents a promise, subsequently fulfilled in full detail and technicality. If the teleology sits a little heavily ('works out its own completeness') and even oddly ('premature accretions'), it is in fact the mixed metaphors which give the passage its vitality. They are characteristic and without question calculated ('no theory or principle works in isolation'); not a sign of slackness but the chosen expressions of a conscious aversion to 'a perpetual striving after the abstract idea or law of change, the constant "accentuation", as it is called, of principles in historical writing'.[94] The teleology is inescapable, of course. Consider another passage, also quite characteristic, this time from the opening of the third volume, on Parliament in the fifteenth century:

Under the monotonous detail there is going on a process of hardening and sharpening, a second almost imperceptible stage of definition which, when new life is infused into the mechanism, will have no small effect in determining the ways in which that new life will work. In the record of asserted privilege may be traced the flashes of a consciousness that show the forms of national action to be no mere forms, and illustrate the continuity of a sense of earlier greatness and of an instinctive looking towards a greater destiny.[95]

The attribution of such 'instinctive' striving or unconscious premonition is of course a central characteristic of programmatic or 'Whig' historiography, yet for all this the passage is alert and thoughtful in the vitality and precision of its diction. There is never a sense, in reading Stubbs, that a theory or programme had merely taken over from history.

'Life', 'forms', 'mechanism', 'expansion', 'consciousness', and above all the frequently expressed dialectic of 'spirit' and 'machinery' hint very broadly at a familiar and pervasive nineteenth-century metaphysics. The controlling thought is that of the relation and interaction between what is variously called spirit, energies, life, and its vesture or necessary embodiment in what Stubbs most often called 'machinery', through which it finds coherence and identity, and effective means of self-expression as

[93] *ibid.*, ii. 2.   [94] *ibid.*, iii. 519.   [95] *ibid.*, p. 2.

political will. It is a relationship thought of as a kind of historical striving for more adequate, concentrated, expanded and self-conscious forms. The elements of the creative tension are introduced by Stubbs in the opening sentences of the *Constitutional History*:

The growth of the English constitution, which is the subject of this book, is the resultant of three forces, whose reciprocal influences are constant, subtle and intricate. These are the national character, the external history, and the institutions of the people.[96]

The nation is given concrete expression, and realises its identity through its institutions, through a creative interaction with circumstance. The recurrent metaphors of the book can be seen, in retrospect, to group themselves around these three elements: spirit, life, energies, 'formative power'; pressures of all kinds; and a machinery progressively more coherent, definite and comprehensive, consciously wielded as the expression of national will. The native and latent spirit or life of the constitution is, essentially, Germanic freedom, but it runs, initially, uncoordinated and unselfconscious, in narrow, local and habitual channels. In it, custom has not reached the level of constitutional political action, and its political expression is no more than a multiplicity of essentially similar tiny units. To find its embodiment in the larger, conscious and coherent unity of the nation was the work of history and of the Norman. For a time – a time of despotism – native energies and Norman machinery are independent, the latter clamped on the former as an external, alien force.[97] Their growing together in organic fusion makes the constitution – though the phrase is not in Stubbs' vocabulary – a true concrete universal, conscious of itself: 'the commixture of race and institutions was so completed as to produce an organization which grew into conscious life'.[98] The nation realises its unity and identity;[99] it 'becomes one and realises its oneness'.[100]

We may if we wish speak of this underlying metaphysic as Hegelian, provided that we recognise that in doing so we consult our own intellectual convenience rather than refer, so far as we know, to an immediate influence. The search for a specific influence, in fact, may well be vain, a piece of naive pedantry which only distance in time makes plausible. The metaphysical

[96] *ibid.*, i. 1. [97] *ibid.*, p. 289. [98] *ibid.*, p. 551.
[99] *ibid.*, p. 444. [100] *ibid.*, p. 545.

formula for creativity and self-development we have been considering was, it may well be, by the mid-nineteenth century, even for someone so determinedly unphilosophical as Stubbs, so pervasive and diffuse an influence that it is pointless to attempt to particularise. Beginning, essentially, in the aesthetic thought of late eighteenth-century Germany, as an attempt to grasp the nature of the created aesthetic object and the artist's relation to it, it had permeated and become an organising principle in many different branches of thinking: in philosophy, poetics,[101] theology,[102] in the distinctively German moral concept of self-cultivation or the development of personality (*Bildung*),[103] and even, through the influence of Hegelian philosophies of history, in politics. It was no doubt inevitable that it should at some point become an organising metaphysic for the English, Burkean thoughts with which it has some initial affinities, as it had already done, up to a point, in the political thought of Coleridge.[104]

It is also inevitable that it should produce, for us, tantalising family resemblances in works influenced by it. There is an obvious, but in terms of any mutual influence quite irrelevant analogy, for example, between Stubbs' idea of the nation taking possession of the machinery used by the Normans as the means of its oppression, and making it the instrument of its political unity, will and self-consciousness, and Marx's account of the proletariat entering into possession of the instrument of its exploitation, the industrial plant and world markets created by capitalism, and turning it into the means to the expression of man's species being in autonomous social labour. There is also, of course, a vaguer though possibly more relevant similarity to Carlyle, whom Stubbs seems to have admired, though there is too much Whig optimism and Burkean stress on continuity in Stubbs for there to be any close correspondence with the essentially relativistic and discontinuous view of history in Teufelsdröckh's clothes-philosophy.[105] Closest of all, perhaps, are the analogies with an author for whom Stubbs had no sympathy at all: Herbert Spencer. There are clear

---

[101] See particularly M. H. Abrams, *The Mirror and the Lamp. Romantic Theory and the Critical Tradition* (New York 1958), ch. VIII.

[102] E.g. Stephen Prickett, *Romanticism and Religion. The Tradition of Coleridge and Wordsworth in the Victorian Church* (C.U.P. 1976).

[103] See Wilhelm von Humboldt, *The Limits of State Action*, ed. J. W. Burrow (C.U.P. 1969), Editor's Introduction.

[104] In the concept of the 'Idea' developed in S. T. Coleridge, *An Essay on the Constitution of Church and State* (1830).

[105] Carlyle, *Sartor Resartus* (1838).

coincidences in conception and even in vocabulary in their respective elaborations of the central idea. The development of the English constitution according to Stubbs would be very adequately described by the Spencerian formula of evolution, as a transition 'from an indefinite, incoherent homogenity to a definite, coherent heterogenity'.[106] Yet Stubbs, accused of being influenced by Spencer, might well have felt, like a Darwinian accused of claiming descent from a chimpanzee, that a radical and distasteful mistake had been made. Of course, distaste does not preclude influence, but the link may lie further back, in Spencer's indebtedness, freely acknowledged, to Coleridge's 'Idea of Life', borrowed in turn it seems from Schelling.[107]

To take leave of Stubbs with a discussion of a formula does him an injustice; perhaps enough has been said earlier to correct any misleading impression from this. Yet it is well, perhaps, to leave him with a thought which connects him, in a more than merely professional way, with his age, for he does not offer many such opportunities. Intellectual flirtatiousness was never one of his vices or virtues; his guiding lights were few and steady. This in no way impairs his achievement, but it confines it. Stubbs made the history of institutions a far richer and more suggestive thing than any mere historical technician could have done, impressively vindicating his claim that it could be educative, though many among the generations of history undergraduates who got bits of it up may not have found it so. In 1893, Frederick Harrison published a squib in the *Fornightly Review* entitled 'The History Schools: An Oxford Dialogue', in which he makes his undergraduate protagonist observe, among other complaints, that 'When we come up to Oxford we never seem to get out of an infinite welter of "origins" and primitive forms of everything.'[108] Harrison's polemic is not particularly impressive; it contains numerous distortions, and Harrison himself was too obviously an interested party, being a leading spokesman for a positivist variety of Whiggism by now called 'Sociology', but it gives voice to what may well have been a common disillusionment.

Herbert Paul, the biographer of J. A. Froude, writing in the early years of this century, said that Froude, as Regius Professor, 'made more impression upon the undergraduates in a few months than

---

[106] Herbert Spencer, *First Principles* (1904), 1st edn. 1862), p. 321.
[107] D. Duncan, *Life and Letters of Herbert Spencer* (1908), p. 541.
[108] Reprinted in F. Harrison, *The Meaning of History* (1894), p. 132.

Stubbs had done in as many years'.[109] Stubbs himself lamented his sparsely filled lecture rooms. The technicality of his subject was against him, but his immediate successor, Freeman, seems to have fared little better with the world-historical ruminations he offered his Oxford audiences.[110] The ability to arouse enthusiasm usually implies good relations with the *zeitgeist*. Froude, lecturing in the 1890s on Elizabethan seamen, had a bracing and apparently welcome message for patriotic young England. The older patriotic and populist impulse which underlay '*Die Germanische Rechtsgeschichte*' belonged essentially to the age of post-Napoleonic liberalism. Now it was overlaid by time and scholarly technicality: the passionate devotion to legal antiquities of Grimm and Kemble rendered down, to Stubbs' dismay, into examination questions.

Stubbs' academic legacy may well have seemed more arid than he deserved – though no historian who has Maitland as his most obvious heir has really the right to complain of his posterity. But to speak of Froude and the Imperialist exuberance of the nineties is to anticipate. We have not yet done with the earlier, liberal-Teutonic enthusiasms, for though Stubbs embodies them most impressively he exemplifies them only in part. There was much, which we still have to consider, in possible responses to the early English past, of which Stubbs' work carries only a tinge, just as there was much in his intellectual milieu which influenced these responses, but to which Stubbs is only a guarded witness. This is not, of course, a criticism. Historians have no duty to make themselves available to intellectual history (it has sometimes been thought that they have a duty not to do so, but that is another issue). But it does mean that for a fuller picture we need to attend to a more impressionable and impulsive mind. Though, for example, the presiding metaphor of Stubbs' *Constitutional History* may be central to Romantic aesthetics and much else, there is an unrelenting sobriety and professionalism which forbids us to speak of his work or its author as Romantic. Stubbs' capacity for Romanticism exhausted itself early, in a Puseyite High Churchmanship and a liking for medieval architecture.[111]

Freeman, by contrast, though only two years older – he was born in 1823 – never threw off the Romantic enthusiasms and cast

[109] Herbert Paul, *The Life of Froude* (1905), p. 410. For the reception of Stubbs' lectures, *ibid.*, p. 384. Paul was an undergraduate at Oxford in the 1870s.

[110] Stephens, *Life*, ii. 429. James Bryce, *Studies in Contemporary Biography* (1903), pp. 288–9.

[111] Hutton, *Letters*, p. 21.

of mind of the 1840s, his formative years, though in some respects he changed their direction. Gruff pedant and country magistrate as he was, he was a Romantic in almost everything: in his *Schwär-merei* and his Byronic philhellenism, in the lush intemperance of his libertarian rhetoric, in his racialist nationalism and sympathy with oppressed nationalities, in his Tacitean primitivism and populism, and in a note, seldom altogether silent in his historical writing, of apocalyptic excitement. The cultural matrix of Romanticism is something to be borne constantly in mind in reading him, or we shall approach him with historical sympathies half-unawakened: eccentric and obsessive though he undoubtedly was, some of his peculiarities are not literally peculiarities; they are generic: intensifications at the most. It is to Freeman therefore, and to J. R. Green who shared so many of his interests without his oddities, that we have to turn for ampler, more overtly emotional and more widely responsive versions of how the early period of English history could be felt and understood in mid-Victorian England. Stubbs and Freeman stand to each other as the Hallam and Macaulay of their day. It is a minor expository inconvenience that Stubbs was a far greater historian than Hallam, Freeman something considerably less in achievement and popularity than Macaulay.

III

THE DEMOCRAT

Freeman and the unity of history

CHAPTER 7

Teutonic freedom and municipal independence

The making of a democrat[1]

Freeman, a generation younger than Macaulay, eagerly read the volumes of the latter's *History* as they appeared,[2] and always spoke of their author with admiration. The two men had much in common: a combative, enthusiastic nature which, unchecked, sometimes ran to vulgarity and fierce polemic; an aversion to mathematics and field-sports;[3] political ambitions and an excited interest in public affairs which waned a little as they grew older; and a love of roll-calls of the great dead. The last, indeed, and a delight in historic continuities, a sense of connection with the English past, uninhibited by any sense of that past as alien and obscure, may be seen as defining characteristics of the Whig historian, though they are less marked, or at least less exuberant, in Hallam or in Stubbs. For Macaulay and Freeman, such Whiggism was not so much a political requirement as an overflowing necessity of temperament, and it was comprehensively satisfying; neither cared much for any modern literature except Scott, though Macaulay's taste in earlier literature was wider. Belonging to generations brought up on Percy's *Reliques* and Scott's *Lays*, they were drawn – in Freeman's case almost exclusively – to epic and ballads, and tried to write them.[4]

Both were child prodigies, and their situations, as leisured private scholars in easy circumstances (at least in Macaulay's later years), were similar. In both cases they outgrew an early rearing in

---

[1] Strictly Freeman's claim to the title could be disputed, since he never altogether reconciled himself to one man, one vote. See W. R. W. Stephens, *Life and Letters of Edward A. Freeman* (1895), i. 147–8; ii. 441. But it was one he always applied to himself.   [2] *ibid.*, i. 165. Also ii. 473.

[3] A description which also applies to Gibbon. Freeman's objection to field sports, however, was a principled one.

[4] Stephens, i. 82–3.

Toryism and Biblical fundamentalism: the child Macaulay's start-ling imprecation 'Cursed by Sally; for it is written, Cursed is he that removeth his neighbour's land-mark' is matched by the young Freeman's refusal to believe that the earth went around the sun because of the verse in Psalm 104 'He hath made the round world so sure that it cannot be moved'.[5] Both – and here the similarities become coincidences – fell as children under the patronage of the *grande dame* of Evangelicalism Hannah More, though Freeman was fond of remarking that unlike the older historian he had not offered her 'a glass of old spirits'.[6] There is also a more remarkable coincidence: in both cases their life's work was anticipated or, in a sense, begun, in the composition of university prize essays: Macaulay's on 'The Conduct and Character of William the Third' and Freeman's unsuccessful effort submitted for the Chancellor's English Essay Prize at Oxford, for which the subject set in 1846 was 'The Effect of the Conquest of England by the Normans'. In both cases the strongly Whig line taken in the works by which they are remembered is clearly adumbrated in these early efforts.[7]

But it was only by a gradual transition that Freeman came to take this position, and the writing of the prize essay seems to have provided a vital impetus; as an undergraduate High Churchman he had further to travel to his historical Whiggism than had Macaulay. Moreover the differences are, of course, as instructive as the similarities. Macaulay's was the Whiggism of the *Edinburgh Review* and Holland House, in which an exuberant rhetoric was consciously tempered by a tart, deflationary shrewdness. Free-man's liberalism was the Byronic and Mazzinian creed and rhetoric of the 1830s and 1840s: dealing in vague images of liberation and heroic populism rather than adjustment, passionate on behalf of oppressed Greeks and Italians. The assimilation of these enthusiasms to English Whig notions of continuity can be seen as the central intellectual and emotional task of Freeman's life, and though it can be argued that he found more or less intellectually acceptable formulae, the currents of sentiment, as we shall see, never entirely coalesced.

He was not helped in this task by any practical experience. Apart from fighting, unsuccessfully, two parliamentary elections, acting as a conscientious magistrate, and playing a leading part in

[5] Trevelyan, *Life*, p. 21; Stephens i. 19, 28.
[6] Tevelyan, p. 20; Stephens, i. 6.
[7] Trevelyan, p. 61; Stephens, i. 74.

the anti-Turk agitation of 1877–8,[8] he lived essentially as a private scholar, and later professor. Macaulay dramatised and, as it were, historicised his political experience with a parvenu's zest, but that experience, and the desperate realities of English politics during his young manhood, gave him a grasp on the contemporary, and, later, even some sense of its tedium. Freeman was not only an outsider but belonged to a more settled England, with more room for political self-indulgence. His absorbing and combative interest in foreign affairs inevitably took on a leader-writer's facile authority; it is no surprise that he was a frequent writer of letters to the newspapers; Stubbs, presumably, would not have approved. It gave Freeman's historical Whiggism scope and generosity as well as venom, and even a kind of grandeur, but at a perceptible cost in realism: a gaudy solemnity became its habitual tone.

His philosophy of history was in any case more hectic and grandiose than Macaulay's jubilant but essentially rather mundane and occasionally bathetic Scottish belief in progress: it was Arnoldian, redemptive, almost apocalyptic. For it mattered, too, that while Macaulay was a product of the Cambridge of the 1820s (the Cambridge, he would have added, of Bacon and Newton), Freeman's university was the Oxford of Thomas Arnold, Pusey and Newman. Freeman, though a High Churchman, was greatly impressed by Arnold's lectures; hearing his Inaugural as Regius Professor of History was a formative intellectual experience. It was, he said in his own Inaugural over forty years later, from Arnold that he 'first learned what history is and how it should be studied – first learned the truth which ought to be the centre and life of all our historic studies; the truth of the unity of history'.[9] He also greatly admired Arnold's *History of Rome*.

Freeman, in his writing for the reviews, consciously modelled himself on Macaulay, and caught well, or helped to form, the tone of exasperated common sense and superior knowledge which marked the style of the *Saturday Review*, for which he wrote much in the 1860s and 1870s. He could be witty; his celebrated persecution of Froude was unfair and malevolent,[10] but his attack on Kingsley is quite funny as well as cruel and pedantic; it is the more striking because Kingsley's boyish enthusiasms seem, after the lapse of a century, divided only by a hairsbreadth from

---

[8] For this, and Freeman's part in it, see R. T. Shannon, *Gladstone and the Bulgarian Agitation, 1876* (1963).   [9] Stephens, i. 66.
[10] The fullest account of this is Herbert Paul, *The Life of Froude*, ch. 5.

Freeman's own. He mocked Kingsley's 'ultra-Teutonism' and found his lectures 'throughout frightfully earnest' but 'never once decently serious'.[11] But in Freeman's own historical writing, high-Victorian prophetic solemnity is unqualified. J. R. Green, an airier spirit, who dealt with Freeman with an admirable and rather awesome candour, wished that he had written more as he talked, and complained of 'a sort of undertaker-solemnity'.[12] Freeman conceived The History of the Norman Conquest, there can be no doubt, as national epic, but it is sometimes easier to think of it as a patriotic oratorio, with music by Stanford or Sullivan, with banked massed choirs, respectively high-collared and low-necked, mustachioed and muslined, pomaded and bunned, and the Whiggish sound of a great Amen.

Arnoldian prophetic seriousness was, it seems fair to assume, one model for Freeman's high solemnities, but Arnold was not the only or in the short term the most obvious Oxford influence. Tractarianism was virtually inescapable in the Oxford of the early 1840s, and Freeman had already taken an eager interest in the Tracts before he went up. He seems to have had no personal contact with Newman or Pusey, unlike Stubbs, who naturally encountered the latter at Christ Church, but one of the fellows of his own college, Trinity, was Newman's curate Isaac Williams. The scholars of Trinity seem to have been as earnest a body of young High Churchmen as one might expect. How far Freeman was at this time from Whiggism of any kind is seen in his following what seems to have been a common practice and absenting himself from chapel on the annual occasion of prayers for the deliverance of 1688; 'Did not go to Chapel because of Dutch Bill.'[13] But he had little bent for theology; his High Church enthusiasm took another, almost equally topical form: ecclesiology, the study of Gothic or 'Christian' Church architecture and church restoration. At one point he contemplated becoming an architect,[14] though, unlike William Morris, caught up in some of the same enthusiasms at Oxford a decade later, he never went so far as to enter an architect's office.

Freeman's mature historical writing is almost inseparable from his interest in architecture, and we shall have to look at its

---

[11] The Saturday Review, xvii (9 April, 1864), 446–8. For attribution of Saturday Review articles see M. M. Bevington, The Saturday Review (New York 1941), pp. 343, 345.
[12] Stephen (ed.), Letters of John Richard Green, pp. 222, 302.
[13] Stephens, i. 49.   [14] ibid., i. 51. 61.

significance later. For the moment it is enough to notice that the period of Freeman's undergraduate High Churchmanship was not so distinct from his later nationalist and racialist interests and his cult of 'Teutonic' democracy as it may immediately seem. True the most obvious political and historiographical resting-place for an ecclesiologist was a spiritual home in the thirteenth century, a repudiation of virtually every development since the later Middle Ages, and perhaps a kind of Carlylean Tory Radicalism; the stance, variously modified, of Pugin, Ruskin and William Morris, though Morris – it is one of his many points of similarity with Freeman – also later shifted his enthusiasm from the feudal and chivalric high Middle Ages to the period of the Norse sagas and primitive Teutonic democracy. But Freeman did not take what might have seemed the prescribed path. Ruskin was too near a contemporary to be a mentor as he was to the younger medievalists, and Freeman's references to 'Ruskinesque fools' are characteristically impatient;[15] among other points of difference Freeman rather disliked Italian Gothic and liked railway viaducts.[16] Carlyle, whom Stubbs admired with reservations, Freeman found merely an unintelligible ranter.[17]

But though Freeman's architectural and historical interests became more eclectic, though he shed his Toryism and embraced Teutonic democracy, though his High Churchmanship dwindled to a liking for ritual, a distaste for Puritanism and a marked sympathy with Eastern Orthodoxy, and even his Christianity to vestiges of a kind of Arnoldian-providential philosophy of history, this early Tractarian and ecclesiological period left its traces, though it did not, as in J. A. Froude's case, scar him for life. The transition – emancipation, it is tempting to say – was not so very great in some respects, nor, it seems, particularly painful. Of course, it is easy to see how an interest in medieval architecture could become, as it seems to have done in Stubbs' case, a step to more general archaeological or historical interests.[18] More specifically, for all its insistence on the 'Catholic', there was a marked strain of nationalism in the Gothic revival in its earnest Victorian phase. Baroque and neo-classical architecture – for which Freeman retained an abiding contempt – were rejected, as they were by Pugin and later by Ruskin, as unsuitably foreign as well as gimcrack and pagan.

[15] *ibid.*, ii. 304.   [16] NC, iii. 329.   [17] Stephens, i. 93; ii. 68.
[18] See above p. 150 and n. 11. Green also shared the interest, Stephen, *Letters*, p. 10.

But above all we can trace in Freeman the persisting influence of his Tractarian and ecclesiological period, not in any particular idea but in the antiquarian pedantry which became one of his most noticeable characteristics. Freeman's pedantry has become a by-word, not unjustly: a fanatical fussiness over such things as historical nomenclature and spelling. It seems not to have been noticed how far this is a transference of a fundamental ecclesiological trait. The Cambridge Camden Society, the leading ecclesiological organisation, was notorious for the severity and rigour of its dogmatism in matters of historical 'correctness': the unorthodoxy of a lancet too many, a wrongly placed tower or clerestoried aisle drew instant, passionate anathemas.[19] Freeman himself seems to have noticed something of the similarity when, with a rather rare flash of irony, he once, later in life, dated a letter 'day of Godwine's return',[20] parodying the Tractarian habit of dating letters by saints' days. But the comparison also works, of course, the other way round. There are several letters, for example, written by Freeman, while still a fellow of Trinity, to his fianceé, on the death of her sister. They are typical ecclesiological letters of the period: rather vague about the deceased, conventionally pious in their consolation, keenly excited and precise about the proposed inscription on the tomb: 'above all you must have "who *deceased*", not "who *died*", the latter word being, I believe, *never* found in ancient tombs of those who are not dead but sleep in Christ'.[21] The ostensible point is theological, and it is also quite typical, but it is easy to see here too the Freeman who was later to be fanatical over Saxon diphthongs and his misguided determination to call the battle of Hastings by what J. H. Round called 'the excruciating name of Senlac'. The frenzy of Freeman's devotion to the revival of what he thought of as historically 'correct' forms, including political and constitutional ones, was a mutation of the ecclesiological antiquarianism of the 1840s.

In the transformation of the Tory, High Church Scholar of Trinity into the Somerset magistrate, Teutonic racialist, and democrat, a number of public, personal and academic events appear to have combined. Freeman was already a sympathiser with oppressed nationalities and therefore in European terms a liberal; he himself dated his lifelong identification with the cause of Greece from seeing a Panorama of the battle of Navarino as a

---

[19] James F. White, *The Cambridge Movement. The Ecclesiologists and the Gothic Revival* (C.U.P. 1962).   [20] Stephens, ii. 73.   [21] *ibid.*, i. 93.

child.[22] It is hardly possible, too, that he should not have shared some of the excitement of many of his undergraduate contemporaries in 1848, though he seems to have been less stirred than some; he did not go to Paris like Clough, or like J. A. Froude set a band to play the Marseillaise under the Vice-Chancellor's window,[23] though his subsequent obsessive hostility to Napoleon III and the Emperor Franz Joseph may owe something to liberal disappointment and a sense of betrayal. Far more immediately important though was his engagement in 1844. Marriage would mean leaving Oxford; it was also opposed to the Tractarian ethos and clearly incompatible with membership of the society founded in Freeman's rooms in the same year called 'The Brotherhood of St Mary', devoted to the study of 'ecclesiastical art upon true and Catholic principles', which soon evolved into a quasi-monastic guild for the regulation of religious life.[24] There is a sense of growing distance and a touch of the embarrassment a young man feels in confronting old friends with the new version of himself in the jocularity with which Freeman, by 1854, was excusing himself from attending a meeting of the Ecclesiological Society: 'I really fear whether a profane person like me, a carnal west country alderman, in a white hat and brown holland trowsers, would not be somewhat out of character . . . I should be afraid of being torn to pieces like Hypatia.'[25]

The most specific intellectual influence, however, was academic, and it seems to have arisen directly from the Chancellor's prize essay on the Norman Conquest. Freeman naturally consulted the leading works on the period, chiefly Palgrave, Thierry and Kemble. One wonders if the authorities knew what they were doing. The Saxon period was still – or rather, it was again – the lost heritage of the radical ancient constitutionalist. Thierry's *Histoire de la Conquête de l'Angleterre par les Normands* (1825), in particular, was a manifesto of Romantic nationalism and populist sympathies. Freeman came to disapprove of it. It was unscholarly, and exaggerated the perpetuation of the division between Norman aristocrats and Saxon plebeians.[26] It was in fact not Whig history, but a version of the radical 'Norman Yoke' theory, though

---

[22] *ibid.*, p. 12.
[23] Waldo Hilary Dunn, *James Anthony Froude. A Biography*: vol. i. *1818–1856* (O.U.P. 1961), p. 98. For the nationalist sympathies of English liberals, see Christopher Harvie, *The Lights of Liberalism. University Liberals and the Challenge of Democracy 1860–1886* (1976), ch. 5.
[24] Stephens, i. 58.   [25] *ibid.*, i. 168.   [26] *Hist. Ess.*, 1st series, pp. 101–2.

Thierry's account is obviously modelled on the distinction, traditional in French historiography, between the Frankish nobility and the Gaulish Third Estate in France. But Freeman must have felt an answering pang when Thierry explicitly compared the Saxons under Norman rule with the Greeks under the oppression of the Turk.[27] Freeman's identification with the Saxons – always to him 'the English' – was to be his point of personal access to the Romantic excitements of the European liberal nationalism of his day; the Norman Conquest was his historical consolation for not belonging to an oppressed nation; Hastings and the Fall of Constantinople, Harold and Constantine Palaeologus were always to be coupled in his mind.[28] The effects of the earlier oppression, in so far as it was not simply seen, in the vein of English Whiggism, as essentially superficial and even beneficial, had been undone; the latter was still to be.[29]

Kemble's work, too, was more in the line of radical ancient constitutionalism than any other recent English work of early English history. A member of the great theatrical family, Kemble was a former Benthamite and radical who as a young man at Cambridge in the 1830s had taken part in the abortive Spanish rising under General Torrijos which formed such an exotic interlude in the early life of the Cambridge 'Apostles'.[30] But Kemble, as we have seen, in his studies with Jacob Grimm in Germany had also imbibed from source the Romantic–Tacitean cult of the primitive Teutonic democracy of the *mark*-community. It is true that by 1849 he had learnt some Whig caution. In the preface to *The Saxons in England*, written in 1848, he made the same obvious contrast as Macaulay was concurrently drawing in his *History*, between English continuity and stability and the revolutionary tumults of the continent; it may also have been relevant that Kemble, a somewhat raffish figure whose periods of

27 A. Thierry, *Histoire de la Conquête de l'Angleterre par les Normands*, 11th edn, 4 vols (Paris 1858), i. 10–11. For the 'patriotic' (as distinct from radical) nineteenth-century enthusiasm for the Saxons, whose landmarks are Scott's *Ivanhoe* (1819), Bulwer Lytton's *Harold, Last of the Saxon Kings* (1848), Kingsley's *Hereward the Wake* (1866) and Tennyson's *Harold* (1877), see Asa Briggs, *Saxons, Normans and Victorians* (Historical Association, Hastings 1966), and Andrew Sanders, 'Some aspects of the use of Anglo-Saxon subject matter in Victorian literature' (unpub. Cambridge M. Litt. thesis, 1975).

28 'The King who died upon the hill of Senlac finds his only worthy peer in the Emperor who died before the gate of Saint Rômanos', *NC*, ii. 44. Cf. *ibid*., p. 336; iii. 400, 404.

29 *ibid*. Cf. *Historical Essays*, 3rd series (1879), p. 446.

30 See Dickins, *John Mitchell Kemble*. Also Peter Lewis Allen, *The Cambridge Apostles. The Early Years* (C.U.P. 1978), pp. 97–101.

sobriety were intermittent, was vainly aspiring at the time to the Chair of History at Cambridge; the book is dedicated, hopefully, to the Queen. Kemble was also a profound scholar, perhaps the best of English early medievalists before Stubbs,[31] who did not, in the manner of the radical uses of 'the ancient constitution', simply present Anglo-Saxon England as a paradise of freedom and equality. He recognised, though he also lamented, that Anglo-Saxon society was becoming steadily more feudalised and its constitution more monarchical.[32] But there is an unmistakable Romantic nostalgia for the freedom and relative equality of the early days of Saxon colonisation, and for the small self-governing bond of kinsmen united in the primitive democracy of the *mark*-community.[33]

Freeman was captivated; the immediate academic source for the enthusiasm for early Teutonic democracy which he was proclaiming so loudly by the mid-1850s, and which he never lost, can hardly have been other than Kemble. Freeman's eleventh-century nationalism and newly found democratic sympathies eroded some of his High Church prejudices. As early as 1846, clearly as a by-product of his work for the prize essay, we find him writing to his fianceé of his preference for an elective kingship 'as was done in the Saxon times'.[34] In 1854, writing to a friend about the latter's Romanist tendencies, he admits that 'my present studies have given me a push the other way, and my faith in B. Gregory VII is somewhat shaken, as the sender over of those abominable Norman thieves', and he continues with a reference to 'the laws of King Cnut of blessed memory'.[35]

It is worth stressing the historiographical origins of these political and religious opinions, because alongside his reputation for pedantry Freeman as an historian has another, equally unappealing, for the anachronistic intrusion of contemporary political ideas into history. Round, his chief enemy, called him 'a democrat first, an historian afterwards'.[36] The German historian Pauli complained to Stubbs that 'radicalism and republicanism will continue to peep through the monarchical constellations of the twelfth century'.[37] Bryce, in his generally sympathetic essay on Freeman, commenting on his best-known epigram that 'History is

[31] See the opinion of Stubbs, above p. 130 and of Maitland, *Collected Papers*, iii. 456. Freeman admired his work, a little unwillingly it seems, Stephens, i. 366.
[32] *The Saxons in England*, ii, bk 11.   [33] *ibid.*, i. 53–68.   [34] Stephens, i. 88.
[35] *ibid.*, i. 103.   [36] J. H. Round, *Feudal England* (1964), p. 303.
[37] Quoted Hutton, *Letters*, p. 184.

past politics, and politics is present history,' remarked that 'Freeman was apt to go beyond his own dictum about history and politics, for he sometimes made history present politics as well as past.'[38] We need not defend Freeman against charges of anachronism to point out that Round's criticism, and to some extent Bryce's, are misleadingly put; in fact if Round's 'first' is chronological it is literally false. Freeman did not simply inject his contemporary politics into history; it would be truer to say that apart from history he had no contemporary politics at all. All his opinions were rooted in history; they were derived from his conceptions of the past. He did not so much look to old English democracy to justify modern Reform Acts as accept extensions of the franchise because he thought them archaeologically correct, as an ecclesiologist might approve the 'restoration' of an Early-English window of the 'correct' form in place of a Perpendicular one.

His interest in contemporary English politics, though genuine and irritable, was feeble and flickering by comparison with his feelings for the eleventh century or the thirteenth. There is sometimes in his comments on contemporary life a Victorian liberal hostility to court flunkeyism and snobbery, and a little hankering for a republic:[39] some resentment, too, of the political influence of the landed gentry, which could in a sense be said to have denied him the coveted seat in Parliament.[40] But these were tepid resentments compared with his denunciations of historical inaccuracy and false views of the past, and his disappointment that his own historical writing was not more popular.[41] Even his sympathy with movements of national liberation, the origin of his most vivid and vehement interest in the contemporary world and a source, undoubtedly, of his interest in the Norman Conquest, had itself, according to him, a primarily historical basis, derived from the time when, as a child poring over the map of Europe – historical geography was always an interest of his – and comparing it with that of Europe before the Revolution, he noticed their differences.[42] He felt, clearly, as Macaulay said of Burke, 'like an antiquary whose shield had been scoured'.[43] Ever afterwards he regarded Austria with detestation as an expansionist, parvenu

[38] Bryce, *Studies in Contemporary Biography*, pp. 274–5.
[39] E.g. *Historical Essays*, 4th series (1892), pp. 386–7.
[40] See Harvie, *The Lights of Liberalism*, pp. 177–82, for Freeman's electioneering.
[41] Stephens, ii. 228, 325, 339, 381, 405.   [42] *ibid.*, i. 12.
[43] Macaulay, 'Southey', *Essays, Works*, v. 331.

power, as France was also.[44] In his hatred of the latter he came to mourn the loss of the old 'middle-kingdom' of Burgundy, both as a buffer against France and a reminiscence of the glories of the old Carolingian Empire.[45] It was entirely characteristic that in 1871 he should have been passionately in favour of the 'restoration' to Germany of Alsace (always 'Elsass' to Freeman), irrespective of the wishes of the inhabitants: the democrat was overborne by the political antiquary: 'I have ventured to speak of historic right because it is that upon which the whole thing turns. Some persons will, of course, cry out "pedantry", "antiquarian rubbish"; I shall not be greatly troubled if they do.'[46]

Even the remark that 'History is past politics' is significantly balanced by 'politics is present history'. Contemporary politics, that is, became interesting to Freeman by being seen as part of the historical continuum, part of an unfolding and recognisable historical pattern. It is impossible to imagine him, as a member of Parliament, giving to a budget speech of his hero Gladstone[47] the minute attention devoted, for example, to the nature of Anglo-Saxon kingship in the appendices to *The Norman Conquest*. There is a strong sense in which Freeman was not at all interested in politics as the conduct of contemporary public affairs. No one could have been less what Bagehot liked to call 'a man of business'. He was interested in English politics not so much for its own sake as because he found it full of the resonance of the past. There is even a sense in which it is wrong to speak, as is always done, of his historical writing as essentially political history: this is true perhaps if the implied contrast is with social or economic or institutional history, but what excites him is not politics, for which he shows little taste or comprehension, but an idiosyncratic kind of cultural and universal history. What Freeman was interested in was heroes and restorations and the superimposition and inter-penetration of cultures – which he tended to speak of as races; his first book, a history of architecture,[48] epitomises the rest. The modern event for which he most ardently longed, the eviction of the Turk from Constantinople and the first Orthodox mass in the

---

[44] See particularly 'The Holy Roman Empire' and 'Frederick First King of Italy', *Hist. Ess.*, 1st series. [45] *Hist. Ess.*, 4th series, p. 87.

[46] Stephens, ii. 3–4, 8. Green, a less antiquarian democrat, rebuked him for this: 'Your indifference to the will of the people themselves is of the old Tory and Metternich order.' *Letters*, p. 262.

[47] Freeman admitted that he found budgets and financial matters incomprehensible. Stephens, i. 235, 269; ii. 179. [48] *History of Architecture* (1849).

reconsecrated church of St Sophia,[49] would have been for him not so much a desirable contemporary political occurrence as a kind of historical consummation, a final binding-up of the wounds of time.

It is this essentially historical, even antiquarian character of all Freeman's interests that we have to bear in mind in considering the first results of his newly acquired democratic sympathies in the 1850s. Nevertheless, the nearest he ever came to a practical political concern, apart from his later role in the anti-Turk agitation of the late 1870s, was his interest, at this time, in federalism. The combination of his comparative and historical interests and his sympathy with nationalist movements issued in 1863 in the first volume of his projected *History of Federal Government*, dealing primarily with ancient Greece; it was a mark of the fragility of this interest that the projected second volume, dealing with more recent times, was never written, but the initial impetus was a contemporary problem. The new national states would require constitutions, and Freeman's reading, chiefly it seems in Guizot, as well as his English predisposition in favour of the institutions of local self-government, convinced him that these should generally be federal.[50] Leagues of cities for a time fascinated him (he always loved historical parallels): Grote on the Achaean League in the latter days of Ancient Greece (the last, as well as the first, flickerings of 'freedom' and 'national' independence also had a special fascination for him), and Sismondi on the Lombard League in medieval Italy, in particular.[51] Grote and Sismondi are, as it were, the joint godfathers of his project on federal government.[52] Inevitably, in time he came to be disappointed by the reality of the new states. Italy proved overcentralised and philistine; Greece drove him almost to despair.[53] Bulgaria, still gratifyingly vague and potential,[54] and Montenegro, satisfyingly small and, to put it mildly, unbureaucratic, became the focus of his hopes.

There are some hints that the aridity of merely constitutional questions, when unredeemed by antiquarian interest, played a part in his abandonment of the work on federal government,[55] though

[49] *Hist. Ess.*, 3rd series, p. 449.   [50] Stephens, i. 171, 194, 240, 270.
[51] See 'Ancient Greece and Medieval Italy' (first pub. 1857); *Historical Essays*, 2nd series (1873).
[52] 'Sismondi and Grote should always lie open at the same moment,' *ibid.*, p. 8.
[53] Stephens, i. 343; ii. 45.   [54] Stephens, ii. 45.   [55] *ibid.*, i. 289.

more immediately important was the interruption of the project in favour of work on the Norman Conquest in the hope, disappointed until much later, of obtaining the Oxford Chair of History, vacated by Goldwin Smith.[56] In fact Stubbs was preferred, and it is a slightly odd thought that we may owe both the latter's *Constitutional History* and Freeman's *History of the Norman Conquest* to Goldwin Smith's resignation at that point. Meanwhile, however, before his interest in federalism waned, it had taken Freeman, naturally, to Switzerland, and in Switzerland he experienced a kind of epiphany, the incarnation of Demos in the form of a political myth made visible.

Despite the rather technical nature of the information on federal systems he ostensibly sought, Freeman seems, in any case, to have gone to Switzerland in an exalted mood, rather as a radical of a different tradition might have gone to Paris, city of revolutions.[57] Freeman, who concentrated on Paris all his combined Francophobia (which left him free to love the French provinces, consoling himself with the reflection that they were not originally 'French' at all)[58] his hatred of great capitals (he also hated London)[59] and his detestation of Napoleon III, seems to have gone gladly to Paris only once, in 1871, as he said, 'for a glimpse at ruins'.[60] Geneva he approached in 1863 with a pilgrim's excited reverence. Not, of course, for Calvin's sake, or Rousseau's, but 'I never was in a republic before, and I feel in a sort of paradise. I venerate every bill on the wall which has "République" at the top.'[61]

Switzerland as the home of liberty and hardy mountain simplicity was a powerful myth in English minds, long epitomised in the story of William Tell, in which, of course, Freeman did not literally believe. But the Swiss pikeman, the leveller of the battlefield in the later Middle Ages (like the English archer at Agincourt) who had broken the imperial armies and the chivalry of Austria in defence of his home and independence, had a mythic universality for others besides Freeman; Ruskin, for example: 'it was all for you and your sake that the grapes dropped blood from the press of St Jacob, and the pine-club struck down horse and helm in

---

[56] *ibid.*, pp. 335, 342–3.
[57] E.g. Alexander Herzen: 'If I might only see the Hôtel de Ville, the Café Foy in the Palais Royal where Camille Desmoulins picked a green leaf, stuck it on his hat for a cockade and shouted "à la Bastille".' *My Past and Thoughts* (tr. Constance Garnett, 1968), 4 vols, ii. 646. [58] Stephens, i. 295; ii. 306. *Hist. Ess.*, 4th series, p. 93.
[59] Stephens, ii. 211, 233. [60] *ibid.*, ii. 18. [61] *ibid.*, i. 286.

Morgarten Glen'.[62] The alpine shepherd, type of a noble simplicity, had long been recognised in English constitutionalist sentiment as a kind of unspoilt rustic cousin:

> Two voices are there; one is of the sea
> One of the mountains . . .[63]

Despite their formidable later reputation as professional soldiers, the Swiss of Morgarten could also be thought of as exemplary of the civic humanist's ideal of the nation in arms. Classical parallels were almost obligatory for 'the Marathonian tale':

> While Waterloo with Cannae's carnage vies,
> Morat and Marathon twin names shall stand;
> They were true Glory's stainless victories,
> Won by the unambitious heart and hand
> Of a proud, brotherly and civic band,
> All unbought champions in no princely cause
> Of vice-entailed Corruption . . .[64]

Gibbon similarly pointed a civic humanist moral, speaking of his two abandoned projects, on the history of Florence and 'The History of the Liberty of the Swiss': 'the one a poor, warlike, virtuous republic, which emerges into glory and freedom; the other a commonwealth, soft, opulent, and corrupt, which by degrees, is precipitated from the abuse to the loss of her liberty'.[65] Freeman was fully alert to the Byronic contrast at least, an alertness sharpened by renewed fear of the designs of Napoleonic France. He wrote of the citizen soldiery of Switzerland (he was always responsive to the idea of the nation in arms),

With what different feelings does one look upon them from the instruments of selfish ambition at which one shudders in the streets of every town in France! These are the descendants of the men who fought at Morgarten and at Sempach; they are the grandsons of the men who died upon their mountains when the sham democrats of Paris came to bind the yoke of Liberty, Equality and Fraternity upon a people more free, more equal, and more fraternal than themselves.[66]

The Swiss myth in fact was a composite one, composed of a harmony of equality and order ('Equality by Prudence governèd')[67] in a Spartan yet pastoral simplicity, as well as national independence.

[62] Ruskin, *Praeterita. An Autobiography* (O.U.P. 1978), p. 102.
[63] Wordsworth, 'On the subjugation of Switzerland' (1807).
[64] Byron, *Childe Harold's Pilgrimage*, iii. LXIV.   [65] Gibbon, *Memoirs*, p. 77.
[66] 'The Landesgemeinde of Uri', *Saturday Review*, xv (30 May 1863), 687.
[67] Wordsworth, 'The Town of Schwytz', *Memorials of a Tour on the Continent* (1820).

All these by now standard enthusiasms seem to have helped to predispose Freeman's mind as he went to seek his treasure beneath the mountains, while his contemporaries scaled the high peaks in search of sublimity, a form of athleticism and scenery-tasting he held in contempt.[68] The most recently supplied aspect of Freeman's preconceptions was provided by Kemble's theory of the *mark*-community, with its reference to the solemn 'Ding or court' of the Gà or shire at which 'thrice in the year the markmen assembled unbidden'.[69] It was such an assembly which Freeman saw in Switzerland in 1863 and 1864; it was Kemble's view of the *mark* as the nuclear cell of all Teutonic society which for Freeman made the Swiss literally political, as well as racial, cousins, and their surviving archaic institutions the equivalent of an archaeological site. Federalism was less interesting than political fossil-hunting: he seems to have felt a palaeontologist's excitement and awe at his discovery of this perfect specimen, the contemporary embodiment of the Tacitean myth. The revelation became one of the landmarks of his life. Years later, arriving for the first time in Spoleto, where the arches of Diocletian's palace were exciting to him as the first stirring of the Romanesque – he was always susceptible to the awesomeness of the primal spring – he wrote to his daughter that it was 'like getting one's fellowship or seeing one's first *Landesgemeinde*'.[70] His strong belief in the latter's constitutional significance is attested by his placing his description of it at the opening of *The Growth of the Constitution*.

It is a well-known passage, if any prose of Freeman's is well known, and he repeated it in several places, but it is best given in his original words, as he wrote them for the readers of the *Saturday Review* in 1864.

To the true student of political history – to him to whom the present and the past are alike realities – the scene is one which has not its parallel of earth. It is the realization of a dream; it is the bringing before the bodily sight of all that has been the object of the fondest imaginations of years. To stand, with the clear heaven above and the mountains on either side, and see the descendants of the men of Sempach and Morgarten discharge the immemorial rights of Teutonic freemen, is a sight which may well make us doubt whether we are in the common world or in some paradise of our own imagining. There, not in fancy, but in reality, is the eternal democracy, well-nigh as eternal as the hills that guard it – the constitution which was of immemorial antiquity in the days of Tacitus, and which, since the days of Tacitus, has suffered no interruption save during the

[68] Stephens, i. 216. Cf. Stephen, *Letters of John Richard Green*, p. 309.
[69] Kemble, *Saxons*, i. 74.   [70] Stephens, ii. 96.

momentary havock of the hordes of revolutionary France. The most ancient crowns of Kings and Popes and Caesars are things of yesterday beside the patriarchal honours of the Landammann of Uri.[71]

Freeman, clearly, was in that state of vibrant awe or exultation in which men feel themselves in the presence of living myth or even, sometimes, attach themselves to it, like Gibbon treading for the first time with a lofty step 'where Romulus stood, or Tully spoke, or Caesar fell'[72] or Macaulay witnessing the passage of the Reform Bill as already an historical event.[73]

At the risk of some repetition, it is worth analysing the content of Freeman's democratic epiphany. There is, for example, an interesting antitype of it, comparable in the luxuriance of its rhetoric, written a generation later and also dealing with the origin of political society: the opening of Frazer's *Golden Bough*. Frazer's well-known night-scene, with its evocation of the gloom and irrationality of primeval savagery marks the victory of the positivist over the Romantic conception of origins; the innocence of the pristine has been replaced by the darkness of the primitive. Freeman's generation, though it had begun to make the new geology part of its culture – Freeman, like Green, was a close friend of the geologist Boyd Dawkins and sometimes asked his advice – was still close to a time when the days of Creation were within the imaginable range of a few thousand years; close enough to be able to surround the idea of the primal with the glow of the world's first morning ('well-nigh as eternal as the hills that guard it').

Ostensibly Freeman's revelation was political, though the sense in which it was will bear examination. What matters, apart from the documentation of Tacitus, is the pristine transparency of this small, face-to-face polity; its negative virtues in the absence of kings or bureaucrats; and, above all, its historic associations which, unknown to the participants, extend beyond the range of the Teutonic world: we cannot attribute to the freemen of Uri 'any clear notion that the best description of his yearly assembly is to be found in a Roman writer nearly eighteen hundred years ago – still less that one point of attraction to the thoughtful stranger is the analogy which that assembly presents to the institutions of a still older Grecian city of which he probably never heard the name'.[74]

---

[71] 'The Landesgemeinden of Uri and Appenzell', *Saturday Review*, XVI (21 May 1864), 622.
[72] Gibbon, *Memoirs*, p. 84.   [73] See above, p. 70.   [74] *Saturday Review*, XVI. 623.

Even the charm of the setting had, of course, its historical authorisation: 'With the old Teutonic feeling which looked on a town as a prison, the Dêmos of Uri pitches its Pnyx under no meaner canopy than the sky.'[75]

The subject of the sovereign people's deliberations was not important; in the later article just cited Freeman admitted, with only the smallest perceptible irony, that it concerned, on this occasion, a licensing question: how late in the evening should dancing be permitted. Democratic assemblies can admittedly get excited over anything, but there was not much occasion here, obviously, for what Horner would have called 'the heat and pride of the debate',[76] nor is it clear that Freeman would have responded to it if there had been; his conception of popular government, whatever it was, was never agonistic. He clearly greatly liked, as he described it, the Teutonic orderliness and even stiffness of it all, the almost ritual enactment of the democratic process. He emphasised proudly to Stubbs the conservatism of these Swiss democrats,[77] and was anxious to show his readers how far this kind of face-to-face democracy was from mob rule (Macaulay was an identified opponent here).[78] 'Such a democracy as this is quite consistent with all external respect for authority' and with 'a large influence on the part of a sort of natural aristocracy'.[79]

But though democracy in the 1860s may have needed such defence, Freeman, for so keen a democrat, never seems to have felt much complicity with the process of discussion by which the people's will was supposedly ascertained. He had neither Macaulay's love of oratory and the parliamentary occasion, nor Bagehot's more low-key liking for the rational interchange of sensible men as a way of doing business. Green, who shared all Freeman's democratic enthusiasm, combined it with a boyish love of tumult: 'a crowd of Florentines shouting themselves hoarse on their Piazza are a greater and a nobler thing than all the Emperors that ever breathed'.[80] Freeman, on the contrary, always speaks of democracy in terms of unanimity; what stirred him was not debate but ratification, the approbatory clashing of spear on shield and 'the most spirit-stirring of earthly sounds, when a sovereign people binds itself to obey the laws which it has itself decreed, when thousands of voices join as one man in the rehearsal of one solemn

---

[75] *ibid.*, xv. 687.   [76] See above, p. 89.   [77] Stephens, ii. 298.
[78] *Hist.* Ess., ii. 130–3.   [79] *Saturday Review*, xv. 686.   [80] Stephen, *Letters*, p. 309.

formula'.[81] Democratic politics for Freeman was not theatre, much less a way of coping, but liturgy. Much of his preference for face-to-face democracy seems ultimately a ritual and sensuous one; only on such a scale could 'the people' be seen and heard and its unanimity be made manifest: taking a decision becomes a ritual of solidarity.

Freeman, apparently the most political of the 'Germanist' mid-Victorian historians – Stubbs being typed as 'constitutional' and Green as 'social' – was in fact the least interested in political processes. He had little or nothing of Stubbs' understanding of the complex interactions of selfish human behaviour operating through institutions; he had none of Green's response to the vital untidiness of contemporary life, whether in Italy or in the East End of London. Yet they too clearly felt, in the same way, the sensuous appeal of the face-to-face democracy of the town-meeting. It was this in part at least which underlay the idealisation of the notion of the village-community. The economic ideal of the *mark-community* as a body of co-proprietors made, it is true, little appeal to them, and unlike Kemble they largely discounted it, Green remarking merely that 'the toil necessitated by the system of common cultivation was severe'.[82] But Kemble's picture of the small group of settlers 'all recognizing a brotherhood, a kinsmanship or sibsceaft',[83] and the accounts by Stubbs, Green and Freeman of the village in its forest clearing, and the gathering of the folk-moot in the open air by its sacred tree or hill, have the obvious pathos of intimacy and a satisfying comprehensibility.

It was Green who excelled in this kind of evocation; his picture of the small Saxon town of the eighth century in *The Conquest of England* has the appeal of a primitive painting or of an illustration in a child's history book; no doubt it inspired many:

All the features of English life, in fact, all its characteristic features were already there. We see mills grinding along the burns, the hammer rings in the village smithy, the thegn's hall rises out of its demesne, the parish priest is at his mass-book in the little church that forms the centre of every township, reeves are gathering their lord's dues, forester and verderer wake the silent woodland with hound and horn, the moot gathers for order and law beneath the sacred oak or by the grey stone on the moor, along the shore the well-to-do salt-men are busy with their salt-pans, and the fishers are washing their nets in the little coast hamlets, and setting apart the due of fish for their lords.[84]

[81] NC, ii. 340.   [82] J. R. Green, The Making of England (1882), p. 187.
[83] Kemble, Saxons, i. 56–7.
[84] J. R. Green, The Conquest of England (2nd edn 1884), p. 7.

It is a less egalitarian picture than the parallel one in the earlier volume, *The Making of England*, of the free village-community;[85] there are lords and reeves, dues and, no doubt, tithes. The change is in itself regrettable to Green, but the later picture has, perhaps almost unintentionally, much the same charm as the earlier one for all that: its self-evidence and self-sufficiency, its compact symmetry, its sense of community and satisfying limits.

It would be wrong, in spite of this, no doubt, to go to the opposite extreme and deny all significant content to the cult of primitive Teutonic democracy, even in Freeman's case. It raised for him, as an enthusiasm for face-to-face democracy in the modern world has always done, genuine dilemmas; it constitutes, in a curious way, a qualification of his nationalism and of his Whig complacency, and it links his sentimental and antiquarian Teutonic republicanism to earlier civic humanist notions of republican virtue, giving him, what has not always characterised Teutonists, a love, not indeed of capitals, but of cities and civic independence.

Free cities and Imperial Rome

But this enthusiasm in Freeman was not primarily civic humanist, though there were similarities; it was philhellenic. Republican Rome, Livy and Plutarch, meant little, certainly less than the greater Emperors, though Caius Licinus and the Gracchi get occasional honourable mentions; Cicero had none of the influence over him that he had over Macaulay. He is never as explicit as Green about Plutarchian 'virtue' but he would no doubt have agreed when Green spoke of Madame Roland in the authentic tones of English Whiggism:

She is the child of Plutarch and Rousseau. Her creed of political and social faith, though it was life and death to her, is merely the string of silly paradoxes which Rousseau built up into a revolutionary philosophy, – original innocence of man, – original equality of the race, – social contracts, – human perfectibility, – and the like. Hollow ideas of this sort found congenial expression in the hollow rhetoric of Plutarch, the child of great 'decadence'. Nothing in the world is so intolerable as the taste for 'phrases' which their study of Plutarch gave to the French Revolutionists.[86]

Freeman shared to the full the Whig distaste for 'magnificent

85 *Making*, ch. IV.   86 Stephen, *Letters of John Richard Green*, p. 370.

theories and massacres in the cause of humanity'.[87] His own classical references, though copious to the point of obtrusiveness, are overwhelmingly Greek. But they are not, for once, instances of an idiosyncratic pedantry; they are the rhetorical patter – Timoleon and Cleisthenes, Marathon and Plataea and Pnyx – of the English philhellenes, which all his life was a natural patois to Freeman.[88] We have already seen how they pervade his response to the *Landesgemeinde*; the experience, like virtually all his experiences, came to him freighted with historical allusion. He had gone to Switzerland in 1863 with his head full not only of Kemble and Tacitus but of Athenian democracy and the Achaean League.

His chief source was Grote's *History of Greece*, which he had reviewed eulogistically in the *North British Review* in 1856. Freeman was in all things an enthusiast, and, at least in the 1850s and 1860s, highly impressionable;[89] they were his *Lehrjahre*. A handful of historians became intellectual mentors whose influence he never cast off: Arnold, Kemble, Palgrave, Sismondi, Grote, Finlay. Each, henceforth, had possession of a layer of his mind. He was generous with acknowledgements and never attempted to disguise his debts: to reconcile these mentors was necessarily to place, compare and bring together virtually every important political–cultural strand and epoch in the history of Europe: Ancient Greece, Imperial Rome, Byzantium, Tacitean democracy, municipal independence, Greek and Italian nationalism. To bring these together in a synthesis, which he called, after Arnold, establishing 'the Unity of History',[90] was also to assure himself of the reconcilability of the constitutive elements of his own mind.

In the pigeon-hole marked 'democracy' Grote was sovereign over the sub-section 'Greek' (though Freeman preferred Gladstone's more democratic treatment of the Homeric assemblies)[91] as Tacitus and Kemble were over its Teutonic counterpart. Freeman's philhellenism was, apart from a love of the Greek language, purely political, and it takes one as close as anything except his various hatreds to an understanding of what politics, at least in the 1850s and 1860s, meant to him. Cultural life, apart from architecture and epic literature, interested him hardly at all,

[87] *Hist. Ess.*, 1st series, p. 45.
[88] For this see W. L. St Clair, *That Greece Might Still Be Free*.
[89] Reading Grote was, he said, 'an epoch in a man's life', *Hist. Ess.*, 2nd series, p. 150.
[90] 'The unity of history' (The Rede Lecture 1872) printed with Freeman, *Comparative Politics, Six Lectures Read Before the Royal Institution*, 1873 (2nd edn 1896).
[91] 'Gladstone's Homer', *Hist. Ess.*, 2nd series, p. 84.

unless it could be subsumed into the categories of public life or political ideas. He always spoke of the cultural legacy of Greece, except its language, with a kind of jealousy, as though of a too successful rival: 'Athenian poetry and speculation have overshadowed the glory of Athenian democracy; Sophoklês and Plato have dimmed the brighter fame of Kleisthenes and Periklês';[92] he made the same complaint about the civic and cultural life of medieval Italy.[93] Freeman fully shared, if not always from the same sources, the Aristotelian and civic humanists' belief that participation in the life of the polis was the highest form of human life; we see man 'in his highest character as a member of a free state'.[94]

Above all this is true of the city-state: 'in the single city, each full citizen has his intellectual and political faculties sharpened to the highest pitch. Athens and Florence could reckon a soldier, a statesman, or a diplomatist, in every head of a free household.'[95] The decisive advantage of the city-state, counterbalancing the obvious disadvantage of almost incessant warfare, was the political education it gave its citizens;[96] there may be some influence of Arnold here, by whom political education was much stressed.[97] Freeman's references to this quality of the city-state have an un-Whiggish wistfulness: representative democracy can be only a tepid recreation of its virtues,[98] though 'No means of improvement, save the unattainable standard of the Athenian Assembly, is equal to that offered by a good system of local Self-Government'[99] (the note here refers us to Tocqueville). The attraction of federalism for him is chiefly that it offers a chance of perpetuating at least some shadow of the virtues of the polis in an age of large states.[100] There is no possibility of the literal recreation of the former after the establishment of standing armies, just as the *Landesgemeinde* of Uri is essentially a charming fossil.[101] Freeman's discussion of the disadvantages of the city-state is like Macaulay's,[102] but the tone is warmer and there is a marked nostalgia. Freeman had, as we have seen, no condescension towards the citizen-soldier and a

---

[92] *ibid.*, p. 3.   [93] *ibid.*, p. 4.   [94] *ibid.*, p. 156. Cf. pp. 7, 336.   [95] *ibid.*, p. 15.

[96] Freeman, *History of Federal Government in Greece and Italy* (2nd edn 1893), p. 29.

[97] Thomas Arnold, *Introductory Lectures on Modern History* (delivered 1841–2) (6th edn 1874), esp. pp. 13–19. *History of Rome* (new edn 1857), 3 vols, i. 18.

[98] *Fed. Govt.*, pp. 31, 64, 67–8.   [99] *ibid.*, p. 82.

[100] *ibid.*, p. 69.   [101] *ibid.*, p. 49; *Saturday Review*, xvi. 623.

[102] Like Macaulay in 'Machiavelli' and 'Mitford's Greece' (see above), he stresses the consant warfare and its total character. *Fed. Govt.*, pp. 42–6.

very marked traditionally radical hatred of standing armies.[103] Bryce wondered that Freeman, who hated militarism, should so have loved describing battles.[104] It was an easy paradox: Freeman loved a battle, best of all when it could be seen as a clash of cultures or races, but he cherished the amateur spirit; in practice he tolerated a professionalism such as that of King Harold's housecarls[105] if it could be presented as a Tacitean brotherhood-in-arms.[106]

Yet there is little sign that Freeman much entered into the actual process of democratic life in the Greek city-states; he left that to Grote. Thucydides, though he evoked an awed admiration, clearly repelled him; that clinical coldness was not Freeman's style at all.[107] What he liked was the myth, the confrontation with Asiatic despotism – so like, to him, the Eastern Question of his own day[108] – and the roll-call of heroes. Yet his enthusiasm was not simply dissipated in rhetoric. What it gave him, of larger importance in his work, was a sympathy with the concept of civic autonomy. A city too was bounded, compact, comprehensible, like a *Landesgemeinde*, with the added advantage of being more permanently visible.

Such a liking was not an invariable trait in the 'Germanist' historian; there is a note of approval in Stubbs' recording of Tacitus' Germans' dislike of cities.[109] As a Tory, Stubbs seems to enjoy finding a good word for one of Macaulay's butts, the county member of Parliament. The system of county representation was the peculiarity and, it is implied, the glory of England. 'If it had not been for the county representatives forming a body of independent men, unvarying in number and position, the representative system might have died out altogether, or become powerless as it did in other countries.'[110] English liberty was rural, not urban.

The country or village communities are a system common to all Teutonic races, and their whole administration is founded in freedom, in the spirit and discipline

---

103 E.g. Stephens, *Life*, ii. 198–9. Cf. 'What can Greece want with an army? Surely Switzerland is the model for a country in that sort of position; no army, but every man a soldier.' *ibid.*, i. 334.

104 Bryce, *Contemp. Biog.*, p. 291.   105 NC, iii. 473, 501. Also i. Appendix KKK.

106 *Comparative Politics*, p. 169; *Growth of the Constitution*, p. 48. Only Freeman could have referred, in the latter, to 'what is undoubtedly a trace of the Teutonic *comitatus*, the fagging of our public schools'.

107 *Hist. Ess.*, 2nd series, pp. 99–100.

108 E. A. Freeman, *The Chief Periods of European History. Six Lectures read in the University of Oxford, 1885* (1886), pp. 5–6.

109 CH, i. 92.   110 *ibid.*, p. 316. Cf. CH, iii. 608.

of the ancient free allodialism. The town or burgher communities are, on the other hand, founded on privilege, spring from a state of servitude . . .[111]

Stubbs insisted, more vehemently than Green or Freeman, on the purely Teutonic origins of English freedom, owing nothing to Greek ideas or Roman municipal traditions.[112] He felt a Christian distaste for the ancient world, particularly the Roman,[113] which they did not share, and it underlay his determination, which they disapproved of, to make the distinction between ancient and modern history a real and firm one.[114]

Green's love of municipality, by contrast, lay at the centre of his view of the world. Born into a family of Oxford tradesmen, he seems to have carried the resentments of the Town with him into the University, in which he never felt at ease.[115] One of his essays is a bitter account of the stifling of Oxford's older municipal life by the overmighty clerical corporation which had grown up alongside it and overwhelmed it.[116] It was no doubt this which sharpened the sense of conflict so evident in another of his major essays, on a town in a similar situation, Bury St Edmunds.[117] Green's essay neatly inverts Carlyle's *Past and Present*, though it is not quite certain how far Green intended this. Carlyle mentions the tensions between Abbey and townsfolk, but he emphasises not only the patriarchal rule of Abbot Samson but also the fact that the whole town, brought into being by the abbey and the cult of the saint, is in a sense St Edmund's tomb, 'in one of the brick niches of which dwells the present respectable Mayor of Bury'.[118] Green takes up the story at a different point, with the aged Samson's concession of the town's charter, and tells the story of the townspeople's long, sometimes violent, struggle to preserve and enlarge their liberties against the manorial overlordship of the abbey. It is, in Green's telling, the story, in miniature, of the emancipation of the English people from feudal oppression. The freedom of the borough for Green derived from the source of all Teutonic freedom, the folk-moot, and it was the boroughs which had been the frail arks in which that freedom had been brought safely through the deluge of the Norman Conquest: 'The town-motes of the Norman reigns tided free discussion over from the

---

[111] *EEH*, p. 111.   [112] *ibid.*, pp. 197, 334.   [113] E.g. *ibid.*, p. 237.   [114] *SI*, p. 16.
[115] Stephen, *Letters of J. R. Green*, p. 14.
[116] 'The early history of Oxford', *Stray Studies from England and Italy*, 1st series (1876).
[117] 'Abbot and town', *ibid.*
[118] Carlyle, *Past and Present* (Everyman edn), p. 55.

Witenagemot of the old England to the Parliament of the new.'[119]

But there was another form of municipality, older, grander, directly linked with the civic life of antiquity, if ultimately less fortunate than the more modest English developments in local self-government. Green recognised in it another story of liberty than the English: it was a story in essence derived from the writers of the Scottish Enlightenment, from Smith and Robertson in particular – a fact apparently, when Green was writing a century later, entirely forgotten – but it had become standard among the continental liberals of the first half of the nineteenth century. For Green's generation it was the story told by Sismondi for Italy and Thierry for France, of the revival of a spirit of liberty from the twelfth century onwards in the town communes of the continent, and stemming from it another political tradition and another rhetoric of liberty from the one to which Englishmen were accustomed. It was a rare act of magnanimity in an English Whig historian to recognise this as Green did, prompted by his democratic sentiments, and his love of Italy and of the relics of Italian municipal grandeur; to sympathise with the medieval 'democracy of traders and craftsmen struggling to be free',[120] and the alien form of political eloquence derived from it:

Instead of the basis of property on which Teutonic freedom had rested, this new freedom took for its basis man himself . . . .. It stands now in direct opposition to the speech of Teutonic, of constitutional liberty, of the freedom based on custom and slow development, which, at the hour of Italian decadence, revived again in the Parliament of the Plantagenets. To Englishmen the eloquence of Garibaldi or Victor Hugo is almost unintelligible, but it is fair to remember that this type of free speech, and not our own, the eloquence of sentiment rather than of reason, is the type which is dearest and most intelligible to half the lovers of freedom throughout the world.[121]

Freeman's civic sympathies fell somewhere between Stubbs' and Green's but much nearer the latter's. They were in part architectural. Helped by trains, Freeman made travel an essential preparation for historical writing.[122] It was a trait he shared with the Liberal Anglican historians – Arthur Stanley was an almost heroic traveller in the services of history – inspired, possibly, as in their case, by admiration for Arnold;[123] J. C. Hare, introducing the

[119] Green, *Stray Studies*, 2nd series, p. 88. Cf. *Short History*, pp. 92–3.
[120] 'Como', *Stray Studies*, 2nd series, p. 36.
[121] *ibid*. pp. 40–1.
[122] See Freeman, *The Reign of William Rufus and the Accession of Henry the First* (O.U.P. 1882), 2 vols (henceforth cited as *WR*), Preface, i. p. viii. Cf. Stephens, *Life*, i. 109.
[123] Duncan Forbes, *The Liberal Anglican Idea of History* (C.U.P. 1952), p. 140.

latter's *History of Rome*, spoke of 'the most remarkable among his talents, his singular geographical eye'.[124] To the latter quality Freeman added his own acute sense of the historical testimony of architecture, though he never took it to the lengths of Ruskinian moralism. But there was clearly a massive difference in weight and intensity between Freeman's attempts to decipher the lessons of urban topography, and of architecture as cultural or strategic self-assertion, and Macaulay's visits to battlefields and travels in search of associations. Green's and Freeman's work in town history represented a revitalisation and immense imaginative extension of the older piecemeal antiquarianism. Freeman complained bitterly of 'minds which cannot understand that the tracing out of the features and history of a city may be as truly a scientific business to one man as the study of the surrounding *flora* and *fauna* is to another'.[125] Such work rested, of course, in part on the growing network of local archaeological societies, references to whose papers are frequent in Green's and Freeman's footnotes, and to which they themselves belonged. It needed, besides imagination and accuracy, a sense of historical perspective and an eye for comparison. Freeman, in particular, loved to compare his specimens, running them through his mind, feeling out their structure, arranging and cross-referencing. Thus Exeter, for example, perhaps his favourite among English cities, called up not only associations but analogies: with Marseilles, as a town whose Latin name had endured; with Bourges and Chartres, Le Mans and Caen as Celtic hill-forts in unbroken occupation; and in its site, and, by contrast, in its relation to its river, with Bristol and Châlons.[126]

It was Green, as Freeman readily acknowledged, who was the pioneer: 'it was from him that I first learned to look on a town as a whole with a kind of personal history, instead of simply the place where such and such a church or castle was to be found'.[127] Green himself complained – he found Freeman one culprit – of the abandonment of archaeology to 'country parsons and old maids'[128] and its practice 'as a study of ecclesiastical architecture slightly tempered by an enthusiasm for Roman camps and old helmets'.[129] His own conception was very different:

There is hardly any better historic training for a man than to set him frankly in the streets of a quiet little town like Bury St Edmunds, and let him work out the

[124] Arnold, *History of Rome*, Introduction, i. p. vii.   [125] *Hist. Ess.*, 4th series, p. vi.
[126] Freeman, *English Towns and Districts* (1883), p. 56.
[127] *ibid.*, p. ix; Cf. NC, iv. Preface.   [128] *Stray Studies*, 2nd series, p. 85.
[129] *ibid.*, p. 86.

history of the men who lived and died there. In the quiet, quaintly-named streets, in the town-mead and the market-place; in the lord's mill beside the stream, in the ruffed and furred brasses of its bishops in the Church, lies the real life of England and Englishmen, the life of their home and their trade, their ceaseless, sober struggle with oppression, their steady unwearied battle for self-government. It is just in the pettiness of its details, in its commonplace incidents, in the want of marked features and striking events that the real lesson of the whole story lies.[130]

Bryce describes Green, in a strange town, 'darting hither and thither through the streets like a dog trying to find a scent'.[131]

Green's feeling for humdrum activity, obscure, repetitive, slowly transforming, so reminiscent of Carlyle and George Eliot, is an aspect of that extension outwards and downwards of the Whig tradition referred to in an earlier chapter. Freeman's urban perceptions were more channelled, predictable and official: an eye for the lie of church and castle and city wall, and their implications. (Green characteristically remarked of the ecclesiastical parts of *The Norman Conquest* 'I wish your church wasn't so Bishopy.')[132] It is doubtful if he would, like Green, have noted, in Troyes, the whirl of the stocking looms and the cotton bales piled in the courtyards as 'the continuation of an industrial energy which reaches back for eight hundred years'.[133] But Freeman's eye for urban topography immensely enriches his histories of the Conquest and of the reign of Rufus, giving the spare narratives of the Chronicles a solidity of location and a visual immediacy which was the sediment of hours, some spent with Green, pacing quiet streets in Normandy and Maine, tracing the invisible outlines of vanished walls and towers, or in exalted, erudite contemplation of great buildings, accompanied by imprecations against restorers and the vandalism of Renaissance and Revolution, of *préfet* and *maire*. Sometimes, it is true, the history becomes more like an antiquary's tour, the Norman chapters an historical companion to Cotman's *Antiquities of Normandy*, which he often cites; William the Conqueror's and his son's campaigns in England and Maine become an inventory of town histories.[134] Occasionally the effort strains into a Macaulayan bathos:

of the mighty pile which now commands the Fécamp valley, that huge length of nave which almost rivals our own St Alban's, that central tower so stately in its simple majesty, that Lady Chapel where the rich work of later days contrasts with the stern dignity of the thirteenth century, not a stone had yet arisen.[135]

[130] *ibid.*, 1st series, pp. 218–19.   [131] Bryce, *Contemp. Biog.*, p. 153.
[132] Stephen, *Letters of J. R. Green*, p. 302.   [133] Green, *Stray Studies*, 2nd series, p. 20.
[134] E.g. *NC*, iv. 160; *WR*, i. 318.   [135] *NC*, iv. 87.

But such a love of cities, bounded and visible – one suspects that Freeman liked hill-sites best not only for their antiquity but because they could be taken in at one glance – bearing in their varied architecture and in the configuration of street and precinct and mound the tangible evidence of a continuous past, could hardly fail to be accompanied by a sympathy with the municipal freedom which meant so much to Green. It was, predictably, for Freeman less a matter of internal politics, more of external independence. He did not mourn so much as Green for the usurpation of the rights of the citizenry by a civic oligarchy, though he noted the latter's restrictiveness and privilege,[136] but more for the extinction of the city as a political unit; a 'free city' was for him not one in which aldermen were kept in their place but one owning no earthly superior except perhaps the distant emperor; it was a kind of nationalism in little, and in some ways the more satisfying for it.

The tone of Freeman's references to it is, of course, necessarily elegiac. The day of the free cities was over. In France, or rather, in what he obstinately insisted on regarding as the lost lands of the empire usurped by the Duchy of Paris, their subjugation aroused his indignation: 'Independent Orange, besides its Prince, its Bishop and his Chăpter, had its Parliament, its University and its Con-sults. All that it seems to have now is a Mayor.'[137] But he was forced to recognise, reluctantly, the centralising tendencies also at work in the 'new' states whose rise he had so applauded, and he continued to hope for federal solutions for them: 'no lover of Italy could bear to see Milan and Venice and Florence and the Eternal City itself sink into dependencies of the Savoyard', he had written in 1857.[138] He feared too for the Hanse towns in a united Germany, and would only admit that elsewhere 'the loss of local freedom has *perhaps* been outweighed by admission into a wider national unity'.[139]

In Freeman's philosophy of history and politics as he set it out in *Comparative Politics* (1873), the city-state, though part of the story of political freedom, was ultimately an abortive experiment. It was, as it proved, the good fortune and the achievement of the Teutonic world to have passed, in the most privileged case of England, from village community and tribalism to the modern political unit, the nation-state, with no purely civic episode such as

[136] E.g. *ibid.*, p. 208.   [137] *Hist. Ess.*, 4th series, p. 93. Cf. on Le Mans *WR*, ii. 219.
[138] *Hist. Ess.*, 2nd series, p. 50.   [139] *Chief Periods*, p. 203, italics mine.

the whole Greek and Roman world had experienced. And in the nation-state the political invention of representation made good, in another form, the loss of the ancient liberty of face-to-face democracy. This was a typical, though in its detail fairly novel version of English Whig constitutionalism: bland, progressive and optimistic. In it, England preserved her traditional role of political pathfinder and instructress of the nations.

But if we take Freeman's work as a whole, we have a rather different, more grandiose but less complacent story, tinged, as we have already seen, with regrets not altogether appeasable, and made complex by divided sympathies. It was not only that Freeman's ideal story would perhaps have ended in federalism, with the English constitution as a successful aberration, or that a vote in a general election was a somewhat meagre consolation for the many-sided personal development of the ideal Athenian democrat. There was also an undeniable emotional pull towards an idea of universal history, with Rome at its centre, in which England was inescapably, however glorious her destiny, essentially peripheral. In this wider and longer perspective, even the Whig's vaunting of England's constitutional continuity was muted a little.

There is an essay of Freeman's, entitled 'French and English Towns',[140] in which he generalised his insights into urban historical topography, which is relevant here. It is one of his most attractive shorter pieces, vivid and reflective in his usual comparative vein; it is little detraction from its merits that a similar but briefer treatment of the same themes had been published earlier by Green.[141] Freeman's love of provincial France and his Francophobia, which he usually managed to rationalise into a hatred of Paris and the French nation as an entity, was always a source of some emotional confusion to him; here he managed to think it through, at least partially. For once, though the specifically political message is the contrary, the balance of advantage, not only in grandeur but in one kind of continuity, lies with 'all that revolutionary havoc has left of an old French city'.[142]

But the essay is not only an evocative meditation; it is also an enquiry. Why are there so many more French hill-top cities than English ones? Why does the French city surpass the English in the picturesqueness of its streets and the size of its churches? Why do French cities more resemble each other in size, neither very

[140] *Hist. Ess.*, 4th series.   [141] Green, 'Rochester', *Stray Studies*, 2nd series.
[142] *Hist. Ess.*, 4th series, p. 25.

small nor very large? The typical French town is 'the old, respectable, steady-going local capital, which has been the local capital since the beginning of things, and which seems as if it must go on being the local capital to the end of things'.[143] It is not in all respects that France is more centralised than England. 'No town in England has been a capital for many ages, in the same sense that these old French towns are still capitals.'[144] They have, often, judges and a bar; they are centres of education and social centres in a way now unknown in England, but for which Edinburgh supplies the best British parallel; the hotels of the *noblesse* are still sometimes inhabited by their owners. There is not, as there frequently is in England, the division between the civil and the ecclesiastical capital of the district; the dioceses coincide with the departments, while English dioceses do not usually coincide with counties.

Such questions and observations are now commonplace; then they were a new kind of history, a comparative urban history and historical travelogue which Green and Freeman did much to create. The latter part of Freeman's essay offers answers, but the essay is above all a celebration of continuity: of the Gaulish hill-stronghold, the memory of it often perpetuated not only in site but in name, which became a Roman city; Christianity in turn plants itself, not in missionary outposts, but in the still surviving centres of Roman urban life; the churches rise on the sites of the temples. The cities survived the barbarian invasions. The Middle-Ages draws its protecting walls around the suburbs, while the line of the Roman wall makes the inner *cité*.

So it is at Limoges; so it is, in a more striking shape, in the wonderful city of Le Puy. There the *cité* still sits on the height of the rock, with no small remnants of the walls that fenced in that marvellous church, raised high on soaring arches, with the dwellings of priests and nobles around it. There too is the lowlier *ville*, home of burghers and friars, gathering at the foot and on the slopes of the hill. One almost wonders that one does not find, as at Chur and at Syra, one form of worship practised at the top of the hill and another at the bottom.[145]

Even such an attractive characteristic feature of the English cathedral city as its close is a sign of novelty; in England the city grew around the church, or at least the bishop entered the existing city as a great potentate, but 'in the immemorial city, where the bishopric was as old as the Christian empire, there was no room for a distinct ecclesiastical quarter'.[146]

[143] *ibid.*, p. 27.   [144] *ibid.*, p. 29.   [145] *ibid.*, p. 41.   [146] *ibid.*, p. 43.

It is an essay, quite apart from its intrinsic merits, to set, in Freeman's work, beside the death of Harold at Hastings, the repeated yearnings for a reconsecrated St Sophia, and the settlement in the spring of 1863 by the freemen of Uri of their *Tanzfrage*. Its themes lay, with them, at the vital centre of his thought and feelings. Inevitably he repeated them elsewhere, with what R. T. Shannon happily calls his 'variant repetitiousness',[147] sometimes more rhetorically and emphatically. The overt political message of the essay is clear. What the civic has lost, in England, the nation has gained. England's earlier and firmer national unity happily prevented any such flowering of civic life; the nobility lived on their estates in a more serene countryside.[148] It is oddly, and not without strain, that Freeman finds himself the spokesman of centralisation, but even at the emotional moment when William the Conqueror receives the surrender of Exeter Freeman remembers that he is an English Whig historian. Exeter held a special place for him, as the most continental of English cities, in the continuity of its life from Celtic times, and in the chance he fancied it might have had, as capital of its remote region, as a free English civic commonwealth. But Exeter was not to become as Bern and Florence.[149] English history was characterised, as Freeman remarked when considering the similar case of Lincoln, by 'the steady advance of the whole realm, as opposed to the most brilliant development of particular cities'.[150]

But it was not only civic independence which, half-unwillingly, Freeman responded to, but antiquity and continuity. True France held the advantage only in the physical sense; English civic continuity was to be found in her institutions.[151] It was a point Green made more emphatically, in the context of the same argument:

Oxford is not so old or so grand as Rouen, but the chief magistrate of Rouen has dwindled into a Government official, while the Mayor of Oxford, if he has but command of nine policemen, of whom one is superannuated and the rest incapable, is still the lineal descendant of the mayor named in the charter of John.[152]

But such is Freeman's joy in the antiquity and grandeur of the cities of France and the zest of his rhetoric in their celebration that

---

[147] Shannon, *Gladstone*, p. 81.   [148] *Hist. Ess.*, 4th series, p. 42.   [149] *NC*, iv. 148.
[150] *ibid.*, p. 208. Cf. Green, *Stray Studies*, 2nd series, p. 45.
[151] *Hist. Ess.*, 4th series, p. 48.   [152] *Stray Studies*, 2nd series, p. 116.

even national peace and equity and lineally descended mayors were bound to seem, in that context, a poorish consolation.

Even the scouring completeness of the English conquest and settlement, and the exterminations of Welshmen, the accounts of which normally gave him so much pleasure,[153] as the necessary foundation of England's Teutonic homogeneity in race and institutions, took on, in Freeman, a shade of wistfulness when it came to towns:

> The grass which once grew over the temples and houses of Deva and Aquae Solis, the grass which still grows over the temples and houses of Calleva and Anderida, is the best witness to the difference between the English Conquest of Britain and the Gothic, Burgundian, and Frankish conquests of other lands.[154]

To rejoice, as he and Green and Stubbs frequently did, that the village and tribal boundaries of the English settlement were preserved in modern parish and diocesan ones, was well enough.[155] As Freeman put it on his own behalf, 'The Teutonic settlement in this island becomes more of a living thing to one who finds that the boundary of the land which Ceawlin won from the Briton abides, after thirteen hundred years, the boundary of his own parish and his own fields.'[156] But it seems a slightly rustic and even meagre compensation for 'those ancient cities of central Gaul, which, now, no less than in the days of Caesar and in the old time before him, still sit, each one as a lady for ever, by the banks of their ancient rivers or by the proud crests of their everlasting hills',[157] and the rhetoric marks the difference.

Freeman's celebrations of continuity, in fact, always take on a particular sonorousness when the continuity is Roman and imperial. The medieval empire, what Stubbs called 'the curse of the imperial system',[158] had many attractions for Freeman: as Teutonic; as combining universality with a wide latitude for civic autonomy; and as the grandest example of continuity that Europe could show. In so far as Freeman found difficulty in being a Whig historian it was partly because he wanted to be a Whig on a European scale. Even Switzerland was precious to him not only as republican and federal but as a severed fragment of the Empire: 'Basel, Basilia, in her very name brings up thoughts of Empire.'[159]

---

[153] Stephens, *Life*, p. 415.   [154] *Towns and Districts*, p. 54.
[155] E.g. Stubbs, *EEH*, p. 15; Green, *Stray Studies*, 2nd series, p. 449. Freeman, *Hist. Ess.*, 4th series, p. 235; *NC*, i. 8.
[156] *NC*, v. pp. ix–x.   [157] *NC*, iii. 147, 'a lady for ever', Isaiah, 47.7.
[158] *CH*, i. 6.   [159] *Chief Periods*, p. 198.

Part of his detestation of Napoleon III and Franz Joseph derived from his sense that they were impostors, illegitimate pretenders to the imperial title.[160] Freeman's nostalgic imperialism owed something to his hatreds: the medieval Empire had been the buffer against the relentless aggrandisement of the duke of Paris and his heirs in the West,[161] as Byzantium against the Turk in the East.

But there were deeper and more mysterious sources. Freeman's mind was in some respects almost a medieval one. He had a medieval feeling for the universal and for the local and particular which sometimes jarred with his Teutonic tribal nationalism. Some of the themes and formulae of a medieval universal historian like Eusebius[162] seem to have come naturally to him, quite apart from any question of influence, though we must no doubt make allowance for his long exposure to the Chroniclers, as well as the continuing influence in the nineteenth century of Christian and apocalyptic conceptions of history, as we see in Arnold.[163] In part of his mind Freeman was always, as he admitted, 'democrat as I am', captive to eternal Rome: 'the Romanorum Imperator semper Augustus, impressed me with considerable awe – wherefore I have the more loathing for these miserable pseudo-Caesars in Austria and France'.[164] Green disapprovingly noted his tenderness for emperors. Their travels in Italy together, in fact, seem to have been less harmonious than those in France. Freeman felt that Italy seduced Green too far from his Teutonic allegiance, Green that Freeman's imperialist sympathies led him to undervalue Italian civic freedom:

with all your architectural devotion you could still find room for enthusiasm whenever an emperor came on the stage. There was no indifference when you stood before the figure of Frederick or the tomb of Henry. It was only when you stood before some memorial of the people that you took refuge in your sketching book.[165]

Freeman himself admitted divided loyalties confronted by 'the assertors of the venerable rights of the Roman Caesars and . . . the assertors of the new-born freedom of the commonwealth of Lombardy'.[166] Freeman was accustomed to claim always that 'As far at least as our race is concerned, freedom is everywhere older

---

[160] *Hist. Ess.*, 1st series, p. 162. *Chief Periods*, pp. 151–2.
[161] *Chief Periods*, pp. 195–8, *Hist. Ess.*, 1st series, p. 131; 4th series, p. 87.
[162] Beryl Smalley, *Historians in the Middle Ages* (1974).
[163] Arnold, *Introductory Lectures*, pp. 29–30.   [164] Stephens, *Life*, p. 237.
[165] Stephen, *Letters*, p. 309.   [166] *Hist. Ess.*, 1st series, p. 274.

than bondage'.[167] Confronted by a situation in which venerability told the other way he became less partisan than usual.

There is no mystery about the immediate sources of Freeman's imperialism: the remoter source may have been Arnold, but the more direct one was Sir Francis Palgrave. In 1858, writing to the historian of Greece, George Finlay, Freeman said, speaking of Palgrave: 'I make my historical system out of an union of you two. Between you you work out that the Roman Empire did not die in 476, but lived on as long as you please after. You do the East, which has been forgotten, he the West, which has been misconceived.'[168] It was no casual compliment. In the course of lectures on European history he delivered in Oxford many years later the same influences are still dominant.[169] In Finlay he found the resources for his sympathetic interest in Byzantium and the pathos of its end; the Christians of the East were now, as it were, a lost nation on the grandest racial, religious and imperial scale, a submerged empire.

But of the two there is no question that Palgrave exerted the more comprehensive influence.[170] The themes – continuity, empire, apocalypse – which in Freeman are muted by his allegiance to Teutonic democracy and his diluted Christianity, are openly proclaimed by Palgrave. If the latter's was also in some respects a medieval mind it was one which knew and confidently asserted its medieval dogmas, which Green called 'great twaddle'.[171] Palgrave's basic historical scheme was the traditional patristic one of the Four Empires, of which Rome would be the last. Rome, in all her wickedness, had the grandeur of God's chosen instrument.[172] Quite apparent too, in Palgrave, is the Renaissance German conception of the *translatio*, the transmission from the Italians to the Germans of the imperial authority.[173] Palgrave adopted the idea of the *translatio*, not surprisingly, not only as a necessary feature of the providential historical scheme, preserving Rome for the consummation of all history,[174] but as an

---

[167] *Growth of the Constitution*, p. x.   [168] Stephens, *Life*, i. 237.

[169] Published as *Chief Periods of European History*.

[170] 'I got my imperial ideas from Palgrave, strengthened by Finlay.' Stephens, ii. 68.

[171] Stephen, *Letters*, p. 153.

[172] 'The history of Normandy and England' (1851) in Sir R. H. Inglis Palgrave (ed.), *The Collected Historical Works of Sir Francis Palgrave* (C.U.P. 1921), i. chs 1 and 2. Ch. 1 is entitled 'The Fourth Monarchy'.

[173] See Kliger, *The Goths in England*, pp. 41ff.

[174] 'History therefore becomes a continuous drama', etc. Palgrave, *op. cit.*, i. 2. See also 'This devolution of authority from Rome . . .', pp. 4–5.

instance of a truth more familiarly proclaimed by the political experience of England. Apocalyptic history foresakes the imagery of Daniel for the primmer language of the English Whig: 'No method of reforming ancient institutions is so safe and efficatious as that which can be produced by an examination of their original nature.'[175]

Freeman's vocabulary was, of course, more circumspect, less Eusebian and Biblical than Palgrave's, but there is no doubt that he derived from him the notion of the Roman empire as the centre of universal history,[176] and with it the tang of providential and apocalyptic ideas. He even made it into a kind of personal theodicy, as a substitute for more orthodox Christianity.[177] But he was also fascinated by the empire as, in Palgrave's terms, history's greatest example of continuity; he seems sometimes to have felt it required of him an almost global kind of Whiggism which, as we have seen, co-existed uncomfortably with more parochial Whig and democratic loyalties. He was fascinated, above all, by the joints in the universal-historical machinery he had constructed out of Arnold and Palgrave and Finlay, by the moments of transition and amalgamation and their surviving architectural evidence. The concept of the *translatio*, though he does not use the actual term and there is no evidence that he was aware of its source, was always deeply stirring for him: 'The vigorous youth of the Teutonic race had decked itself in the Imperial garb of elder days, and appealed to the proudest associations, both of the old and of the new state of things.'[178]

The Aryan brotherhood

Freeman, in fact, had an archaeologist's fascination with the superimposition of cultures, and with reading history – above all, of course, through architecture – as a palimpsest. It was part of the attraction to him of Byzantium that it was 'Greek and Roman at once',[179] and this too which made Ravenna 'for me the grandest place in the world'.[180] This is a theme to which we shall have to return in the next chapter. The counterpart of Freeman's fierce

[175] 'The rise and progress of the English Commonwealth' (1837), Palgrave, *Works*, vi. 7.
[176] See particularly *Chief Periods*, passim.
[177] Stephens, ii. 389.　　[178] *Hist. Ess.*, 2nd series, p. 20.
[179] NC, v. 506; cf. 'The Byzantine Empire', *Hist. Ess.*, 3rd series (a review of Finlay).
[180] Stephens, ii. 15. Cf. 'The Goths at Ravenna', *Hist. Ess.*, 3rd series.

racial antipathies, in fact, was inclusiveness. He loved the moments of amalgamation because they swelled the team of the righteous. He had a schoolboy's love of World Elevens, heroic brotherhoods and roll-calls of heroes of all the ages: it was Whig piety become ecumenical in scale. Race, of course, was the adhesive agent. As he said, quite self-consciously, 'Ethnological and philological researches ... have opened the way for new national sympathies, new national antipathies, such as would have been unintelligible a hundred years ago.'[181] What Freeman could do with such an opening and the powerful identifications it licensed – powerful at least to him – is frequently apparent: 'We have our part in the great deliverance by the wood of Teutoberg; Arminius, "liberator Germainiae", is but the first of a roll call which goes on to Hampden and to Washington.'[182]

But the circle of Teutonic kin was not the outer edge of the newly acquired racial sympathies. Freeman's Teutonic exclusiveness had its extension in an 'Aryan' inclusiveness. The concept of an Aryan race and stock of institutions, derived from the philological discovery of the Indo-European family of languages, captivated Freeman, as it did so many other scholars of his generation. His *Comparative Politics* was his attempt, analogous to Sir Henry Maine's work on the development of law,[183] to reconstruct the subsequent history of the primitive stock of Aryan social and political institutions. It was into this context that he fitted his idea of the branching history of Aryan freedom; one, the classical line, leading to the impasse of the city-state; the other, the Teutonic, leading directly from the village-community to tribalism and the nation-state and the invention of representative government. It was thus that Freeman offered his understanding of the relevant 'science' as the comparative base for his varied historical and political interests, just as the History of Civil Society had given a comparable intellectual and comparative framework to Macaulay. The reception of *Comparative Politics* seems to have been disappointing,[184] but though bold it was in no sense an eccentric work. Stubbs, for example, though he did not share Freeman's excitement, and when told of the subject of Freeman's lectures commented that it was 'largish',[185] wrote that it was 'quite lawful to work back, through obvious generalisations and comparisons

---

[181] *Hist. Ess.*, 3rd series, p. 179.   [182] *Chief Periods*, p. 64.
[183] See Burrow, *Evolution and Society*, ch. 5.   [184] See Stephen, *Letters*, p. 405.
[185] Hutton (ed.), *Letters*, p. 164.

with the early phenomena of society in other nations, to the primitive civilizations of the Aryan or the Indo-Germanic family'.[186] It was only an extension of the German historians' idea of a common original stock of Teutonic institutions which could be reconstructed comparatively using Scandinavian and Icelandic as well as German and English evidence.

The concept of an Aryan race and the importance scholars in the second half of the nineteenth century attached to it now seems an arbitrary and unrewarding limitation of sympathy and interest. To Freeman it seemed the exact reverse. His interest in general history is less distant than it may seem from his love of *Landesgemeinden*, and not only because the latter stood for him as a type of the early Aryan as well as Teutonic polity; the similarities, which he cherished, with Homer's Achaeans were those of literal family resemblance. The Aryans were the free aristocracy of the world, the antitype of the slavish Asiatic, represented chiefly by the Turk. The Aryan brotherhood was far more to Freeman than an organising principle for the comparative history of early institutions. His mind, on one side, was always strongly synthetic and reconciliatory. Just as he always wished to combine the modern authors who had influenced him into a harmonious canon, so it was always his concern to tie up the threads of the European past in terms of the relationships which chiefly interested him: kindred, continuity and recapitulation. The Aryan concept was a powerful auxiliary.

He was always anxious, for example, that neither modern nor ancient history should be undervalued at the expense of the other; in the later nineteenth century it was a relevant concern. Sometimes his claims for modern history have, understandably, an *arriviste* assertiveness.[187] His roll-calls of Teutonic worthies are clearly offered in conscious imitation of classical epic. The notion of an overarching Aryanism in race, language and institutions reaffirmed for him in 'scientific' terms the lesson he had already learnt from Arnold, of the Unity of History. It bound together every valued cultural tradition and every revered hero, Greek, Roman and Teutonic, into one exalted brotherhood, in common descent from the Aryan ancestors, dim but noble figures in the misty splendour of the world's dawn: 'the forefathers, as yet one in speech and brotherhood, of Kleisthenês the son of Megakles, of

---

[186] *CH*, i. 32.   [187] 'The unity of history' in *Comparative Politics*, pp. 197, 218.

Caius Licinus and of Simon of Montfort'.[188] Freeman in pan-Aryan mood takes on the office of bard, and custodian of the great traditions of the race, to a tribe which is no less than the whole European family of nations; it is sometimes hard to repress the rival image of a garrulous nanny of formidable memory, attempting to reawaken family pride in a careless generation by heroic tales of glamorous, distant, deceased great-uncles.

That he should have despised non-Aryans was predictable; the displays of his racial prejudices during his visit to the United States, for example, confirm the worst that the twentieth-century reader could believe of him. What seems at first sight curious is that so passionate a believer in Aryan kinship should, in a European context, have been so cantankerous and unrepentant a Teutonic racialist. Celts, for all that they were Aryan brothers, were objects of an obsessive hostility and contempt; some Aryans were more Aryan than others. The corollary of his tribal inclusiveness was, just as naturally, exclusivity. There often seems something studied, a kind of nursery ferocity, about Freeman's racial prejudices. He admitted that the feeling of race, unlike that of nationality, was in a sense artificial, the product of scholarly theory; he also insisted that it was 'a political fact' none the less.[189] And in his own case, if racial prejudice, at once gruff and pedantic, was one of the chief traits out of which he constructed the 'carnal west country alderman' who had replaced the young ecclesiologist of Trinity, it came to fit very close. Very occasionally we may suspect a trace of self-parody, as though easing a button. The tone is perhaps not quite certain when, for example, he prefers the Arab to the Turk, 'at least inflexional, against a dirty agglutinative'.[190] But there was nothing particularly eccentric in moralising grammatical forms; Max Müller based a whole philosophy of history on doing so.[191] It was, after all, little more far-fetched than Ruskin's detection of spiritual degeneration in excessive foliation of tracery.[192] Though Freeman enjoyed pedantic jokes, it is nearly always safe to refuse him the benefit of the doubt.[193] It was as a

---

[188] *Comparative Politics*, p. 34.   [189] 'Race and language', *Hist. Ess.*, 3rd series.

[190] Stephens, *Life*, ii. 259.

[191] See Burrow, *The Uses of Philology in Victorian England* in R. Robson (ed.), *Ideas and Institutions of Victorian Britain. Essays in honour of George Kitson Clark* (1967), pp. 198–204.

[192] Ruskin, *Lamps of Architecture* (1848) (1903 edn), pp. 111–22. He later, of course, recanted some of this, p. 122n.

[193] E.g. 'But Eadgyth has been charged with far heavier offences than this. She seems to have been in some degree smitten with her husband's love of foreigners.' *NC*, ii. 46.

consciously crusty Teutonic racialist that Freeman stumped
Europe. In France he liked to try to distinguish honest Scandinavian Normans from the wretched 'Gal-Welsh'.[194] Generally, as
one might expect, Freeman's Aryan ecumenism was chiefly evident
in his negotiations with the past, Teutonic exclusivity in those with
the present. Even in the present there could be a distinction
between the historic present and the mundane one. The Risor-
gimento was for him one of the greatest events of his own time,
and he compared Garibaldi, by allusion, to the Emperor Frederick
II.[195] Italy itself, however, he treated, as Green noticed with
annoyance, in standard English fashion, as a museum.[196]

It is not surprising either that in his dealings with English history
Teutonic homogeneity was required and foreigners were not
wanted, except as adoptive sons or in the quarantined safety of
historical analogy. It is to Freeman's view of English history that
we now have to turn, but we need also, as a distant point affording
perspective, to retain what we know of his love of inclusiveness
and his response to other forms of connection than the continuities
of English constitutionalism. It was to the victory of that continuity over its greatest threatened hiatus that Freeman devoted his
intellectual prime. His last book, *The History of Sicily*, the child of
his old age, was its complement. England and Sicily were antitheses: one the type of homogeneous nationality and the purest
unbroken development of Teutonic institutions, the other the
palimpsest of Europe: two images of temporal relation, the natural
continuity of organic growth and the architectural superimposition of forms. Sicily had the attraction of an historical microcosm,
England that of a pure ideal type. The foundations of both lay
deep in Freeman's mind. It is in their rivalry and interplay that we
shall find the nature and limits of Freeman's English Whiggism.

---

[194] Stephens, i. 295.   [195] NC, iii. 92.   [196] Stephen, *Letters*, p. 309.

CHAPTER 8

Conquest, continuity and restoration

Whig history and the making of England

Untainted, except marginally, by scepticism, unsecured by the
trenchancy of argument and proof which made Stubbs' demon-
strations of his Whig position, even when questionable, an intellectual discipline, Freeman's strictly constitutional views, though
vehemently expressed, usually have a complacency even beyond
the normal run of historic Whiggism. It would not be true to say
that he took no deep interest in constitutional questions; some
specific issues held an antiquarian fascination for him, and he
discussed them in detail in the appendices to *The History of the
Norman Conquest*, which make up a substantial part of each
volume. But his general expressions of constitutional opinion
tended to be incantatory rather than argumentative. Though he
responded to venerability in institutions as in everything else, and
though continuity of institutions was one of the most important
attributes of that concept of Englishness on which he rested his
sense of identity, he was not, nor would have claimed to be,
primarily a constitutional historian. The idiosyncratic, ponderous
vitality of the *Norman Conquest* lies elsewhere. After Stubbs'
Constitutional History appeared he relied on it heavily and
openly; he privately described his task in the constitutional section
of his final volume as being 'to translate Stubbs into thunder and
lightning'.[1]

Stubbs gave added precision to Freeman's views but did not
change their direction. In vaguer shape, the opinions of the
rejected prize essay he wrote at Oxford[2] seem to have coincided
with those he held over a million words later at the end of the
second volume of *The Reign of William Rufus*. Their essence was

[1] Stephens, *Life*, ii. 88.　[2] *ibid.*, i. 75.

the traditional Whig belief that the Conquest was at most a disturbance, not a breach, of constitutional continuity. William the Conqueror and his successors accepted the letter if not the spirit of the existing constitution; the 'laws of Edward the Confessor' were dormant, never dead. The old English constitution was restored in improved form by the constitutional movement of the thirteenth century, whose hero was Simon de Montfort, and confirmed for good by Edward I, who makes a restorative, Fortinbras-like appearance at the conclusion of *The Norman Conquest* and, more strikingly, after the death of Harold, in the kind of consolatory spiritual reincarnation of which Freeman was always intensely fond.

The advance of feudalism and centralisation was already occurring before the Conquest; the latter intensified and accelerated the process. In the long run the effects of the Conquest were beneficial, though not because Freeman held anything like the Carlylean 'pot-bellied Jutes and Angles' view of the nation's forebears, in which Stubbs clearly saw some merit.[3] But Freeman accepted the view that the Norman kings, by repressing the anarchic political tendencies of feudalism, confirmed the nation's unity, and the Angevins, by shaking the people into unified opposition, averted the loss of freedom by stealth which occurred elsewhere.

Much of this was derived, with full acknowledgement, from Stubbs.[4] But the earlier coincidence of Freeman's original view of the Conquest[5] with Stubbs' was not surprising. Both, after all, owed the same initial debt to Palgrave, and Palgrave had presented the Whig doctrine of continuity in its blandest and most optimistic form.[6] Freeman said a number of times that he made up his view of the Conquest by striking a mean between the opposite views of Palgrave and Thierry, the two chief authors whom he had studied for his early essay.[7] It was a way of saying that he aimed at a balance between the extremes of the Whig and the radical position, for Thierry held a version of the thesis of a persisting 'Norman Yoke'. Yet though, in opinion, Freeman was far closer to Palgrave, much of the imaginative life of his history derives from a modified version of Thierry's vicarious bitterness.

The Norman Conquest, in fact, has the familiar optimistic shape of loss and restitution, and its dramatic force is if anything

---

[3] See above p. 143.   [4] NC, v. chs XXIII, XXIV.   [5] NC, i. chs I and III.
[6] E.g. Palgrave, *Normandy and England*, Works, iii. 349.   [7] NC, i. p. xiv.

impaired by the fact that the loss is only superficial. Its crisis, the subject of its central volume, the year 1066, the year of King Edward's death and Harold's election, of Harold's defeat and William's coronation, is a self-contained tragedy. But Freeman's history throughout offers its readers an indulged sense of desolation and loss which no merely Whiggish constitutional blandness could achieve or would require. Freeman tries in fact to write a national tragic epic within a Whig tradition which is itself consolatory and jubilant. The combination is not always easy, the circumstantial cheerfulness giving an unwanted air of masquerade to the tragedy, as though the actors would rise to take a final curtain and applaud the author; in Whig history there are no important irrevocable losses; the long run compensates for all. Alternatively, though more rarely, the relentless prospective cheerfulness seems rebuked by the tale itself. Godwin may have been a Whig ('something very like the distinction of Whig and Tory can be traced as far back as the eleventh century');[8] 'the good old cause' may have been 'truly that for which Harold died on the field and Waltheof on the scaffold'.[9] But 'hindsight as foresight makes no sense',[10] and Godwin, Harold and Waltheof died, presumably, without the consolations of history.

In its broadest sense Freeman's is perhaps the most Whiggish of all histories, not only in its opinions but in its narrative. The sense of historical perspective is omnipresent, overwhelming the mere happening, the latter sometimes, not through Freeman's fault, only dimly or meagrely discernible in the sources. In compensation Freeman offers a luxuriant allusiveness. Actions are performed not principally in their immediate circumstances, but in the dense medium of 'history' thickened by every available device of reminiscence, analogy and anticipation of future repetition, restoration or fulfilment. 'As the father had made his way to England almost in the wake of Aelle and Cissa, so the son made his way into England more nearly in the wake of Cerdic and Cynric'[11] is Freeman's preferred way of saying that Duke Robert landed at Portsmouth rather than Pevensey.

For a more meditated example, not from *The Norman Conquest* itself but highly characteristic, consider Freeman's extended

---

[8] *ibid.*, ii. 240.
[9] Stephens, i. 125.   [10] W. H. Auden, 'Secondary Epic'.   [11] WR, ii. 405.

rumination on the entry into Exeter of the two Williams, the Conqueror and the Deliverer. It is worth quoting at length.

The entry of William the Deliverer through the Western Gate forms the balance, the contrast, and yet in some sort the counterpart, to the entry of William the Conqueror through the Eastern Gate. The city had resisted to the utmost, when a foreign invader, under the guise of an English king, came to demand her obedience. But no eighteen days' siege, no blinded hostage, no undermined ramparts, were needed when a kinsman and a deliverer came under the guise of a foreign invader. In the army of William of Normandy Englishmen were pressed to complete the Conquest of England; in the army of William of Orange strangers came to call her sons to the work of her deliverance. In the person of the earlier William the crown of England passed away for the first time to a king wholly alien in speech and feeling; in the later William it in truth came back to one who, even in mere descent, and yet more fully in his native land and native speech, was nearer than all that came between them to the old stock of Hengest and Cerdic. The one was the first king who reigned over England purely by the edge of the sword; the other was the last king who reigned over England purely by the choice of the nation. The coming of each of the men who entered Exeter in such opposite characters marks an aera in our history. And yet the work of the two was not wholly alien to each other. The later William came to undo the work of the earlier, so far as it was evil, to confirm it so far as it was good. With the one began the period of foreign domination which seemed to sweep away our ancient tongue and our ancient law. With the other began that period of internal progress, every step of which has been in truth a return to the old laws of England before the Noman set foot upon her shores. And yet, after all, William the Conqueror did but preserve what William the Deliverer came to restore. His conquest ruled for ever that England should remain an undivided kingdom, and, in so ruling, it ruled that the old laws and freedom, trampled on indeed but never trampled out, should live to spring up again in newer forms. When the one William renewed the laws of Edward, it was but a link in the same chain as when the other William gave his assent to the Bill of Rights. In the one case the invader came to conquer, in the other he came to deliver; but in both cases alike the effect of his coming was to preserve and not to destroy; the Conqueror and the Deliverer alike has had his share in working out the continuous being of English law and of English national life. The unwilling greeting which Exeter gave to the one William, the willing greeting which she gave to the other, marked the wide difference in the external aspect of the two revolutions. And yet both revolutions have worked for the same end; the great actors in both were, however unwittingly, fellow-workers in the same cause.[12]

The analogies and contrasts drawn here have a function in spelling out a broad interpretation of English history, but the recitation of parallels and resemblances-in-difference, in varied recapitulations, was a repeated feature of Freeman's writing. Identity of name always acted on him as a challenge to comparison and antithesis: Edward the Elder and Edward I; the English

[12] *Towns and Districts*, pp. 74–5.

Margaret who was King Malcolm's queen, the English Margaret who was James V's.[13] We shall have to consider the significance of this later. For the moment we are concerned with these traits essentially as stylistic recipes for thickening the texture of an historical narrative otherwise threatened with baldness. In attempting to write an extended and detailed narrative history of a period so remote and relatively poorly documented, Freeman faced wholly different problems from those of Macaulay. When Macaulay tried to apply the techniques of the novel to history he was able to draw on sources in genres which had themselves helped to shape the development of the novel: the seventeenth-century interest in the portrayal of character, and the passion for writing memoirs or 'histories' of one's own times: Halifax, Clarendon, Burnet, Grammont. Lacking such aides, and having instead the terser, less exploratory and circumstantial narratives of the Chroniclers, Freeman's historical tableaux were necessarily in shallower relief. He was almost forced, though temperamental sympathy and a sense of its appropriateness to an archaic society would no doubt have led him to it in any case, to another of the novel's sources, epic. Epic conventions for temporal connection have in any case, of course, much in common with the perspectives of Whig history: the *Aeneid* is a Whig poem. Epic was one of the influences under which Whig historiography grew up, and both draw on some of the same psychological roots: ancestral pride and a sense of destiny. The novel, though it tells a story, by its proliferation of detail and picaresque freedom of incident gives more to the immediate moment.

Freeman, in resolving to write a detailed narrative on a large scale (two volumes before 1066 is reached), faced immense problems of realisation and narrative connection. The former he attempted to solve in part by travel and attention to town and architectural history. For individuality of character and narrative coherence the allied devices of epic convention and Whig perspective became all-important. Minor characters are identified through genealogy and place of origin, destiny and posterity, which tend to be invoked on each of their appearances; J.H. Round was cruel to Freeman's errors of fact here.[14] Freeman was, of course, more fortunate with his Norman than his English worthies. Defeat is said to be an orphan; it also, in this instance, carried the penalty of

[13] *NC*, iv. 513; i. 52. [14] E.g. Round, *Feudal England*, p. 251.

an anonymous posterity. Freeman's muster-roll of the invaders,[15] on the other hand, is Whiggishly diversified by references to parts played by their descendants in the constitutional struggles of the thirteenth century. The assembly of William's nobles, genealogically and topographically attended in the usual manner, has a genuine portentousness, full as it is of premonitions of the strange connections to be made by the Conquest:

His fame still lives, far away from the forest of Lions and the hill of Arques, where the minster and castle of Brecknock look forth on the vale of the Welsh Axe, and on the mountain rampart which, when Arques was beleaguered and defended, still guarded the realm of Gruffydd the son of Rydderch.[16]

In Freeman's treatment of the English, however, the difficulty of combining epic convention and historical fact is sometimes apparent in risks of bathos of which he seems unaware. Not, of course, because of defeat, which calls for epic treatment more readily than it lends itself to Whig optimism, but because historical Whiggism and epic alike have difficulty in accommodating mere futility and inconsequence.

Thither came the Ætheling Eadgar, once more to try the chances of the last representative of the House of Cerdic. Thither came Gospatric with the forces of his Northern Earldom, the men of the still independent England beyond the Tees ... Thither came the exiled Merlswegen ... Archill ... Siward the son of Æthelgar ... [17]

This heroic last muster of the English nobility after Hastings gets a forceful irony from the ensuing inglorious débâcle, which unfortunately seems unintended by the author. Even the roll-call of notables of Harold's army, dignified, one would think, beyond any risk of bathos, as a muster of the doomed, gains an additional, unwanted pathos from Freeman's determination to make 'the Staller Esegar', 'Ælfric of Gelling', 'Godric the Sheriff', into 'names to be cherished wherever the tongue of England is spoken'.[18] Pious Whiggism straining beyond its familiar bounds becomes revivalist, and, if it presumes on rights of allusion given only by an established canon, ludicrous, whatever the merits of the case. Freeman consciously set out to establish a national pride in early English history and to promote Teutonic heroes to parity with those of classical history and epic. Rather as J.R.R. Tolkien

---

[15] NC, iii. chs XII, XIII.   [16] *ibid*., iii. 132.
[17] *ibid*., iv. 255. I have retained Freeman's spelling of Saxon names.
[18] *ibid*., iii. 425.

attempted to rescue the Teutonic lore of elves from the nursery, and D.H. Lawrence to take the 'Anglo-Saxon' idioms of sex from the public domain of market-place and playground into the bedroom, Freeman was attempting, not, in his case, to cleanse or transfer, but to create resonances where none existed.

Often, inevitably, he was shouting 'echo' to an unresponsive wall. Even the sympathetic Green was cruelly unmoved by Freeman's single-handed attempt to establish Harold as a patriotic and tragic hero: 'he is *so* dull, so exactly the glorified image of the respectable grocer who wishes to die a vestryman'.[19] But at least Harold and Hastings have the inalienable dignity of catastrophe, and we have it on high authority that 1066 is memorable. Freeman's attempts in earlier volumes to engage the reader's sympathies by patriotic partisanship have, when applied to a period as remote as the early eleventh century and earlier, an air of artificiality. If one did not know Freeman one might suspect it of being assumed, like a tourist's towpath preference for Oxford or Cambridge, to give a factitious interest to obscure and uninteresting events. It is not just that, but Freeman's excitement, which sometimes catches with unfortunate accuracy the tone of bellicose journalism conducted from a safe distance, often seems a rather solitary self-indulgence. He insists, too, on retaining, in a period of opaque characters and obscure motives, the convention – no mere convention, of course, to a follower of Arnold – of moralistic historical judgement, though patriotism seems to make up the greater part of morality, and Freeman generally sounds less like a judge than a proud or anxious relative. His concern extended to in-laws: 'It is some slight comfort to find that a man who was honoured with the hand of a sister of Æthelstan was at least not stained with any such frightful crimes as those which have handed down the names of Arnulf and Herbert to everlasting shame.'[20] We can only speculate how many readers needed comforting or shared Freeman's pride when in 1016 'the standard of England waved again over fields on which the English arms were often crowned with victory, and where defeat at least never was disgrace'.[21] These patriotic vivacities give some idea of Freeman's problems; the latter are directly visible when, as occasionally, he seems to give up, clinging to his Chronicler like a drowning sailor to driftwood, and admitting as much by the kind of inert and

[19] Stephen (ed.), *Letters of J. R. Green*, p. 442   [20] NC, i. 195.   [21] *ibid.*, p. 383.

barely intelligible plot-synopsis which all readers of history and opera-goers recognise:

On a later visit to Rouen he received the cession of Evreux from Hugh. Herlwin now waged war against Arnulf with some success, for he slew Balzo, the actual murderer of William, and sent his hands as a trophy to the Norman capital. But in the course of the year Hugh contrived to reconcile Arnulf to the King and the King reconciled Arnulf and Herlwin.[22]

The context, of course, helps a little.

Bryce, recognising that *The Norman Conquest* was never as popular as Freeman had hoped, thought it should have been three volumes rather than five.[23] Certainly the quickening of interest in the reign of the Confessor (the second volume) is noticeable, and the third, covering the year of the Conquest alone, has a genuine if overstressed poignancy and dramatic power. Even the largely unavoidable externality of the view of character is sometimes overcome, as in the expository *tour de force* in which Freeman presents Harold's situation, when offered the crown, in the form of something like an imaginary soliloquy which has a very plausible intensity of fear, guilt, pride and ambition as well as being a lucid survey of the prospects of his reign and gathering dangers. It is a considerable narrative achievement, at a cost only in careful subjunctives.[24]

Yet there were other, more continuously available ways in which early English history, even as far back as the English settlement, could be imaginatively rendered, as Green showed in his two books *The Making of England* and *The Conquest of England*, and without confining himself to the institutional rigours of a Stubbsean treatment. The attraction of the earlier period lay, as Green saw, not in its dynastic or political affairs but in its essentially colonial character. The central protagonist was the English people engaged in settling their land. It was in fact a multiple protagonist: the controlling theme was the gradual expansion, convergence and coalescence of the small coastal pockets of settlement; the initial obstacle to a comprehensive settlement, and the achievement of a national political life as 'England', was not so much the conquered Britons, though they fought hard, as the untamed land itself. It is not at all hard to appreciate the appeal of this. If for Freeman the Norman Conquest

[22] *ibid.*, p. 211.
[23] Bryce, *Contemporary Biography*, p. 286. It had been Freeman's original intention to make it three volumes. [24] *NC*, iii. 23–7.

was his retrospective consolation for being unable to play, in his own day, as it were, the role of the English Kossuth or Mazzini, for Green, and clearly in some degree for Kemble and Stubbs also, the attraction of the earliest period of English history lay in the vicarious experience it offered of the free self-reliance and co-operation, the awe-inspiring isolation, and the heroic confrontation of man and virgin nature, of a colonial, frontier society.

It was exhilarating and refreshing to think of times when the valley of the Itchen and the Icknield way were paths into dark, tangled woodlands, and when small groups of kinsmen had laid their axes to the great forests of Charnwood and Arden and the Weald. Sharon Turner had used the colonial analogy,[25] though with little Romantic complicity. Kemble's imagination was clearly stirred, however, to identification with the small groups of families colonising the wastes of their new land.[26] But it was Green who above all gave colour and imaginative depth and intensity to the English experience as, initially, a colonising one. In *The Making of England* the modern reader is reminded of Conrad's Marlow and his evocation, at the beginning of *Heart of Darkness*, of pre-Roman England as a dark, unknown land and the estuary of the Thames as a kind of temperate Congo: 'Sand-banks, marshes, forests, savages, – precious little to eat fit for a civilized man, nothing but Thames water to drink.' But Marlow agrees with Green about the Romans themselves: 'They were no colonists; their administration was merely a squeeze, and nothing more, I suspect.' In Marlow's vein, Green had made the obvious comparison of the Romans with colonial administrators; he emphasises the extent of the barbarism and raw nature on which the Roman authority was superficially imposed,[27] though sufficiently to exhibit what was for Green the curse of Roman civilisation, not, as in earlier accounts, vice and enervation but the width of its social inequality: 'the union of material wealth with social degradation that lay like a dark shadow over the Roman world'.[28] Rome continued to supply its exemplary warnings: corruption to the Augustan politician; poverty in the midst of wealth to Green, the former East End parson. Indeed, inequality seems to take on for Green some of the explanatory generality of 'luxury' for the eighteenth century; it was the depression of the free ceorl in

---

[25] Turner, *Anglo-Saxons*, i. 19.   [26] Kemble, *Saxons*, i. 67–8.
[27] Green, *Making*, pp. 7, 13.   [28] *ibid.*, 45; cf. pp. 14, 153.

the latter days of Saxon England that deprived it of vitality and left it a prey to fresh waves of invasion.[29]

Green did not altogether neglect the opportunities for pathos in the fate of the Britons; he made telling use, for example, of the cave-excavations of his friend Boyd Dawkins, making the Celtic brooches and sword hilts found in a cave above Settle epitomise the plight of the fugitives.[30] But the chief identification is, of course, with the invading English: 'The mosaics, the coins, which we dig up in our fields, are no relics of our fathers, but of a world which our fathers' sword swept utterly away.'[31] Post-Roman Britain is not primarily for Green a land of crumbling, echoing ruins of greatness and civilisation, though he is not entirely indifferent to its picturesque opportunities, as well as the valuable evidence supplied by the excavation of a Roman site, as at Bignor. But Green's main perspective is, of course, that of the settlers, to whom the villa's ruins are a blackened heap of goblin-haunted stones.[32]

Above all he stresses the existing wildness of the land, not the desolation created by the invaders but the great tracts of forest and fen which condition the boundaries of their settlements and form the chief barriers to their progress:

the clearings along the river valleys were still mere strips of culture which threaded their way through a mighty waste. To realize the Britain of the Roman age we must set before us the Poland or Northern Russia of our own; a country into whose tracts of forest-land man is still hewing his way, and where the clearings round town or village hardly break the reaches of silent moorlands or as silent fens.[33]

The Making of England, in fact, rests far more on the nineteenth-century's achievements in geology and archaeology and such auxiliaries of philology as the study of place-names (to whose importance as a source Kemble had drawn attention)[34] than it does on the Chronicles. Like the studies of towns, it is a new kind of history, embodying a new sense of the significance of landscape, both in its malleability and its resistance, in explaining the character of the settlement and the subsequent administrative organisation of the settled people. Place-names too are records of settlement, and preserve a wilder past, when places of comfortable familiarity still belonged more to nature than to man.[35]

Above all it is the forests which dominate the earlier parts of

[29] *Conquest*, p. 361.　　[30] *Making*, p. 67.　　[31] *ibid.*, p. 148.　　[32] E.g. *ibid.*, p. 45.
[33] *ibid.*, p. 153.　　[34] *Saxons*, i. 61–3 and Appendix.　　[35] *Conquest*, p. 5.

Green's two books: the life of the invaders is the Tacitean life of the forest-clearing; against the darkness of the great woods the fires which mark the presence of man also mark their transitions.[36] In Roman times, gleaming through the dark, 'the beacon-fire which blazed on the cliffs of Dover to guide the vessels from the Gaulish shores to the port of Richborough proclaimed the union of Britain with the mainland',[37] Other fires proclaim other cultures; with the coming of Christianity the pagan burial-fires burn no longer 'and instead of resting beneath his mound like Beowulf, on some wind-swept headland or hill, the Christian warrior slept with his fellows in his lowly grave beneath the shade of the village church'. But the old pagan festivals remain as mementoes: 'Easter-fires, May-day fires, Midsummer-fires.'[38] The fire of the hearth, too, is a refuge for the men of the North from a too oppressive nature,[39] but it also marks, like the beacon, an outpost of a conquest not so much ethnic as human. Saxons, Angles, Jutes, even Vikings, become, in their struggles with nature, not merely pirates and destroyers of tradition, but types of 'Man', agents, in their own way, of civilisation and polity.[40]

The message of Green's evocation of England as a land

> Thick with wet woods, and many a beast therein[41]

is, of course, a characteristically Whiggish sense of gratitude. Few of his readers can have regretted times when the wolf roamed the Cheviots and 'the wild bull wandered through forest after forest from Ettrick to Hampstead'.[42] But there was no Macaulayan perfunctoriness about it, and no vulgar triumph. In fact Green's treatment of this theme is actually more consistently Whiggish than Macaulay's, involving not merely self-congratulation at the outcome but a conveyed admiration amounting to reverence for the early settlers, not mere pirates and destroyers of tradition, but pioneers. The English settlement becomes a great unconscious drive to unity, to England.

The study of such a tract as the Andredsweald would show the same ceaseless struggle with nature – Sussex-men and Surrey-men mounting over the South-downs and the North-downs to hew their way forward to the future meeting of their shire-bounds in the heart of the Weald, while the vast herds of swine that

---

[36] *ibid.*, 131.   [37] *Making*, p. 3.   [38] *Conquest*, pp. 9, 11.   [39] *ibid.*, pp. 54–62.

[40] Cf. Carlyle on the forest-felling of the Northmen: 'A more legitimate kind of valour that; showing itself against the untamed Forests and dark brute Powers of Nature, to conquer Nature for us.' *Heroes and Hero-Worship* (1841) (Everyman edn), p. 269.

[41] Tennyson, 'The coming of Arthur', *Idylls of the King*.   [42] Green, *Making*, p. 10.

formed the advance guard of the Cantwara who were clearing their way westward along the Medway, pushed into the 'dens' or glades in the woodland beyond.[43]

The accomplishment of a national cohesion was as much an achievement as the conquest of the land itself. Apart from the church, its chief agent and symbol in later times, with all that it brings of inequality and subservience – the old dialectic of freedom and civilisation is still at work in Green – becomes the itinerant royal courts

pounding in through the muddy roads, horsemen and spearmen, thegn and noble, bishop and clerk, the sumpter horses, the big waggons with the royal hoard or the royal wardrobe, and at last the heavy standard born before the king himself. Then follows the rough justice-court, the hasty council, the huge banquet, the fires dying down into the darkness of the night, till a fresh dawn wakes the fore-runners to seek a fresh encampment.[44]

Freeman had not the imaginative eye for this; his abilities in visual evocation were almost entirely architectural and literally descriptive. Though he shared Green's and Stubbs' delight in the preservation of old administrative boundaries with their reminiscence of tribalism, his love of maps was essentially political and his topographical eye essentially urban; his imagination needed more impressive evidence of the work of man than tillage of ground once gripped by the roots of trees. The English settlement meant above all, to him, the guarantee of the racial homogeneity of the English people. The degree to which there was any Celtic admixture, the extent to which the Britons had been exterminated, driven out, enslaved, or their women bred from, by the invaders, was an old and often disputed question. For Freeman, Teutonic prejudice apart, near-homogeneity of race was vital as the basis of a natural political life and organic political development. Assimilation of alien races was possible, as with the Normans in France, but it was an article of his nationalist creed that homogeneity of population was a prerequisite for a natural, spontaneous and hence free political life; thus, Sicily could enjoy a high civilisation but never a self-governing polity.[45] The nation was the natural unit of political existence, and the historical basis of the nation was the idea of kinship, real of adoptive.

The Ottoman empire was abhorrent to him, among other reasons, as the polar antithesis of this natural unit: a denationalised bureaucracy – the result of the recruitment of the state service

[43] *Conquest*, p. 5.   [44] *ibid.*, p. 31.   [45] *Hist. Ess.*, 3rd series, p. 480.

by the tribute of Christian children – imposing its will on an inert population.[46] In Freeman's hatred of the Ottoman there were many different cultural layers: an Herodotean sense that the barbarian empires of the East were the natural enemies of European civilisation; an almost medieval detestation, not apparently abated by the etiolation of his own Christianity, of the 'infidel'; an eighteenth-century conception of 'oriental despotism' as the political antitype of the European polity; and last, a Romantic antithesis between the mechanical and the organic.[47] It is, of course, the last which concerns us here. He took a predictable pleasure in showing, after Kemble, that the political organisation of the parish, the hundred, the shire and the state had been created, not by imposition from above, but by organic amalgamation of smaller into larger units.[48] It was to this gradualism that the coincidence of the modern shire with the ancient tribal area, as in Norfolk and Suffolk, testified.

But despite all this, Freeman's imagination did not really respond to the age of settlement as Green's and Stubbs' did. Of course he treated it in less detail, and his essentially political treatment and his almost exclusive reliance on the Chronicles were particularly disabling here, but these were perhaps only symptoms. He was at once too much and too little of a Whig: too much of one, that is, fully to identify with a society with so little of a discernible past. It is a paradox, in fact, in a sensibility such as his; the Whig is bound to venerate origins, yet the conception of the unprecedented is in a sense outside his range. Freeman did his best with Aryan and Tacitean analogies, but it was not really enough. One suspects that the early medieval emperors, with their, as it were, adoptive past as heirs of the Caesars, were, if not more admirable, more real to him. Freeman's writing in the earlier volumes of his history only kindles as 'England' grows in a grandeur which makes its downfall the more pitiful, and develops an accessible literature to preserve and celebrate its own achievements, its past.

Conquest and the limits of restoration

Where Freeman was not wholly a Whig was in a delight in restoration almost greater than his love of continuity. It was a

---

[46] *ibid.*, p. 352.   [47] E.g. *Chief Periods*, pp. 6, 168.
[48] *Comparative Politics*, pp. 76–80.

need in him to enjoy, simultaneously if possible, the satisfactions both of self-congratulation and of elegy; by sentiment, if not altogether in his opinions, he was part-Whig, partly nostalgic radical. Where he differed, more than Kemble or Green, from the radical ancient constitutionalists, was in what he chiefly lamented. He recognised the features of later Anglo-Saxon society which Kemble and Green deplored – the depression of the free ceorl, the moves towards feudal dependence – but he did not, at that point, particularly dwell on them.[49] It is not primarily the political and social effects of the Norman Conquest, in accelerating and intensifying these, that mark for him the national tragedy of the eleventh century, though he can always become irritable with the authoritarian sophistries of Norman lawyers when occasion demands,[50] but the more obvious loss of 'national' independence and the domination of foreigners. 'Our national being', not the constitution, was the protagonist of Freeman's history; a composite concept which included race, culture, language and national autonomy as well as 'free' Teutonic institutions.

Freeman's diagnosis of the decadence of England in the first half of the eleventh century, in fact, implied that it was essentially superficial, stemming from the court and the crown, and chiefly from the fatal marriage of Æthelred to the Norman princess Emma, which gave England a Norman-hearted king in Edward the Confessor.[51] England was worm-eaten by the Norman favourites of the king, the advance-guard of William.[52] But it was at least dramatically essential that England should approach its doom bright with an ironical false dawn of renewal, and rich with reminiscence of past glories to resound in its falling: the remembered splendour of 'glorious Æthelestan', the day when the Emperor of Britain was rowed on the Dee by eight vassal kings;[53] heroic recollections of Brunanburh and Maldon, enshrined in a stirring epic literature; victories over the Welsh; glorious defeats by the Danes. The history of the Anglo-Saxon monarchy was not in fact particularly glorious, but Freeman was determined that the standard which waved over Harold on the hill at Hastings should carry the battle-honours of four centuries: 'There, high above the host, flashed the Dragon of Wessex, the sign which had led

---

[49] NC, pp. 88–96. *Growth of the Constitution*, pp. 53–4.
[50] E.g. *WR*, i. 4, 335–6; ii. 262–3. Cf. *Growth of the Constitution*, pp. 126–47.
[51] NC, i. 301–2.
[52] *ibid.*, ii. 28–30, 69–71, 124–38, 393–8, 346.   [53] *ibid.*, i. 53, 61, 65.

Englishmen to victory at Ethandun and at Brunanburh, at Pensel-
wood and at Brentford, and which had sunk without dishonour in
the last fight beneath the heights of Assandun.'[54]

The possibility of a renewed and fuller national life is represented by Godwin, England's first great parliamentarian, and his
son Harold. Godwin's return from exile to chasten Edward and
expel his foreign favourites is a revival of the traditions of
Teutonic democracy, and Godwin, himself a deliverer, a type of
William of Orange and Simon de Montfort.[55] Harold's election, as
the first king of non-royal blood, so often made a reproach to him
by historians for his ambition, becomes in Freeman's telling an
almost Smilesean triumph for merit.[56] Freeman's treatment of the
house of Godwin, in fact, is peculiar to himself. No other historian
had cast them in this heroic role, and it had become customary to
blame them for England's weakness.[57] Whatever its merits as
history, and they do not seem substantial, Freeman's narrative
undoubtedly gains from this blighted spring. As the crisis
approaches, he makes full, Niebuhrean use of contemporary
superstition to thicken the atmosphere of doom: the ominous visit
of Halley's Comet;[58] the personal guilt of Harold's broken oath to
William and the sinister nodding of the Holy Rood of Waltham as
he kneels before it in prayer;[59] William's dedication of his
daughter to a convent in exchange for a favourable wind (he
becomes, inevitably, 'the new Agamemnon');[60] and the dying
Edward's prophetic dream of a withered tree sending forth green
shoots, which Freeman makes into the central image of his
History.[61]

After Hastings, where the bloody field is strewn with Homeric
quotations (it seems strange that Freeman did not find room for
the parallel from *Beowulf* for Harold's burial in a cairn on the
sea-shore), the English have, of course, the obvious pathos of
the defeated and dispossessed: the consoling legends of an oppressed people; [62] the flight of young men, 'the wild geese of their day',
to serve in the Emperor's Varangian guard at Constantinople,[63]
and the proud, bitter memories which Freeman liberally supplies.
Chester, for example, the last city to submit to William, recalls
'The old City of the Legions, the river on which Eadgar had been

[54] *ibid.*, iii. 475.   [55] *ibid.*, ii. 319; i. 522.   [56] *ibid.*, iii. 21, 254.
[57] Contrast with Freeman's account, Green, *Conquest*, pp. 539–40, 566–7, 583.
[58] NC, iii. 71–4, 9–13.   [59] *ibid.*, pp. 240–53, 428–30.   [60] *ibid.*, pp. 395.
[61] *ibid.*, pp. 9–13.   [62] *ibid.*, iv. 262–6, 290–2.   [63] *ibid.*, pp. 627–32.

rowed by vassal Kings, the minster where the English Basileus had knelt with his vassal kings around him, the walls from which men could look out on the land which Harold had added to the English realm . . . '[64]

But in Freeman's mind more was borne down at Hastings than a people which, since its early colonising adventure, had acquired a history and a place among the nations. Hastings (always of course 'Senlac' to him) was the symbolic conflict not of races but of two cultures and two epochs in European history. The Normans themselves are treated by Freeman with respect: they are Teutonic brothers, still close, despite their veneer of French manners, to their Scandinavian origins. Ostensibly conquerors, they come to be reclaimed: 'The Norman was a Dane who, in his sojourn in Gaul, had put on a slight French varnish, and who came into England to be washed clean again.'[65] But in the short term, as bearers of continental ideas and culture, they are, no less than the English, representative. Hastings was, Freeman's account at several points implies, a clash of two worlds: feudal hierarchy against Teutonic freedom, the age of heroes against the coming age of chivalry, Epic versus Romance.[66] The conflict was epitomised in the contrasting military tactics: the English still fought comradely, on foot; the Normans in the new fashion, as two distinct classes.[67] Beleaguered England gains an additional poignancy as the last redoubt of the elder world:[68] a position of which Harold's diplomatic isolation in the year of the Conquest and the Pope's blessing of William's banner are the immediate signs.

The rival invasion from the North in the same year, by Harold's brother Tostig and the Norwegian king Harold Hardrada, emphasises the European scale of the conflict and further enforces, though superficially it might seem to contradict, its message. Freeman's treatment of it is adroit. It is not only the aggravated difficulty of Harold's position, making him seem to fall beneath an accumulation of blows rather than one, nor just that the two invasions offer obvious scope to Freeman's love of historical parallels and heavily stressed ironies, that give it its dramatic significance. Hardrada was well qualified, as Freeman realised, to play the role of the last and greatest of the Norse pirates.[69] If the

---

[64] ibid., p. 312. [65] Growth of the Constitution, pp. 73–4, cf. NC, iii. 403–4.
[66] NC, iii. 275–6, 289, 452.
[67] ibid., i. 272; ii. 128–9; iii. 472. [68] ibid., iii. 274–7.
[69] ibid., pp. 342, 346.

invasion from France was portentous, the Northern one was full of echoes of the past, pagan and barbaric. Hardrada, with his giant stature, his polygamy, his huge ingot of gold which twelve strong youths can hardly lift, is, in the account of the poet Snorre which Freeman skilfully used, a semi-legendary figure from an older world, emerging for the last time out of the fjords of the North.[70] Between the two invaders the English Harold and his realm become, though Freeman does not say so explicitly, a kind of mean, happily combining freedom and civilisation, between the old pagan barbarism and the new papal and feudal Europe. Harold's victory over the Northerners at Stamfordbridge, 'the last triumph of pure and unmixed Teutonic England',[71] enables that England to stand, in her last fight of all, as the undisputed head and glory of old Teutonic Europe. Its fall becomes, explicitly this time, a kind of *Götterdämmerung*: 'in that Twilight of the Gods, when right and wrong went forth to battle, and when wrong for the moment had the victory, the brightest light of Teutonic England sank, and sank for ever'.[72]

Freeman's cultural confrontation, though complicated in some respects by his refusal to accept the Normans as really French, contains strong elements of a pair of long-lived popular stereotypes: honest English manliness and simplicity set against the artificial varnish of French manners, which for Freeman found their fantastic apogee in 'the tinsel fripperies of chivalry'.[73] It was a polarity which often had, in English eyes, clear connotations of masculinity and effeminacy, as well as honesty and deceit, home-spun and courtliness. We have already seen it in Macaulay; Freeman's version has the merit of precise cultural and historical location. He handles it with a lighter touch than some of his contemporaries – Kingsley is, of course, the unapproachable stan-dard-bearer – but his homosexual kings, William Rufus and Richard Cœur de Lion, seem appropriate exemplars of the exclu-sive ethic of chivalry[74] as the unacceptable, unassimilably 'French' element deriving from the Norman connection, just as the alleged-ly virgin Edward the Confessor stood for and patronised its clerical fifth-column.[75] Rufus was Freeman's epitome of the class ethic of chivalry: 'William Rufus is my ideal gentleman, *probus*

---

[70] *ibid.*, pp. 340–1.   [71] *ibid.*, p. 367.   [72] *ibid.*, p. 517.
[73] *Essays*, 1st series, p. 126.   [74] NC, v. 482–3. WR, i. 169, 172.
[75] NC, ii. 66–7, 120, and Appendix C.

miles, preux chevalier, "officer and gentleman", and all the rest of the humbug,' he wrote to a friend.[76]

Historically, Freeman's contrast was the same transition from barbaric freedom to feudal hierarchy that Kemble and Green regretted, but in Freeman, somewhat in defiance of the evidence but aptly for a narrative history, the confrontation became national, dramatic and ultimately military. But it was also cultural, social, literary and religious. The reproach levelled against the English army by the Norman chroniclers (analogous, as Freeman notes, to the reverse accusation against the French at Agincourt), that they spent the night before battle carousing while their future conquerors knelt in prayer, is embraced by Freeman as a scene with a special pathos:

> We shall hardly deem the worse of our countrymen, if that evening's supper by the camp fires was enlivened by the spirit-stirring strains of old Teutonic minstrelsy. Never again were those ancient songs to be uttered by the mouths of English warriors in the air of a free and pure Teutonic England. They sang, we may well deem, the song of Brunanburh and the song of Maldon; they sang how Æthelstan conquered and how Brihtnoth fell.[77]

And though uppermost here is Freeman's own lament for the old English heroic poetry for which he cared more than any later literature, the religious contrast made by the Chronicler is answered too, elsewhere. Just as he could, as he admitted, sometimes see Whigs in the eleventh-century, so, predictably, like Archbishop Parker,[78] he could see Romanists and Anglicans. Norman power provided a bridgehead, in England, for the claims of Rome.[79] There were distinct ecclesiastical styles: Edward the Confessor's establishment at Westminster of the continental form of monasticism is contrasted with Harold's foundation at Waltham, where the canons lived 'like Englishmen, each in his own house'.[80] Freeman would not have missed the Tacitean resonance.

Just as the monk cared only for his own soul, the knight of chivalry cared only for his own class. 'Chivalry, in short, is in morals very much what feudalism is in law; each substitutes purely personal obligations, obligations devised in the interests of an exclusive class, for the more homely duties of an honest man and a good citizen.'[81] The fopperies of chivalry were a later development from which the Normans of the Conquest were themselves

[76] Stephens, *Life*, ii. 80.   [77] *NC*, iii. 452.
[78] D. C. Douglas, *English Scholars*, p. 19.   [79] *NC*, ii. 67.
[80] *ibid.*, p. 460. Cf. pp. 451–2, 509–10.   [81] *ibid.*, v. 482.

exempt. But they were a result nevertheless, and with them, far more widely and indelibly, the associated un-English taste for French and Celtic Romance. For Freeman the most grievous, because irrevocable, consequences of the Conquest were cultural. Estranged by a gulf of taste and language from his older literature, the Englishman was culturally disinherited and the loss was irretrievable:

> In nothing do we seem so utterly cut off from our earliest forefathers as when we turn to the oldest words of English speech, to the songs of days when England was yet beyond the sea, when the crews of the three keels had not yet crossed the whale's path to seek them a home in the conquered land of Britain. If there is anything truly national in the world, it is the old heroic songs of the English folk.[82]

There was nothing studied in Freeman's mourning for the literature and language of Anglo-Saxon (the phrase itself was abhorrent to him) England. References to 'this abiding corruption of our language'[83] carried overtones of the common philological doctrine, held by England's most influential philologist Max Müller,[84] that linguistic change is in a sense degenerative, a process of grammatical corruption, but chiefly they express an un-Whiggish sense of irrevocable disinheritance. At one point he compares displaced Teutonic words to men going into exile,[85] but there could be no general restoration to summon them back.[86] Freeman is a nostalgic cultural radical, determined to do what he can to reverse the verdict of history. His tone, normally jubilant or self-indulgently elegiac, here becomes strenuous and embittered. It is well known that he set himself to write as 'pure' an English as possible, untainted by words of Latin or French origin. In revising earlier editions of *The Norman Conquest* he had, he said, 'often put a good English word where I had at first allowed a stranger to creep in'.[87]

The effects on his writing of a voluntarily depleted word-hoard have not been generally approved of. It affects a primitivism which was clearly deliberately acquired: the style of his earliest writings is quite unlike it. Like Pre-Raphaelite painting and the earnestness

---

[82] *ibid.*, p. 586.   [83] *ibid.*, p. 547.

[84] An influence Freeman acknowledges, *ibid.*, p. 522n. See also pp. 538–9, and F. Max Müller, *Lectures on the Science of Language* (1st ser. 1861; 2nd ser. 1864).

[85] *NC*, v. 546.

[86] Freeman himself makes the contrast with the political 'restoration' of ancient freedom. But 'in literature and language this cannot be. There, when the stain has once fixed itself, it can never wholly be wiped out.' *ibid.*, 596.

[87] In the Preface to the 3rd edn. of *NC*.

of Victorian Gothic, Freeman's restricted diction and syntactical austerity represent an attempt, conducted with revivalist zeal, to use archaism as a means of cleansing and renewal; as usual the achieved effect is an almost fetidly intense, gamey Victorianism. Freeman's diction was of course not only restricted but necessarily in some measure deliberately archaic; there are times, though their preferred periods were different, when one is reminded of Rossetti's searching of old Romances for 'stunning' words,[88] though Rossetti's eclectic sensationalism was actually the reverse of Freeman's austerity: Strawberry Hill Gothick to Gilbert Scott's pedantry. It is perhaps not altogether Freeman's fault if his freely employed 'strove', 'deem', 'tarry', 'of a truth', 'recked little', having for long been readily available to less serious revivalists, have such a pasteboard Gothicky flavour. He was also predictably fond of inversions: 'came not', 'failed him not'.

Freeman said he wrote as though to be spoken aloud, but what he had in mind was not the tone of conversation – we have already seen that Green wished he had written more as he talked – but a kind of skaldic chanting.[89] His own analogy was poetry, and by this he clearly means epic and ballads, for he cared for little else. It is a prose of short, grammatically simple sentences, with few conjunctions, participles or adjectives, constituting a style which seems best described as neo-barbaric: a succession of unqualified, at times almost ritualised assertions, unspeculative and unequivocal: 'but', 'because' and 'although' are rare. Freeman's preferred ways of expressing consequence – 'And so it was', 'And so it proved', and above all 'It was ruled' – imply not so much scientific connection or causal inevitability as doom or destiny, and the heroic fatalism of the Sagas. The most striking characteristics of Freeman's style are the result less of archaic diction than of the deliberate avoidance of grammatical flexibility: a ballad-like syntactical and rhythmic monotony whose few variations come not from the subtle play of adjectival nuance or metaphorical allusion, or the modulation of relative clauses, but from the manipulation of repeated patterns of parallelism and inversion, of which we have already seen something in the extended quotation, earlier, in the passage on the two Williams.[90]

These patterns were fundamental to Freeman's view of history – how fundamental we have still to consider – and in that sense the

---

[88] John Dixon Hunt, *The Pre-Raphaelite Imagination, 1848–1900* (1968), p. 44.
[89] 'just as if it were verse', quoted Stephens, *Life*, i. 346.   [90] Above, p. 196.

style was an apt vehicle. The most instantly recognisable feature of his prose, in fact, is the successive repetitions of the subject noun, as though with a distrust of unsupported relative pronouns:

> The crown which had passed to Eadward from a long line of kingly forefathers, the crown which Harold had worn by the free gift of the English people, the crown which the first William had won by his sword and had kept by his wisdom, now passed to the second of his name and house.[91]

Nouns and repeated pronouns fall on the ear like successive blows of Thor's hammer; the result is predictably sometimes a headache. Freeman found a style appropriate to his conception of his role and task – good for crescendo and quasi-liturgical recapitulation, vulnerable to bathos – at a high price in suppleness and nuance. At its best his prose makes a stirring and dignified noise.

He was irritated by complaints of his repetitiousness and clearly disappointed by the reception of his works. There was more than vanity in this; there is something of the bitterness, like Ruskin's though far less painfully intense, of a baffled messianism. In his references to the medieval translator of 'silly tales of Brute and Arthur' there is a venom which hints not very obscurely at a more contemporary hurt: 'The first sinner has had his following; he has done his work. To the mass of Englishmen Arthur and his fantastic company seem more their own than Hengest and Cerdic.'[92] The glance at Tennyson was oblique but the self-reference was patent and marked by a rare sense of defeat. It was the jealousy of the bard who sees his role as guardian of the tribal lore usurped, whose folk prefers the songs of the stranger; and it was the fault of the Norman Conquest. Since Englishmen adopted Arthur as the national hero 'it has been a hard task to make them feel as they ought to the heroes of their own blood, towards Arminius and Theodoric, towards Hengest and Cerdic and Æthelstan'.[93] It had not been for want of trying on Freeman's part, but despite his efforts no cyclic formula of renewal seemed to offer reassurance. English language and sentiment had suffered an uprooting, and 'the change is only and wholly evil'.[94] It seemed to defy his whole conception of history.

If Freeman's Romantic primitivism and sense of lost cultural identity did not find what seems its obvious political counterpart in a radical ancient constitutionalism, but co-existed instead with many jubilant celebrations of English political continuity, it was

---

[91] WR, i. 16.　　[92] NC, v. 592.　　[93] *ibid.*, 597.　　[94] *ibid.*

not because he was more tolerant of a legal than a cultural or linguistic eclecticism. He would no more have spoken, as Blackstone had done, of English law as improved, by successive importations, 'by the accumulated wisdom of divers particular countries'[95] than he would have rejoiced in the varied 'richness' of modern English. The English constitution was, on the contrary, autochthonous and organic, with a highly developed immune system for rejecting alien innovations: 'New and foreign elements have from time to time thrust themselves into our law; but the same spirit which could develop and improve whatever was old and native has commonly found means sooner or later to cast forth again whatever was new and foreign.'[96] Freeman was a Whig constitutionalist not because he valued purity less in constitutional law than in language and literature but because its restoration seemed easier.

The shapes of Freeman's version of English history are complex, but, with the one exception considered above, always optimistic and restorative. It is, at one level, a series of swings of the pendulum, representing the respective dominance of constitutionality and arbitrary rule, of English and foreign influences, the latter invariably centred on the court. But the emphasis is always on the moments of restoration and renewal. Thus Edward the Confessor gives way to Harold, Henry III to Edward I, the Tudors and Stuarts to 'the glorious name of William of Orange'.[97] It is this pendular movement which is marked by Freeman's obsessive fascination with historical types or parallels; the key figure in each such movement appears almost invariably accompanied by his counterpart from the corresponding later moment: Godwin by de Montfort, Harold by Edward I, and, on the opposite side, Edward the Confessor and the rebuilder of his abbey and his shrine, Henry III. Freeman's extended meditation on the abbey and the shrine is one of the great rhetorical set-pieces of his history. Though marked by even more than his customary dense allusiveness, it is a striking piece of high-Victorian eloquence, less syntactically insistent than usual in Freeman and given an unaccustomed touch of ambivalence by his love of architecture and hatred of Protestant vandalism. The abbey is not, as in Macaulay, a temple of reconciliation, but a battleground epitomising England's history, where the honours paid to Edward's shrine, fittingly 'the work not

[95] Blackstone, *Commentaries*, i. 64.
[96] *Growth of the Const.*, p. 20.   [97] NC, v. 583.

of English but of Italian hands', mark the rise and fall of English and foreign influences.[98]

These oscillations are enclosed in two larger cycles, the lesser providing the trajectory of Freeman's book, the greater coinciding with English history itself. The first runs from the marriage of Æthelred to the mid-thirteenth century, with its crisis in 1066, when the national life seems overthrown for ever. Of course it is sleep not death, and Magna Carta and the Oxford Parliament proclaim its revival.[99] This was a standard Whig pattern, though Freeman's emphasis, properly in a narrative history, was less on the survival of institutions, more on the ultimate fusion of the two peoples, conquerors and conquered, in a renewed national homogeneity which could again provide the basis for political life. It mattered crucially, of course, to Freeman, that the Norman was a Teutonic brother: this graft would take.[100] It was a situation which appealed to his love of assimilation and amalgamation. In the reign of William Rufus, too, his rather overdeveloped sense of historical irony, as well as national pride, was gratified by the defeat of Norman armies by Rufus with the aid of his English subjects.[101] In Rufus' successor Henry I, English-born though of foreign race, and married to a native queen, a descendant of Ælfred, the green tree begins to return to its place, as Freeman was fond of saying, borrowing the imagery of the dying Edward's prophetic dream.[102] The resolution of the whole work is the constitutional movement of the thirteenth century, confirmed by the reign of Edward I,[103] symbolically important to Freeman as the first king since the Conquest to bear an English name, and to retire from continental entanglements to pursue the proper business of an English king, chivvying the inhabitants of the Celtic fringe: 'the conqueror of Wales and Scotland, seems truly like an old Bretwalda or West-Saxon Basileus sitting once more on the throne of Cerdic and of Ælfred'.[104]

But room had, of course, to be made for later development, and the greater cycle is completed, it seems, or virtually so, in Freeman's own time. Godwin and de Montfort are sometimes joined in a triptych by Gladstone: a joke to Freeman's friends.[105] 'We have advanced by falling back on a more ancient state of

98 *ibid.*, iii. 32–41.   99 E.g. *ibid.*, v. 394, 726.   100 *ibid.*, i. 149.
101 WR, i. 10, 72.   102 NC, iii. 112. Cf. iii. 11, and v. 331.
103 *ibid.*, v. 730; iv. 724.   104 *ibid.*, iii. 522.
105 Stephens, *Life*, ii. 201, 203. Hutton, *Letters of Stubbs*, pp. 162, 183n.

things; we have reformed by calling to life again the institutions of earlier and ruder times.'[106] That Liberalism was the truest conservatism, while the Conservative rested his faith on 'recent' innovations like hereditary monarchy and the lord of the manor, was one of Freeman's favourite paradoxes.[107] It was not an uncommon argument; Gladstone, as Christopher Hill points out, employed it.[108] Green made the same point about the reform of the municipal corporations.[109] It was reassuring, and understandable when most examples of democratic institutions were still ancient rather than modern.[110] In Freeman it was far more than a debating point; it was fundamental to his view of history. Of course, in the dominance of the cycle there is inevitably a sacrifice of Whig continuity in favour of revival or restoration. Freeman's pattern for English history is notably less linear than Macaulay's. But this was no real problem: linear continuity is fundamentally assured by the preservation at all times of the spirit which resists and ultimately casts out innovations.[111] The price, a mystical distinction between what the constitution really was and what, at a given time, the courts thought it was, was one, after all, which Whig historians were used to paying, though Freeman paid it more extravagantly than most. What gave the assumption plausibility, above all, for Freeman, was the gratifying closure of the great cycle.[112] It is victors who write Whig history, and resurrection casts doubts on even the most well-attested death. Retrospective Whiggism and hints of apocalyptic resolution could co-exist, after a fashion, as the shape of English history, so long as that history remained ultimately kind to Whigs.

Only once, in his first published paper,[113] did Freeman deliberately confront and attempt to argue through the dilemma of restoration as the potential adversary of continuity. The *casus belli* was architectural; architecture was always almost as important to him as constitutions, and at this point it was more so. In this instance, as in all others, Freeman wished to satisfy the claims of the past, but which past? In architecture in the mid-nineteenth

---

[106] *Growth of the Constitution*, pp. 21, 158. Cf. *NC*, v. 596.
[107] *Hist. Ess.*, 4th series, pp. 386–7.
[108] Hill, *Puritanism and Revolution*, p. 112.
[109] Green, *Stray Studies*, 2nd series, p. 120.
[110] But Green admitted it was 'a little discouraging to see that our greatest steps in advance are only a recurrence to older freedom'. *ibid.*, p. 103.
[111] *Growth of Const.*, p. 20.   [112] *ibid.*, p. 158, 'the cycle has come round'.
[113] *Principles of Church Restoration* (1846).

century it was clearer to him than to his contemporaries that it spoke with two voices, one urging restoration, the other preservation. We have seen him, in a later instance, repudiating continuity – the English language as it has developed – for a forlorn revivalism which he knew to be hopeless. The starkness of the choice, the anguish of the tone, were uncharacteristic; normally he made his Whiggism and his love of restorations at least superficially cohere. But when, as a young man, he confronted the urgently topical problem of architectural restoration, his vote had been, on the whole, the other way. He deserves credit, in fact, as one of the earliest protesters against the excesses of church 'restoration', anticipating Ruskin and William Morris. Imprecations against the devastations of the restorer crop up throughout his writings. Yet he had been active in church restoration himself, and in his early essay he weighed the case with a judiciousness uncommon both in the ecclesiological circles to which he then belonged and in his own mature writing on nearly all subjects.

The ancient building was a favourite analogy of the Burkean Whig, an image of endless renewal without loss of identity, of repairs and even additions and improvements entirely compatible with the essential integrity and continuity of the structure. Burke had invited the French National Assembly to regard their country's constitution as a dilapidated old mansion to be lovingly renovated. Stubbs saw an ancient church – he probably had his own, at Navestock, in mind – as an epitome of English history: 'every old building, church or not, has a history for every broken stone'.[114] Ruskin, who wrote in the same terms about Oxford Cathedral,[115] also reversed the metaphor: hasty, pattern-book building was the expression of a rootless, improvised way of life.[116] The ancient building as an image of continuity was, in constitutionalist terms, an untroubling metaphor; Freeman himself continued to use it in this way.[117] But in architecture itself this complacency was fatally disturbed by the activities of the zealous 'restorers' of medieval churches. Ecclesiology, as practised in the 1840s, most notoriously by the Cambridge Camden Society, was conceived as a prescriptive science and a radical one; ecclesiologists aspired to discover and propagate the 'correct' style of medieval church architecture, not only for church building but for 'restoration'. Genuinely medieval work of an incorrect or inferior

114 Stubbs, *EEH*, p. 3.   115 Ruskin, *Praeterita*, pp. 179–80.
116 Ruskin, *Seven Lamps*, pp. 325–8.   117 *Growth of Const.*, p. 20.

kind was ruthlessly dealt with. J. M. Neale, the President of the
Society, with deliberate provocativeness, declared he would support the pulling down of Peterborough Cathedral if it could be
replaced by 'a Middle Pointed cathedral as good of its sort'.[118]

It was Freeman who posed the central dilemma, in a paper much
discussed in ecclesiological circles at the time, and put the case for
continuity, if not quite so emphatically as Ruskin in *Seven Lamps
of Architecture* or as Morris was to do in his manifesto for the
Society for the Preservation of Ancient Buildings,[119] when it had
become apparent that the chief danger to ancient buildings was
not neglect but 'restoration'. The restorer's creed, Freeman said,
should be 'one hard, unswerving law . . . the building is simply to
be brought back to what we know or reasonably suppose from
analogy to be its original state'.[120] But what are we to understand
as 'its ancient condition'; how can we freeze at a single moment
the development of a church;

> where a church has received changes in several styles of architecture, where
> perhaps a vista of Romanesque arches is terminated by a lancet triplet or a
> gorgeous Flowing east window, and itself supports a Perpendicular clerestory,
> what is to be done? It cannot be maintained that all is to be reduced to its original
> condition; that the history of the building is to be destroyed.[121]

Freeman was not at this point prepared to condemn absolutely all
destruction, but his sympathies are clear. A medieval church
incorporating the work of successive ages is an icon of 'the state of
the Church, her hopes and her fears, her persecutions and her
triumphs, her prosperity and her corruptions'.[122]

If, in literature and language Freeman was something like an
embittered ancient constitutionalist, in architecture he became an
increasingly consistent and wholehearted Whig. In his historical
writing he embraced every opportunity of enumerating as a form
of historical perspective the traces of the past inscribed on the land
by the monuments of different ages. In his chapters on William the
Conqueror's campaigns, for example, Normandy is seen as a
palimpsest: geological,[123] prehistoric,[124] Celtic,[125] Roman[126] and
Scandinavian;[127] some of its features and associations are soon to
be transferred to parts of England and Wales in the names of their

---

[118] White, *The Cambridge Movement*, p. 168.
[119] J. W. Mackail, *The Life of William Morris* (1901), 2 vols, i. 342–4.
[120] *Church Restoration*, p. 5.   [121] *ibid.*, p. 12.   [122] *ibid.*, p. 8.   [123] *NC*, iii. 165.
[124] *ibid.*, pp. 235–6.   [125] *ibid.*, p. 147.   [126] *ibid.*, pp. 203–4, 291.
[127] *ibid.*, pp. 117, 123, 127, 149.

lords.[128] In buildings he came not merely to tolerate but to be fascinated by the strange conjunctions and evidences of re-use and adaptation which made them emblems of historical continuity: the concentric circles, Roman and Norman, of Pevensey;[129] the re-used Roman brickwork of St Alban's Abbey; the flat, fluted pilasters of the cathedral at Autun;[130] the eleventh-century church inside the great Roman gate of Trier.[131] Above all there was Palermo:

Here and there a column rich with the foliage of Corinth, set in a niche in some street corner, reminds us that Palermo once was Roman. Here and there columns of strange form, bearing legends in characters strange to European eyes, are made to serve again in church or doorway, to remind us that Palermo once was Saracen.[132]

Increasingly he came to love all evidences of the past. 'I am so conservative', he admitted, 'that I don't like pulling down anything .... Keep everything.'[133] He was deploring, here, the destruction which made way for the Victor Emmanuel monument in Rome. Understandably the new regimes in Italy and Greece proved less Whiggish in their attitudes to their country's chequered pasts. It was a patriotic vandalism which Freeman's view of his own country's history scarcely allowed him consistently to deplore, but he did so none the less. In Athens he condemned also the narrowness of an archaeological interest devoted purely to the classical past. The interest of Athens lay in its whole history, 'but to the pedant who is satisfied to grope among the details of two or three arbitrarily chosen centuries, the unity of history has no meaning'.[134] He regretted particularly the destruction of the medieval Frankish tower on the Acropolis:

The excuse for the barbarous deed was that inscriptions might be found in its ruins. To some minds the chance of finding a shattered stone with an *alpha* or a *beta* graven on it seems to be of more value than the preservation of a living monument of an important part of the world's history, a period which its very incongruity makes attractive.[135]

Freeman wanted – a large concession from him – even the evidences of Turkish rule preserved.[136]

[128] *ibid.*, pp. 129, 132.   [129] *ibid.*, iii. 402.   [130] *Hist. Ess.*, 4th series, p. 128.
[131] *Hist. Ess.*, 3rd series, p. 117.   [132] *ibid.*, p. 447.   [133] Stephens, *Life*, ii. 341.
[134] *Hist. Ess.*, 3rd series, p. 302.   [135] *ibid.*   [136] *ibid.*, pp. 290, 302–3.

Alpha and omega

Though sometimes in practice conflicting, and though they gave a character to Freeman's responses to the past that was potentially contradictory compared with more simply restorative or progressive views, his two loves, the rival seductions of purity and palimpsests arise from the same source. They are the two faces of continuity, simple and complex. It seems inadequate here to speak of a love of the past; it was more like a craving for the past to be eternally present, an ultimate denial of time; for

> New things and old co-twisted, as if Time
> Were nothing . . .[137]

Restoration and preservation represented rival means to essentially the same end: the former gave a promise of possession of a fragment of the past in its integrity; preservation offered 'the great whole' with the scars of its grafts as evidence of its comprehensiveness. Where Freeman's sympathies and sense of identity were most strongly engaged for the suffering subject, nothing less than virtually a total resurrection could satisfy him, a scouring of all traces of the alien and a wiping of all tears. Where he could take a more generously disinterested and ecumenical view, he wanted as much preservation as the case allowed. Much depended also, of course, on the prior expectation. Where continuity could be confidently assumed and thought of as organic, intrusions were an unwelcome threat; on the other hand, unexpected juxtapositions and conjunctions of apparently wholly distinct cultures and epochs, conveyed a message of continuity and connection the more welcome for being unlooked-for. The greater the incongruity the more striking the lesson. Freeman loved such apparently bizarre conjunctions: the Frankish Dukes of Athens;[138] the thought that the temple of Athene had been successively in continuous use for pagan, Orthodox, Catholic and Islamic worship;[139] finding the familiar names of Western medieval history in the Greek of a Byzantine geographer.[140] The jumbled, layered texture of the past became itself a source of delight and reassurance.

The co-existence of epochs is, of course, even more obvious in Freeman's delight in restorations, his pleasure in cycles and

[137] Tennyson, 'Gareth and Lynette', *Idylls*.   [138] *Hist. Ess.*, 3rd series, pp. 301–2.
[139] *ibid.*, p. 300.   [140] *ibid.*, p. 413.

recapitulation. In such recapitulations the heroes of Freeman's canon seem often not merely to recall each other but virtually to coalesce: the Whig honours-board becomes a record of almost literal metempsychoses. In the same way Freeman's love of comparison seems sometimes to become something more. Macaulay, for example, shared Freeman's liking for classification and analogy, but he kept it in a separate compartment from his celebrations of continuity and his lists – in his case often ranked class-lists – of heroes. Freeman did not. Classification runs, in him, with no decisive break, into older ways of conceiving similarity; analogy becomes virtual identity. Sometimes, clearly, we have merely analogies such as any historian might draw: William the Conqueror and Theodoric, for example, as monarchs ruling by a kind of legal fiction of continuity.[141] Sometimes, again, we have an obsessive parallelism, the kind of playing with names and repetitions and antitheses which often makes Freeman seem like a structuralist *avant la lettre*. Thus it was through Margaret, wife of King Malcolm, 'that the old kingly blood of England passed into the veins of the descendants of the Conqueror' and 'another marriage, the marriage of another English Margaret – widely different as was the sister of Henry the Eighth from the sister of Eadgar Ætheling – completed the work which the earlier marriage began'.[142]

But in Freeman's favourite examples, in the constant coupling of his heroes, there is more than analogy. English history for Freeman is not a source for sociological classifications, it is a drama of rebirths and resurrections, as when 'the great Assembly which welcomed the return of Godwine rises again to life in the Parliaments of Earl Simon and King Edward'.[143] There is a re-enactment of roles: 'the part of Godwine is played again by Simon of Montfort'.[144] Edward I 'reproduced' the life of Edward the Elder: 'if not Ælfred himself, at least his unconquered son, seems to rise again to life in one who at once bore his name and followed in his steps' and 'the Scot and the Briton once more bowed to an Eadward of England'.[145]

In all this there is something closely akin to the patristic, medieval idea of historical typology, to the concept of *figura*. As Auerbach puts it in a classic essay, 'Figural interpretation establishes a relation between two events or persons, the first of which

[141] NC, v. 56–7.   [142] *ibid.*, iv. 513.   [143] *ibid.*, p. 724.
[144] *ibid.*, i. 522.   [145] *ibid.*, p. 33.

signifies not only itself but also the second, while the second encompasses or fulfils the first.'[146] The aptness of this description to Freeman is obvious, and in both cases the function is the same, to establish, in Freeman's phrase, 'the unity of history'. Originally it was used to bring the Old Testament history into the scheme of salvation offered in the New.[147] Moses was for St Augustine a prefiguration or type of Christ, *figura Christi*; Noah's ark is a *praefiguratio ecclesiae*.[148] Later, typological thinking was made to play the same role in subsequent secular history, giving it eschatological significance by bringing it into the overall scheme of salvation; restoring monarchs are types of the Messiah, oppressed peoples typify both captive Israel and mankind in bondage to sin. Figural interpretation is the binding agent of history, bringing together Old and New Testaments, classical and Christian, religious and secular histories, into one eschatological story.[149]

Of course, some broad features of figural thinking are common to all conceptions in which history is presented as a single meaningful drama. Auerbach's general characterisation will fit all Whig histories: 'in this light the history of no epoch ever has the practical self-sufficiency which, from the standpoint both of primitive man and of modern science resides in the accomplished fact'.[150] In Freeman, too, as in many Whig historians, Manichaeanism was never far off; in his case it is the English and foreign influences which contend, perennially it sometimes seems, for mastery in English history which resemble a parochial version of St Augustine's two cities whose conflict gives its meaning to secular history. The view of the Normans as both cruel oppressors and instruments of providence was a traditional one going back to Geoffrey of Monmouth;[151] the providential ordering of English history is much more overtly proclaimed in Turner, Hallam and Palgrave than in Freeman. But the strong traces of figural thinking in Freeman are something else again, more specific and therefore tantalising. As with the concept of the *translatio*,[152] we cannot be sure how far he was conscious of it as a specific concept in his thinking, or how far he was aware of its origins. Certainly he could have been influenced by some of his primary sources, Gildas

---

146 Erich Auerbach, 'Figura', *Scenes from the Drama of European Literature* (Gloucester, Mass. 1973), p. 53.
147 *ibid.*, p. 52.   148 *ibid.*, p. 38.
149 Hanning, *The Vision of History in Early Britain*; Frances Yates, *Astrea*.
150 Auerbach, *op. cit.*, p. 58.   151 Hanning, *op. cit.*, p. 128.   152 Above, p. 187.

for example, though there is no evidence that he was. When, speaking of Switzerland, he says that 'Achaia . . . lives in a figure in the mountain land',[153] it is hard to know how much weight of suggestion to attach to the use of the word 'figure', a rare if not unique one in his work.

But though the question of any direct medieval influence on what it seems fair to call Freeman's figural thinking must be left open, there is little doubt about the more recent sources for the eschatological strain in his writings; they were his mentors, Arnold and Palgrave. Arnold accounts for much; it may not be accidental that the formula of repeated cycles of national history within an overarching scheme of salvation, which, as Duncan Forbes has shown, was characteristic of Arnoldian history,[154] was, transposed into secular and purely national terms, Freeman's pattern for English history. Arnold's view of history is, not surprisingly, explicitly apocalyptic. Modern history contained 'the first acts of a great drama now actually in the process of being represented, and of which the catastrophe is still future',[155] but 'it appears to bear the marks of the fulness of time, as if there would be no future history beyond it'.[156] Anxiously scanning the signs, Arnold could see only in the Slav an historic potentiality still unfulfilled, and therefore the prospect of a respite.[157] Palgrave's philosophy of history, as we saw at the end of the last chapter, is avowedly the medieval and Biblical one of the four empires, of which Rome is the last.

Freeman's thought is not, of course, openly eschatological. He disagrees, in fact, with Palgrave, though only to replace his view of eternal Rome by one of his own typical cycles:

By one of the strange cycles of history, we who dwell in the wide world of modern times, the world of continents and oceans . . . have in some points come back to the state of those who dwelled in the narrow world of the earliest times, the little world of islands, peninsulas, and inland seas.[158]

It was emotionally that Freeman participated in thoughts inspired by the eschatological drama. If his historical thought was not literally apocalyptic, it had, as it were, the smell of apocalypse about it, a tremulous and awed sense of portentousness in the

---

153 *Chief Periods*, p. 198.
154 Forbes, *The Liberal Anglican Idea of History*.
155 Arnold, *Introductory Lectures*, p. 25. 156 *ibid.*, p. 29.
157 *ibid.*, p. 30. 158 Freeman, *Chief Periods*, p. 176.

times, 'an age as strange and memorable as any that went before it'.[159] The world was to be made new, the former things restored. 'Every step that has been taken towards the unity of Germany and Italy is not a step towards something new but a step back again towards something old.'[160] Freeman's hatred of the 'pseudo-Caesars' of Austria and France seems to owe something to a sense of the apocalyptic scale of their importance.[161] They figure in his writings like twin Beasts from *Revelations*, delaying by their delusion of mankind the final resolution. Now that Greece is free 'Must we deem that the last struggle of the sister peninsula has been made in vain? that the elder two-headed bird of prey must tear at his will the entrails of Milan and of Venice, and his younger single-headed brother gorge himself for ever with the blood of Rome? Will force for ever trample upon right?'[162] Of course, literally we should not speak on Freeman's behalf of a final resolution: 'History has no beginning and no ending.'[163] But Freeman's historical imagination seems bounded, no less than Arnold's, by the notion of a Slav empire in the Near East. Imaginatively, for him, the reconquest of Constantinople would have been a kind of consummation and ultimate restoration; he spoke in appropriately metaphysical terms of 'our captivity – for the captivity of Eastern Rome is the captivity of all Christendom'.[164]

In so far as Freeman could not make a literal apocalypse the end of history, his emotional commitment to the notion of an ultimate restoration or eternal cycle throws into even sharper focus another feature of eschatological history, the belief that, since all ages are equally elements of the divine plan, all are in a sense coeval. As Augustine had put it, 'If God's knowledge contains these things, they are not future to Him but present.'[165] Palgrave placed this thought on the first page of his *History of Normandy and England*: 'The events appearing to us consecutive are essentially consentaneous . . . the beginning and the end are simultaneous in the designs of Him who is Alpha and Omega, the First and the Last.' For Freeman too, alpha and omega were invariably one; if he was torn between restoration and continuity as forms of

[159] *ibid.*, pp. 175–6.   [160] 'Historical cycles', *Hist. Ess.*, 4th series, p. 252.
[161] *Chief Periods*, pp. 150–2.
[162] 'Ancient Greece and Medieval Italy' (first pub. 1857), *Hist. Ess.*, 2nd series, pp. 30–1.
[163] Quoted Stephens, *Life*, ii. 341.   [164] *Chief Periods*, p. 169.
[165] Auerbach, *Scenes*, p. 43. See also Frank Kermode, *The Sense of an Ending. Studies in the Theory of Fiction* (O.U.P. 1967), p. 25.

triumph over time it was because they offered alternative images of eternity: the tying of the ends of history into its eternal circles and the architectural palimpsest as the symbol of the co-existence of all ages.

Freeman's cycles are nothing like the sociological model, the *corsi* and *ricorsi* of the Machiavellian political scientist, from which the latter hopes to learn the formula of historical change; Freeman has little interest in their dynamics. Still less, of course, are they the occasion for a shrug and a murmured 'plus ça change': they are 'the wonderful cycles of history'. Sometimes, with a little Whiggish deference to notions of improvement, they can sound reminiscent of the Romantic metaphysician's conception we found in Stubbs, of a recreation of an earlier state at a higher level, as a more definite and comprehensive embodiment of the active spirit, but this is not really Freeman's language, and when it occurs in his thoughts on English history it is probably Stubbsian or merely traditionally Whig in origin. Freeman's cycles are more like the recurrent geological upheavals of a disturbed landscape in which, with each surge of the earth, different eras of its past are recurrently revealed. What is wrong with this image, of course, is its relativism. Freeman's own historical optimism consisted essentially in his ability to ignore or at least not to dwell on the fact that theoretically the notion of cycles proved the resilience of evil as much as good. But what excited him was not transcendence but the cycle itself, eternal recurrence, alpha and omega. History seems constantly engaged in an almost liturgical recreation or resurrection of itself, giving repeated historical disproofs of irrevocable extinction.

But the notion of progress seems to have had no appeal for him except as restoration. Such inventions as the telegraph or political representation were estimable to him because they enable us to revive the virtues of the closely knit polity of the ancient city-state on the larger scale of modern political life.[166] The suspicion remains that the latter is second-best; that the earlier state was the more vital and authentic, though brittle.[167] With so much that was reactionary and Romantic in his temperament and ideas, it is surprising that Freeman did not become a hater of modernity in all its forms: that he insisted on being consoled. Of course, restora-

---

[166] 'The highest use of the discoveries of natural science has been to raise large states to the political level of small ones.' *Chief Periods*, p. 185.
[167] See above, p. 175.

tion, as distinct from mere repetition, is conceptually dependent on some notion of continuity, some element of persisting identity. The Whig idea of continuity secured Freeman's own sense of identity; applied in its widest, most novel form, as the concept of a single Aryan race, it guaranteed the integrity of European history; but it was resurrection, not progress, that gave that history the shape of victory.

In all this there was a threat to traditional Whig conceptions of history which went beyond any difficulties experienced by Freeman himself in reconciling continuity and restoration. True the intensity of Freeman's love of cycles was peculiar to himself. The apocalyptic tone, though not so eccentric as a twentieth-century reader may find it, was to become less prominent, not more, in English historiography. It is best seen both as a Christian residue and as a legacy of Romanticism and the prophetic, messianic European mood prevalent in the years following the Revolutionary and Napoleonic upheavals.[168] One is inclined, perhaps, to say therefore that Freeman belongs with the geopoliticians and historical seers of the nineteenth and early twentieth centuries, Gobineau, Marx, Chamberlain, Spengler, Toynbee, rather than with the main body of English historians. In saying so, however, we unfortunately reinforce a tendency to categorise the intellectual activities of the past too glibly and rigidly. Palgrave, for example, was precisely the same combination of historical mystic and antiquarian pedant as Freeman himself. It would be more accurate to point to the pedantry rather than the mysticism as a danger to historic Whiggism, but in Freeman the two are linked. In both there is a devotion to the past so intense as to amount to a reluctance to recognise it as irrevocably past. If we think of this as merely an accentuation of Whig piety and the doctrine of continuity we also have to recognise it as one which Whiggism could accommodate only in strictly regulated amounts.

Whig historiography – to repeat what has been said before – depends on a fine balance of interest and allegiance between the present and the past. In Freeman the balance tilts decisively towards the latter. Superficially this seems not to be so; Freeman became notorious among a new generation of more dispassionate professional historians for Whig anachronisms, for arbitrarily introducing present concerns into past history. In a sense this is true; Freeman's Whiggish sense of history as a single drama was

[168] J. H. Talmon, *Political Messianism* (1960).

developed, as we have seen, almost to the point where every moment became contemporary. But – again to repeat an earlier point – this is radically misdescribed by saying that Freeman introduced 'the present' into 'the past'. Freeman in fact historicised all his perceptions in terms of a single scheme which was neither present nor past. If we wish to be pedantic about it, we can see in that scheme elements of a nineteenth-century intellectual milieu as we can also see much older elements, but it had hardly anything to do with contemporary English politics. The only strong sense in which it was 'present' is that it was Freeman's. In every other sense it is the conception of the past which dominates. Macaulay, identifying Livy as a Whig, though without using the word, said that he contemplated the past with interest and delight because it led to the present. Freeman contemplated the present in a similar spirit only because and in so far as he saw it as recreating the past. Anachronism cuts both ways; Freeman did not defend Godwin because he admired Gladstone; he admired Gladstone because he had persuaded himself that he resembled Godwin. More than to any of his contemporaries, Lecky's remark that we are Cavaliers or Roundheads before we are Whigs or Tories applied to Freeman.

The balance he struck, the ideas of restoration and the figural devices by which he kept a residual hold on the Whig notion of continuity, were too individual to be generally available. Whig historiography, however pious, had never been disinterested, or without a firm view of present necessities. It had been written, in England, hitherto to a notable extent by lawyers and politicians. Scotland had, it is true, produced, if not 'professional', at least 'professorial' historians, but their historical writing, in so far as it was Whig, had typically been conditioned by a conception of social change in which an eager and vigorous understanding of the present state of society was fundamental. In Stubbs, Freeman and Green we have something else: historical scholars with little or no experience of public affairs, with views of the present that were in varying degrees Romantically historicised, and who were drawn to history by what was, in a broad and complimentary sense, an antiquarian passion for the past. It was not only that, of course; there was also the patriotic and populist impulse to identify the nation and its institutions as the collective subject of English history, which made the new historiography of early medieval times an extension, filling out and democratising, of older Whig notions of continuity. It was Stubbs who presented this most substantially; Green who made it popular and dramatic as well as extending its scholarship and imaginative range to include landscape and townscape.

It is in Freeman, in a sense the most traditional of the three, in that he was the most purely a narrative historian, that the strains are most apparent. The assimilation of an essentially Romantic cultural and political nostalgia to the Whig tradition was a precarious achievement. It was one which the future course of English government and society, and the progressive self-disciplining of the antiquarian temperament in the profession of history, would make increasingly hard to sustain. One path, towards which Stubbs, as usual the best Whig of the three, had no apparent inclination, though the more radical Freeman and Green, like Kemble before them, had at least a foot on it, led towards a more broadly cultural and social, or even socialist, version of ancient constitutionalism. This was the route taken, with variations, by medievalist social critics from Cobbett to William Morris, though their motive was often, admittedly, not so much a love of a recognisable past as hatred of the present and a reasonable preference for utopia. The other, naturally the more attractive to the dedicated historian, was to figure in the self-questionings of the historical profession in the twentieth century as the way of emancipation from the confining and distorting requirements of Whig historiography: the study of the past 'for its own sake'.[169]

---

[169] The classic statement, of course, is Butterfield's *The Whig Interpretation of History*.

IV
THE IMPERIALIST
Froude's Protestant island

CHAPTER 9

'Something strange and isolated': Froude and the sixteenth century

The most familiar and most parodied of Victorian historical paintings, after 'And When Did You Last See Your Father?', is surely Millais' 'Boyhood of Raleigh' (1870):[1] the two boys on the beach, their discarded toy boat half-revealed in the foreground; the future courtier and colonist, his pinched, anxious face and foetal pose unfortunately suggesting a rather recalcitrant attitude to the age of expansion, giving an air of expostulation to the seaman who, arm outstretched with nautical precision, at an angle to indicate El Dorado and the Indies rather than Dinard, points an imperious finger seaward.

James Anthony Froude, the historian of Tudor England and a leading promoter of the imperialist excitement of the closing years of the nineteenth century, had drawn, nearly twenty years earlier, his own fleeting pen-portrait of the same imagined scene at Dartmouth three centuries before, in what is perhaps his best-known essay, 'England's Forgotten Worthies', his influential celebration of the mariners and explorers of the Elizabethan age.[2] It was a review of a new edition of Hakluyt, 'the Prose Epic of the modern English nation', as Froude called it, adding that 'What the old epics were to the royally or nobly born, this modern epic is to the common people.'[3] In a curiously blasphemous comparison he drew

a parallel between the rise of the poor fishermen of Galilee to the spiritual authority over mankind, and the seamen who in the days of our own Elizabeth

---

[1] For the presentation of historical subjects in Victorian painting, see Roy Strong, *And When Did You Last See Your Father? The Victorian Painter and British History* (1978).

[2] It inspired Kingsley's *Westward Ho!* and Tennyson's 'Ballad of the Revenge'. See Waldo Hilary Dunn, *James Anthony Froude. A Biography*, vol i *1818–1856* (O.U.P. 1961), pp. 192–3. The analogy with Millais' painting seems unlikely to be accidental, though I have found no confirmation of this.

[3] 'England's forgotten worthies' (1852), repr. in Froude, *Short Studies on Great Subjects* (1898), 4 vols, i. 446–7. (Henceforth cited as *SS*.)

... from the banks of the Thames and the Avon, the Plym and the Dart, self-taught and self-directed, with no impulse but what was beating in their own royal hearts, went out across the unknown seas fighting, discovering, colonizing, and graved out the channels, paving them at last with their bones, through which the commerce and enterprise of England has flowed out over all the world.[4]

Later in his essay Froude envisages the young Raleigh, and his Gilbert half-brothers (Millais censors one), rowing down to Dartmouth 'and listening, with hearts beating, to the mariners' tales of the new earth beyond the sunset'.[5]

Millais turns this, presumably knowingly, into a cryptic image of Froude's kind of imperialism: Elizabethan enterprise, English commerce, the empire of the seas and the empire beyond them, prophetically condensed in the seaman's tense finger and the boy's glazed, brooding eyes. It is tempting to juxtapose this symbolism with that of another image, of a century earlier. In 1762, at the height of the Wilkite agitation, the radical Arthur Beardmore contrived to be arrested while teaching his young son Magna Carta;[6] he seems, in fact, to have inspired what became almost a traditional practice of radicals about to be arrested: Sir Francis Burdett managed the same scene in 1810.[7] Beardmore's lesson to his son was made the subject of a popular print.[8] In the picture, compared with Millais' scene of discipleship, there is none of the excitement and energy expressed in the seaman's tense arm. Instead the atmosphere is grave, serene, almost devotional, a contrast, presumably, to the imminent rude interruption of the arresting officers. The father's finger rests in calm exposition across the sacred text (at cap. XXI, dealing with arbitrary imprisonment), possessively, like a medieval founder-saint's indicating the model of his church The changed direction of the pointing figure in the two pictures, from reverent textual exposition to an expansive, almost frantic exhortation or call to action, offers a Copernican contrast: from the closed world of the immutable ancient constitution to the prospect of an illimitable national destiny; two contrasting uses of the past. Having emancipated itself from narrow legalism, and assimilated the concept of progress, having democratised itself in establishing the colonial origins of the English folk and its institutions, the Whig tradition was ready to assume the responsibilities of empire, and to provide the unfolding charter of Greater Britain.

[4] *ibid.*   [5] *ibid.*, p. 479.   [6] Ann Pallister, *Magna Carta*, p. 60 n. 3.
[7] *ibid.*, p. 69.   [8] *ibid.*, plate I.

But the parable is too pat as it stands. It is an irony, at least, of
course, that the attachment of the new English settlements across
the Atlantic to ancient constitutionalism was to be perhaps more
deep-seated and lasting than that of England itself.[9] But in any
case, the story was never quite told in this fashion by any great
English historian, even by reference and sentiment – it would be
too much to expect detailed narrative: from the grounding of the
Saxon keels at Ebbsfleet to the (still prospective) Imperial Federation. All the ingredients were there, but no Victorian historian was
ever equally committed to all parts of the story; the history of the
English-speaking peoples had to wait until the twentieth century
for its teller, when the tale itself had become an echo of older ways
of thinking. Empire had not been salient in Whig history, though
in the eighteenth century there was naturally Whig sympathy for
the rebellious American colonists who drew so heavily on the
common heritage of political ideas for their justification. The older
histories, though referring to commerce, had essentially been
concerned with constitution rather than expansion. Macaulay,
who might have responded to the challenge, never doubted that
London was the world's hub, and had the self-consciously civilised
man's dismissive scorn for the merely outlandish; the only colonial
venture dealt with in his *History* was a dismal failure.[10] For
dominion over the exotic he looked East, not West or South.
Green was no imperialist, and Freeman frankly a little
Englander,[11] for whom America was interesting chiefly as a
museum of old-English political forms.[12]

As for the avowed imperialists, Froude and Seeley, they lacked
the Romantic Teutonism and the Whig pride and interest in
constitutional development necessary to tell the whole story in the
manner suggested. Seeley told at least its latter part, in *The
Expansion of England* (1883), though not in the Whig–Teutonic
vein; in Froude's case even empire took, in the mass of his work,
second place to religion. 'England's Forgotten Worthies' and the
book he made on the same theme out of his Oxford lectures,
English Seamen of the Sixteenth Century, his articles on the

---

[9] E.g. H. Trevor Colbourn, *The Lamp of Experience. Whig History and the Intellectual
Origins of the American Revolution* (Chapel Hill 1965).
[10] The Darien scheme. *History*, ch. xxiv.
[11] See Freeman, 'The physical and political bases of national unity' in A. S. White, (ed.),
Brittanic Confederation (1892).
[12] Stephens, *Life of Freeman*, ii. 233, 241.

Colonies[13] and his account of his imperial journeys, *Oceana*,[14] were his most influential and popular works, but in the central task of his life, *The History of England from the Fall of Wolsey to the Defeat of the Spanish Armada* (1856–70), a vast, sprawling work of original scholarship, the privateering exploits of the Elizabethan seamen took no more than their share of attention, with a recognition of the role of greed and the element of atrocity. For all the rhetoric in celebration of their bold, free, pioneering individualism, of energies released from age-old shackles of superstition and ignorance, of trackless wildernesses and uncharted seas, it would be misleading to interpret Froude's message simply as a windswept patriotic liberalism. He played a major part in the creation of that rhetoric, now so over-familiar; it represented the more boyish, optimistic side of his nature and it nourished the imperialist political creed he built for himself. But his *History* is the creation of a far more complex, haunted and lugubrious mind than it alone would suggest.

Froude's is in fact one of the representative intellectual and spiritual careers of the Victorian age.[15] Many of the standard ingredients are there, exaggerated to a pitch which he himself at times found almost unendurable: born in a Devon parsonage in 1818, the youngest son of a bleakly stoical, patriarchal clerical household; brother of Hurrell Froude, the brilliant, vehement leading spirit of the early Oxford Movement, who tormented and terrified him;[16] exposed at Westminster to the worst atrocities even a Victorian public school could provide for the forming of character;[17] an undergraduate career at Oriel at the height of the Oxford Movement. A Fellowship at Exeter College and his father's wishes led him to take deacon's orders, which increasing religious doubts soon made abhorrent to him. He, like others, was to blame Tractarianism and the influence of Newman for unsettling his faith. A vestigial Christian, or rather theist, he became like his brother-in-law Kingsley, a fervent and aggressive Protestant, a fact which clearly provided much of the impulse to the study of Tudor England.

---

[13] 'England and her colonies', 'The colonies once more' (first pub. *Fraser's Magazine*, Jan., Aug., 1870; repr. *SS*, ii).   [14] *Oceana, Or England and Her Colonies* (1886).
[15] For Froude's life, see Herbert Paul, *The Life of Froude* (1905), and W. H. Dunn, *op. cit.* Also Dunn, *James Anthony Froude. A Biography*, vol. ii *1857–1894* (O.U.P. 1963). (Henceforth cited as Dunn, i and ii.)
[16] Dunn, i. 18. For Hurrell Froude see Piers Brendon, *Hurrell Froude and the Oxford Movement* (1974).   [17] *ibid.*, ch. 3.

By the late 1840s Froude was, like his friend Arthur Hugh Clough, a man consciously scarred by his century, a victim of the spiritual malaise of the 'enfant du siècle' or 'superfluous man'.[18] His fervid, declamatory novel of spiritual autobiography, *The Nemesis of Faith* (1849), which records his clerical hero's loss of faith, the resignation of his living and his death in despair, led to his resignation of his Fellowship, anticipating his ejection. Froude said of the book, 'I cut a hole in my heart and wrote it with the blood.'[19]

By comparison with this *via dolorosa*, Froude's later career was outwardly placid, at least until his misfortune in becoming Carlyle's biographer. The popularity of his lectures made his short period as Regius Professor at Oxford at the end of his life (he died in 1894) a little more than an honourable public restitution.[20] He himself saw the watershed in his career in his determination 'to have done with insincerity' and proclaim his doubts, and in acceptance of the ideas of Carlyle.[21] As a married man, a prolific though vilified historian and a respected editor of *Fraser's Magazine*, a Carlylean and a Tory Radical whose residual substantive radicalism was increasingly qualified by an adjectival Toryism,[22] and an influential imperialist publicist, Froude clearly came to reject and despise, with an uneasy resentment and pity, his earlier self. As he wrote retrospectively of *The Nemesis of Faith*, 'I have done for ever with the subjective and have got my boat on an even keel.'[23] His autobiographical writings, including his early fiction, suggest both understandable resentment of his father's treatment of him and also a strong desire to identify and be reconciled with him.[24] Froude's mother had died when he was very young, and in marked contrast to Macaulay and Freeman, who grew up surrounded by admiring women, his family life was masculine and, to its youngest member, astonishingly harsh. It would be possible to interpret much of Froude's writing in terms of his relations to his father and his eldest brother, the stern, traditionalist, Erastian – at least in Froude's account – High-and-Dry Anglican parson and squire, and the strident, articulate, intellectual 'Catholic' theologian. No such systematic reduction will be attempted here, but

[18] See e.g. *The Nemesis of Faith* (1849), p. 51. [19] Dunn, i. 131.
[20] Paul, *Life*, p. 384.
[21] Dunn, i. 134, 141, 169–70. Cf. Froude, *Carlyle's Life in London*, i. 311–12.
[22] E.g. Dunn, i. 152–3, 179. [23] *ibid.*, p. 134.
[24] Dunn, i. 46–50, 105. Dunn's first volume incorporates Froude's autobiography, as well as substantial passages from his autobiographical novella, 'The Spirit's Trials'.

these early biographical episodes can seldom be entirely forgotten in interpreting Froude's hatreds, ambivalences and personal myths. He was always to write with nerves on the stretch and obsessions near the surface. The sixteenth century was not a period where they could be laid to rest, nor, clearly, was it Froude's intention that they should.

Froude's account of Tudor England was complicated and in some ways enriched by these ambivalences; the fact that they arose from dilemmas that were religious, moral and personal rather than inherent in historiographical or political tradition was in some ways liberating, distancing him from the more conventional preconceptions with which Whig historians had approached the period. The latter had always stood at an uncomfortable angle to Tudor England. As the source of the English Reformation it was inescapable, but constitutionally it had been made, since Hume's challenging references to Tudor despotism,[25] a source of embarrassment and even shame. Green spoke in the line of his tradition when he said that 'the character of the monarchy from the time of Edward the Fourth to that of Elizabeth remains something strange and isolated in our history'.[26] The apparent servility of sixteenth-century Englishmen was felt to need excuse; Hallam, for example, found it in the popular role played by the crown in the Reformation.[27] The sophisticated Humean view of the period, derived, with modifications, from Bacon and Harrington, that the power of the Tudors arose from their occupation of a unique moment of equipoise between the decline of the feudal nobility and the rise of the Commons, was adopted by Macaulay and Green.[28] More frequent, however, were simply denunciations of the tyrannical nature of Henry VIII and of his 'usurpations',[29] which had, nevertheless, left the fabric of the constitution 'essentially' intact.

Froude, as one might expect of a disciple of Carlyle, had – to speak more temperately than his nineteenth-century liberal critics – no prejudice in favour of constitutionalism. It was a mark, of course, of his lack of interest in constitutional questions that he should conclude his history with the Armada, thereby

---

[25] See above, p. 26.   [26] Green, *Short History*. p. 290.
[27] Hallam, *Const. Hist.*, i. 39.
[28] Macaulay, 'Hallam', *Works*, v. 193–5. Green, ch. VI, sect. iii.
[29] For the reputation of Henry as a tyrant and monster see Valerie E. Chancellor, *History for their Masters* (1970), pp. 51, 76–7.

excluding the constitutional disputes characterising the last years of Elizabeth; Froude's was the history of the English Reformation, not of the Tudor monarchy. It was not only that he took no interest in constitutional questions; there was positive distaste. Sometimes he used the term 'constitutional' pejoratively, meaning the doctrine of government by a balanced representation of interests,[30] which to him was the abnegation of moral responsibility in government.[31] The refinements of constitutional liberty did not concern him; his own conception of liberty was essentially the 'positive' view,[32] the Platonic–Christian conception, mediated probably by Carlyle: freedom consisted in the right ordering of one's life, obedience to the dictates of the moral law – even submission to a moral superior.[33] What interested him in history, politically speaking, was not liberty in the constitutional or liberal sense, but the right use of authority. Clearly no doctrine of essential continuity in England's history could be derived from the moral qualities of her rulers: 'revolutions, reforms, transfers of power from one order to another, from kings to aristocracies, from aristocracies to peoples, are in themselves no necessary indications of political or moral advance. They mean merely that those in authority are no longer fit to be trusted with exclusive powers'.[34]

Froude spoke of the constitution, when he spoke of it at all, loftily, *sub specie aeternatis*, as of a thing destined to pass away,[35] and his tone altogether lacked the stressed pathos which normally characterised his reflections on mutability. Compared with the eternal laws of right and wrong,[36] the constitution was a temporary, external thing, in Carlylean terms a formula; it could even, like all such formulae, become an idol.[37] Froude even condemned the fiction of constitutional monarchy, with a blunt Puritanism worthy of Tom Paine, as 'lies'.[38] Thus there was no call for censure or lamentation over the abrogation of constitutional propriety in moments of crisis, for the constitution was not the timeless essence of political rule, which was the necessary imposition of order, the exercise of the natural authority of the wise over the foolish, but

---

[30] 'Reciprocal duties of state and subject', *SS*, ii. 315. [31] 'On progress', *SS*, ii. 382.
[32] For the classic statement on this, see Isaiah Berlin, *Four Essays on Liberty* (O.U.P. 1969).
[33] E.g. *SS*, ii. 377–81. [34] *ibid.*, p. 380. [35] 'Party politics', *SS*, iii. 440.
[36] 'The science of history', *SS*, i. 27. [37] 'England's War', *SS*, ii. 483.
[38] Dunn, i. 207.

merely a local historical manifestation of it. The assertion that in times of crisis *salus populi* became *suprema lex* was one which a pragmatic utilitarian Whig like Macaulay could strictly endorse. But Froude clearly felt an altogether un-Whiggish satisfaction at such moments, when the facade crumbles and the essence is revealed. He liked strong men and stern measures for the public good. The suppression of the Indian mutiny gave him much satisfaction:

India has been spared the invasion of constitutionalism, and British India (sic) statesmen and generals were free to use both brain and hand. In great extremities the eloquent tongues fall silent. The heart of the nation is in its armies. Constitutional anarchy would have ruined Rome. French soldiers saved the credit of the Revolution. The sword of Cromwell had to rescue the cause of the Civil Wars from the weak generosity of the Long Parliament.[39]

Of course, the stern measures of the sixteenth century, the state executions, the judicial use of torture, the penal laws against Catholics, the extended definition of treason, needed some explanation for ninteenth-century consciences; the doctrine of *raison d'état* must be worked hard to justify them, as Froude almost invariably did, to the horror of Victorian liberals, in, as Freeman said, 'passages at which our moral sense revolts'.[40] Froude was not a hard man; he had, in fact, little of Freeman's boyish delight in a fracas. He was, if anything, more than usually sensitive to the thought of suffering. *The Nemesis of Faith* is suffused with vicarious as well as personal pain.[41] Referring to the vividness of Newman's belief in eternal punishment, he said, 'the minds of most of us would break under the strain',[42] and he used similar words of the Irish famine: 'It is very lucky for us that we are let to get off for the most part with generalities, and the knowledge of details is left to those who suffer them. I think if it was not so we should all go mad or shoot ourselves.'[43] His justification for the asperities of sixteenth-century statecraft, that we must understand it in the light of the dangers to be surmounted,[44] fulfilled the requirements of historical understanding, though to mid-

---

[39] Quoted *ibid.*, p. 204. Macaulay also exulted in the suppression of the Mutiny, though with a little misgiving about his own revengeful feelings. Trevelyan, *Life*, p. 656.

[40] 'Froude's Reign of Elizabeth', *Saturday Review*, xvii (16 Jan. 1864), 80, attrib. Bevington, *The Saturday Review*, p. 343.

[41] *The Nemesis of Faith*, pp. 8–9.

[42] 'The Oxford Counter-Reformation', *SS*, iv. 276.   [43] Quoted Dunn, i. 123.

[44] E.g. Froude, *The History of England from the Fall of Wolsey to the Defeat of the Spanish Armada* (1904 edn), 12 vols, i. 167–8, 337–8, 436, 467; ii. 215–16, 224; iii. 202; ix. 71. (Henceforth cited as *HE*.)

Victorians it seemed Machiavellian. As Carlyle had pointed out in *The French Revolution*, the element chiefly missing in our vicarious experience of the past is fear,[45] though there is a pitifulness in Carlyle's treatment of history's victims which is perhaps less often present in Froude's.

But Froude went further. He was far from being merely the amoral apologist of state necessity; he was intensely the moralist. The scrutiny of character and motive was for him not merely the traditional duty of the historian, it was a dogmatic necessity. There was no Macaulayan briskness and delight in the exercise. In his residual theism it was essential that the better, more honest creed should both attract and produce the better characters and works. It was the proof of its vitality and of the moral government of the world; there was no other.[46] He cannot, of course, apply the doctrine without exception, but sometimes he carries it far. Just as he hated the constitutional doctrine of the representation of interests as amoral, in history he wished to owe no obligations to selfishness or wickedness. There is little sociological distance or irony in his account of the victory of the better cause. In the case of Ann Boleyn, for example, he insists that her guilt, in which he professed to believe, is a matter of vital importance; the injustice done would otherwise be too appalling, and Protestants, by holding her innocent, 'in mistaken generosity, here courted an infamy for the names of those to whom they owe their being, which, staining the fountain, must stain for ever the stream which flows from it'.[47] It was a circularity he was to revert to in other cases, including that of Mary Queen of Scots. This was presumably the kind of thing Freeman had in mind when he spoke of 'one of the wildest and most paradoxical theories that ever entered the head of mortal man', namely 'the infallibility of Henry VIII'.[48]

In so far as Froude's interests were not moral and religious, they were social. For the Whig historian the constitution and Parliament provided the essential protagonist for the story of English history, as the development and fortunes of liberty and its reconciliation with order. Froude had no such enduring political protagonist; only the spiritual one of 'The Reformation' in his own *History*, and the social condition and moral character of the English people themselves.[49] There is in fact a good deal more

[45] Carlyle, *The French Revolution*, Part III, bk ii, ch. iii.
[46] 'Calvinism', *SS*, ii. 14, 45–6.   [47] *HE*, ii. 400. Also iii. 482–3; iv. 239.
[48] *HE*, viii. 72. Cf. iii. 246.   [49] Freeman, *op. cit.*, *Saturday Review*, xvii. 81.

'social history' in Froude than in Macaulay, and in this respect, as
in others, it is tempting to see him not merely as anti-Whig but as a
kind of Tory–Radical. Predictably, in a disciple of Carlyle, he was
always drawn to governmental paternalism, to calls for a responsible aristocracy, to a critique of the inequitable distribution and
misuse of wealth, and to a naked hostility to laissez-faire individualism and political economy.[50] And of course the Tory–
Radical critique of English society, as it had developed from the
1820s onwards, was essentially based on a primitive social history
of England. It was this critique which, in the 1830s and 1840s, had
given such a sharp contemporary relevance to the interpretation of
the sixteenth century, in a fashion very different from the Whigs'
traditional concern with the fate of the constitution, though
Disraeli had rewritten that too, in his Bolingbrokean Tory
version.[51] Cobbett and Pugin had made the Dissolution of the
Monasteries an issue in the contemporary debate over poor-
relief.[52] The people had been deprived of the charitable fund set
aside by pious testators for the relief of their necessities. Disraeli,
supporting them, found the origins of the Whig oligarchy in their
acquisition of the spoils of the monasteries.[53] Whiggism was
founded in robbery. But the Dissolution was, of course, only one
important issue in a whole social and cultural reappraisal of the
Middle Ages and the modern world, and, inevitably, of the
sixteenth century as the watershed. There was, if not yet an
historiographical tradition, certainly a cause, for Froude to
embrace if he would.

The limits of the present book have not allowed for a systematic
account of the radically disaffected, overtly reactionary strand in
the English approach to the past, though it wove itself as a
contrasting thread into the texture of Whig history. But in the
middle years of the nineteenth century, from Southey and Cobbett,
Pugin and Disraeli, to Ruskin and Morris, with a twentieth-
century epilogue in Belloc and Chesterton and, more soberly,

---

[50] See particularly, 'State and subject', 'On progress', 'England's war', *SS*, ii; 'On the uses
of a landed gentry', 'Party politics', *SS*, iii.
[51] See above, p. 18.
[52] W. Cobbett, *A History of the Protestant Reformation in England and Ireland* (1824–7)
(Gasquet edn, n.d.) pp. 84, 93. A. W. N. Pugin, *Contrasts* (2nd edn 1841).
[53] Disraeli, *Coningsby* (1844), bk II, ch. 1. This was, of course, a long-standing debate. See
Pocock (ed.), *Political Writings of James Harrington*, p. 198; Robbins, *The Eighteenth
Century Commonwealthman*, p. 118; Millar, *Historical View*, ii. 438; Hallam, *Const.
Hist.*, i. 78–9.

Tawney, the past, constantly called on for the conception of a medieval utopia, notoriously formed the basis of a radical critique of capitalism and a repudiation of Whiggish complacency about the national history. In this critique, with the Middle Ages as a lost paradise, the sixteenth century – sometimes the fifteenth was also impugned – was clearly designated as the site of the fall: the monasteries plundered, the tranquil, regulated loyalties and industry of manor and guild desiccated by irresponsible greed and commercialism. The links of this critique with eighteenth-century, Country Party forms of nostalgia have not yet been properly explored, though nineteenth-century neo-medievalism has drawn more attention in recent years[54] than nineteenth-century Whiggism; a reflection no doubt, apart from the aesthetic perquisites of the former, of our age's preference, in intellectual history, for the subversive and rancorous over the official and self-congratulatory.

It is nevertheless a curious fact that in the major historical works of the nineteenth century, though the influence of an atavistic (early) medievalism and nostalgic radicalism were strongly felt, the Whig line was held, if only just. Freeman, Green, and even, in historical terms, Stubbs, remained faithful to the Good Old Cause. There is no great Tory Radical narrative 'Decline and Fall of Medieval England'. Cobbett's *History of the Reformation*, vigorous – to say the least – as polemic, was not a work of scholarship; it was culled, according to Gasquet, from the soberly Catholic history of Lingard.[55] Later in the century, one of the leading authorities on the decline of feudalism, Frederic Seebohm, was a hard-headed Liberal-Unionist banker.[56] It may be objected that neo-medievalism was essentially polemical, and found a certain vagueness convenient, but polemical historiography would have been no novelty. More might be said for the view that, as an essentially social indictment, it would have needed a fully developed economic and social history to express it, of the kind to

---

[54] There is no entirely satisfactory general study of nineteenth-century medievalist social criticism. The most comprehensive is Alice Chandler, *A Dream of Order. The Medieval Ideal in Nineteenth Century English Literature* (1971).

[55] Cobbett, *Reformation*, p.v. Lingard, however, makes none of Cobbett's extravagant claims. John Lingard, *The History of England from the First Invasion by the Romans to the Accession of William and Mary* (6th edn 1854), 10 vols. v. ch. II.

[56] The other being Thorold Rogers. See next note. For Seebohm on the decline of feudalism see Burrow 'Village community' in McKendrick (ed.), *Historical Perspectives*, pp. 273–5. For the controversy between Seebohm and Rogers, see Sir Paul Vinogradoff, 'Frederick Seebohm', *Collected Papers*, 2 vols (O.U.P. 1928), i. 272–4.

which Thorold Rogers' *History of Prices*[57] made an impressive contribution, and which was later developed, among others, by R. H. Tawney and J. L. and Barbara Hammond.[58]

The same, however, might be said of Green's *The Making of England*, which also moved far away from traditional political narrative, yet there is no correspondingly elaborate historical lamentation, no version of England's late-medieval undoing. Morris was a poet, not an historian, and Ruskin's denunciations only became circumstantial where the eye could see; his most copiously documented – in his own idiosyncratic fashion – indictment of the corruption, luxury, infidelity and hard-heartedness of the fifteenth and sixteenth centuries is *The Stones of Venice*. Apart from Ruskin's, the most powerful mind in which the medievalist critique found a lodging, of much individuality, was of course Carlyle's, but his major works of history were set outside England, and in *Cromwell* Puritanism was naturally to the fore. *Past and Present* remained an unclassifiable *tour de force*, like Southey's *Colloquies on Society* or Pugin's *Contrasts*. If there is a large-scale narrative history of England by an author essentially Tory Radical in ideas and sentiment it is that of his disciple Froude; that it nevertheless approves Tudor England's break with the past, appears to endorse progress, and celebrates the origins of England's commercial empire, is an inadvertent testimony to the adhesiveness and resilience of basic Whig ideas, as well as to their enduring links with Protestantism. Froude was no Whig, but his *History* ultimately supported rather than challenged a central Whig sentiment: a sense of the privileges the English derived from their history. It lies, as it were, in the debatable lands along the borderline of Whiggism, and helps us to chart its vagaries.

Froude was fond of asserting the conventionality of his historical opinions before he began his *History*, claiming to have been led to his later views by the source material.[59] His enemies spoke of lack of preparation, and conceded him originality of a sort, though they interpreted it as perversity. Goldwin Smith spoke, for example, of 'the extraordinary revolution which he has undertaken to

[57] Thorold Rogers, *A History of Agriculture and Prices in England* (1866), 2 vols.
[58] Especially R. H. Tawney, *The Agrarian Revolution of the Sixteenth Century*, and J. L. and Barbara Hammond, *The Village Labourer*.
[59] *HE*, i. Preface; iv. 239. For an appraisal of Froude's handling of his sources, by an eminent authority, see G. R. Elton's Introduction to the forthcoming Chicago University Press abridged edition of Froude's *History*. I am most grateful to Professor Elton for his generosity in allowing me to see this essay in advance of publication.

effect in this period of English History'.[60] So far as historiographical issues went, Froude may have been right; provided Protestantism was proved the better cause he made few initial demands on his chosen century. He came to write in conscious opposition to established Whig views, particularly, probably, Macaulay's: on Tudor monarchy, on Henry VIII, on Cranmer, on Elizabeth. But his hostility to the Romantic High-Tory version of the English past, brought back from Oxford by Hurrell Froude, surprising his old-fashioned family, was of a more fundamental kind; Tractarianism was a part of his own moral world, though rejected, in a way Macaulay's kind of Whiggism never was. In the Tractarian version,

the Reformation became the great schism, Cranmer a traitor, and Latimer a vulgar ranter. Milton was a name of horror, and Charles I was canonized and spoken of as the holy and blessed martyr St Charles .... Similarly we were to admire the nonjurors, to speak of James III instead of the Pretender; to look for Antichrist, not in the pope, but in Whigs and revolutionists and all their works.[61]

Froude was startled, but not, by his own account, convinced. If he was, he reacted; in his *History* he was to defend the Dissolution, applaud the Reformers, and damn Mary Queen of Scots and all 'sentimental' Catholic versions of English history. Froude, in fact, came to hold a stance unprecedented in English historiography: friendly to Puritanism and to strong monarchy, hostile to the monasteries and by no means tender to early capitalism. It is perhaps no wonder that Green described his *History* as disfigured, among other sins, by paradox.[62] Froude was no party man. He was right, in fact, to present himself as a free spirit, if one excepts bondage to Carlyle and to his own early experiences.

Of course, given the sympathy of High Tories and Tory Radicals – though there were exceptions – with the Catholic Middle Ages, to write a history vindicating the Reformation was, not necessarily intentionally, but in the broadest sense and beyond all cavil over detail, to align oneself with Whiggism of a sort. For though the Whig as constitutionalist might deplore the sixteenth century, the Whig as Protestant – and though not all Protestants might be Whigs, a Whig historian of England must of necessity be

---

[60] Quoted Dunn, ii. 267.
[61] 'The Oxford Counter-Reformation', *SS*, iv. 248.
[62] Green, *Short History*, p. 331.

Protestant – was bound in some measure to cherish it.[63] In the same way the Protestant could not help forming some alliance with Whiggism. It had long been an uneasy alliance, but it was one which could not be escaped.

We have seen what Froude thought of the Whig's fetish, the constitution. For the Whig, Protestantism clearly contained possibilities of enthusiasm not always congruous with his own creed; archetypically the Protestant was the man of a book, not a tradition. Puritan sectaries, like republican regicides in the seventeenth century – they might well be the same – might find themselves inside or outside the Whig pale. Of course, in so far as the Whig tradition was constitutionalist, tolerant and Erastian, it had no concern with theological questions as such. Macaulay, growing up in a Whiggism committed to Catholic Emancipation as a central article of its current political creed, took a strong version of this view; it was persecution that turned sects into factions.[64] And increasingly from the mid-nineteenth century onwards, in an age of attenuated religious belief, it could be a convenience to applaud the Reformation without too much attention to the more theologically self-assured aspects of Protestantism. As Green rather blandly put it, 'The real value of the religious revolution of the sixteenth century to mankind lay not in its substitution of one creed for another, but in the new spirit of inquiry, the new freedom of thought and of discussion, which was awakened during the process of change,' though he admitted that such cheerful latitudinarianism was not characteristic of the sixteenth century itself: 'however familiar such a truth may be to us, it was absolutely hidden from the England of the time'.[65]

An additional secular consideration came to cement the alliance with Protestantism in the broadest sense: the concept of progress. The more progressive tendencies of Protestant communities spoke eloquently for the reformed religion, supplementing more purely theological considerations. The increasing diffusion and scope of continental travel provided material for an informal sociology of religion; the state of inns and beds brought opportunities for

---

[63] The young Macaulay, trying to counter Protestant bigotry and to make the penal laws against Catholics accidental to Whiggism, played down the connection. Our ancestors' hostility 'was primarily not to popery but to tyranny', 'Milton', *Works*, v. 26. Russell, however, stated the connection succinctly: 'Boast as we may of our constitution, had Queen Elizabeth been a Roman Catholic, or James the Second a Protestant, there would have been no liberty in England.' *Hist. Eng. Govt.*, p. 52.
[64] Macaulay, *History*, *Works*, i. 47.   [65] Green, *Short History*, p. 360.

inductive Protestant apologetics, and pyrrhic victories for the purer faith. Catholicism was clearly associated with poverty, flies, dirt and indolence, as well as priestcraft and intolerance, and it was likely there was a causal connection. With Macaulay's sanction, adjacent Swiss cantons of different faiths were examined for relative daintiness, industry and prosperity.[66] Ruskin records this practice of his parents:

> They failed not, therefore, to look carefully on the map for the bridge, or gate, or vale, or ridge, which marked the separation of Protestant from the benighted Catholic cantons; and it was rare if the first or second field and cottage, beyond the border, did not too clearly justify their exulting, – though also indignant and partly sorrowful, – enforcement upon me of the natural consequences of Popery.[67]

Freeman protested against this habit.[68] Froude himself made the same comparisons in Ireland.[69] If Ireland was an awful warning, the condition of the Papal States was an offence to public spirit.[70] Macaulay summed up:

> The loveliest and most fertile provinces of Europe have, under her [i.e. the Roman Church's] rule, been sunk in poverty, in political servitude, and in intellectual torpor, while Protestant countries, once proverbial for sterility and barbarism, have been turned by skill and industry into gardens, and can boast of a long list of heroes and statesmen, philosophers and poets.

Illustration copiously followed.[71]

Such broad sociological categories were useful, for of course it was only in the widest sense that Protestantism could be uncontentious. In detail, the animosities over differences of theology and organisation which in the sixteenth century stretched from Hooker to Cartwright, from Cranmer's prayer book to Puritan 'prophesyings' and hedge-preaching, could hardly fail to be at least palely reflected in historiography, as nuances of approval or distaste. The Burkean Whiggism of the nineteenth century, for example, had acquired as a defining characteristic a marked dislike of the doctrinaire and the zealot, or what Bolingbroke, with

---

[66] Macaulay, *History, Works*, i. 38.   [67] Ruskin, *Praeterita*, p. 227.
[68] 'Protestant and Catholic cantons of Switzerland', *Saturday Review*, xvi (9 Jan, 1864), 51. Bevington does not attribute this article to Freeman, but the style and opinions make it almost certainly his. He produced a similar argument elsewhere. 'National prosperity and the Reformation' (1868), *Hist. Ess.*, 4th series.
[69] Dunn, i. 68–9. *SS*, iv. 297.
[70] Macaulay, *History, Works*, i. 38. Cf. Trevelyan, *Life*, pp. 361–2. It was, of course, a common view. For Victorian impressions of Rome, see Mario Praz, *The Hero in Eclipse in Victorian Fiction*, Appendix II, 'Rome and the Victorians' (O.U.P. 1956).
[71] *History, Works*, i. 37–8.

nice Augustan discrimination, had called 'precise knaves and enthusiastic madmen'.[72] By the mid-nineteenth century, the developed taste for medieval art and architecture added charges of vandalism to those of fanaticism. Earlier, more radical Whigs, especially those from Dissenting backgrounds, like Godwin, had naturally written more approvingly of the sectaries.[73]

On the other hand, the Established Church, founded in compromise and now securely rooted in tradition, might seem a paradigm case of institutionalised Whiggism. The difficulty, of course, was the Church of England's unremitting Toryism, and even, in earlier times, her association with Divine Right and non-resistance, which Macaulay, for one, could never forgive. His treatment of the dilemma this posed for a Whig account of the English Reformation was an exercise in Mandevillian historical irony: men had on the whole done better than they knew, intended or deserved.

> Elsewhere worldliness was the tool of zeal. Here zeal was the tool of worldliness. A king whose character may best be described by saying that he was despotism personified, unprincipled ministers, a rapacious aristocracy, a servile Parliament, such were the instruments by which England was delivered from the yoke of Rome. The work which had been begun by Henry, the murderer of his wives, was continued by Somerset, the murderer of his brother, and completed by Elizabeth, the murderer of her guest. Sprung from brutal passion, nurtured by selfish policy, the Reformation in England displayed little of what had, in other countries, distinguished it, unflinching and unsparing devotion, boldness of speech, and singleness of eye.[74]

The Church of England was born in Erastianism and politic compromise. 'In many respects, indeed, it has been well for her that, in an age of exuberant zeal, her principal founders were mere politicians.' The price was that 'she continued to be, for more than a hundred and fifty years, the steady enemy of public liberty'.[75] Taken in conjunction with his description in the *History* of the gloomy fanaticism of the Puritans, despite a recognition of their positive qualities,[76] it was a somewhat modest endorsement of the English Reformation, and of its theological spirit as a whole: despotism, time-serving and servility on the one hand, uncouth zeal on the other.

But of course the undisputed essence of Protestantism for the

---

[72] Quoted Kramnick, *Bolingbroke*, p. 26.
[73] Robbins, *Eighteenth Century Commonwealthman*, p. 252.
[74] 'Hallam', *Works*, v. 172.   [75] *ibid.*, p. 176.
[76] *History*, ch. 1. Macaulay's judgements on the Puritans are mixed. For a more favourable view see 'Milton', *Works*, v.

Whig does lie nevertheless at the very outset of the English Reformation, in its origin as a national declaration of independence, expressed in the preamble to Henry VIII's Statute of Appeals. English historians, from Tudor times onwards, embroidered the theme of national independence with the colours of Hebraic and Augustinian providential history, with its recurrent moments of deliquency and deliverance, giving to secular history a high-strung apocalyptic tension and sense of special national privilege. As Haller shows, the Protestant historians of the sixteenth century, and Foxe in particular, identified the struggle of the true doctrine of God's word against the corruptions of the Roman Antichrist with the cause of English nationhood, while Elizabeth became, through her providential preservation to ascend the throne, and through the even more clearly providential defeat of the Armada, a type of the monarch as messianic deliverer.[77] Both these themes, and particularly the former, though belonging essentially to Christian apocalyptic universal history, were in this nationalised form to remain powerful in the polite, legalistic Whig history of later centuries.

When Haller, identifying the Augustinian and Eusebian roots of the conception, speaks of the Elizabethan Protestant historians' presentation of English history as 'an age-long contention of English rulers and people against the alien intruders',[78] he also states the central theme of Freeman's *Norman Conquest*, while Foxe's observation on the Norman Conquest itself 'what dangers oft do chance to realms public by foreign marriage with other princes',[79] could well stand as the epigraph to Freeman's work.[80] English history, in sixteenth-century Protestant propaganda, exhibited, as Haller says, 'English rulers faithfully endeavouring or weakly failing to protect themselves and their people against the intrusions of foreign powers and the encroachments of successive popes or their representatives and emissaries upon civil rulers everywhere, but especially in England.'[81] The public excitement over the restoration of the Catholic hierarchy in England in 1851, and the prompt passage of the Ecclesiastical Titles Act were to show in the mid-nineteenth century how much vitality there still was, fostered by more recent feeling against the Tractarians, in traditional English Protestant fears of the pope's emissaries.[82]

---

[77] William Haller, *Foxe's Book of Martyrs and the Elect Nation* (1963).   [78] *ibid.*, 69.
[79] Quoted Haller, *ibid.*, p. 154.   [80] See above, pp. 206, 214–5.   [81] Haller, *ibid.*, p. 154.
[82] See E. Norman, *Anti-Catholicism in Victorian England* (1968).

But in any case the 'foreign-hearted' king,[83] with his foreign favourites and sometimes his sinister complicity in papal designs, became a stock figure in Whig historiography, and not only of the vulgarest sort. In Macaulay's *History* the secret Treaty of Dover was a genuine example, and the crisis of the story was the attempt of James II to reverse the verdict of the Reformation. Seventeenth-century fears of Popish despotism, established by Irish armies and French gold, passed naturally into Whig historiography. But even apart from these then perhaps justified terrors, foreign 'entanglements' offended the sense of national autonomy and integrity, of which Elizabeth's virginity had become the symbol, even though Whigs had to make the best of Dutch and German complications. There was, at the theoretical level, more than pride at stake; national autonomy was a logical as well as historical precondition of the development of a Whig conception of national history, as the nation making itself through the creation of tradition.[84]

The sixteenth-century Protestant conception of the English as an elect nation, itself a nationalisation of a conception of Christian eschatology, helped to foster the sense of national pride, so evident in the interest in national origins, history and antiquities in the later sixteenth and early seventeenth centuries.[85] Equally evident is its eventual transmutation into the celebrations of English stability, prosperity and leadership of Europe in the ways of ordered liberty, which resound so strongly in Hallam and which still contain a more than perfunctory acknowledgement of Divine Providence. English historians like Kemble and Macaulay, brooding gratefully on their country's immunity from the continental disturbances of 1848, had a long tradition of national self-congratulation to sustain them, in which the idea of national integrity and autonomy, vindicated by the Reformation, rescued from the Stuarts, confirmed by the Protestant Succession, was a central one. Even in the cool, wholly secularised vocabulary of a late and partial representative of the Whig tradition, Sir John Seeley, at the end of the nineteenth century, the perennial conflict of national and alien provides him with his conceptual key to the history of English foreign policy: the struggle, since the days of Elizabeth, between a 'dynastic' and a 'national', essentially commercial and imperial, foreign policy, culminating in the eighteenth

[83] Freeman, *NC*, iii. 41.
[84] See Pocock, *Machiavellian Moment*, p. 341.
[85] Haller, *op. cit.*, pp. 225, 232, 240.

century in the victory of the latter.[86] It was the corollary of the familiar Whig story of the conflicts of the Stuarts and their Parliaments and the successful tilting of the balance of the constitution ratified by the accession of the Hanoverian line. Foxe might have recognised some of the ingredients.

The origin of a national foreign policy, for Seeley, lay in the reign of Elizabeth, and its essence was overseas expansion.[87] Seeley's tone, consciously 'scientific' and restrained, was very different from earlier eulogy, but essentially his view of the role of her reign in English history was one more note in a long-drawn chorus of approval. For of course the reign of Elizabeth forms an exception to what has been said earlier about Whig attitudes to the Tudors. As Macaulay said, the Puritans she persecuted lauded her.[88] The Whigs whose constitutional prejudices she prospectively flouted, for the most part forgave her. Millar compared her to Alfred,[89] though Brodie, at least, was predictably sour.[90] For Lord John Russell she was 'the greatest of English, perhaps of all modern sovereigns'.[91] The voluble adulation of the great Queen's subjects had, of course, left a powerful residue. Even in constitutional terms the reign became mythical, identified with the ideal Harringtonian balance;[92] the notion of an Elizabethan golden age passed into popular mythology, where it was identified as the authentic site of Merrie England. Seventeenth- and eighteenth-century country gentry found in it a focus for their social nostalgia.[93] In the seventeenth century, as Hume pointed out, to exalt Elizabeth at the expense of the Stuarts was a natural opposition tactic.[94] In the eighteenth century she was inducted into the Whig canon; Rapin and Bolingbroke united to praise her.[95] Only the Walpolean Whigs, hostile to the notion of the ancient constitution, and intent on peace with Spain, dissented.[96]

[86] Sir J. R. Seeley, *The Growth of British Policy* (first edn 1895; C.U.P. 1922).
[87] *ibid.*, i, pt 1.
[88] *History, Works*, i. 49.
[89] *Historical View*, ii. 446.
[90] Brodie, *Constitutional History*, i. 96, 111–12. Cobbett too, of course, though no Whig, provided a dissentient voice: 'The worst woman that ever existed in England, or in the whole world, Jezabel herself not excepted.' Cobbett, *Reformation*, p. 288.
[91] Russell, *op. cit.*, p. 44.
[92] Kramnick, *Bolingbroke*, pp. 172, 178, 133.
[93] Kramnick, *ibid.*; Haller, *op. cit.*, ch. VII.
[94] Forbes, *Hume's Philosophical Politics*, p. 239. Cf. Haller, p. 228.
[95] Forbes, *op. cit.*, pp. 236, 245. There were some reservations among Whig historians about her arbitrariness, Forbes, p. 255; Colbourn, *Lamp of Experience*, p. 41.
[96] Kramnick, *op. cit.*, pp. 134, 233.

But the most pregnant form taken by these eulogies, though not perhaps the most common, was through the theme of the expansion of English trade and the acquisition of the empire of the seas. For its articulation in the eighteenth century we have to look to the Country Party and Bolingbroke. 'To her we owe that spirit of domestic and foreign trade which is not quite extinguished. It was she who gave that rapid motion to our whole mercantile system which is not entirely ceased.'[97] The polemical edge is obvious, but at first sight it is strange to see Bolingbroke, the spokesman of the nostalgic country gentry, intensely suspicious of the influence of commercial wealth, hailing the expansion of English overseas trade. But as Kramnick points out, it was essentially a view which derived from Bolingbroke's positive conception of the state. 'Bolingbroke's praise of trade could also find its legitimacy in the mercantilist views of the Elizabethans, who saw trade solely as a contribution to the greatness and power of the state. In such a view the social hierarchy neither excludes nor is threatened by the merchant.'[98] In other words it was essentially a nationalist rather than a progressive commercial conception, and implies no general endorsement of the moneyed interest.[99] We shall be able to apply much the same description to Froude's view of empire. But first it is necessary to look in more detail at his notions of English history.

---

[97] Bolingbroke, *Idea of a Patriot King* (1736) (ed. A. Hassall, O.U.P. 1917), p. 118.
[98] Kramnick, p. 199.
[99] The demand for unrestricted trade, by Bolingbroke and others, was directed at the great trading companies, which financed the government through investment in the National Debt. Kramnick, p. 46.

CHAPTER 10

The spirit's trials: Reformation and renewal

Götterdämmerung

In turning to consider Froude's view of English history in more detail we have to consider the possibility that detail may be all there is: that he had no overarching conception of English history at all, certainly not a developmental one. He has, it is true, something like a Whiggish sense of gratitude, more broadly applied in Carlyle's fashion, for the accumulated treasury of 'work', of noble example and material toil inherited from the past; this was, indeed, Carlyle's version of a sense of tradition.[1] Froude's enthusiasm for empire also leads him, as we have seen, to celebrate 'origins' in the classic Whig manner. He has, too, a sense of the significance of English history for Europe in general, or, rather, of a particular moment of it. The most fateful year of that history for Froude was not of course 1688 but 1588; the defeat of the Armada saved the Reformation and thus determined the fate of Europe as a place where life and energy were possible. Though less emphatic, this is reminiscent of the proud Whig notion of England as the political beacon of Europe. We shall find other variations on stock Whig themes later.

But of course Froude's *History*,[2] as we have seen, lacked the Whig's enduring protagonist, the constitution and Parliament. History, for him, was essentially spasmodic, unpredictable in a fashion which went beyond a commonplace rejection of determinism. The spirit blew where it listed. 'The temper of each generation is a continual surprise.'[3] Above all, for him, the determining fact of

---

[1] E.g. *Past and Present*, 'the quantity of done and forgotten work that lies silent under our feet in this world', p. 129.

[2] Froude does note the constitutional significance of the role given to Parliament in the Reformation, and its rising importance in consequence, but it cannot be described as one of the themes of his history. *EH*, iv. 241–2.

[3] 'The science of history', *SS*, i. 27. It is tempting to think Froude may have had the Oxford Movement in mind here, as so often elsewhere.

history was religion; public virtue, polity and social relations were merely its barometers.[4] And 'religion has advanced not by easy and natural transitions, but by successive revolutions, violent leaps, spasmodic and passionate convulsions'.[5]

Yet taken alone the remark is misleading, for the spirit's errant motion is in fact only one moment in an essentially cyclic, recurrent process of decay and renewal, which Froude, like Carlyle, tends to apply to history as a formula. Froude spoke sceptically of philosophies of history, but he had one of a sort and it was essentially Carlyle's. Froude's intellectual subservience to Carlyle, 'my master', is not in doubt. It has his own seal of acquiescence and approval. In the crisis of his life 'Carlyle to me spoke as never man spoke', and 'in all that I thought or attempted I allowed his judgement to guide me'.[6] It was Carlyle's conception of change, with perhaps some subsidiary influence from the sixteenth-century historians themselves, notably Foxe, Hakluyt and Knox, which shaped Froude's *History*, far more than any studies of Tudor England prior to his own.

It was an essentially cyclic and also discontinuous conception, fundamentally at odds with the underlying assurances of historical Whiggism. Of course, in practice it is possible to exaggerate this opposition. The central Whig insistence on continuity and consti-tutional development, though dominant in the eighteenth and early nineteenth centuries, had seldom existed in a pure state; inevitably, as we have seen, it had always been liable to con-tamination from its chief rivals, the nostalgia of the radical, and the Protestant apocalyptic drama of messianic transformation and restitution.[7] The close relation between the comforts of continuity and the consolations of nostalgia has been a major theme of earlier chapters in ths book, while the affinities of an historio-graphical tradition whose central figure is a Great Deliverer with Hebraic and Augustinian notions of captivity and release were inevitably at times close. They tended to become even more so, as we have seen, with the elaborations of historical narrative in the mid-nineteenth century; narrative needs vicissitudes as well as continuity: losses, gains and restitutions.

In Carlyle, the blending of Old Testament sacred drama and German Idealist philosophy,[8] which provided the basis for his

---

[4] E.g. *EH*, iv. 362.   [5] *ibid.*, xii. 481.   [6] Dunn, i. 201–2.
[7] See Pocock, *Machiavellian Moment*, ch. x.
[8] See C. Harrold, *Carlyle and German Thought, 1819–1834* (1934).

view of history, is curiously without incongruity. The first offered a cycle of successive relapse and chastisement: the chequered relations of the chosen people with their jealous God. It became an archetypal Christian historical pattern, a diagnosis for every disaster. It naturally entered into the perceptions of sixteenth-century Protestant historians in a manner Froude must have found congenial. Its secular, classical counterpart, of course, is the exemplary–sociological account of the fall of Rome, in terms of virtue leading to conquest, luxury, corruption of virtue, loss of liberty and destruction. In Carlyle, the hallmark of corruption is dilettantism and hypocrisy, the loss of spiritual force and conviction, the divorce of profession and performance: unreality. History guarantees retribution, a volcanic eruption of inchoate vitality, terrible but cleansing, a return to reality in harsh form, and the hardening of the lava into new shapes, themselves destined one day to decay and break up in similar fashion. The cyclic nature of the process is ensured by the perennial human predisposition to moral sloth and love of ease, to self-deception and imposture: a readiness to tolerate lies and to take the form for the reality: in a word, to idolatry.

It was Carlyle's imaginative achievement, though not his uniquely – Marx's is the other name that comes to mind – to fuse this Hebraic–Christian pattern of idolatry and retribution with a version of the German philosophical accounts of the relations of spirit and matter, creative energy and determinate form. It is through this fusion that his view of culture and institutions, including religion, is relativised and made subtler than a mere iconoclasm, with a recognition of their necessity; they become impostures only in decay. This, of course, is the 'clothes philosophy' of *Sartor Resartus*. The embodiment or clothing of spirit is necessarily a matter of the creation of forms and formulae. After a while the forms become outworn; spirit withdraws from them; they become ghostly, unreal, uninhabited. In some more famous accounts, notably Hegel's, the successive phases of the spirit's incarnation become moments of a developmental sequence, successively more adequate and comprehensive embodiments of universal reason. There is little or nothing of this in Carlyle, though Froude makes an occasional rather half-hearted acknowledgement of intellectual advance,[9] which usually appears, in

---

[9] E.g. *SS*, i. 570; ii. 31; iv. 350, 353; *EH*, xii. 480–1.

Carlylean (here Saint-Simonian)[10] fashion as critical not creative, a solvent of existing forms. Essentially in Carlyle there is not sequence but only the cyclic assurance of the retribution that waits for forms from which the spirit has departed, and the endless self-renewal of the latter. If there is an Absolute Reality it is immanent, as an ever-present possibility of sudden, blinding, life-changing illumination, an immediate access to grace. It is not an historical terminus. Carlyie's conception of history was apocalyptic and messianic, but pluralist; not one but many, a recurring pattern, not a consummation.

This cyclic pattern applied to the history of religion, and hence – given the determining role he assigned to religion, or more vaguely 'belief' or 'conviction', to all history – became from Froude, as early as *The Nemesis of Faith*, a formula of historical dynamics. He returned to it frequently. Sometimes he spoke of it in Hebraic and Carlylean, sometimes in more traditionally classical language, though never, directly, in that of German philosophy. Like the civic humanists of the eighteenth century he was possessed by thoughts of the fall of states and empires through indolence and luxury, though the formula was now sometimes Carlylean rather than Machiavellian: hypocrisy and idolatry became major components of corruption, and faith took precedence over, and created, virtue. The formula, however, is still easily recognisable:

The very same symptoms meet us steadily in the decline of every great people – an old faith, withered in its shell, yet which is preserved in false show of reverence, either from cowardice, or indolence, or miserable social convenience. So Rome fell, so Greece, so Spain, so the greatness of modern Italy. Is this all which we are to expect for the England of Elizabeth and Cromwell?[11]

Nearly forty years later, in *Oceana*, he was still brooding on the fall of Rome and the fate of Britain, though, appropriately, the comparison had become more socially precise and neo-Harringtonian.[12]

In Froude's *History*, the idiom is more distinctly Carlylean. The notion that the Catholic Church in the sixteenth century was a carcass from which the spirit had migrated to become the inspira-

---

[10] In the above account of Carlyle's ideas of history, in order to avoid excessive complexity, I have not spoken of the influence of Saint Simon, but obviously any comprehensive account would have to include it, and especially, as here, the notion of alternating critical and organic periods. For Carlyle's Saint Simonianism, see R. Pankhurst, *The Saint Simonians, Mill and Carlyle* (1957).

[11] *Nemesis*, pp. xxiii–iv. Cf. 'Calvinism', *SS*, ii. 30–1 and *SS*, iv. 355.

[12] See below, p. 282.

tion of Protestantism was accompanied by a characteristically Protestant emphasis, expressed in Carlyle's vocabulary, on the rejection of sham and imposture, 'a monstrous solecism',[13] the carapace of a dead faith. In the Reformation 'the old struggle begins to repeat itself, between the flesh and the spirit, the form and the reality'.[14] In due course, in the nineteenth century, Protesant Bibliolatry would in time become the new fetters.[15] But Froude's treatment is not quite Carlylean in tone. Somewhere in him there was a Whig in exile.

In the Carlylean view of history, just as the spirit is essentially errant, so change is essentially abrupt and convulsive. In registering this as the antithesis of the Whig view, it is tempting to speak of two opposed types of sensibility, and to classify them, as we have already done with Stubbs, and as Carlyle's characteristic imagery, particularly in *The French Revolution*, invites, geologically. A sensibility like Stubbs', as we have seen, is essentially sedimentary, with an acute sensitivity to the effects of almost imperceptible accretion; its geological metaphor is the new uniformitarian geology of Sir Charles Lyell, so vital to the development of nineteenth-century positivism in England, just as its aesthetic counterpart is the late eighteenth-century cult of the Picturesque; it is a Whig sensibility. Carlyle's, by contrast – and here we almost leave metaphor behind – is igneous, saturated, like the paintings of John Martin, with the Vulcanist geology of the earlier nineteenth century; its calculated aesthetic effects are those of the terrible–sublime. Historical change, in *The French Revolution*, is a fearful apocalypse of convulsive heavings, belchings, terrifying crackings of the surface of assumed normality, seas of fire, driven through the vents, overspreading the earth:

Behold the World-Phoenix, in fire-consummation and fire-creation: wide are her fanning wings; loud is her death-melody, of battle-thunders and falling-towns; skyward lashes the funeral flame, enveloping all things: it is the Death-Birth of a World.[16]

Thus the French Revolution, in terms of a rather Teutonic apocalypse. But it is also an old Testament scourging: the fire purifies.

The metal images are molten; the marble Images are become mortar-lime; the stone Mountains sulkily explode . . . Wo to them that shall be born then.[17]

---

[13] *EH*, i. 343. [14] *ibid.*, p. 513. [15] *Nemesis*, p. xviii.
[16] Carlyle, *The French Revolution*, Pt. I, bk VI, ch. I. [17] *ibid.*, Pt III, bk VII, ch. VIII.

It was Froude's misfortune that he did not share Carlyle's enjoyment of iconoclastic frenzy, his exhilarated (and exhilarating) spluttering in the fire-fountains he had conjured up; at most, in Froude, there was an occasional grim, ironic pleasure in retribution. As he once said, admittedly in old age, 'The function of Radicalism in these days I conceive to be the burning up of rubbish ... But the burning process is disagreeable to me, however I may see it to be inevitable.'[18] It seems appropriate that when he saw a volcano he disliked it;[19] it is a pity no similar confrontation is recorded of Carlyle.

Froude's own characteristic imagery was on the whole non-violent, apart from the occasional flash of lightning. He was fond, it is true, of military and naval comparisons for the state, for which he had Carlylean precedent. But for metaphors for historical change his recourse was not to geology but to botany, meteorology and navigation. Seeds sprout, plants grow; at one point, by some odd, unresolved tension between Carlylean retribution and the suggestions of the image, they crush.[20] Lights go out, clouds gather and are dispelled, night gives way to day and 'lengthening daylight'.[21] But above all there was the sea, with its combined suggestion of freedom and featureless illimitability, and the imagery of navigational aids. Froude's well-known diagnosis of the spiritual predicament of his generation makes it sound like the experiences of a peevish yachtsman:

all round us, the intellectual lightships had broken from their moorings, and it was then a new and trying experience. The present generation, which has grown up in the open spiritual ocean, which has got used to it and has learned to swim for itself, will never know what it was to find the lights all drifting, the compasses all awry, and nothing left to steer by except the stars.[22]

The immensity was daunting, but the sense of emancipation was also great.

It was this, above all, which linked his thought and his *History* to the Carlylean pattern of rejection, otherwise alien to the gentler tenor of his own mind. It taught him the release, if not the lurid imagery, of catharsis. In the crisis of his own life he had found the strength to face and proclaim his doubts and suffer for the truth as he saw it, to 'have done with insincerity'[23] and fling himself free of the nightmarish tangle of insoluble theological puzzles which emmeshed him. It was from his renunciation of his clerical gown,

[18] Dunn, ii. 560.   [19] *Oceana*, p. 343.   [20] *HE*, ii. 248.   [21] *ibid.*, p. 469.
[22] Froude, *Carlyle's Life in London*, i. 311.   [23] *ibid.*

his Nessus-shirt as he called it, and his escape from the clerical tyranny of Oxford by the resignation of his fellowship, that he dated his regeneration, his conversion into a solid and useful layman, a resolute Erastian and a devout theist.[24] In retrospect the character he created for himself seems to lack inventiveness and subtlety; like the rather similar version of his friend Fitzjames Stephen,[25] it sometimes needed a certain philistine brutality to sustain it; in his hatred of theology – though religion, as a sense of the ultimate justice of the system of the world, remained the abiding interest of his life – Froude came a little to resemble, with a richer vocabulary, E. M. Forster's unsympathetic public school imperialist: 'I don't think it does to talk about these things, every fellow has to work out his own religion.'[26] But the tension had been great. He said of *The Nemesis of Faith*, the book in which he had, in the modern phrase, 'come out', that 'To myself, writing the book was an extraordinary relief. I had thrown off the weight under which I had been staggering. I was free, able to encounter the realities of life.'[27] The only flames were those in the grate in Exeter College Hall, where his colleague Sewell publicly burnt the book.[28] The suffering, however, was real: rejection by his father and family, public denunciation, loss of livelihood and career.

It would not be hard to see in all this a recapitulation of aspects of the Reformation, especially if, like Froude, one sees Protestantism essentially as 'a refusal to live any longer in a lie'[29] and the English Reformation as a lay revolt against the clergy and the Church.[30] In fairness to Froude we should no doubt try to repress the recollection of Hegel's well-known dictum about history repeating itself first as tragedy and then as farce. Froude was certainly aware of the analogies, and naturally preferred to think of his own life recapitulating history rather than his *History* re-enacting his life. He shared a common thought of his day: ontogeny recapitulated phylogeny. 'I have often thought it is part of the inner system of the earth that each one of us should repeat over again in his own experience the spiritual condition of each of its antecedent eras.'[31]

In the *History*, there is nothing covert about the analogies, if not with Froude's personal life, at least with the circumstances of his own time; he points them unmistakably and sometimes explicitly.

[24] Dunn, i. 126, 131, 143–4, 169–70. [25] *ibid.*, ii. 472.
[26] *A Passage to India* (Penguin edn), p. 51. [27] Dunn, i. 126. [28] *ibid.*, pp. 227–8.
[29] *EH*, i. 548. [30] Dunn, i. 174. [31] *Nemesis*, p. 74.

They go beyond specific instances like his presentation of Knox, which is almost, as he admitted elsewhere, a portrait of Carlyle.[32] The resemblances Froude detected between the Oxford of the sixteenth and the nineteenth centuries formed, in a sense, as his concluding chapter makes clear, the central contemporary lesson of the entire work.

Froude seems always to have thought of Tractarianism and its fate, the success or failure of an attempt to reverse the verdict of the Reformation, as the most momentous issue in contemporary life.[33] The cause seems disproportionate to the possible consequences:

a class of residents which appears to be perennial in that University [Oxford] composed of the young masters [of arts]; a class of men who, defective alike in age, in wisdom, or in knowledge, were distinguished by a species of theoretic High Church fanaticism.[34]

But one cannot wonder at Froude being struck by the sense of familiarity, or of identification, as when, in pre-Reformation Oxford, ' "towardly young men" who were venturing stealthily into the perilous heresy of Greek were eyed askance by the authorities, and taught to tremble at their temerity'.[35] For 'Greek', clearly, read 'German'. The activities of the Oxford-trained Jesuits in the reign of Elizabeth offered even more obvious parallels, and Froude's depiction of Campion, vain, surrounded by an atmosphere of hysterical devotion and adulation,[36] is not exactly a portrait of Newman, whom Froude continued to respect, but of what Newman might have been. And in Froude's picture of Cardinal Pole, the arch-villain of the entire *History*, we seem to see beyond the stock figure of the doctrinaire fanatic, not a portrait, but flickering resemblances to Hurrell Froude:

He belonged to a class of persons at all times numerous, in whom enthusiasm takes the place of understanding; who are men of an 'idea'; and unable to accept human things as they are, are passionate loyalists, passionate churchmen, passionate revolutionists, as the accidents of the age may determine.[37]

Such analogies, perhaps with the exception of the last, were clearly made in full self-consciousness. It is harder to be sure about those in which we seem to see the recapitulation of Froude's own life. Obscurer and subtler, perhaps unconscious, perceptions of

[32] Dunn, i. 199.
[33] E.g. *HE*, xii. 480, 502. Cf. 'The condition and prospects of Protestantism', *SS*, ii. 179.
[34] *EH*, i. 275.   [35] *ibid.*, p. 312.   [36] *ibid.*, x. 467; xi. 50, 52, 90.
[37] *ibid.*, vi. 100.

similarity seem to underlie his *History* and echo some of his own deepest promptings and dilemmas. What is interesting here is not so much just the fact itself, but the ways in which they find quite natural and congenial expression in some of the standard vocabulary and prejudices of English – which means predominantly Whig – historiography, as we have seen them in Macaulay and Freeman: prejudices central, in fact, to their cultivated notions of Englishness.

Perhaps the most obvious case is Froude's notoriously favourable presentation of the character and actions of Henry VIII. In proposing a reappraisal, he employed an essentially familiar and congenial vocabulary, as well as one with special resonances for himself. Even Freeman had conceded that Henry, to him a tyrant and vandal, was 'a King who, with all his crimes, was at least an Englishman':[38] high praise in Freeman's lexicon.

Henry, in Froude's account, is a man caught in the toils, freeing himself and England by a convulsive effort Emmeshed in the tangle of the divorce negotiations and the web of European diplomacy, he is surrounded at home by the superstitious fears and rumours among his own subjects, brought to fever-height in the 'disordered visions' of the Nun of Kent and her cult.[39] French and Italian subtleties are set off against the 'downright honesty' of Henry's emissary, Bonner, at the Valois and Papal courts, with their refinements, their 'graces which . . . transform licentiousness into elegant frailty, and treachery and falsehood into pardonable finesse'.[40] Pope Clement weeps, flatters, dissembles, hysterically tears his handkerchief. At home witchcraft flourishes; the prophetess, with her chorus of 'fanatical friars', shrieks her wild warnings; the great men of the realm are troubled, confused and fearful.[41]

The honest Englishman, confronted by the wiles of polished foreigners, diplomats, priests, or both in one, is a familiar, almost folkloric figure. We have seen him – an honorary Englishman only – in the person of Bentinck in Macaulay's account of the Treaty of Ryswick. There the scene was comedy, the intrigues of the foreigners merely a fatuous burlesque. In Freeman, Harold cuts a tragic and unsuccessful figure in the face of William's diplomacy and his alliance with the Pope. In Froude's account

[38] Freeman, *NC*, iii. 41.   [39] *HE*, ii. 59.   [40] *ibid.*, p. 31.
[41] *ibid.*, pp. 58, 82, 74–5, 82–3, 92.

essentially the same character, sane, forthright, masculine –
Froude insists more than once on the essentially feminine character of Catholic hysteria, another archetypal polarity[42] – is more
like a figure from Romance, a knight held fast by insidious
superstitious terrors and emanations of the lower world. The
Reformation – and Henry – were 'beset not merely with external
obstacles, which a strong will and a strong hand could crush, but
with the phantoms of dying faiths, which haunted the hearts of all
living men'.[43] The king himself was a divided nature. Henry's
theological training had been a misfortune to him[44] – we know
what Froude thought of his own. But Henry's nerve holds, and the
cathartic moment comes.

So Henry spoke at last. There was no place any more for nice distinctions and
care of tender consciences. The general, when the shot is flying, cannot qualify his
orders with dainty periods. Swift command and swift obedience can alone be
tolerated; and martial law for those who hesitate.[45]

The Pope – whose prompt death is made to seem a divine
dismissal[46] – and his frenzied minions are put to flight, the web of
diplomacy cut; the Nun and her friends are executed, Fisher and
More sent to the Tower.

The victory was a spiritual and moral one, a crucial act of
self-emancipation and will, followed by a kind of rebirth. Henry
was 'a new man'.[47] It was also metaphysical: not only vigorous,
decisive action but the breaking of a kind of enchantment, sinister
but essentially insubstantial, dispelled at the touch of reality; the
air clears, the mists are dispersed. The enemy had been, in a sense,
under the same spell: 'In the rough awakening out of their
delusion, as with a stroke of lightning, popes, cardinals, emperors,
ambassadors, were startled into seriousness.'[48] It is a very Carlylean conception, though in no way obviously borrowed. At the
opening of The French Revolution the court of France is itself the
figment of an enchantment, an 'Armida palace', Dubarrydom (not
'ism'); its creatures vaporous as well as vapid, packed off in an
instant by the reality of Louis XV's death.[49] Carlylean too, in
Froude's account, is the notion of Charlatanism, divination and
hysteria as the symptoms of an order in decay and as premonitions
of revolution.[50] Froude obliquely acknowledges the debt in his

---

[42] ibid., i. 328; v. 444; vi. 384.   [43] ibid., ii. 82.   [44] ibid., i. 285.
[45] ibid., ii. 122.   [46] ibid., p. 123.   [47] ibid., p. 166.   [48] ibid., p. 275.
[49] Carlyle, The French Revolution, Pt I, bk I, ch. I.   [50] HE, ii. 74.

reference to the analogy of Cagliostro,[51] on whom Carlyle had written a well-known essay.

In Froude's account of the first act of the English Reformation there seems to be a twofold identification, in which Henry stands for both England and for Froude himself. Froude had known his own catharsis, but also, in his liking for decisive action, it is easy to see the vicarious relief of an essentially perplexed, brooding nature. He altogether lacked the exuberant temperament of the typical Whig historian. His frequent sense of the difficulties of judgement – 'every one is a perplexity to himself and a perplexity to his neighbours' – expressed itself not in detachment – his judgements are vehement enough by any standard – but in agonising, in a constant probing of the sensitive spot. Compared with the innocence of Macaulay or Freeman, Froude seems morally adult but also damaged. Their blindnesses came from a lack, from coarseness and sometimes lack of imagination. Froude's vehemence came from attempts, sometimes strident, to resolve inner doubts. His work, full of moral earnestness, lacks self-enjoyment. His pleasures, fishing and sailing, were not, like theirs, extensions of his cultural interests but escapes from them into a simpler world. He loved the freedom of the sea, the liberating hiatus of a long voyage. On his passage to South Africa he wrote:

> I have been feeding hitherto on Greek plays; this morning I took up Homer instead, and the change is from a hot-house to the open air. The Greek dramatists, even Aeschylus himself, are burdened with a painful consciousness of the problems of human life, with perplexed theories of Fate and Providence. Homer is fresh, free, and salt as the ocean.[52]

His own nature was profoundly melancholy-reflective and not at all Homeric. As he once, admittedly at a bad time, wrote to Kingsley, explaining his dislike of Clough's *The Bothie of Tober-na-Vuolich*, 'From some unhappy idiosyncrasy I am always affronted with anything like rude, boisterous health – physical or moral.'[53] In later life strangers noticed his pathos and gloom.[54] Freeman and he could have sat for emblematic portraits of Schiller's opposed poetic categories, the naive and the sentimental.

'Why, why are we compelled to know anything, when each step gained in knowledge is but one more nerve summoned out into consciousness of pain?'[55] This was the young Froude in *The Nemesis of Faith*, in the 'subjective' vein he came to repudiate. But

[51] *ibid.*, iii. 343. Cf. i. 107. [52] Quoted Paul, *Life of Froude*, p. 257.
[53] Quoted Dunn, i. 131. [54] Paul, *Life*, pp. 269–70. [55] *Nemesis*, p. 17.

consciousness remained a burden, making thoughts of release either exhilarating or dangerously seductive. In Froude, as in Tennyson, whose poetry he admired and felt to be a voice for his own thoughts only second to Carlyle's, strenuousness was at odds with, and in periodic, anxious need of assertion against, a susceptibility to a lapping enchantment, a longing for self-surrender and an infinitely soothing moral obliviousness.[56] 'Manful', for Froude, was contrasted not only with effeminate but also with childish.

The underlying anxiety or need for the reassertion of will may help to explain his much-resented and frequent remarks on the Irish character. Though he constantly condescended to them, and though they appalled him, the Irish fascinated Froude as they did not Macaulay, whose attitude in other respects was similar. The Irishman was a familiar foil to English virtues in Whig history. But in Froude's he becomes an uncanny antitype, of mysterious seductiveness. 'The Irish who had been conquered in the field revenged their defeat on the minds and hearts of their conquerors; and in yielding, yielded only to fling over their new masters the subtle spell of the Celtic disposition.' The English virtues were powerless; 'the stealthy evil crept on irresistibly'.[57] Spenserian imagery – The Faerie Queen had been part of Froude's early reading – seems appropriately called on, each new deputy leaving for Dublin 'with the belief that he at last was the favoured knight would break the spell of the enchantment'.[58] It was what a later generation would call 'going native'.[59] For Froude 'the fatal fascination' represented 'certain perennial tendencies of humanity, latent in all mankind, and which opportunity may at any moment develop. It was not a national spirit ... It was rather an impatience of control, a deliberate preference for disorder, ... a reckless hatred of industry.'[60] Putting aside the question of the justice of the observation, it can be said of Froude, as scarcely of Macaulay, certainly not of Freeman, that he could imagine what it might be to be someone else, lead another kind of life.

The seductiveness of an anodyne irresponsibility, this time in the form of an unquestionable creed, formed a vital element in

---

[56] E.g. Tennyson, 'The Lotus-Eaters', 'Locksley Hall', 'The Palace of Art'.
[57] HE, ii. 130.   [58] ibid., vii. 536.
[59] For a perceptive discussion of this and of the ambiguities of feeling involved, see Eric Stokes, ' "The Voice of the Hooligan". Kipling and the Commonwealth experience' in McKendrick (ed.) Historical Perspectives.   [60] HE, ii. 134.

Froude's violent reaction to his view of Catholicism. His occasional declarations in the *History* of the need to understand all points of view are rather perfunctory and could well seem hypocritical to an indignant Catholic, but it is clear that in a sense Froude did understand, perhaps better than he wished.[61] Near the end of *The Nemesis of Faith* there is a kind of pseudo-resolution. The hero, Markham Sutherland, in self-disgust and despair at the ruin of his life and the loss of all conviction, is saved from suicide in melodramatic circumstances and undergoes conversion to the Catholic Church. If the book had ended there it would have been a Catholic conversion-novel, like Newman's *Loss and Gain*, though more overwrought and less intellectual. And in a sense the *novel*, as the enactment of Sutherland's story, does end there. The narrator's assurance that Sutherland's conversion proved spurious, that the Catholic Church could not hold him, and that he died in despair, has, by contrast, the air of an editorial interpolation rather than the conclusion or resolution of a novel. If we were to trust the tale not the teller, *The Nemesis of Faith* would be, as Newman's subtitle proclaims of *Loss and Gain*, 'the story of a convert'.

One of the complexities of Froude's case is that Catholicism presented itself in his own life and family as novelty, as a sophistical, theoretical, disturbing theological loquaciousness. Except in Ireland he knew it personally in no other form. And in Froude himself there was a strong dislike of intellectual and theological *tours de force* as wanton, irresponsible in another sense than the one we have been considering. His fondness for catharsis was balanced by a deep attachment to the traditional, habitual and inarticulate. It was a Carlylean trait also, of course, but a difficult one for the celebrant of the Reformation and Protestantism and the emancipated mind of the sixteenth century. Yet how better could he defend the ancient ways, in this case the sober traditional ways of the Church of England at its least theological, which he came increasingly to eulogise, usually with some reference to his father, than by defending their origins?

The Tractarians had made a mere unthinking traditionalism impossible, and Froude never forgave them; it was the revolutionary, upsetting character of Tractarianism he found most objection-

---

[61] 'The vexed soul, weary of its doubts, and too impatient to wait till it pleases God to clear away the clouds, demands a certainty on which it can repose – never to ask a question more.' 'The revival of Romanticism', *SS*, iii. 141.

able. It was 'the wild dance' which Newman had led.[62] 'They were
to tear up the fibres of custom by which the Establishment as they
found it was maintaining its quiet influence. They were to raise
discussions round its doctrines, which degraded accepted truths
into debatable opinions.'[63] As for his own generation, 'We had
been floated out into mid-ocean upon the Anglo-Catholic raft' and
left by Newman's defection 'like Ulysses, struggling in the
waves'.[64] Newman's voice from the other shore was seductively
beautiful, but 'I believed that it was a siren's song, and that the
shore from which it came had been strewn for centuries with the
bones of the lost mariners who were betrayed by such enchanting
music.' Froude, a not altogether plausibly wily or resilient Ulysses,
stopping his ears with the rougher accents of Ecclefechan, had
'preferred to steer away into the open ocean'.[65]

The backward gaze, however, remained charged with the
conscious stoicism of the warrior-exile from the rich homelands of
the spirit: not, of course, Newman's kind of Catholicism, but the
ancestral pieties he offered, spuriously in Froude's view, to restore.
Initially it was wet-eyed. In *The Nemesis of Faith* the long
plaintive threnody for lost childhood faith and a disenchanted
world rises to a crescendo of wild yearning: 'Oh, for one look of
the blue sky, when we called it heaven.'[66] It subsides into a more
resigned melancholy, in what is in effect a prose poem, a meditation on the theme of *Götterdämmerung* – a very different twilight
from the crash of Freeman's Saxon Valhalla. The old pagan gods
are gone. 'Far out in the country, in the woods, in the villages, for
a few more centuries, the deposed gods still found a refuge in the
simple minds of simple men, who were contented to walk in the
ways of their fathers – to believe where they had believed, to pray
where they had prayed.'[67] The parable is easy to read, the parallel
the same as that of the ending of Frazer's *Golden Bough* almost
half a century later, but the mood is tender, not ironical.[68]
'Centuries have rolled away, the young conqueror is decrepit now,
dying as the old faith died, in the scenes where that faith first died,
and lingering where it lingered. The same sad, sweet scene is acting
over once again.'[69] Carlyle's iconoclasm was native to him;
Froude, by contrast, was a natural builder of shrines for 'old

[62] 'Oxford Counter-Reformation', *SS*, iv. 329.   [63] *ibid.*, p. 252.   [64] *ibid.*, p. 334.
[65] *ibid.*, pp. 339–40.   [66] *Nemesis*, p. 18.   [67] *ibid.*, p. 20.
[68] In this respect the closer analogy is with Walter Pater's *Marius the Epicurean* (1885),
which deals with much the same theme.   [69] *Nemesis*, p. 21.

clothes'. Perhaps it was only Tractarianism that prevented him from being one more openly. But the moral – Carlyle's moral – was accepted. 'Once, once for all, if you would save your heart from breaking, learn this lesson – once for all you must cease in this world to believe in the eternity of any creed or form at all. Whatever grows in time is a child of time.'[70]

The Nemesis of Faith was an immature work, of which Froude was subsequently ashamed; in it, nostalgia was candidly indulged. But the dual nature of the Carlylean conception of history and mutability, at once Hebraic and philosophical, always allowed Froude a convenient alternative in mood and tone; when the working of Divine Providence called for retribution on shams, retribution is duly provided and even enjoyed. When the mood is elegiac, and a meditation on the mutability of all earthly things uppermost, the necessarily evanescent relation between historic forms and the informing spirit provides a softer vocabulary. Catholicism hated can be treated in the tones of Jeremiah; Catholicism almost loved and lamented in those of Ecclesiastes. The elegiac mood was always recurrent, drawing from Froude a wistful eloquence and nostalgia for the old unquestioned faith, the trodden ways of the past, infinitely distant from Macaulay's and Freeman's robust epic roll-calls.

For of course Froude's kind of respect and tenderness for tradition is nevertheless distinctly un-Whiggish. For Froude the dead are really dead. In the case of the Middle Ages there is poignancy in their remoteness, rather than intimacy in their ready invocation. In place of the Whig's confident appropriation of the past, of which Freeman's eternal present is the *reductio ad absurdum*, there is a sense of disruption and distance.

In the alteration of our own character, we have lost the key which would interpret the characters of our fathers, and the great men even of our own English history before the Reformation seem to us almost like the fossil skeletons of another order of beings.[71]

There is a reminiscence here, of course, of Carlyle's *Past and Present*, where the pathos of remoteness is heavily stressed, where the monk is an extinct fossil species, and St Edmund's Abbey 'an old osseous fragment', a mastodon – in turn recalling Tennyson's 'Nature brings not back the Mastodon.'[72] But it was

---

[70] *ibid.*, pp. 21–2.   [71] *HE*, i. 3.
[72] *Past and Present*, pp. 42, 47. Tennyson, 'Morte D'Arthur'.

not simply a convention for Froude; there is no reason to doubt that the pathetic sense of distance was genuinely felt.

And now it is all gone, like an insubstantial pageant faded, and between us and the old English time there lies a gulf of mystery which the prose of the historian will never adequately bridge. They cannot come to us, and our imagination can but feebly penetrate to them. Only among the aisles of the cathedral, only as we gaze upon their silent figures, sleeping on their tombs, some faint conceptions float before us of what these men were when they were alive; and perhaps in the sound of church bells, that peculiar creation of medieval age, which falls upon the ear like the echo of a vanished world.[73]

This passage, so deliberately resonant, gains further resonances when we know how strongly church bells, for Froude, were linked with ideas of childhood and lost faith; the poignancy becomes self-referential. In the *Nemesis* the references have the unguarded sentimentality of a popular ballad: 'When I go to Church, the old church of my old child days, when I hear the old familiar bells, with their warm, sweet heart music . . .'[74] In the *History*, Cranmer's prayers 'chime like church-bells in the ears of the English child'.[75] Froude had refused to regress, but the refusal was always a matter for strenuous assertion. In the opening chapter of the *History*, a long survey of the state of England in the early sixteenth century, which taken by itself could be the preamble to a work of medievalist social nostalgia, he had explicitly to declare that he was not setting up England in the sixteenth century as a model for the nineteenth — too much had changed for this to be possible — and to disclaim the intention of attacking 'the conclusions of political economy';[76] his other writings, and indeed stray remarks in the *History* itself, make it clear that this inhibition, if not insincere, was at most a local self-denial which he felt no obligation to repeat elsewhere.[77]

Pre-Reformation, pre-capitalist English society, with the single exception of the state of the Church, is presented by Froude as almost unqualified idyll; many themes which were to become favourites with him in his essays, a paternalist state, a placid, conservative, essentially equitable ('not . . . economy but . . . equity')[78] and robust way of life, are here presented as realised. As for the material well-being of the people, in the reign of Henry VIII 'In all points of material comfort they were as well off as they had ever been before, better off than they have ever been since.'[79] For

[73] HE, i. 62.   [74] *Nemesis*, p. 16.   [75] HE, v. 53.   [76] *ibid.*, i. 37 n. 1, 89–91.
[77] E.g. *ibid.*, i. 424. SS, iii. 156–7.   [78] HE, i. 30.   [79] *ibid.*, p. 68.

its time, Froude's chapter was impressively detailed, but the overall picture is essentially not different from that of the polemical medievalists and eulogists of 'merrie England': 'it was a life unrefined, perhaps, but coloured with a broad, rosy English health'.[80] Even the notion of the Church as censor and enforcer of morals is not theoretically repugnant to him, on liberal grounds: it is simply unworkable, too much to entrust to frail human beings. The corruption of the Church was the Achilles heel of this society in otherwise robust health.[81]

Of course, the elements of change are noted: the new Copernican astronomy, the discovery of the new world.[82] Similarly, later, Froude was to make the obvious connection between the growth of Protestantism and the population of the towns, especially the seaports.[83] These things represented the future that Froude, at this point at least, was determined to endorse, but there is no triumph, no exulting, in Macaulay's vein – which, like Kingsley, Froude disliked[84] – at the emergence out of squalor, superstition and ignorance, at the March of Mind or the growth of opulence, about both of which, particularly the latter, he was to develop strong reservations. His special enthusiasm for the Scottish Reformation, in fact, derived – apart from its associations with Carlyle – from its plebeian character, and the fact that it seemed a free motion of the spirit, virtually without prior social or economic base.

Elsewhere the plebeian element of nations had risen to power through the arts and industries which make men rich – the commons of Scotland were sons of their religion . . . the tradesmen, the mechanics, the poor tillers of the soil, had sprung suddenly into consciousness with spiritual convictions for which they were prepared to die.[85]

Ordeal and reward

Though the notion of Protestantism as the creed of 'the England of progressive intelligence'[86] is periodically stressed, what chiefly arouses Froude's interest and shapes his treatment of the Reformation is not the march of mind but, in the phrase he used for the title of one of his early autobiographical stories, the spirit's trials:[87] the harrowing and purifying of the spirit of the Reformation through

---

[80] *ibid.*, p. 46. [81] *ibid.*, pp. 191–4. [82] *ibid.*, p. 61. [83] *ibid.*, iv. 297–8; ix. 337.
[84] 'Lives of the Saints', *SS*, i. 550, 565, 571. [85] *HE*, ix. 243. [86] *ibid.*, xii. 476.
[87] In *Shadows of the Clouds* (1847).

hubris and holocaust, a spiritual progress through ordeal. Martyrdom was, of course, the most intense of these trials, and for
martyrdom Froude's enthusiasm was, as one might expect, almost
unbounded. There were to be several false dawns, and a period of
acute trial, before purgation and a return to something like normal
health. Narrative needs vicissitude, and so, apparently, did Providence in its scheme for England's moral self-education, which is
the underlying theme of the first two thirds of Froude's book.
Again we recognise the symmetry between the individual and the
nation: 'If the obscure and intricate existence of man in this planet
has any meaning at all, he is placed here as a training school for his
character.'[88] It is these vicissitudes which give what shape Froude's
narrative possesses.

Not in fact that the *History* is particularly shapely; Froude's
organisation of his vast work is not notably taut or artful. It is not
ill-organised, but even-paced, leisurely, even sprawling. No one
can mistake the dramatic structure of Macaulay's *History*, even
though it is not the complete work he planned: the ominous
acceleration of James' drive to self-destruction, freedom suffering
wound after wound; the tension building up to the relieving
climax of revolution; the brief moment of national unity and
reconciliation, and then the subsidence into the dour struggle for
the preservation of what had been won. In Freeman's, though it is
less successful, partly through excessive length, the variations in
pace and the pyramidal structure are even more marked. The first
and last volumes are surveys, preparation and aftermath, the
second and fourth each deal with a reign, of considerable length;
the narrative texture becomes closest at the apex, the third, which
deals with the single climactic year of the Conquest. There is
nothing like this in Froude's *History*. It is divided into chapters
thematically, in the manner Gibbon had established, but there is
still something of the annalist about it, as there is of course in
other nineteenth-century narrative histories; it was perhaps in part
a consequence of Froude's frequently proclaimed and violated
purpose to let the *History* speak for itself.[89] Perhaps not surprisingly, Froude's response to the virulent attacks, led by Freeman,
on his alleged inaccuracy, was to print yet more documents
verbatim, for which in turn he was abused.[90] Yet it is still possible
to make out the high points in the history, the moments of crisis,

[88] *SS*, iii. 455.
[89] 'The science of history', *SS*, i. 35–6; also *ibid.*, p. 409.   [90] Paul, *Life*, pp. 80, 98.

trial and reward in the Reformation's tutelage by events and its own errors: it is the story of national and religious freedom incompletely won, abused, lost, chastened and confirmed. Largely, of course, the events themselves impose such a pattern, once the Reformation is taken as the protagonist; it corresponds to the reigns of the last four Tudor sovereigns. The rebirth of Protestantism with the accession of Elizabeth and its salvation in the defeat of the Armada would be salient in any Protestant history; indeed, had long been so. But Froude's own preoccupations give them a peculiar emphasis and unity. His treatment of the breach with Rome we have already seen. His handling, too, of the reign of Edward and of the Catholic pseudo-restoration of Mary's reign, have the stamp of individuality and, perhaps more unexpectedly, at times of Whiggishness.

Froude's sense, sometimes conscious, sometimes no doubt latent, of the essential consonance between individual and collective life, gives his history the character not so much of epic as of a morality or passion play, a drama of sin, expiation, redemption and reward. Though Henry, in the opening act of the Reformation which we have already considered, is clearly made in some degree to represent or embody England and Englishness, Froude does not use individuals typologically as Freeman does. His conception does, however, require representative victims; in his view of the Protestant martyrs there is even a strong resonance of the conception of a vicarious atonement which, in traditional theology, had become so abhorrent to him: 'in their deaths they assisted to pay the purchase money for England's freedom'.[91]

But the first notable victim was, morally speaking, smaller fry. Ann Boleyn was, superficially, the Reformation enthroned. But 'the king, professing to be acting upon principle alone, had divorced a Catholic princess to make way for a friend of the Reformation. The sense of duty had been real, but it had been tainted with private inclination'. Ann's guilt and fall were the retribution. 'The high purposes of Providence were not permitted to be disfigured with impurity by the intermixture of worldly intrigues.'[92] Froude dwells with ironic satisfaction on Ann's brief triumph, giving at length the account from Hall of her coronation procession, and adding a grim premonition of its reversal, her return journey to the Tower and execution: 'we escape from this scene of splendour very gladly as from something unseasonable';[93]

[91] *HE*, ii. 258.   [92] *ibid.*, iii. 482–3.   [93] *ibid.*, i. 480.

it is in fact virtually the only scene of Tudor pageantry reproduced in the *History*. Froude was probably attracted to the ironic effect by Carlyle's comparable though kindlier use of the same device in speaking of Marie Antoinette,[94] itself no doubt a reminiscence of Burke's famous rhetorical *tour de force*. But it illustrated, too, one of his guiding conceptions; 'unseasonable' refers to the fate of Queen Catherine, but it seems to have a wider implication. The Reformation was not yet triumphant, nor yet deserved to be.

The proof was the reign of Edward, Protestantism's premature victory. Impatient irreverence and doctrinaire intolerance proved it still unworthy, while the moral corruption of the times – Froude makes much of the spirit of commercial greed, the sufferings of the smallholders and Latimer's denunciations[95] – showed that its mission of spiritual regeneration had for the time being failed. England under Somerset and Northumberland was a topsy-turvy carnival of misrule, one of whose symptoms, for Froude, was a reversal of the – to him – natural moral hierarchy: Catholics were better than Protestants. 'The moral relations of good and evil were inverted; and between Mary, the defender of a dying superstition, and the Lords of the Council, the patrons of liberty and right, the difference so far was as between the honest watch-dog and a crew of howling wolves.'[96]

Froude's sympathy with Latimer's social ideals, and with the poor men dispossessed in the break-up of traditional social bonds, is his own, but there is also much that is reminiscent of Macaulay in his treatment of this reign, possibly unconsciously on his part, though it seems unlikely to be entirely coincidental. There is, for example, a reference to the (typically Macaulayan) notion of a natural 'recoil' of public sentiment against extremes.[97] There is a passage which echoes Macaulay on the demoralising effects of revolutionary times.[98] Above all, though this at least is almost certainly coincidence, there is Froude's attitude to Wyatt's rebellion early in Mary's reign. Froude is grateful for its failure: 'The Protestants would have come back to power in the thoughtless vindictiveness of exasperated and successful revolutionists . . .'[99] Just as the Protestant extremists seem to resemble the Shaftesbury-

[94] *French Revolution*, Pt III, bk IV, ch. VII.
[95] *HE*, iv. 298, 359–63.   [96] *ibid.*, v. 30–1.
[97] *HE*, v. 289. See above p. 86 and n. 105.
[98] *ibid.*, iv. 349–50, 506. Cf. 'Hallam' and 'Temple', Macaulay, *Works*, v and vi.
[99] *HE*, v. 350.

ian Whigs, the unacceptable face of Macaulay's 'great party', the Wyatt rebellion resembles that of Monmouth the pseudo-deliverer, as the premature trial of strength by the men of extremes and the demonstration of their weakness. Protestantism was still to be educated through suffering.

The notion of an historic winnowing, a burning away of dross, was a favourite one of Froude's. Lollardry, for example, was 'an untimely birth'.

The Church was reprieved for a century. Its fall was delayed till the spirit in which it was attacked was winnowed clean of all doubtful elements – until Protestantism had recommenced its enterprise in a desire, not for a fairer adjustment of the world's good things, but in a desire for some deeper, truer, nobler, holier insight into the will of God.[100]

The whole conception of a 'premature revolution', though expressed in Froude's characteristically moralistic and religious terms, seems a very Whiggish one,[101] and of course there is much in his accounts of the chastening of extremism which brings him very close to standard Whig endorsements of the middle course; his hatred of the theological and doctrinal is a counterpart to the Burkean's detestation of the theoretical and doctrinaire. Froude hated theologians more than Macaulay disliked theoretical republicans or Stubbs and Freeman lawyers.

The most obvious qualification to this, of course, is Froude's Puritan enthusiasm for the Protestant martyrs, his discovery of glamour in their mostly humble social positions, and in what an unsympathetic idiom might have called their fanaticism. But even here there is a disguised affinity with Whiggish sympathies and aversions of a Burkean kind. Vital to Froude's account of the martyrs, distinguishing them from the 'peasant theologians' and 'voluble rhetoricians', for whom Froude felt a distaste which seems at once Carlylean and decorously Anglican,[102] was their earnestness, attested beyond dispute by their deaths, and a strongly imputed simplicity. Apart from Latimer, Froude liked his Protestants dying rather than preaching. He took Foxe's familiar picture of the humble, untaught man or woman, confounding the learned authorities of the Church by the simple power of God's word, and turned it to his own essentially nineteenth-century

---

[100] *ibid.*, i. 503–4.
[101] There may just possibly be an influence on Froude here, however, of the characteristic Liberal Anglican notion of the 'false spring' in history. See Forbes, *Liberal Anglican Idea of History*, pp. 26–7. [102] *HE*, iii. 185; v. 81.

purposes. They became the witnesses not to theological beliefs but to an earnestness of conviction which, in so far as it was not purely negative, was essentially ethical: to their 'weariness of unreality' and 'the fundamental axiom that the service which man owes to God is not the service of words or magic forms, or ceremonies or opinions, but the service of holiness, of purity, of obedience to the everlasting laws of duty'.[103]

It was, in fact, Froude's peculiar achievement to make the language of sixteenth-century Protestant faith consonant and almost identical with that of nineteenth-century earnest doubt. He constantly insists on the undoctrinal character of Protestantism at its sturdiest. In the writings of Latimer, in the depositions against the martyrs, 'we find no opposite schemes of doctrine, no "plans of salvation", no positive system of theology'.[104] Knox was 'a man pre-eminently of facts, and untroubled with theological subtleties'.[105] The martyrdoms were the victories of something essentially practical and even inarticulate over the men of doctrine. And here it is possible to see the underlying affinities between the Carlylean and the Burkean endorsements of dumb practice, between Carlylean earnestness and Whig empiricism. Latimer, for example: 'His deepest knowledge was that which stole upon him unconsciously through the experience of life and the world.'[106] And for Froude, as for the Whig, the justification of revolution is never speculative and theoretical, but only sheer necessity. For him the Reformation was justified essentially and only because the alternative – and here the Whig pragmatist would part company and Froude becomes simply Puritan – was acceptance of institutionalised pretence, living a lie, the service of a graven image inwardly known for what it was. And though the perception of the unreality seems owed in part at least to the discoveries and the march of mind, the actual breaking of the shell and the marking out of the new paths for the spirit was essentially the work of the humble and simple, inspired by their reading of the vernacular scripture: 'Intellect, as it ever does, followed in the wake of the higher virtues of manly honesty and truthfulness.'[107] Poor men and women, 'in tough contact with reality, had learnt better than the great and educated the difference between truth and lies'.[108]

Because he felt it to be wanton, factitious and therefore essentially theoretical, Froude always hated Catholic revivalism, which

---

[103] ibid., i. 506, 512.   [104] ibid., p. 512.   [105] ibid., iii. 400–1.
[106] ibid., p. 573.   [107] ibid., p. 548.   [108] ibid., i. 510.

of course connoted Tractarianism, while he was always tender, if sometimes condescending, to a purely traditional and inarticulate faith.[109] For the Marian restitution, however, and above all for Pole as Papal emissary, there was no mercy. Mary's reign becomes a satisfying demonstration of the futility of a Catholic restoration. Though Froude admits that the country was still predominantly Catholic in sentiment – the Protestant Reformation in England was the victory not of numbers but of the more vigorous conviction[110] – and that with a more judicious policy matters might have gone differently, the spirit of persecution is made to seem so native to Romanism that the issue is foregone. The efforts of the Catholics are made vain by the impassioned honesty of the martyrs, but also by Providential decree.[111]

At this point, of course, the Whig, the Protestant and the Carlylean again coincide, in treating outcomes as vindications. In Carlyle, because his vocabulary and choice of outcome were thought eccentric, this was often condemned as the worship of success or the doctrine that might is right. In Whig historiography it is the familiar retrospective detection and benediction of the forces of progress. To speak less cynically then of 'backing winners', all, of course, are still informed by the notion of Providential direction. For Carlyle it seems to have been most signally demonstrated as retribution. 'I should not have known what to make of this world at all', he once said to Froude, 'if it had not been for the French Revolution'.[112] Froude's acknowledgement of divine guidance is open, though occasionally complicated by the Carlylean use of the word 'fact' for essentially the same thought. Providence had turned down a premature curbing of the powers of the Church in the Middle Ages, and was complimented: 'It was ordered otherwise, and doubtless wisely.'[113] Providence in the sixteenth century favours a union of the crowns of England and Scotland.[114] And Providence decides, irrevocably, against the Marian Catholic revival.

Pole's embassy, the reconciliation of England with the Pope, Mary's marriage and hopes of an heir, become, in Froude's account, an ironic comedy of sentimental illusion and fatuous false

---

[109] E.g. iv. 298.   [110] *ibid.*, vi. 150, 561; xii. 482.
[111] For the providential nature of the Reformation, see, e.g. *ibid.*, ii. 476.
[112] Froude, *Thomas Carlyle. A History of the First Forty Years of his Life, 1795–1835* (1890).
[113] *HE*, i. 93.   [114] *ibid.*, iv. 146.

hopes, mocked by the reality of Bonner's fires and the steadfast-
ness of the martyrs' faith.[115] Mary's phantom pregnancy becomes
a symbol of futility just as for Catholics its supposed reality had
been one of hope. Pole's messianic language about it, making
Mary a type of the Mother of God,[116] is made to seem an
archetypal case of Catholic sentimentality and bombast, essentially un-English. This is reminiscent of Macaulay's similar though
more peripheral scene, Castlemaine's embassy to Rome.[117]
Froude, it has to be said, here shows the more delicate touch and
the deeper irony. Macaulay's method was schoolmasterly
annotation; in Froude the reader, and perhaps the author himself,
is carried by the rhetoric into complicity with the pathos of
reconciliation and restitution, only to find that he has participated
in a masquerade, 'the Whitehall pageant'.[118] Neither historian –
though Vatican rhetoric and Latinity may have constituted a
special case – has any liking for or, it seems, much understanding
of, the courtly cultures of their chosen periods, judging them by
the standards of what has to be called middle-class and post-
Addisonian simplicity. Froude gives no recognition, perhaps not
surprisingly, since our own awareness of it is relatively recent,[119]
of the prevalence of Biblical, figural and especially messianic
language applied to rulers in the sixteenth century; to Elizabeth, in
fact, more than Mary, in a fashion Froude also found absurd.[120] In
Mary's case, however, he makes it seem a distinctively Papist trait.

It presents him, of course, with an invaluable image of Providential rejection, and a kind of historical irony of which he was fond,
though his other effects of this kind are usually more ruminative
and moralising. On the death of James V of Scotland, for example,
after the defeat of Solway Moss: 'To such an end had the blessing
of Paul III, and the cap, and the sword, and the midnight mass,
brought at last a gallant gentleman.'[121] In his reflection on the
defeat of the Armada, Froude seems for once betrayed into a pure
secularity, but no reader attuned to the judgemental Carlylean
connotations of 'reality' and 'fact' will take the final comment at
face value:

The names on both sides, either by accident or purpose, corresponded to the
character of the struggle; the St Matthew, the St Philip, the St James, the St John,
the St Martin, and the Lady of the Rosary, were coming to encounter the Victory,
the Revenge, the Dreadnought, the Bear, the Lion and the Bull: dreams were

[115] *ibid.*, v. 495.   [116] *ibid.*, pp. 444, 461.   [117] See above, pp. 75–6.   [118] *HE*, v. 495.
[119] Frances Yates, *Astrea*.   [120] *HE*, x. 319.   [121] *ibid.*, iii. 534.

ranged against realities, fiction against fact, and imaginary supernatural patronage against mere human courage, strength, and determination.[122]

All this, of course – except the last – could be found more crudely expressed in traditional Protestant providentialism. In its story of the preservation of God's people and his Word, the accession of Elizabeth was, along with the scattering of the Armada, naturally the greatest mercy and deliverance. But Froude, apart from a sentence or two which could be intended as a representation of the popular mood – 'The black dominion of priests and priestcraft had rolled away, like night before the coming of the dawn'[123] – does not crow, but soberly stresses the dangers and complexities. Rightly, no doubt, but it was also typical of his handling of the reign. This was the age, by his own account, which had first drawn him to the sixteenth century. Amid the tangled desperation of *The Nemesis of Faith* it appears briefly as a glowing image of release and renewal: 'The dazzling burst of the Elizabethan era was the vigorous expansion of long-imprisoned energy, springing out in bounding joyous freedom.'[124] It was the traditional picture, tuned to the purposes of a personal and needed myth. In his *History* too, Froude endorsed the traditional eulogy in one respect with a complete complacency, making a modern adaptation of the notion that Elizabeth's reign had seen an ideal balance between classes: the social and economic questions which had been so acute and distressing in Edward's reign had been solved. 'When religion revived, the country righted of itself.'[125] In Elizabeth's time 'the yeomen and peasants were living in a golden age. The war of class, the struggle between rich and poor, had ended.'[126]

But, except in the exploits of the seamen, the mood of exuberance was hard to sustain, naturally enough, amid a mass of complex detail, much of it uncongenial to Froude. Over half his book is devoted to the reign, including, necessarily, a great deal on diplomatic negotiations and intrigues. That any historian of the period should be often baffled and irritated by Elizabeth herself is also understandable and even appropriate, though Froude's was the first really critical treatment of her after centuries of adulation. But there is something more significant here than the inevitable dousing of a myth in scholarly detail, or the reappraisal of a character. The latter is in some ways symptomatic of Froude's

---

122 *ibid.*, xii. 378.   123 *ibid.*, vi. 105.
124 *Nemesis*, p. 98.   125 *HE*, iv. 362.   126 *ibid.*, x. 479.

treatment of the reign as a whole, and of ambivalences in his own attitude to what it seemed to represent. For fanaticism, though still present, was now under control. The Reformation, still heroic because still in extreme danger, was nevertheless to settle into a kind of normality, into a 'solid and secular character',[127] which, it seems hardly necessary to add, was precisely the character Froude, after passing through his own martyrdom for truth, had consciously chosen for himself. Inevitably what was missing was the high nobility and purity of purpose of the time of greatest trial. It was towards normality in this sense, not abridged, as in his first chapter, into a model, and seen through a medieval mist, but extensive, with its compromises, its mixed moral homespun, clearly visible, that Froude was ambivalent. It is not surprising, therefore, that he was most attracted to what was vaguely portentous in it, as well as direct and vigorous; to what could be seen as the glinting promise of a distant high destiny, in the privateering and ocean voyages;[128] it is no doubt creditable that he gave them no excessive attention. But, this apart, Froude had wanted a pragmatic and tolerant Protestant regime, an Erastian Church, a lay-dominated society, and that was what, by and large, he had got. The question was whether he could like it. It was also, of course, a question about how far he would find it possible to be a Whig.

At several points in Froude's *History* he attempts, in a manner reminiscent of Macaulay though less vivid, portraits of the various warring elements in the nation, and suggests the necessity of each, or what each represents, and of their ultimate reconciliation in a *via media*.[129] It is true that such large-minded ecumenism was not altogether typical, and that the Catholic party, in so far as it represented dogmatic and priestly authority, had no appeal for him, or if it had it was an appeal which it would have shattered him to admit to himself. But as the simple, practical, unselfconscious piety of laymen, standing unquestioningly in the old paths and following in the ways of their fathers, it had a role he openly respected and even admired. His writings are freely sprinkled – it is a Carlylean theme, of course – with assertions of the spiritual health of such taciturn conservatism.

The strongest nations are the most reluctant to change, and in England especially, opinions, customs, laws hold their ground because they exist, although their logical defences may long have crumbled . . .. Healthy people live and think more

[127] *ibid.*, vi. 194.   [128] *ibid.*, viii. ch. XLVII.   [129] *ibid.*, i. 173.

by habit than by reason, and it is only at rare intervals that they are content to submit their institutions to theoretic revision.[130]

Such revision is occasionally not gratuitous but necessary, and it calls for a different moral type. Without the spiritual vigour and the bold, open eye of the heroes of the Reformation, England would have been condemned to the fate of Spain: an increasingly rigid enforcement of dogma no free intelligence could believe, and moral and material stagnation or degeneration.[131] But reverential habit was essential ballast;[132] it represented healthy normality. This is a little reminiscent of Stubbs' descriptions of the complementary characters of Saxon and Norman, as well as of Macaulay's Cavaliers and Roundheads. In another form, Froude's is the familiar Whig balancing of continuity and indispensable adaptation. It was this *via media* that the reign of Elizabeth essentially, if only partially successfully, established.

Yet Froude remained, if not discontented, at least restless, not, here, for ancient stability but for uncompromising spiritual heroism. In approaching the 'normality' of Elizabeth's reign it was not only that he disliked some specific features of the compromise, the retention of episcopacy and the 'fiction' of the apostolic succession, though he had personal reasons enough for that. In general he longed for something bolder and more clear-cut, sickening of Elizabeth's 'artifice' and prevarications, turning from them with relief to follow Drake into his simpler world.[133] It seems ironically hard on Froude that history should have provided so stern a test of his pragmatism as Elizabeth. She had no sympathy with 'the nobler aspect of Protestantism, with its deep, passionate loathing of falsehood'.[134] With her, equivocation was a system. Froude wished her otherwise, yet uneasily suspected she might have been right. 'Had she taken her place as the leader of Protestant Europe ... the result might have been as much grander as her course in itself would have been more honourable and straightforward.'[135] The subjunctive was a sad concession. Froude admitted the outcome would have been uncertain, and 'her first duty was to her own people'.[136] But the actual, successful outcome was not quite enough. He would have liked a moral symmetry of ends and means, rather at odds with his usual readiness to justify almost any measures, including torture, for the internal security of the state.

---

[130] *ibid.*, vi. 114.   [131] *ibid.*, viii. 5.   [132] *ibid.*, iv. 232.   [133] *ibid.*, xii. 35.
[134] *ibid.*, x. 339.   [135] *ibid.*, xi. 338. Cf. p. 499.   [136] *ibid.*, x. 326.

But the contrast that troubled him here was not between humanity and ruthlessness but between honesty and deviousness.[137]

We can perhaps best see the nature of Froude's ambivalence if we consider two contrasting types of character in the *History*: it was a polarity Froude himself occasionally made explicit, notably in the contrast he drew between Cecil and Latimer.[138] First there is what we may anachronistically call the conservative or Burkean Whig statesman: fundamentally attached to the old ways, but a pragmatist, capable of recognising the need for adaptative change but not moving before he has to; anxious to reconcile, knowing when to concede. The highest example of this type in the *History*, made congenial to Froude by forthrightness, was Henry VIII. 'Like all great English statesmen he was constitutionally conservative, but he had the tact to perceive the conditions under which, in critical times, conservatism is possible.'[139] Henry 'possessed the peculiarity which has always distinguished practically effective men, of being advanced, as it is called, only slightly beyond his contemporaries'.[140] Cranmer has something of the same qualities, reverence for the past and a perception of the necessity of change.[141] Elizabeth, disfigured by her idiosyncrasies, makes a third. The Church of England is their joint creation.

In the long run it worked, ratified by history as 'an anticipation of the eventual attitude into which the minds of the laity would subside'.[142] Yet as a compromise 'from the first it has been endured with impatience by those nobler minds to whom sincerity is a necessity of existence'.[143] For of course another name for the pragmatic Whig is 'trimmer', and this Froude never was. There was another side to him, not conservative, much less Whig, which, prompted by an impatience of complexity in his own nature, responded, in the 'right' cause, to intransigence and recklessness of consequence. His commitment to a middle course came not from any mundane liking for middle courses, but because he was equally drawn to both extremes: a yearning for a world of absolute freedom, purity and transparency – which he called 'honesty' – exactly balancing a wistful traditionalism. The type of such approved intransigence, of course, was not the doctrinaire, the man of an institution or a system, but the inspired prophet,

---

[137] Cf. Macaulay, above, pp. 76–7.   [138] *HE*, v. 438 n. 2.   [139] *ibid*., i. 165.

[140] *ibid*., ii. 480. This is reminiscent of Bagehot's (less flattering) remark about Peel, published in the same year: 'He was converted at the conversion of the average man.' Stevas (ed.), *Collected Works of Walter Bagehot*, iii (1968), 245.

[141] *ibid*., v. 54.   [142] *ibid*., vii. 249.   [143] *ibid*., viii. 249.

far-seeing but down-to-earth: Latimer, Knox, and their archetype Carlyle. Robust, inarticulate conservatism and uncompromising prophetic testimony, piety and 'love of truth', formed the poles to which Froude's sympathies were drawn;[144] the pragmatic Whig statesman was the necessary mediator, a vital concession to what another idiom would call the reality-principle.

In the conclusion to Froude's *History* it was the conservative Whig who was uppermost, in what is essentially an adaptation – it would be interesting to know how conscious – to Froude's own interests of the Whig concept of the necessary or timely revolution; the lesson is enforced, as usual, by a comparison with the continent. Just as, according to Macaulay, England has been saved the violent upheavals of his own era because she had had a constitutionalist revolution in the seventeenth century, while the French had doomed themselves then to subsequent and more destructive revolution by their acceptance of despotism, Froude held that the English Reformation, by which alone the Protestant cause in Europe had been sustained, had provided a bulwark against a subsequent atheism, against which Catholic regimes had proved ineffectual. To be on the side of religious innovation in the sixteenth century was to be on the side of religion itself, of the reverent theism to which Froude still clung, in the nineteenth: 'To the countries which rejected the Reformation, freedom never offered itself again in the dress of a purer religion. It returned upon them as revolution, as the negation of all religion.'[145] Seen in this way, the significance of the Reformation was ultimately conservative.

The spirit's migration and the promised land

But Froude's conclusion does not quite stop there. Once again history and individual life coalesce in a vague promise for both, that 'those who adhere at all costs to truth, who cling to her though she may lead them into the wilderness, will find beyond it a promised land where all their sacrifice is restored to them'.[146] How far Froude himself felt recompensed is a matter of guesswork, but in so far as this represented a hope for Protestantism collectively we can be surer; it was disappointed. Froude was not a

[144] *ibid.*, xii. 481.   [145] *ibid.*, p. 479.   [146] *ibid.*, p. 481.

Broad Churchman in the strict sense – if there can *be* a strict sense; not of he confession of Thomas Arnold or F. D. Maurice, though many of his sympathies were the same. Baron Bunsen had offered, as it were, to induct him by giving him a scholarship to study theology in Germany, and he had refused.[147] His nationalism was native to him and his positive conception of the state derived from Carlyle and the documents of the sixteenth century rather than the Broad Churchmen.[148] But it is clear that he looked, in their spirit, for some wider, more tolerant, essentially ethical renewal of undogmatic Protestantism, and that he saw the most hopeful signs in Germany.[149] It was always a distant hope. Protestantism, he thought, was in decay, given over to sectarian theological disputatiousness and Bibliolatry.[150] There were even nightmarish moments when the thought obtruded, and had to be rejected, that Catholicism might be the only vital form of contemporary religion.[151] Signs of renewal were hard to discern: 'The Puritan has swept the house and garnished it; but as yet we do not see any symptoms showing of a healthy incoming tenant.'[152]

Fretful at the tardiness of the spirit to reinvest, Froude resorted increasingly to a conservative patriarchalism, including an idealisation not so much of the Middle Ages as of the respectably Anglican, still predominantly traditional and rural past of the eighteenth century.[153] The prophet disappointed could revert to the parson. For if Carlyle was the type of the prophet, the archetypal conservative for Froude was his own father. Increasingly he seems to have come to idealise his stoical, old-fashioned family life, though it was always a tendency with him. Even in *The Nemesis of Faith*, with his sufferings recent, an image of it, as it was or might have been, hovered in front of him. According to his fictional hero 'surely we at home . . . repeated over again the old

---

[147] Dunn, i. 148–9, 151–2.

[148] In contrast to his fellow imperialist Seeley. See R. T. Shannon, 'John Robert Seeley and the idea of a national church' in R. Robson (ed.), *Ideas and Institutions of Victorian Britain* (1967). Also Deborah Wormwell, *Sir John Seeley and the Uses of the History* (C.U.P. 1980).

[149] 'Her theology is undergoing change. Her piety remains unshaken.' *SS*, iii. 188. But Froude, regretting the separation of English and German forms of Protestantism at the Reformation, admitted that 'If the lines in which their minds have flowed seem to be converging at last . . . the remote meeting-point is still invisible.' *HE*, ii. 297. Froude, like Macaulay, sometimes spoke of the affinity between the Teutonic nations and Protestantism, e.g. *HE*, i. 510; iii. 397–8; *SS*, iii. 158.

[150] 'Prospects of Protestantism', *SS*, ii.

[151] 'Revival of Romanism', *SS*, iii.   [152] *SS*, i. 584.

[153] E.g. *SS*, ii. 169, 363, and 'The Oxford Counter-Reformation', *SS*, iv. 237–44, 254, 264. But see also the more critical view in *SS*, iii. 170.

patriarchal era in its richness'.[154] Froude came to take his father as
the type of Anglicanism when 'the Church was perhaps in the
healthiest condition it had ever known': ethical rather than
doctrinal, unself-consciously traditional, with the parson, or
'squarson', virtually a lay patriarch among his parishioners.[155]
The picture was, of course, part of his revenge on Tractarianism.
The kind of adjustments to intellectual change which Froude
accepted unreservedly on behalf of sixteenth-century Catholics he
continued to grudge in his own time, and to blame the Tractarians
for thrusting them upon him. But the patriarchal idyll had a wider
relevance for him than this, and a perennial appeal which seems to
have grown with the passage of time.

Froude's essays, in fact, at least from about 1870 onwards, are
notably more pessimistic and reactionary than the *History* he had
just concluded, where nostalgic conservatism is always balanced
by the presentation of sixteenth-century Protestantism as something luminous, energetic and bold. There may be other reasons
than the passage of time. The essays were naturally more
uninhibited; we have seen the same in Macaulay, though his essays
preceded the *History* and were more radical. More significantly, in
dealing with sixteenth-century Protestantism an unhappy
nineteenth-century doubter could find something like his own
denials expressed in a mood of confident affirmation; the sea of
faith was then at the flood, even if Froude needed to dilute it a
little to make it reach his own residue. But in turning to the
modern England with which many of the essays dealt, he found
nothing, except the prospect of empire, so vicariously invigorat-
ing.

The nation depicted in Froude's essays[156] is essentially one out
of control, and he contemplated the probable nemesis of 'progress'
with alternating despair and bleak satisfaction. It is hard not to
read with a slight sense of irony the passages in the *History* which
make the familiar association between Protestantism, commerce
and the populations of the towns, when one has read Froude's
pastoral dream of a time 'when the giddy whirl of industry and
progress will cease among us', and when 'the soil will again be
divided among unambitious agricultural freeholders'.[157] Froude

[154] *Nemesis.*, p. 74.   [155] *SS*, iv. 237, 241.
[156] Particularly 'England and her colonies', 'Reciprocal duties', 'On progress', 'The
colonies once more', and 'England's war', *SS*, ii; and 'A landed gentry' and 'Party
politics', *SS*, iii.
[157] *SS*, iii. 404.

knows it is fantasy – 'a peasant proprietary is a dream' – but it was one he found a pleasure in indulging, very different from the playful *frisson* conveyed by Macaulay's New Zealander; there is a grim satisfaction in his no doubt consciously anti-Macaulayan vision: 'The grass will grow in the streets of Manchester. The Clyde will eddy round the rotting wrecks of the Glasgow merchant-ships and the plough will pass over the gardens of its merchant princes.'[158] Retribution was again overdue.

Froude's jeremiads, his denunciations of political economy and irresponsible plutocracy, his calls for paternal government and aristocratic leadership, his frequently stressed concern at the disappearance of the smallholder, the swollen population of the towns and the unhealthiness of urban life and industrial work, all echo, of course, the Tory Radicalism current in his youth. Other aspects of the lament were of more recent origin, notably a mass electorate and the rising power and competition of the United States.[159] A good many of these anxieties and yearnings were to find a ready audience around the turn of the century, among a people moved rapidly towards democracy and less inclined than previously to celebrate the development of their constitution; who had begun increasingly to worry about their international position, about 'national efficiency'[160] and the poor physique of recruits, to admire the military virtues, and to flourish their patriotism. Froude's message found a response in generations which also listened to Dilke and Seeley, recited Kipling and Sir Henry Newbolt, admired Baden Powell and excused Jameson.

But more interesting in Froude's social writings than the echoes of Tory Radicalism, or their use as a sounding-board for contemporary anxieties, is something more unexpected, the strong, one is tempted to say unmistakable, resonances of an older critique still. With a surprising insistence and accuracy, with one important and quite conscious qualification, Froude speaks the language of Bolingbroke and the eighteenth-century Country Party. After almost a century of the dominance of Burkean progressive Whiggism, it is tempting to speak of a 'Harringtonian revival'. It is hard to know quite how conscious this is on Froude's part, though obviously he had read his Harrington. The list of common or similar preoccupations is striking: denunciations of political par-

---

[158] *ibid.*, pp. 404–5.   [159] E.g. SS, ii. 180–1; iii. 439–40.
[160] G. R. Searle, *The Quest For National Efficiency. A Study in British Politics and Political Thought, 1899–1914* (1971).

ties as given over to faction (not his word, but the sense is the same) rather than the national interest; distrust of mobile paper-wealth, and a belief that land alone is the basis of patriotism and public spirit, and that a free peasantry is the only adequate recruiting-ground for a country's defence;[161] a sense that a nation may – will – destroy itself if devoted merely to the individual pursuit of gain while public virtue and responsibility are lost;[162] all these are recognisable echoes if not literal reiterations of the stock themes of Augustan pessimism. Froude had clearly long been familiar, as we have seen, with the theory of the 'cycle of corruption' on which that pessimism had rested. It is not an echo, it is the thing itself:

Virtue and truth produced strength, strength dominion, dominion riches, riches luxury, and luxury weakness and collapse – fatal sequence repeated so often, yet to so little purpose. The hardy warrior of the mountains degenerated into a vulgar sybarite. His manliness became effeminacy; his piety a ritual of priests; himself a liar, a coward and a slave.[163]

Only the last sentence, with its characteristic diction ('manliness', 'a liar') and the inevitable reference to 'a ritual of priests', speak to us of the nineteenth century.

There are omissions and changes, of course, some important. Froude, as we have seen, is not concerned with liberty. He sees and fears the loss of public spirit, but possible constitutional consequences do not concern him; he has made the nineteenth-century transition from 'polity' to 'society'. He rejects the notion of a constitutional balance as mechanical, specifically with reference to Harrington;[164] it was too close to the notion of social life as an interaction of interests, which he detested. Nor is there really any specific hope or call for a regenerator, at least in public, though he greatly admired Caesar, on whom he wrote a short book in which he compares him with Christ;[165] in private there is some sign of vague yearnings for a dictator: 'a Chamberlain dictatorship'.[166] But Froude comes closest of all to the Augustans in the increasing importance assumed for him, once he had done with Tudor England, by the example of Rome and her decadence.[167] It is not a merely vaguely moralising concern; it is diagnostic and specific, though to judge by his references one would take Horace for his

---

[161] E.g. *SS*, ii. 202, 399–400.   [162] *SS*, iii. 439–40.   [163] *SS*, ii. 30.
[164] Froude, *Oceana*, p. 15.   [165] *Caesar, A Sketch* (1879), p. 494.
[166] Quoted Paul, *Life*, p. 346.
[167] 'England and her colonies', *SS*, ii. 202. *Oceana*, pp. 9–10, 28, 386. *Caesar*, pp. 5–7.

chief source: the disappearance of the independent free cultivator; the vast, rootless population of the towns, their suffrage bought by doles, devoid of all virtue and public spirit; the decay of public life and inevitable military and moral decline. The parallels for Froude were clear; he had the imperialist's pitying despair of 'the poor little street-bred people'.[168]

The only escape from the impasse, in fact, was empire. There, with unlimited land, the smallholder could rise again. Carlyle, and of course many others, had pointed to emigration as the remedy for the surplus population of the towns, and attempts had been made to organise it. But Froude's brochure for the colonies has a special quality and emphasis. For one thing it has become political; Froude wants not only emigration but empire, greater Britain. His conception is not quite so much a question of power-politics as was that of his contemporary Sir John Seeley, but it contains that aspect: 'Queen among nations, from without invulnerable, and at peace and at health within.'[169] But essentially what Froude wanted was not so much power, nor simply a better life for individual emigrants, but renewal for the nation, release from the whirligig of 'progress' in which she was trapped, and from 'An England of brick lanes and chimneys, an England sounding with the roar of engines . . . with artificial recreation-grounds, and a rare holiday in what remained of wood and meadow.'[170] The sense of constriction is powerfully conveyed. The images in which Froude expressed his myth – it seems fair to use the word – of the colonies are similar to his metaphors for sixteenth-century Protestantism: air, sunlight, fertility, space, emancipation.

No doubt these are things a man might legitimately see in Natal or New South Wales, compared with England, and Froude responded to them on his travels. The impression remains that it was above all the vague potentiality of the colonies that appealed to him, which he might fill in imagination almost as he chose. Predictably the reality was sometimes disappointing, just as Free-man found in the newly emancipated nations of Europe in which his own hopes were invested. There was even a moment of clear-sighted pessimism, in Honolulu, when Froude realised that he did not like the reality of imperialism at all, as he

[168] Kipling, 'The English flag', *Barrack Room Ballads*.
[169] *Oceana*, p. 11.   [170] *ibid.*, p. 386.

wondered at the nature of our Anglo-American character, which was spreading thus into all corners of the globe, and fashioning everything after its own likeness. The original, the natural, the picturesque, goes down before it as under the wand of the magician. In the place of them springs up the commonplace and the materially useful.[171]

This was rare, but inevitably the colonists had sometimes shown little regard for Froude's plans for them. There was a note of admonition in the way he addressed New Zealand. The inhabitants should not 'renew the town life which they leave behind them ... They will grow into a nation when they are settled in their own houses and freeholds, like their forefathers who drew bow at Agincourt or trailed pike in the wars of the Commonwealth.'[172]

From the first chapter of Froude's *History* to *Oceana*, thirty years later in his life and three hundred and fifty in the life of the nation, the circle is closed. The traditional virtues he had seen and celebrated in the slow-paced rural England of the early sixteenth century, and whose demise he had regretfully but stoically seemed to accept, were precisely those to be recreated in his colonial smallholder's paradise. In the colonies, 'Children grow who seem once more to understand what was meant by merry England.'[173] And if the New Zealanders were disappointing there was one people who answered the specifications perfectly. As Freeman had seen Homer's Achaeans and Tacitus' Germans in Swiss patriarchs, Froude found in South Africa the virtuous and hardy Romans of the Republic: 'The Boers of South Africa, of all human beings now on this planet, correspond nearest to Horace's description of the Roman peasant soldiers who defeated Pyrrhus and Hannibal.'[174] In the devout, old-fashioned patriarchal households of the Cape Dutch Froude clearly found a charm and serenity he found nowhere else in the colony. 'They are precisely what their ancestors were two hundred years ago.'[175] What the Boers had not lost, the English might recover, an idyll of self-sufficiency, stern morality and apple-cheeked children, in new lands 'where the race might for ages renew its mighty youth'.[176] For Froude, no less than for Freeman, the future held hope because, and in so far as, it might recreate the past.

---

171 *ibid.*, p. 351.   172 *ibid.*, pp. 245–6.   173 *ibid.*, p. 17.
174 *ibid.*, p. 42.   175 Quoted Dunn, ii. 407.   176 *Oceana*, p. 10.

CHAPTER 11

Postscript

Nineteenth-century historians occasionally protested against one of the constraints of their art: its sequential arrangement.[1] In history events might be simultaneous which, in narrative, become extended. Carlyle pointed this out,[2] echoed, as so often, by Froude.[3] It is a caution worth bearing in mind in any retrospective consideration of the themes of the present book. The reader, judging subjectively, may legitimately feel that the road from Macaulay to Froude has been a long and weary one. But this is an illusion, as well as perhaps a failure, of art. The first volumes of Froude's *History* appeared only four months after the publication of Macaulay's last, in December 1855. It is quite proper, with no more than the usual caveats, to speak of a Whig historiographical tradition, from Rapin in the early eighteenth century to Hallam and Macaulay, Stubbs, Freeman and Green. But the authors considered in this book, even those who, unlike Froude, can without apology be called Whig historians, do not necessarily represent evenly spaced moments in that tradition. It is only with this reservation, as well as with as full a recollection as possible of each author's idiosyncrasies, that we can begin to consider in what sense if any the sequential arrangement of this book may correspond to any kind of cultural story.

There are, of course, some obvious connections. The example of Macaulay's *History* exerted a marked influence on the ways Freeman certainly, and probably Froude too, for all his antagonism to Macaulay, undertook their own tasks, and this helps to give the work of all three a certain homogeneous character. All aspired to be vivid, readable and stylish; some of Freeman's bitterness

---

[1] J. Burckhardt, *Civilization of the Renaissance in Italy* (trs. H. Trevor (Chapel Hill, 1965)), p. 1.
[2] Carlyle, 'On history', *Works* (Ashburton edn 1885–8), 17 vols, xv. 499.
[3] *HE*, ix. 522.

against Froude almost certainly derives from a sense that they were rivals for Macaulay's mantle, and that Froude had anticipated him. Stubbs, of course, was a different case, aiming at a more purely professional and academic audience, but in his own fashion Stubbs, like Macaulay, was an initiator and a portent, setting new standards of scholarly rigour and professionalism: he was to have, in fact, much the more extensive and numerous progeny, supported by the new educational institutions, though that story has not been treated here. Finally, Green's *Short History of the English People* is another obvious 'successor' to Macaulay's work, in its readability, its immense popularity, and in the way it made basic Whig notions vivid and appealing for a wide audience. It has not been dealt with here – its scale is different from that of the works considered – but its earlier parts contain abridgements of the work of Freeman and Stubbs, as well as anticipations of his own later books which we have considered briefly. The chief difference from Macaulay's kind of Whiggism lies clearly in the more populist or democratic character the Whig story assumed in the hands of the three medievalists.

So much is obvious. But in considering in what sense if any the authors treated here may be thought of as culturally representative, we become immediately aware of a fact which, though it may testify to the reactionary nature of historians, also owes something to the fact that immensely long and learned historical works take a long time to write. It is a kind of cultural lag. By comparison with earlier Whig histories, for example, including Hallam's, Macaulay's was a distinctively nineteenth-century achievement: the work of a man who had read his Scott. But by comparison with those appearing only a decade or two later, what distinguishes it is the strong flavour of an eighteenth-century mind; it is redolent of Augustan England and the Scottish Enlightenment, mediated, of course, through Holland House and the early Edinburgh Reviewers. Trevelyan spoke of Macaulay as so devoted to the culture of earlier days, up to the end of the eighteenth century, as to be almost entirely cut off from that of his own time. Both Freeman and Froude, by contrast, are products of Romanticism, Freeman epitomising its excitements, Froude its melancholy. But they too wrote guided by enthusiasms and concerns which, by the time their histories were completed, had begun to seem old-fashioned: in Freeman's case the liberal-nationalist fervour which reached its European climax in 1848 and which had inspired the German Romantic devotion to the study of legal antiquities and primitive heroic literature earlier in the century; in Froude's the Oxford theological battles of the 1830s and 1840s which he was still, in a sense, re-fighting in the conclusion to his *History* thirty years later. In one respect, it is true – and this provided one reason for treating him last – Froude, in his imperialist tracts caught a mood of the immediate future rather than one receding into the past, but this was only marginally represented in his *History*.

If we consider them as representing the next moments in a story beginning with Macaulay we may be chiefly struck, presumably, by the brevity with which the idea of progress, often thought of as the dominant conception of Victorian historiography, actually holds sway. In Macaulay it is held in steady balance with Whig piety, itself a residue of an older atavistic legalism. In Freeman and Froude, in their different ways, a Romantic nostalgia constantly qualifies even their most robustly optimistic affirmations, and threatens to cancel their endorsements of the course of English history and to make poignancy and regret their dominant mood. Of course this results from our choice of examples: Stubbs and Green would make a rather more optimistic story, and there are other Victorian historians whom we have not discussed.

It would, in fact, be reckless and misleading to appear to make a handful of authors fully representative. Nevertheless, it does seem that, in relation to a confident, self-congratulatory historiographical tradition, Romanticism both gave and took away. It gave narrative colour and density and an extended imaginative range, making the past accessible in new ways, and it inspired a detailed scholarly attention to remote periods, extending the Whig story again where, under earlier scholarly criticism and the influence of Enlightenment notions of civilisation, it had begun to contract. But it also invested in the past a love and regret which the Whig notion of a flexible tradition, as developed by Burke and, in collusion with progress, by Macaulay, could hardly consistently contain, as well as projecting back into it a conception of nationality which later historians have found anachronistic. It is in fact in Stubbs, whose old-fashioned Toryism insulated him from the excessive nostalgia of Froude's Tory Radicalism or Freeman's liberal variety, who seems best to preserve, in the 1860s and 1870s, a sense, sober, admittedly, compared with Macaulay's, of the reality and possibilities of progress.

For the aversions Freeman and Froude in their different ways felt towards basic aspects of modernity, 'Romantic' again seems an appropriate adjective. For Freeman – and in this he was joined by Stubbs and Green – it was bureaucracy and centralisation that were abhorred; for Froude it was commercialism, laissez-faire and industrialisation, which Freeman did not so much accept as simply refuse to notice. They did not, of course, write their major works on periods which forced them to consider these things, but the alert reader could hardly mistake where their sympathies lay.

Of course, there was in Macaulay an innocent blindness to, or determination not to see, some of the costs of progress, and the loss of this might well be called an access of realism. But politically what was missing in Freeman and Froude, by comparison, was the space allowed for confident and up to a point creative political activity, within a framework of constitutional continuity and accountability, which Macaulay's residual civic humanism had added to his Whig feeling for the enduring and slowly changing body of law and tradition. Burke had made the same conjunction and held the same balance, when, contrasting the energy of living tradition with the inertness of a rigid ancient constitution, embodied in the mouldering records in the Tower, he had hopefully seen the former epitomised in the great aristocratic families, combining public spirit and experience with the sense of continuity.

Burke had made his contrast in the form of an exhortation to the Duke of Richmond. And it was perhaps less plausible to expect the same combination of qualities in 'the English people' considered as a whole, though in Stubbs' account of the fusion of local Saxon 'life' and central Norman 'machinery' to form an embodied and conscious political freewill, as the story of the English constitution, we see a kind of parable of it. But in turning to celebrate, as their subject virtually required, the continuity of institutions and the anonymous creativity of the folk, the early medievalists necessarily lost some of the sense of intimacy with political activity and its possibilities which Macaulay had conveyed with so much art. Inevitably, in tilting the balance towards institutions, they gave, even if unintentionally, an impression that was more deterministic – or, in Stubbs, providentialist. In Freeman, though he tried to retain, even where it was inappropriate, a hold on personality and a Macaulayan sense of intimacy, the deterministic impression is in fact strongest. Freeman deprives his historical agents of both autonomy and individuality by turning them into types, always doomed to repeat the same roles in the closed circle of a known national destiny. His references to face-to-face democracy are inevitably wistful; representative government, though he tried to celebrate it, conveyed a sense of exclusion and second-best; the old problem of reconciling civilisation and liberty had not been solved. The feeling for locality, always inherent in a Burkean tradition – it was a form of the patriotism of Burke's 'little platoon to which we belong' – was explored and tended by the medievalists; the feeling for the centre, for Parliament as the ultimate expression, rather than merely the guardian, of political freedom, though Stubbs in his austere vocabulary retained it, was perceptibly less in Freeman and Green. The Macaulayan balance was tilted towards the institutional and traditional.

In the next generation of medieval historians, the liberal impulse itself seemed largely spent, and in that sense Stubbs, Freeman and Green represent an episode, with its own character and coherence. Paul Vinogradoff, writing in the introduction to his *Villeinage in England* in 1892, spoke of the waning of enthusiasm for the cult of primitive Teutonic democracy as a consequence of disillusionment with liberal social democracy in Europe after 1870 (he was a Russian, and it coloured his account), and of the newer attitudes to medieval history as a product of conservative reaction.[4] Vinogradoff's analysis was oversimplified, as Maitland immediately pointed out to him,[5] but that early medieval history was no longer written in a spirit of liberal democratic ardour was true. Charles Petit-Dutaillis, in the preface to his revision of Stubbs for the new generation, made a similar point to Vinogradoff's but saw the consequence of liberal disillusionment only as a cooler and more objective temper in historical writing.[6]

But the disillusionment came, of course, too late to affect the medievalists with whom we have been concerned. In so far as they were resentful, it was of the results of an earlier phase of modernity, the vogue for commissions and administrative rationalisation which had characterised the 1830s after the extension of

---

[4] *Villeinage in England*, p. 31. A similar interpretation is offered in Alfons Dopsch, *The Economic and Social Foundations of European History* (New York 1969), ch. 1.

[5] On this, see Burrow, 'Village community', in McKendrick (ed.), *Historical Perspectives*.

[6] C. Petit-Dutaillis, *Studies and Notes Supplementary to Stubbs' Constitutional History* (1908), p. xiii. For a full treatment of the reaction against Whiggism see P. Blaas, *Continuity and Anachronism* (The Hague 1978). I regret that this substantial and very thorough study became available to me in English too late for me to make proper use of it in this book.

the franchise had produced a reforming Whig government, and which, of course, was still continuing. It was no doubt natural that, with further extensions of the franchise and the development of the party machines in the later part of the century, national politics should seem to middle-class men of letters more remote and uncontrollable and less congenial than before, and understandable that idealisation of the growth of the constitution should have waned in consequence. This, however, was a rather later development. In Froude, it is true, and in his fellow imperialist Sir John Seeley, it is possible to see in their positive distaste for parliamentary traditions, and the history organised around them, some influence of the anxieties created by the prospect of mass electorates, but their aversion really had older sources, Carlyle and Comtean positivism respectively.[7]

In Froude, of course, one might see the Macaulayan balance tilted not towards tradition but in the opposite direction, towards the exaltation of bold decisive action; Froude could recognise and appreciate, with no Whig squeamishness, the creative political energy of a man like Thomas Cromwell. What he lacks, of course, in Whig terms, is a sense of the continuities of public life, of evolving political traditions as the controlling context of political activity. Political action of real significance comes to seem necessarily naked, convulsive and essentially revolutionary.

It is true that the role of Froude's 'Whig' statesman as conciliator, (Cranmer, Elizabeth) is like that of Macaulay's William or Halifax, while in Froude's account Henry VIII and even Thomas Cromwell perform similar functions to those of the Long Parliament or the Whigs of 1832 in Macaulay: that of seeing in time the secular changes in the world at large and making the necessary innovatory adjustments to them. But the changes introduced by the Reformation are apt to seem, despite Froude's assurances of their necessity and inevitability, more gratuitous than those of the seventeenth or the nineteenth century, and in a sense Froude even wishes them to seem so; he is something like a determinist only when it suits him. The Reformers whose cause Froude embraced were more radical men than the Whig constitutionalists of later times, and Froude could not, even by a retrospective endorsement of an undoctrinal Anglican Erastianism, escape the implications of his commitment to a radical revolution, nor did he altogether wish

---

[7] For Seeley, see Wormell, *Sir John Seeley and the Uses of History.*

to. His acceptance, moreover, of the social and economic changes of the sixteenth century (not to mention his despair at those of the nineteenth) to which he admitted that Protestantism was related, was so much more grudging than Macaulay's hearty endorsement of virtually all such changes, that the sense of desperation and revolutionary vehemence in Froude's writing is not fundamentally mitigated by the element of Whiggish pragmatism. The vehemence was a reflection, of course, of the turbulent character of sixteenth-century history, but also of Froude's own lack of interest, at the political level, in the more enduring and slowly developing aspects of English public life – an interest enlarged, admittedly, among Whig historians to the point of hypertrophy.

Froude's view of history is not without a sense of the possibilities of action, but it would be hard to see it, in political terms, as confident or optimistic. He has his own strong sense of tradition, embodied, above all in the conservatism of the patriarchal household. But despite his essentially civic humanist belief in the patriotism, public spirit and military virtues of the independent smallholder, it seems in him ultimately a private rather than a political ideal, of an idyllic security and self-sufficiency, because he refuses to link it, as a Harringtonian would have done, to a theory of the constitution.

We can also see in Froude something it is tempting to call the unavailability of the civic humanist ideal, though these are not, of course, the terms in which he poses the problem. In so far as it is consciously a problem for him it takes a recognisably Romantic form, as a revulsion from the cramping of human possibilities in professional specialisation. His own choice of profession had cost him much anguish and the problem had at one time been acutely personal; arguments of this kind are debated by the hero of *The Nemesis of Faith* before his fatal assumption of orders.[8] In a later essay, entitled 'Representative Men', Froude took up the theme in a different context: the need to offer ideal examples to the young for veneration. The problem here was cultural eclecticism, the variety of available ideals: 'We have no moral criterion, no idea, no counsels of perfection.'[9] But while Froude recognises the practical dilemma ('the *man* is sacrificed to the profession',[10]) the consciously demotic solution offered, essentially the Carlylean notion of work and duty, is likely to strike the modern reader as an evasion: 'Our work lies now in those peaceful occupations which,

[8] *Nemesis*, pp. 2–5.   [9] *SS*, i. 581.   [10] *ibid*., p. 596.

in ages called heroic, were thought unworthy of noble souls.'[11] In the *Nemesis of Faith*, the answer was more direct, heartfelt and significant: 'When we come home, we lay aside our masks and drop our tools, and are no longer lawyers, sailors, soldiers, statesmen, clergymen, but only men.'[12] The wholeness and highest exercise of human faculty once seen as found in the public domain is here openly identified only with domesticity.[13]

In speaking of the balance in Macaulay's *History* between progress and tradition, activity and given institutional context, we inevitably made the histories which followed it, with the exception of Stubbs', seem like a decline, even a symptomatic one. Yet it seems sensible also to recognise Macaulay's achievement for what it was, a *tour de force* owing as much to personal temperament and experience as to the availability of intellectual traditions, and unlikely to be repeated. It was not, after all, the theme itself which was novel, but only the vigour with which Macaulay sustained it. Coleridge, for example, had attempted, more woodenly, in his *Constitution of Church and State*, to reconcile stability and progress in a constitutional balance between the landed and commercial interests, and Disraeli had symbolised the reconciliation in the marriage of his hero and heroine in *Coningsby*. So rather than speak of the Whig tradition declining, and being finally abandoned by the hard-headed professionals of the next generation, we may equally well choose to think of it as having worn out its issues, and speak of its fragmentation. We could even talk, more positively, of forms of adaptation.

We can see one example of this if we follow another aspect of the Macaulayan balance, the equivocation, as we might choose to say, which was considered in chapter 3, between the practice of piety and the endorsement of it: what might be called first and second order veneration. There is, as we saw there, a knowingness, a distance, in Macaulay's reference to the older Whigs' veneration for constitutional precedent, which there is not, generally, for example, in Burke, who is also of course convinced of the utility of such political feelings and habits. Burke that is, not only approves, he also participates, though with sophistication. In Macaulay the sophistication seems to have gone a stage further and become

---

[11] *ibid.*, p. 590. [12] *Nemesis*, p. 67.
[13] Pocock speaks relevantly of a 'shift towards privatization, toward the admission that in a commercial society the individual's relation to the *res publica* could not be simply civic or virtuous'. *Machiavellian Moment*, p. 436.

ironic distance, though the piety is still in its own way real. When we come to the obvious third figure, Walter Bagehot, in his thoughts on the constitution, the two have become wholly distinguishable, and are epitomised in the two parts of the constitution, the efficient and the dignified. Bagehot approves of the venerability of the constitution, as something, as he says, 'taking'. He can hardly be said to participate in the liturgy, unless approval counts as participation.

What we see here is the detachment of the Burkean political style, pragmatist, gradualist, even still in its self-conscious and utilitarian fashion reverent, from the historical myth from which it was derived and by which it had been inspired. And of course the style is more flexible than the myth; the latter, as we saw in chapter 2, made heavy demands on the character of English history, including the demand for unbroken continuity and the requirement that England must be shown to be in some sense a privileged and exemplary nation. But the endorsement of the Burkean political style as such makes no such extravagant demands, which is no doubt as well for its advocacy in the later twentieth century. It requires only the inductive assurance that on the whole – the examples need not even be English, though the positive ones still tend to be – gradualism has 'worked' better than revolution.

This detachment of an aspect of Whig ideas from the parent historical stem seems, in fact, typical; Whig history, that is, except literally as a standard way of writing the history of England, did not so much die or decline as break into tributaries in which much remains recognisable: whether some or all of them eventually ended in backwaters is beyond the scope of this book to enquire. An instance of this fission is provided, for example, by Maitland's seminal contribution to what became, in the early years of this century, a fashionable and explicit creed, Political Pluralism. In Maitland's advocacy of the real personality of groups we find, still clearly evident, the features of the Burkean Whig style, but virtually no elements of the Whig national historical myth, though France, as always, continues to provide the warning of her dreadful alternative.[14]

Seeley is another case in point, though of a different sort. He was certainly a Whig historian in Butterfield's wider sense of one

[14] Burrow, *op. cit.*, pp. 275–81.

for whom history was essentially embryology, deriving its point from present concerns. He is at the opposite pole of Whiggism from Freeman, not so in love with the past that he must make the present its recreation, but fundamentally so little concerned with it that he found its interest almost exhausted by its proven capacity to produce the present (he also had an interest in the possibility of inductively deriving from it a knowledge of historical laws). But for him, as for any good Whig, the story of the English past, at least from the reign of Elizabeth onwards, was a single progressive drama, with an answer to the question 'What is the general drift or goal of English history?'[15] Seeley professed to find 'constitutional liberty a completed development, and therefore an exhausted topic'.[16] But it is clear that his tastes would have led him to a different perspective in any case. He strongly disliked the traditional kind of Whig parliamentary story: political contentiousness, 'parliamentary tongue-fence', erected into an heroic myth. He wanted something both more ecumenically national, and gruff with *Realpolitik*: 'the temptation of our historians is always to write the history rather of the Parliament than of the State and Nation'.[17] Anticipating Namier, he attacked, very effectively, the notion that political parties had exhibited a doctrinal continuity across a hundred and fifty years.[18] The continuity, and the relevance at least of the more recent period in English history – and Seeley was interested in no others – and the 'large conclusion' to which it led, was constituted not by 'the mere parliamentary wrangle and the agitations about liberty'[19] but by the fact of colonial expansion. We must 'begin to think of England as a living organism, which in the Elizabethan age began a process of expansion, never intermitted since, into Greater Britain'.[20]

Seeley, in fact, is an example of Butterfield's dictum that in the nineteenth century the Whig interpretation of English history became the national interpretation.[21] It had, in a sense, as a nineteenth-century historian might have said – as Seeley virtually did say – 'done its work', which Butterfield identified as helping the English to retain continuity with their past in the nineteenth-century transition to democracy.[22] For of course the strictly

[15] Seeley, *The Expansion of England* (2nd edn 1899), pp. 1, 8.   [16] *ibid.*, p. 140.
[17] *ibid.*, p. 30. Cf. *The Growth of British Policy*, i. 1–2.
[18] Seeley, 'History and politics', *Macmillan's Magazine*, xl (1879), 371–5, 452–8.
[19] *Expansion*, p. 10.   [20] *ibid.*, p. 142.
[21] *The Englishman and His History*, pp. 2, 79.   [22] *ibid.*, p. 79.

constitutional history of the twentieth century has so far been exceptionally uneventful and uninventive by comparison; we have made no leaps in the dark. The Parliament Act of 1911, even the admission of women to the franchise, though bitterly contested, were hardly 'shooting Niagara'.

The Professor of History at Cambridge in the early part of the nineteenth century, William Smyth, wrote in his published lectures that 'The distinction between those who incline to the popular part of the constitution and those who incline to the monarchical exists to this hour, and can only cease with the constitution itself.'[23] We have seen other similar declarations; they would have seemed eccentric in the later years of Victoria's reign. But in the middle years of the century the issue of the franchise, for Macaulay and Freeman in particular, continued to give a relevance to references to constitutional continuity. The Whig histories of these years, with which this book has chiefly been concerned, formed a half-way stage between the strict legalism of the ancient constitutionalist, of which the Whiggism of the early nineteenth century, despite its alliance with progress and utility, still, as we saw, contained strong resonances, and the later dispersion of the Whig tradition we have just been considering. It was this unique and naturally relatively short-lived intermediate position which gave much of their point and distinctive character to the Whig histories written in these years.

But by the end of the century, in becoming the 'English' interpretation, and losing even the most residual connection with constitutionalist or party polemics, Whig history obviously ran the risk of death by inanition, for lack of opponents. For Seeley the great lesson to which English history led was Imperial Federation. When it failed to materialise there was nowhere for this kind of national 'Whig' history to go except into a vague and diffuse patriotism, which, of course, Seeley also hoped to arouse.

If the Whig tradition could be said to have moved in one direction away from Parliament and the constitution towards the nation-state in its external relations, it could also move away from politics in the opposite direction, downwards as it were, not upwards: into a cherished sense of the continuities of English life witnessed by the land itself. This was not new, of course:

[23] William Smyth, *Lectures on Modern History* (1840), p. 124. For Smyth, see K.T.B. Butler, 'A "Petty" Professor of Modern History', *Cambridge Historical Journal*, ix (1948), no. 2. Also Peter Allen, *The Cambridge Apostles*, pp. 132, 213.

something a little like it had formed the inspiration of the Elizabethan antiquaries; it is visible, too, in Wordsworth. But here also, at the end of the Whig line so to speak, there lay a differently focussed patriotism and awareness of continuity, with a reverence for the past and tradition like Freeman's, often combined with a positive distaste for aspects of the present. Of course it would be an oversimplification to see this as in any direct way derivative from the Whig sense of the past. The chief Victorian precursors look like Carlyle or George Eliot, though Green, something of a Carlylean though also a good Whig, seems a likely intermediary as well. But the acute awareness of continuities in Hardy, or in a different form in Kipling's *Puck* stories, reaching out to a vision of England and of the historic relation of the inhabitants and their land, clearly offers some of the same reassurances and sense of identity provided by Macaulay in the vicarious experience of parliamentary traditions or, more directly perhaps, by the identification and celebration of the English by Stubbs, Freeman and Green. Even what may be thought of as the central theme of Whig history, the reconciliation of progress and tradition, once it is made historically imprecise and symbolic, is presumably perennial. In the contrasting symbolism of the wych-elm and the role of the male Wilcoxes in Forster's *Howards End*, it is possible to see something like Macaulay's reconciliation, transposed into other and more generally suggestive terms.

But it is not only in such abstracted and symbolic terms that something akin to Whig history seems perennial. The class of purposive and justificatory historical myths of which English Whig histories are a distinguished sub-species is unlikely to be dispelled by any changes in the professional practice and ethics of historians. This is so not only because analysis may be impotent against prejudice, or because even being made to read learned articles in historical journals seems not so incompatible as might have been hoped with continuing subscription to some form of political Manichaeanism. It is because, even in the conditions of exasperated tribalism in which such myths flourish most vigorously, the facts appealed to on both sides may be perfectly true: the Apprentice Boys did play a part in the defence of Londonderry. What gives such history its continuing power is not falsehood, or for that matter truth, but the sense of continuing identity, expressed in re-enactments by ritual or riot. The enemy of such myths is not truth but individualism, the dissolving of the sense of collective identities and temporal continuities – a fact which explains and justifies our ambivalence towards them.

Similarly, in historical writing itself the enemy of 'Whiggish' history is not truth or the dedication to its pursuit, but a measure of nominalism, a willingness and even determination to see differences in similarities: analysis in fact. But this also explains why, as a tendency, Whiggism is perennial here also. For we need of course, sometimes, to see continuities in differences, and to tell stories. Butterfield rightly noted the connection of Whig history, in the wider sense to which he gave currency, as the subordination of the past to the present and its treatment as something essentially embryonic, with abridgement.[24] Conversely it tends to evaporate in the detailed treatment of episodes and the concerns of the particular past moment. Significantly the classic demolition of English Whig history was accomplished by Namier not by a rival story but by a cross-section.[25] But in history we often necessarily speak of, and tell the stories of, entities more enduring than individual human lives: crown, parliament, the constitution, the working class, 'science', or for that matter 'the Whig tradition'. In doing so we postulate their identity: Whig history is a form of reification. In telling their history we try, presumably, to qualify; to show change-in-identity. But this is to tell a story, and there is an innate Whiggishness in stories as such, not only in their presentation of a continuing protagonist but in the ways in which, in a well-told story, the parts are subordinate to the whole: the criterion of relevance is contribution to the story's climax or resolution.

Of course in speaking of this as Whiggish we have stretched the term in a manner which has now become generally understood, using it in a sense in which Marxist histories or histories of science, for example, may – characteristically – also be Whig histories: Whig that is, in construing history as a kind of teleology, of which the present or some preferred future becomes the goal, and in the light of which the earlier 'stages' of the past are appraised functionally, for their 'contributions' to, 'anticipations of', or in all too many cases, 'failure to' contribute to the resolution of the preferred story. As in earlier, literally Whig, history, the protagonist (working-class consciousness, for example – though any approved development can be thought of in the same way) can

---

[24] *The Whig Interpretation of History*, p. 24.
[25] L.B. Namier, *The Structure of Politics at the Accession of George III* (2nd edn 1957).

become a kind of pilgrim, struggling through vicissitude, self-delusion and even ordeal, to self-realisation and self-awareness. Such histories still, of course, retain the capacity, after the manner of Whiggism, to inspire, and to create heroic traditions.

Yet we tell historical stories, as we employ general concepts, because we must; a condition of permanent obstructive adherence to the particular, however salutary as a challenge, becomes tediously unhelpful. In this plight we may think of the greatest achievements in story-telling: the nineteenth-century novel, in the hands of George Eliot or Tolstoy, with its multiple perspectives which are nevertheless placed and controlled within the architecture of the plot and the moral vision of the author; the analogy, of course, if we think of the subsequent history of the novel, also suggests the less appealing prospect of a modernist playfulness in the plotting of historical works.[26] But the precondition of the nineteenth-century novel's multiplicity of perspectives contained in a unity was the godlike omniscience of the author. In history we make our stories on sufferance, because of the disparity in scale, ironically concealed in the ambiguity of the word 'history', between the history we tell and the history we tell it about. To write with some ironic sense of that discrepancy seems the precondition of writing as a modern historian, conscious that people in the past told their own stories, of which they, not we, were the point. We can avoid, that is, writing as though we told *the* story. For in the disparity of scale between 'history' and history, the joke is surely on us, and it is one which Whig history of all kinds consistently ignores. The shield of Aeneas foretold the history of Rome, but the shield of Achilles, which told no story, was the more comprehensive social document.

The historians treated in this book who seem to have been most aware of this were Stubbs and Froude, the former in his practice, the latter, who was of course in most senses no Whig, as a conscious awareness,[27] which affected his practice little. In his own *History*, his sense of the flow of things is as assured, his judgements on those who did not feel it in time sometimes as vehement, as those of any Whig. Of course it is possible for us to envy that confidence, rather as Froude himself clearly in some

---

[26] See the interesting discussion of such possibilities, more sympathetically described than here, in Sheldon Rothblatt's review of John Fowles' *The French Lieutenant's Woman* in *Victorian Studies*, xv, 1972.

[27] 'The science of history', *SS*, i. 1, 20.

sense envied, while repudiating, what he took to be the Catholic's implicit acceptance of dogma. It would not be hard to idealise the episodes of English historiography described here, aided by the elegiac quality which tends to attach to the conclusions of historical works, often reflecting not so much anything in the history itself as the fact that the story told about it is reaching its end. Such celebrations then characteristically adhere and become assimilated to the traditions they speak of. The warmth and intimacy, for example, of G. M. Young's appraisal of the mid-Victorians makes him a kind of bridge to them and hence in a sense a continuation. Similarly and more directly Butterfield's celebration – in time of war – of the Whig tradition, in *The Englishman and His History*, which he had earlier so effectively criticised, now seems a late example of it.

But our best chance of understanding and enjoying the mid-Victorian historians considered here lies in an initial admission of their remoteness. There is a good deal that may offend us in their coalescence of various kinds of self-confidence; the mental image of a plethoric Victorian tourist shouting at the waiters in a foreign hotel is occasionally inescapable. It expresses itself, characteristically, with an exuberance born not only of the sense of national achievement and privilege, but of confidence in the relation between author and reader. On us, inevitably, such conviviality sometimes jars; and the grand gesture in the now empty theatre becomes absurd. Whig historiography stood four-square to its age; there was no suggestion that it was addressed to the happy few, or that it appealed to the justice of posterity against the spirit of the times. Posterity has on the whole avenged itself for this neglect. Macaulay will presumably not lack readers for a good while to come, and Stubbs will enjoy affectionate and respectful remembrance in the small circle of medievalists. But on the whole the great Victorian histories now seem like the triumphal arches of a past empire, their vaunting inscriptions increasingly unintelligible to the modern inhabitants: visited occasionally, it may be, as a *pissoir*, a species of visit naturally brief.[28]

Yet they can still offer much enjoyment, in their energy and zest, of which we would deprive ourselves by an excessive puritanism; here the analogy with the tourist, an insular, Protestant Victorian visitor in Rome, prim and baffled amid the alien extrovert

[28] E.g. Gareth Stedman Jones, 'History: the poverty of empiricism' in R. Blackburn (ed.), *Ideology in Social Science. Readings in Critical Social Theory* (1972), pp. 98–100.

grandeur,[29] turns against ourselves. But most of all what they continue to offer is the characteristic pleasure afforded by past historical writing, the complex historical experience of seeing one society and culture refracted through another, both of them, in this instance, our own and not our own.

[29] G. Eliot, *Middlemarch*, bk II, ch. xx.

Index